TRACK & FIELD COACH'S SURVIVAL GUIDE

Edward L. Wallace, Jr.

PARKER PUBLISHING COMPANY
West Nyack, New York 10994

D1457111

Library of Congress Cataloging-in-Publication Data

Wallace, Edward L., Jr.
  Track & field coach's survival guide : practical techniques and materials for building an effective program and success in every event / by Edward L. Wallace, Jr.
    p.   cm.
  ISBN 0-13-616491-9 (paper). — ISBN 0-13-616509-5 (spiral)
  1. Track-athletics — Coaching.   2. Track-athletics — Training.
I. Title.
GV1060.675.C6W35   1998
796.42—dc21

97-26552
CIP

Thanks to North Central College and the Chicago Board of Education for permission to use their forms and photos. Every effort has been made to contact the athletes pictured in the other photographs. Many of them are from the author's private collection acquired through more than 30 years of coaching.

Printed in the United States of America

10   9   8   7   6   5   4   3   10   9   8   7   6   5   4

ISBN 0-13-616491-9 (paper)   0-13-616509-5 (spiral)

ATTENTION: CORPORATIONS AND SCHOOLS

Parker books are available at quantity discounts with bulk purchase for educational, business, or sales promotional use. For information, please write to: Prentice Hall Career & Personal Development Special Sales, 240 Frisch Court, Paramus, NJ 07652. Please supply: title of book, ISBN, quantity, how the book will be used, date needed.

PARKER PUBLISHING COMPANY
Career & Personal Development
West Nyack, NY 10994

On the World Wide Web at http://www.phdirect.com

DEDICATION

I am eternally grateful to my wife Donnie for the patience she manifested as she endured and suffered the trials and tribulations of being married to a dedicated track coach. There has to be a special crown in heaven for her.

ACKNOWLEDGMENTS

To coach Lou Tortorelli, now deceased, who gave me my first opportunity to coach track in Chicago at Dunbar High School. As his assistant, I learned about quality and specificity in coaching and I have never forgotten that lesson. I also thank Gerald Richard, whom I consider an unappreciated coaching genius, who — unbeknownst to him — taught me how to make something out of nothing. I can never forget Mr. Sidney Miller, of Chicago State University, who sat with me on many occasions as we swapped track trivia and coaching techniques for hours on end. I also remember coach Len Jereczak, who showed me by example that distance runners can be developed in an urban setting. Many thanks to my brother, Paul Wallace, who would come to track meets and remind me of things that I might have overlooked with my athletes during the course of a hectic and tiring track season. I also appreciate the example set by coach Henry Springs who, through his tremendous success at Wendell Phillips High School, inspired me to become a track coach in the Chicago Public Schools. I would be unfair if I failed to give credit to my oldest son, Michael, who adamantly reminded me of the great influence that the mind has upon athletic performance. Credit has to be given to coach Anthony Rainey of Luther South High School who showed me the importance of people skills in coaching today's athletes.

ABOUT THE AUTHOR

Edward L. Wallace, Jr., is a track and field coach with more than 30 years experience in the Chicago Public Schools. He also coached at North Central College. He was elected to the Illinois Track Coaches Hall of Fame in 1990 and has developed over 200 state qualifiers and 500 league champions and won 57 championships in track and field. Wallace has also served as a training advisor to two-time world power lifting champion Franklin Riley, coached Willye White toward the end of her career, a five-time Olympian and two-time Olympic silver medalist in the long jump in Naperville, Illinois, and is currently assistant coach at the University of Chicago. He also mentored U.S. national discus champion Josephine Delavina.

Wallace earned his Bachelor of Education degree from Chicago Teachers College and a Master of Science in physical therapy and exercise physiology from George Williams College, Downers Grove, IL. During his career as health and physical education instructor, he was selected Outstanding Secondary Educator of America and also developed and taught a course in exercise physiology and body mechanics, the first of its kind in the Chicago Public Schools.

A frequent speaker at track and sports medicine clinics, Wallace has had sports articles published in *Track and Field Quarterly Review, Iron Man Magazine* and *Runner's World.*

FOREWORD

Edward Wallace is one of the finest coaches in the United States of America. He established a superlative record of coaching during the 1960s at Englewood High School, at Collins in the 1970s, at Whitney Young Magnet High School in the 1980s, at Steinmetz High School in the late 1980s, and at North Central College in the 1990s, which covers his contribution of over four decades in the Chicago area.

During these four decades, Coach Wallace has developed six high school All-Americans, 300 Illinois state finalists, and 500 public league champions — 10 Chicago Public League cross-country championships and 27 Chicago Public League championships in track and field. He has also developed five Division III All-Americans in two years as jump coach at North Central College.

Coach Wallace has also worked with world-class athletes — for example, Olympian Willye White (long jump), and Josephine Delavina, Philippine national champion in the discus throw. He subsequently served as training advisor to Franklin Riley, two-time national and world champion in power lifting.

His knowledge base encompasses both scope and depth. He is academically superior in the fields of anatomy, physiology, sports medicine, psychology of coaching, exercise physiology, strength training, historical aspects of physical education, and management of a department of Health, Physical Education, and Recreation at the secondary level.

Coach Wallace has had articles published on strength training and techniques in track and field events, and has made many presentations at the Illinois Association for Health, Physical Education, Recreation, and Dance and at the Midwest District of the AAHPERD. He is well-versed in pedagogy both theoretical and applied.

His personal library is unequaled in my experience as a teaching professional of thirty-five years. He is highly intelligent and pragmatic both in his personal and professional endeavors. He is at once warm, friendly and people oriented in his communication with students and peers. He is task-oriented while working toward consensus with groups, and he is an excellent decision-maker. His character and personal habits are exemplary and his integrity the highest. I have found him to be the most honest and principled person I know.

Sidney G. Miller
Associate Professor; HPER Member;
Illinois Track and Cross-Country Coaches
Association Hall of Fame, 1979; Past
President, Chicago District IAHPER;
Past Vice President, School/Comm
Health, Midwest District, AAHPERD

ABOUT THIS RESOURCE

This resource is for all track and field coaches — those with years of experience, those who are just beginning, and those who are struggling with a minimum of equipment and facilities or none at all. Above all, it's for coaches who are seeking to learn more about coaching track and field events. If you want to broaden your program and include more events, increase your technical know-how, or find greater efficiency in juggling numerous responsibilities, read on.

Contained within these pages are many revolutionary training methods that were developed because of the hardships and difficulties common to many American coaches. These techniques are guaranteed to turn any program around. They will prove to be valuable, first for the impoverished program, and second, for anyone who cares to use them.

Reading *Track & Field Coach's Survival Guide* will take you on a coaching adventure; sit back and relax. You are about to embark on an intellectual journey through a most unusual collection of coaching methods. This trip will be worth it.

First of all, some general suggestions for knowledge seekers: I advise you to read. Read this and other books and periodicals devoted to track and field. Don't depend upon one book to supply all the answers. Before the ink dries on this publication, somebody will have discovered something new. I will be the first to admit that I don't know all of the answers. Nobody does. But I know a lot of them. Thirty-six years of toiling in the vineyard has taught me so much. Start with the books in my bibliography and read everything you can get your hands on.

Go to track clinics, sports medicine seminars, weight-training clinics. Don't be afraid to ask questions of anybody and everybody who is willing to answer them. Attend the NCAA championships; attend all the big meets. Talk to world-class athletes and their coaches. Most of these people will be glad to discuss their event with a knowledgeable person. I have had the pleasure of conversing with and learning from Brian Oldfield, Willie Davenport, Mal Whitfield, Samson Kimobva, Willye White, Ira Murchison, Wilma Rudolph, Tom Tallez, Ted Haydon, Stan Wright, Brooks Johnson, Rick Wolhuter, Norbert Shemansky, Dave Bethany, Aubry Dooley, and Jesse Owens, to name a few. I am not name-dropping to make an impression; talking to world-class athletes and coaches will reveal information and advice that you will not find in most textbooks. Ask and you shall receive.

In the *Track & Field Coach's Survival Guide*, I describe workouts that were done in a park, on a sidewalk, in the streets, in a swimming pool, or in a parking lot with makeshift equipment. That was all I had at the time; I had no other choice and the parents understood. You may be held liable for not using the proper equipment if it is available. Running and jumping on these unforgiving surfaces and practicing with improper equipment when you have better are *not* recommended! If you have no other choice but to use substandard facilities and equipment, examine all of the possible hazards and problems that could occur with its use and eliminate them. Inexperienced use of improper equipment and facilities is a dangerous enterprise; look before you leap! On a more positive note: Because I was prudent in my use of these substandard facilities and equipment, I have never experienced a serious injury in 36 years of coaching track and field. I must admit, however, that shin splints were a constant problem until I learned how to prevent their occurrence.

Early in *Track & Field Coach's Survival Guide*, I discuss how periodization, plyometrics, body mechanics, and exercise physiology can be exploited in lieu of certain amenities that most American coaches have as a matter of course. Before I delve into specific training programs for each event, I will give some space to psychology and motivation as they relate to human performance. Experience has taught me to believe that mental preparation is infinitely more important than physical preparation. I am always amazed that a few well-placed words can manifest an unbelievable modification in an athlete's performance.

Finally, I will attempt to dissect and probe all the finer points on coaching each event in the track program. I have coached these events in a different way from everyone else out there (which is certainly safe to say since all of us are different and no situations or circumstances are the same). Take what you can use and discard the rest.

When I began coaching in the early sixties, I was in a school that lacked minimum equipment, facilities, and personnel to run a decent program. Under such circumstances, schools don't really expect a program and its coaches to succeed; they're not looking for coaches to develop champions in events other than the sprints and relays. I was told to forget about the field events and the distances, but I refused the "advice."

Great sprinters are extremely rare and I knew I could not, and would not, base my program on the hope that these inordinately gifted athletes would be a common occurrence in a typical high school population. But I expected to find some speed, and I needed to learn ways to develop this trait when I discovered it. From these people can come relay teams, middle-distance runners, long jumpers, pole vaulters, high jumpers, and weight lifters. This doesn't mean that sprinters can't be found. Often, blazing speed is not clearly evident on initial observation but it is possible to enhance a latent gift with a proper training program.

Most coaches do an outstanding job with sprinters. You don't have to be exceptionally creative if the athlete is gifted, but you can do a much better job — even with these people — if you are resourceful. Great sprinters have trained in long halls and short halls, on streets, in alleys, on sidewalks, in parks, on bridle paths, in plowed fields, parking lots, and playgrounds with and without an indoor season. However, the field events and the longer running events will place greater demands on your creativity and work ethic. The mission of this book is to explore how — through innovation and imagination — to transcend a lack of certain amenities and prevail. It can be done. It has been done. It is being done.

It is not enough to know the latest techniques and scientific methods. You must know how to adapt these methods to an unfriendly coaching environment and situation. You may have to raise funds when you have an inadequate budget or none at all. You may have to make equipment when there is none. You will have to learn how to improvise facilities when it is necessary. You will have to make a way out of no way. How is this accomplished? All of this — and more — is covered in *Track & Field Coach's Survival Guide*.

CONTENTS

Section 1

EXERCISE PHYSIOLOGY AND BODY MECHANICS

A practical and common-sense approach to the often difficult sciences of exercise physiology and body mechanics as they relate to track and field. There is just enough information about the above-mentioned sciences to assist a coach in understanding how to apply this science in the most effective manner for a particular situation.

Track coaches are sometimes intimidated by the terms and concepts covered in this section, but unless you learn some of this you will not fully understand why you do what you do in track and field. Additionally, you might not understand why you should not do what you may have been doing wrong. I know why some coaches are turned off by this; I have attended clinics and read literature written by PhDs who have never coached track and field — people who needed to come down from their ivory towers and use plain English. I have seen coaches walk out of such seminars in disgust. What we have here is a failure to communicate. I will communicate. I promise to be practical.

PERIODIZATION

Let us take a look at periodization. What does this concept mean? It means simply changing your program periodically. It means changing from general to specific. Changing from easy to difficult. Changing from quantity to quality. Changing to eliminate boredom. Most sensible coaches have been doing this anyway. We have always known that variety is the spice of life — and so it is with training. The $64,000 question is, "What is the most effective way of doing all of this periodization?" How often do you change? From what to what? What are the physical and psychological rationales for these changes? Who said so?

I will answer the last question first. The Russians said so. The Bulgarians said so. The Eastern Europeans said so. The Canadians said so. The Western Europeans said so. And because this system is so effective, we are being outsprinted, outhurdled, outhigh-jumped and outpole-vaulted all over the place. We seldom win an international middle-distance or distance race any more.

Periodization means changing at a set period of time. Most books written on the subject suggest that you change every six weeks. This rule is not set in stone; sometimes it is best for a high school athlete to change every four weeks. It depends upon the athlete you are working with. The technical journals talk about macro cycles (yearly); mini cycles (monthly) and micro cycles (weekly or daily). There are also general preparation periods; specific preparation periods; precompetitive, and competitive periods. There are usually four to five periods, and each period will last four to six weeks. The fifth and final period is often called a peaking period. Most coaches usually advocate a twenty-week season starting in mid-January and ending the last weekend in May. Simple arithmetic will give you five periods of about four weeks or four periods of about six weeks — depending upon how long your season lasts.

Remember that I am attempting to convey a simplified but practical version of this subject. If you choose to dig deeper into this subject, there are many books devoted to periodization. The mission of this book, however, is to give you enough information to implement this concept in your track and field program without having to wade through an inordinate amount of data that may not serve any useful purpose. The main purpose of periodization is to prepare an athlete physiologically for optimum performance on a given day. If this can be accomplished without analyzing every nuance and chemical reaction in the anaerobic and aerobic functions of the Krebs cycle, then why not? But you do need to know and understand enough basic physiology to accomplish what you intend to in training and to predict with a certain amount of accuracy the outcome of this training. To know less than that is to do a disservice to your athlete.

Why periodize? In all athletic endeavors a good foundation will prepare an athlete for the rigors of top-level competition. It will give the body the ability to endure a season that is certain to place tremendous demands on the heart, lungs, muscles, and circulatory system. If you periodize, the muscles will not traumatize through prelims, semifinals, and final heats of intense competition. They will be able to recover and do it all over again the next week. They will be able to perform when called upon to give their all. They will not self-destruct.

This is a lineup of the contestants in a high school physique contest. We raised over $2,000 in one session. Most of these athletes were members of the track team. Many of these students were state and conference champions in track and field. The weight training that these athletes did in preparation for this contest was excellent preseason training for the indoor track season. We killed two birds with one stone.

This section is general as it relates to periodization. In the following sections, as I cover each event, the specifics of the system will be spelled out in greater detail.

Cycle 1 — The General Preparation Period

This is a four- to six-week period of time — any longer and the athlete will get stale and bored; research tends to corroborate this notion. I also discovered by empirical observation that when you begin a cycle, it takes about two weeks for the training effect of this or any cycle to be manifest. Athletes tend to enjoy this cycle because you can literally do everything. The objective of this period is to develop every physical aspect of the body in a nonspecific way. Volume is important here; the emphasis is on quantity instead of quality. Play a variety of games, for example, basketball, soccer, volleyball, touch football, and dodgeball for aerobic and anaerobic endurance. We also swim, jump rope, weight train, and do gymnastics and tumbling, supplemented with various kinds of calisthenics. Some easy plyometrics are introduced. The distance runners begin gradually to build up their mileage through fartlek and long runs. Some technique work is included. This is primarily a fun and recreation period. The athletes who thought that track and field was all drudgery are pleasantly surprised at how enjoyable all of this can be. But if the team had to compete during this period, they would be able to perform at a very high level because of their total fitness.

Cycle 2 — The Specific Preparation Period

In this period, things begin to look more like track and field practice. There is an increase in event-specific drills and a decrease, but not an elimination, of games, swimming, and such. We still play an occasional game of soccer or basketball, but these are included as a reward for having good practices. Speed work is also increased, but the training emphasis is on quantity.

Though it is not advocated by most authors, you will find that some sort of speed work is an integral part of all five cycles. This point was the central theme in Brooks Johnson's book on track and field, *The Winning Edge.* Johnson felt that speed work should be an important part of an athlete's training program all year — that in order to run fast and race competitively, speed work must be included in the workout at all times.

Another extremely important factor in training is the duration of each workout. From what I have read in regard to physiology and from attending a coaching seminar given by the Bulgarian national strength coach, Angel Spassov, workouts lasting over one hour will compromise the body's endocrine system. To be more specific, production of testosterone, the male hormone, levels off fifty minutes into a workout and begins to decline after one hour. Therefore athletes (male and female) are working at a testosterone deficit if they train beyond an hour's time. (Incidentally, females have testosterone in their systems, but not in the same quantity as males.) Athletes who consistently overtrain feel a need to use anabolic steroids — which contain artificial testosterone — in order to compensate for poor training methods. Workouts that last too long tend to produce too much of a catabolic substance, cortisol, and no progress can be made until it is removed from the system. Steroids mask the catabolic effects of cortisol so that an athlete can continue to train unwisely. When I learned of this phenomenon, I immediately began to reduce the amount of time my athletes trained, and I never regretted this change in my training philosophy. This knowledge also solved some other training problems that puzzled me for several years. More about this later.

In light of the above information, you might wonder if a volume or quantity training program can be justified. Certainly. You can do all the things that are necessary in a typical workout if you are organized. An athlete can run all of the repeats or intervals that the runner needs in one hour or less. If extra work is needed, then train twice a day. Research on the virtues of twice-a-day training was covered in the periodical *Soviet Sports Review*, published by Dr. Michael Yessis; it states that progress can be significantly enhanced by using twice-a-day training sessions. However, your athletes must be psychologically and physically mature enough to handle this extra work. They must also be highly motivated and gifted juniors or seniors in high school before I would suggest this kind of advanced training.

In this second phase of training, introduce interval and repetition running. I also advocate hill or stair running. Increase the amount of time devoted to sprint drills; plyometrics and weight training become more intense. Everything gradually becomes more track-specific. You can imagine, from all the above suggestions, that there are enough training modalities to maintain variety in the program. This variety will aid in eliminating boredom — the enemy of physical improvement.

Several things are happening in this cycle. If you embarked on cycle one in mid-January (the starting time for most for most high schools' indoor seasons), then this cycle places you in the middle of your indoor track season. At this juncture, you will have to set priorities. Do you want to peak for your indoor championship or do you continue to work for your peak in the last week of May? Remember that your team will be able to perform quite well during this cycle, but the best is yet to come. Also consider the tremendous psychological advantage that your squad would have if you won your indoor league championships without peaking for them. This happened to several of my teams. We had a tremendous psychological advantage over our opponents during the outdoor season. If you don't win your indoor championships, your team should always understand that your peak performances are to be expected in May. If your athletes can't handle this philosophy, then modify this cycle and peak for the indoor championships. You have to know your athletes and make your periodization decisions based on your team's ability or inability to deal with long-range goals.

Cycle 3 — The Precompetitive Phase

Now your workouts are really beginning to look more like track and field workouts. Runners are running, hurdlers are hurdling, jumpers are jumping, and throwers are throwing. This is the real thing. You are getting as event-specific as is possible in your given situation. This is the part of the year where a lack of facilities and equipment can be a decided handicap — if you let it. This is the time that your creative juices should flow. Later on in this book, I will cover in more detail how you can brainstorm in regard to each event, but let us continue to look at periodization.

We are still in the quantity aspect of our training year, but speed is the emphasis now. We are trying to fill our hour of training with anaerobic speed work. There is a great deal of lactic acid in the muscles, and discomfort comes with this kind of training. There is an increased emphasis on repetition running and back-to-back sprinting. Your distance runners are doing more tempo runs and fast intervals. We are doing a great deal of running at "goal pace." Plyometrics are becoming more intense; weight training is heavier. Your jumpers and throwers are more concerned with a large amount of event-specific work. Maximum results are possible in competition, but your athletes will find it difficult to duplicate this in practice because of the sheer volume of work you are asking them to do. Remember, all of this work is to be done within 50 to 60 minutes.

This period is characterized as the precompetitive period, but is precompetitive in name only. You have probably concluded your indoor season and are beginning to launch your outdoor season. During this time, you may be competing in relay carnivals and dual and invitational meets. *You are competing.* Don't push your athletes too hard during this time, or they can lose their competitive edge. Some coaches fail to prioritize, and often lose key runners to injury by pushing them too hard before they are physically ready. It is not wise to require your sprinters or anyone else to go through four events of prelims, semis, and finals during this period. You are asking for trouble. Wait until the next cycle to ask your athletes to give their all at a track meet.

Cycle 4 — The Competitive Season

The intensity of effort in training is increased to another level. During the earlier cycles, training was the priority. Now competition is the major focus. You basically sharpen, rest, and compete. You taper during the week because you are preparing for the most important meets of the year. You do not train through these meets as you did in the previous cycles. You make an effort in training to simulate competitive situations on your hard days. Training is all-out but infrequent, because you are preparing for Saturday's meet. Schedule only one meet per week during this cycle; rest and restoration are of major importance at this time. The time to compete at a high level is almost upon you; swimming, running in the water with a wet vest, massage, and just plain rest and relaxation are highly recommended. Check the athletes' pulses before, during, and after practice. Purchase a nitro stick and have them check their urine once a week. Ask your athletes how they feel every day. They will appreciate your concern.

Cycle 5 — The Peaking Period

If you have followed each cycle carefully, your athletes are ready for their personal best. Ideally, you want their best to occur at the state or national meet. The things you say and do in these final weeks are crucial.

This is the most difficult time of the year for a coach. In cycle four, the workouts were event-specific; you attempted to duplicate the stress that the athletes would face in competition. Now, things are becoming more complicated. You have to determine your training program by what transpired in competition. This is a period where speed and underdistance work are emphasized. The workouts are shorter and the rest periods are longer. Pay close attention to proper technique and try to simulate meet conditions. Limit intense workouts to once a week. Then you rest and compete. Your athletes will begin to wonder why practices are so easy. What you do the day before the meet is also extremely important. A few weeks ago, a Romanian coach told me the best thing to do the day before a meet is to warm up and run a few (two to four) hard 80 — 90 meter sprints at 90 — 100% effort. It seems the nervous system needs stimulation the day before competition. This idea is hot off the press. I tried it. It works.

Some of your athletes may want to train harder during this time. If it makes them feel better, let them—but monitor this activity closely. Athletes may need a specific workout for their individual needs. Keep careful records to determine how each athlete responds to certain workouts. Some will need more speed work, others will require more overdistance, and some will need more rest. You will have to know your athletes.

PLYOMETRICS

In 1960, I was stationed in the army and I met a soldier who played center for our base basketball team. He was only five foot nine. He could dunk a basketball with ease. I was told that he developed this remarkable ability by jumping with light weights. I never forgot this lesson. A few years later, while warming up for an Olympic weight-lifting contest, several of the lifters got involved in an impromptu vertical jumping contest. One of the lifters jumped and touched the top of the basketball backboard. I never forgot that lesson either. This was in the early sixties when nearly everybody connected with athletics believed that weight-lifting would make you musclebound and slow. They were wrong. I can remember people challenging lifters (not to be confused with bodybuilders) to sprints and getting their clocks cleaned. One lifter beat a runner in a sprint who had allegedly run a 9.8 100 yard dash. I did not forget that lesson either. The term *plyometrics* was not known at the time of these demonstrations of extraordinary speed and jumping ability. I also knew little or nothing about fast-twitch and slow-twitch muscle fibers, but I learned from simple observation that in spite of popular opinion, weight lifting did not make you slow. In fact it seemed to make you faster. When I became a track coach in 1962, very few coaches were using plyometrics and weight training to supplement their track workouts. Plyometrics is still a relatively new concept and its proper implementation is often misunderstood.

What is plyometrics? It is basically a form of exercise that consists of an organized system of jumping, bounding, and leaping with and without weights. This system of training was officially devised and developed by a Russian coach, Yuri Verhoshansky. The first information about plyometrics in America was published in the *Soviet Sports Review* in the early 1970s by Dr. Michael Yessis. The term *plyometrics* was first used by Fred Wilt in 1975. Plyometrics became an accepted training method in America in the early 1980s. When I used a crude form of plyometrics in the early 1960s, I was twenty years ahead of my time.

I successfully utilized plyometrics long before I understood why it worked so well. This method of training helped several relatively average athletes on my team become city and state champions. Several years later, I learned that this method improved the function of an athlete's fast-twitch muscle fibers. I also learned that gifted sprinters and jumpers possessed a high percentage of fast-twitch muscle fibers. One of the best ways to stimulate these fibers is through the incorporation of plyometrics into their training program. Fast-twitch muscle fibers are white in color; they can exhibit great power and are often referred to as class IIa or IIb fibers (see Figure 1-1 on page 10). Fast-twitch fibers are also developed by certain kinds of weight-lifting activities. Plyometrics, combined with weight training, is largely responsible for the 70-foot shot put, the 8-foot high jump, the 9.8 100 meters, the 60-foot triple jump, and a host of other world-class performances. Any athletic event requiring speed and power has its own set of plyometric drills that are designed to exploit an athlete's event-specific talents.

Plyometrics is also periodized. If this method is not properly introduced into an athlete's training program, severe damage can be done to the musculature. Milder forms of hopping and jumping should be included in the earlier cycles. A more difficult form of plyometrics like box jumping, depth jumping, and jumping with weights should be introduced in later cycles. The specific details of this valuable training tool are explained in detail when I cover each event separately.

BODY MECHANICS

Geoffrey Dyson, Tom Ecker, and Fred Wilt wrote extensively on body mechanics. The study of physics as it relates to human motion is a fascinating endeavor, but you don't have to work with complicated formulas in order to use this valuable method in your coaching efforts. A basic, common-sense approach will suffice. For example, Sir Isaac Newton wrote this about the three laws of motion:

1. *The law of inertia.* Objects at rest will stay at rest until acted upon by an outside force. Objects in motion will stay in motion until acted upon by an outside force. In plain English, a thing won't move until something or somebody moves it, and once it is moving, it won't stop until something or somebody stops it.

2. *Force = Mass × Acceleration.* In plain English, a big, fast person can generate more force than a small, slow person.

3. *For every action there is an opposite and equal reaction.* In plain English, the harder you push back on the starting blocks, the faster you will go forward from the starting blocks. The harder you throw a rubber ball down, the higher it will bounce up!

Try to remember these illustrations; they will apply more often than you realize. This is not a mechanics textbook, but I must introduce a few more essential physical laws in order to give you enough information to understand why certain techniques are necessary in helping your athletes to perform more effectively:

Center of gravity. This is the exact mid-point of the body. When the arms are raised or lowered, or if there is a bending at the torso, the center of gravity will move up, down, or even outside the body. The center of gravity must also be in line with — or directly above — the force delivered, in order for the force to be manifest with optimum effectiveness.

Figure 1-1

A BASIC CHART OF VOLUNTARY MUSCLE FIBERS

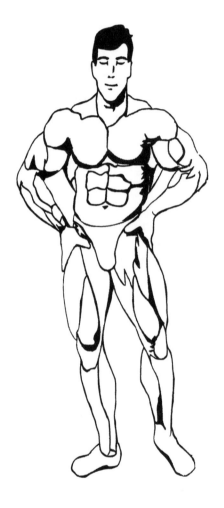

FOUR MUSCLE FIBER TYPES

I	slow oxidative	slow
IIa	fast oxidative	fast fatigue resistant
IIab	fast oxidative	fast inter- mediate resistant
IIb	fast glycolytic	fast fatigable

Summation of forces. To deliver force in a track and field event, the largest and strongest body part should initiate the movement first, followed in rapid sequence by progressively smaller body parts, that is, legs first, torso second — and finally the arms.

Conservation of rotary momentum. Long levers deliver power; short levers are fast. For example, when a spinning figure skater brings the arms closer to the body, the skater rotates faster. Any body part brought closer to the center of gravity will move faster.

Impulse = force × time. The longer a force is applied, the greater the resultant force becomes.

There are at least forty additional physical laws related to track and field events. However, if you remember and understand the above examples, you will find that the rest of the laws are somehow related to these few examples, and you will be pleasantly surprised that you will be able to analyze most track and field events without much difficulty. When you internalize the above seven principles, most of the technical aspects of the mechanics of athletics will begin to make sense. As I begin to cover each event in a more specific way, I will refer to these physical laws to illustrate the rationale of the various techniques relative to that particular event.

EXERCISE PHYSIOLOGY

Some successful track coaches have developed world-class athletes without knowing very much about exercise physiology, body mechanics, periodization, or plyometrics. Most of their expertise was gained through years of trial and error. Knowledge of at least some basic scientific principles can speed up the learning process. If you can understand how a particular workout affects certain athletes physiologically, you are better equipped to assist them in reaching their potential. I have heard coaches saying all kinds of ridiculous things about what a certain training program is supposed to accomplish and they are totally unaware that their programs were next to useless. In many cases their programs were highly *contraindicated*. Often these programs manifest more "error" than trial. That a number of coaches have accidentally discovered a few reasonably effective methods of developing the extremely rare genetically gifted athlete is no justification for lack of understanding of basic physiological principles.

One big physiological mistake that many coaches make is the excessive use of jogging as a training method. Jogging can be valuable as a part of a warm-up and warm-down, but beyond this, jogging is not the way to go. An athlete's warm-up should include some activity designed to simulate the range of motion and speed that he or she will experience in competition. Jogging has very little, if any, positive effect on the fast-twitch muscle fibers. If athletes are expected to compete without injury, they must stimulate their fast-twitch muscle fibers by sprinting in their warm ups.

Jogging does very little to improve cardiac output, oxygen uptake, anaerobic endurance, leg speed, and aerobic endurance. You cannot learn to run fast by running slowly. So let us investigate the above variables and the best training modality for each physiological characteristic:

Cardiac Output

This is the capacity of the heart to deliver oxygen (via the blood stream) to the rest of the body. The best way to improve this function is through interval training. Interval training is the act of running repeat 400s, 300s, 200s, or 100s at a pace slightly slower than race or goal pace. The heart rate at the end of each repeat is about 160–180 beats per minute; the next repeat is started after a 1–2 minute rest. The pulse rate should return to 120 beats per minute during this interval of rest. If the pulse rate fails to return to 120, the athlete is running too fast or the workout is too difficult. The athlete walks or jogs during the recovery period. An easily administered test of the effectiveness of an interval training program is a gradual decrease of the athlete's resting pulse rate during the track season.

Oxygen Uptake

In a nutshell, this is the ability of the body to absorb oxygen. No one can absorb 100% of the oxygen inhaled, but some world-class distance runners have been known to absorb 60% to 80% of the oxygen they inhale. Most of a runner's oxygen uptake capacity is reputed to be acquired prior to puberty, but it can be improved 30% by running repeat 800s. Oxygen uptake can be measured by the Astrand Bicycle Ergometer Test (Astrand, per Olaf. *Text Book of Work Physiology*, New York, McGraw Hill, 1977.)

Capillarization

Long-distance running is the best exercise prescription for stimulating an increase in the number and extent of the capillaries that nourish the musculature. As the capillaries increase in number, more oxygen is delivered to the body via the blood stream. This long-distance running is not jogging; it is running. Some of our more experienced athletes can run 10 miles at the pace of 6–7 minutes per mile. Running these distances at a reasonable speed can prevent most injuries that are associated with jogging. Why? When you jog, there is a greater "G" force on the touchdown of each stride, causing a tremendous shock to the knees, shins, and feet. When I instructed distance runners to run rather than jog, injuries to their lower extremities were dramatically reduced.

Anaerobic Endurance

The longest race in high school competition is three miles. There is a large anaerobic component in middle-distance running, that is, 800, 1600, 3200, and three mile. Interval running and repetition training are two methods usually recommended to improve anaerobic endurance. About ten years ago, I attended a track and field clinic held at Camp Olympia, in Upson, Wisconsin. The subject of the most effective method to achieve optimum anaerobic endurance was hotly debated by some of the best coaches in the world. It was concluded that the most effective method for developing this trait was repetition training. Repetition training is characterized as running repeat 300s, 400s, 600s, 800s, and 1600s faster than race pace. The rest period between these runs is determined by the pulse rate. An athlete should wait until the pulse returns to 120 beats per minute before starting the next repetition. This rest period may take from 3–6 minutes, depending upon the fitness of the athlete. The chronic physiological response to this kind of training is an increase in the reserves of phosphocreatine and other blood buffers in the liver and blood stream, which neutralize the onset of the fatigue poison, lactic acid.

Aerobic Endurance

The purpose of long continuous runs and tempo runs is to raise the anaerobic threshold. The anaerobic threshold is that point at which the speed of the run causes the body to switch from aerobic to anaerobic running. At this point, the runner is unable to absorb enough oxygen to continue running aerobically. Two runners can be running at the same pace; one could be running aerobically and the other could be experiencing the pain of anaerobic distress. The runner experiencing the distress has a low anaerobic threshold. With improved conditioning of the aerobic mechanism (the heart, lungs, and capillaries), this runner will eventually be able to run at a faster pace aerobically. You can gradually raise the anaerobic threshold by doing long runs at a speed that places demands primarily on the aerobic mechanism. Use this formula: 220 minus your age $\times$ 60% to 80% = pulse rate. All this means is that at some point in training, an athlete will be able to run at a faster pace without making any serious demands on the anaerobic system.

Leg Speed and Turnover

Speed is a function of the nervous system and its effect on the white (fast-twitch), muscle fibers. The coordination and distribution of these two characteristics are hereditary, but everybody is capable of improving speed. Every sprinter who lines up in the eight available lanes of a world-class competition has to be heavily endowed with a high percentage of white muscle fibers. However, there are hundreds of talented athletes that never make it that far merely because they are poorly trained. Speed can be dramatically improved by proper training. One of the most important factors in athletic training is specificity. To run fast — you must train fast. A few years ago, I was asked to speak at a track clinic that was held in St. Louis, Missouri. Later that day, I listened to Brent McFarland, the national coach of Canada speak on sprinting training. His talk was extremely interesting and informative. He stated without any reservations that his sprinters did speed work all the time. He concluded that if sprinters are gifted by genetics with an abundance of fast-twitch muscle fibers — and since slow running has no positive effect on these fibers — then distance running is a waste of time and energy for these people. Arthur Jones, the inventor of the revolutionary Nautilus machines, stated in an article in the December issue of *Iron Man* magazine, that endurance exercise will cause fast-twitch muscles to atrophy, causing these fibers to diminish in strength and compromise their explosive qualities. It seems that coach McFarland and Arthur Jones are on the same page.

During the track season, the coach should expect sprint training to stimulate the sprinter's musculature to hypertrophy. Intense and explosive exercise has the tendency to stimulate muscular growth. Strength in the weight room should also increase; a concomitant effect will be a significantly increased vertical jump and standing long jump. If these things fail to occur, something is wrong with the training program. Constant observation of the growth of a sprinter's quadriceps, gluteus, hamstrings, and gastrocnemius muscles can also help to determine the effectiveness of a sprint-training program. The late Arthur Steinhaus wrote in a research paper, "From Morpurgo to Muller — Fifty Years of Research," that it is not the amount of work that makes you strong, it is the intensity of work that makes you strong. Arthur Jones also has stated that you can train hard and you can train long, but you should not do both. Sprinters who are trained with intensity (faster and harder) will get stronger. And in this case, strength is speed.

Charlie Francis, the author of the book *The Charlie Francis Training System* also states that the failure to train can result in injury. If a sprinter's body is not accustomed to moving fast, it will not manifest optimum efficiency at maximum speeds when it is called upon to do so in competition. The SAID principle (specific adaptation to imposed demands) is a concept that is based upon just plain common sense. Sprinters have to experience demands required of them in competition in their practice sessions. If this does not happen on a regular basis, you cannot expect sprinters to survive the pressures that will confront them at the conference, state, and national meets.

Though the mission of this book is to communicate better ways of building a successful track program when confronted with a less than ideal situation, a basic grasp of the science will make your job easier. You must know the importance of exercise physiology in order to optimize the value of your workouts. You can dig a little deeper into this fascinating subject with books devoted exclusively to it. If you continue to study your craft, you will be able to transcend the ubiquitous difficulties that plague the "forgotten coach's" track and field program. As I cover each event in a more specific manner, I will refer to basic physiological principles to justify certain workouts. Workouts that are not physiologically sound will not be very effective, and your athletes may become victims instead of benefactors of your program.

EFFECTIVE WORKOUTS

Finally, before I leave the subject of exercise physiology, I would like to discuss the unfortunate malady of overtraining. For too many years, I was often not certain if athletes were overtrained until it was too late to do anything about it. Like most coaches, I did the obvious things to determine this. I kept a careful record of their performances and always asked how they felt each day. A decline in performance was one subjective sign. Minor ailments and frequent colds were also indications that something was not right. These were all subjective observations, however, and I needed something of a more objective nature. I was aware of the methods used by the Russians, but there was no way I could have a physician at my training site for every workout. There are, however, several objective ways to determine an athlete's fitness. An athlete's resting pulse rate is a tremendous indicator of level of fitness. A resting pulse rate that is higher than usual is a good sign that the body has not recovered from previous workouts or competitions. Another excellent sign of overtraining is a decline in grip strength. Keep a bathroom scale available and check athletes' grip strength by having them squeeze the scale; record the results of these efforts from time to time. Check your athletes' vertical reach jump. If this does not improve during the season, it could be an indication of a lack of recovery from workouts or competitions. The nitro stick is a relatively inexpensive method of checking the extent of an athlete's fatigue. The appearance of excessive nitrogen in the urine is a very accurate measure of an athlete's level of recovery. If one or more of these measures indicates that the athlete is overtraining, it would be a good idea to reduce the training load or give the athlete a few days of rest.

Considerations When Designing a Workout

When you design a workout, there are several factors that need to be considered in your lesson plan. Before you require your athletes to do anything, you should ask the following questions:

1. What month of the track season is it?
2. What stage of the periodization process are we in?
3. What systems of the body do I need to affect at this time?
4. Is there enough variety in the training program?
5. How long should the workout be today?
6. Should I "train through" or should I taper for the next meet?
7. Have I planned for individual differences?
8. Did I check for signs of overtraining?
9. How long and how intense was yesterday's workout?
10. What are the weather conditions today?
11. Have I scheduled enough time for a warm-up and warm-down?
12. How can I make optimal use of the available facilities and equipment?

For your convenience, I have made a chart to illustrate the systems of the body primarily affected by certain training modalities. The *entire body* is involved in whatever training program you design, but each workout will have an optimum effect on a specific system or systems.

Training Modality	System(s) Affected	Expectation
Long runs (6–15 miles) pace 6–8 min/mile	capillaries, slow-twitch muscle fibers, some cardiac improvement	improved aerobic endurance
Tempo runs (3–5 miles) pace 5–6 min/mile	oxygen uptake — anaerobic and aerobic metabolism — slow-twitch muscle fibers	improved anaerobic endurance
Interval training (200s, 300s, 400s with a 1–2 min jog between each repeat) pace slower than race pace	the heart — class IIa fast-twitch muscle fibers	improved cardiac output and some speed
Repetition running (repeat 1600s, 800s, 600s, and 400s) faster than race, Rest between reps 3–6 minutes	anaerobic metabolism — fast-twitch muscle fibers (class IIa) increased phosphates and blood buffers	improved anaerobic endurance and speed
Long sprints (repeat 100s, 150s, 200s, 300s) complete recovery between repeats	fast-twitch muscle fibers (class IIa and IIb) improved anaerobic metabolism increased phosphates and blood buffers	speed endurance anaerobic endurance
Short sprints (repeat 30s, 40s, 50s, 60s, etc.) 90%–100% effort with complete recovery between repeats	fast-twitch muscle fibers (class IIb), improved nerve stimulation and muscle innervation	speed — muscle hypertrophy and increased power, improved turnover

This is not all there is to periodization, plyometrics, body mechanics and exercise physiology. To know every nuance of these subjects, you will have to read; study; attend seminars, workshops, and clinics; and study again. Entire graduate school programs are devoted to each of the above disciplines. The purpose of this book is to give you enough information about these subjects to implement them in your training program. I also introduced these topics so that in later sections you will be able to appreciate the rationale and logic behind certain suggestions that I will offer in regard to training methods and techniques. I have attempted and will continue to attempt — to bring these physical and physiological concepts from the ivory towers of academia into the realm of common sense and reason. Remember that a few successful coaches have managed to develop champions with little or no knowledge of sports science, the school of experience is long and difficult. How many athletes' dreams are you willing to frustrate as you proceed through unnecessary years of trial and error? None, I hope.

If you happen to be a coach working under desperate conditions, a basic knowledge of scientific principles can help you overcome some of the logistical and administrative difficulties you are bound to face. In spite of them, your athletes will enjoy unprecedented progress, and also fewer injuries and plateaus. This same science will enable you to transcend the lack of facilities, equipment, and supplies you have inherited. You are not alone in this dilemma; many countries around the world are working in situations that are similar to, or worse than, what we have. In spite of their circumstances, they are beginning to run American athletes off the track. Many of these countries have never had state-of-the-art equipment, and yet they dominate all of the distance events and most of the field events. Many of the Eastern Europeans have had to work with archaic equipment, under conditions we Americans would characterize as primitive, yet these countries are developing world class athletes by the thousands. Cubans, Canadians, Africans, Jamaicans, and Western Europeans are breaking world records at an unprecedented rate with substandard equipment and facilities. With the proper use of science, you can do it too.

Section 2

MAXWELL MALTZ AND SUGGESTOLOGY

A look at mental attitude and its impact on human performance. It explains how such intengible concepts like belief, faith, concentration, and the power of suggestion can be exploited to help an athlete to realize his or her physical potential.

Several years ago, one of the most successful cross-country coaches in the country, Joe Newton of York High School in Elmhurst, Illinois, spoke at a track clinic held at Oak Park High School located in Oak Park, Illinois. His topic was distance running, but as he covered the physiology and training methods related to his topic, I began to feel that his approach to distance running transcended the physical. Most of the coaches in attendance knew how to design workouts and physiologically sound training schedules, but it was Joe Newton who was winning most of the cross-country meets in the state of Illinois. Illinois produces some of the best distance runners in the country and Joe and his teams seem always to be a little bit better than everyone else. As I focused on his presentation, Joe recommended a book that he felt was partly responsible for the winning attitude of his nationally ranked cross-country teams. That book was *Psycho-Cybernetics* written by Maxwell Maltz. After reading this and other books on the awesome power of the mind, I understood why some coaches seemed to be so successful so often. The great coaches seldom agree on training methods, but they all emphasize the value of a proper mental attitude. Whatever the mind can conceive and believe, the body can achieve!

USING THE MIND-BODY PHENOMENON

How many times have you heard the accounts of ordinary people performing superhuman feats of strength and endurance under stress and dire circumstances? Consider the frail mother who lifted the rear end of an automobile off her child to save his life. Or the sailor who threw a 700-pound bomb overboard to save his ship. History is full of stories about people who accomplished magnificent feats of strength and endurance just because they had to. Great coaches like Johnny Wooden, Vince Lombardi, Knute Rockne, Joe Newton, Percy Cerutty, and Arthur Lydiard have learned how to get their athletes to perform at a level that exceeded their apparent physical limitations. Some athletes, without the aid of coaches, have also developed the ability to call upon their inner reserves of mental and spiritual powers whenever the situation required it.

Science tries to explain some of this mind-body phenomenon. Most athletes and coaches are aware that certain chemicals and hormones are secreted into the blood stream under stress. Substances like epinephrine and endorphins can cause chemical and physical reactions that trigger the sympathetic nervous system to react in a dramatic manner. However, some superhuman efforts cannot be reduced to mere psychological and physiological rationale. Often, extraordinary athletic behavior seems to defy logic; this supernatural level of human performance never ceases to amaze me. In this chapter, we'll explore some avenues of the mind-body phenomenon. Scientists and exercise physiologists

One of track and field's greatest motivators, Al Carius of North Central College, doing what he does best — motivating an athlete.

have told us a great deal about their disciplines as it relates to human performance, but we have only scratched the surface of the psychological aspects of athletic endeavor. In my thirty-plus years of coaching, I have witnessed numerous physical achievements that transcended all logic.

Belief. The Bible is filled with accounts of miracles based on the power of faith and belief. Jesus states in Mark 9:23, "If thou canst believe, all things are possible to him that believeth," You don't have to be religious (but it helps), to know that this statement is true. Any coach who has been involved in athletics for any length of time has seen many athletes do things that would confound any rational prediction. Their physical preparation and training in no way indicated that they in question would accomplish what they did. Belief is an intangible and rather esoteric concept, but whatever it is, the attainment of belief in you and your program must occupy a central focus in your approach to your athletes. All of the physiology, body mechanics, periodization, resistance training, and plyometrics are useless without belief. It is imperative that you sell yourself and your program to your prospective athletes. I have seen coaches who knew little or nothing about the latest techniques in track and field accomplish things with their athletes that confounded the experts. Let me rephrase "Without faith, it is impossible to please God" to "Without faith, it is impossible to do much in track and field."

Have you ever heard of the placebo effect? A recent example of this effect is the experiment that was done with anabolic steroids and its effect on muscular strength. Two groups of athletes were given pills that were supposed to be the anabolic steroid, dianabol. Only one group was given the real thing; the other group was given a fake pill — a placebo. After several weeks of weight training, they were tested. There was no significant difference in the improvement in strength of the two groups. Several years ago, the University of Illinois swimming team was given wheat germ oil in an effort to improve their endurance. The team's improvement in endurance was dramatic and significant. On a subsequent occasion, the swimmers were given just plain oil that was alleged to be wheat germ oil. Their improvement was also dramatic and significant. This is the placebo effect. I have no scientific explanation for this, but I am convinced that the altered state of mind is the key to extraordinary achievement in athletic endeavors — or any endeavor. I don't really understand how an automobile works either, but I drive one every day. Therefore, I can offer a few practical ways to harness this useful tool.

Accentuate the Positive

Always say positive things about your athletes every day. Negative reinforcement has been known to get immediate and temporary results with athletes, but over the long haul, this approach will prove to be counterproductive. It is also imperative that you think, act, talk, and behave in a positive manner around your athlete at all times. A negative attitude can be perceived subconsciously by a sensitive athlete. Be careful. Because of their unique situation, coaches must make a special effort to contribute only positive feedback to their athletes. Many athletes are inundated with all kinds of negative situations at every turn. A coach has to make every effort to be a psychological oasis for his or her team. You have a formidable task before you — more formidable than mere workouts, training, and competition. A stray negative word or thought from you can raise barriers to progress that the most scientific and well-planned training program may not ever overcome.

Most of the literature devoted to the study of the mind seems to emphasize the vast importance of the subconscious or the unconscious mind. The subconscious is intangible and is not easily amenable to scientific investigation anatomically, but its effect on the body is easily observable on an empirical level. Whenever its incredible power is released, superhuman endeavor is often the manifestation.

The subconscious mind has certain characteristics that must be understood before it can be used to elicit a positive change in behavior. The subconscious mind is unable to reason. If you can penetrate athletes' subconscious and communicate with them on this level, you can help them to reach their physical potential, but, several factors must be present. You must have rapport based on trust with your athlete. The athlete must have a belief system — belief in you, belief in self, and — if you will — belief in some higher force. You must constantly reinforce a positive attitude in the athlete by constant repetition of positive affirmations. You must turn every setback and defeat into a positive experience. Athletes have to be told that every workout, every weight lifted, every competition is bringing them closer to their goal. Athletes must be made to believe that they are involved in the best training program on earth. If this is how they begin to feel, their bodies will respond optimally to every workout. Proverbs 23:7 states, "For as he thinketh in his heart, so is he."

If it is at all possible, your athletes should not discuss their training or their beliefs as they relate to track and field with anyone who is known to have a negative attitude. Great athletes are a different breed and often what they believe or say may seem unrealistic to the average person. Most average people are average because they think average. What they say can have a deleterious effect on the athlete's psyche.

The subconscious mind can have a profound effect on the body's physiology. An athlete's response to training and competition can be influenced by his or her state of mind. A well-placed positive statement can work wonders. I have seen athletes make miraculous improvement in times or distances overnight when they became convinced that this improvement was possible.

Stress Goal Setting

Setting goals is often a difficult process for an athlete. It helps to tell them that these goals will be confidential — that this will be a well-guarded secret between coach and athlete. Some guidelines must be established to help the athlete in preparing these goals. I usually ask an athlete to decide on four goals: short-range goals (indoor season), intermediate goals (outdoor season), long-range goals (league and state championships), and ultimate goals (college or university and beyond). Establishment of goals can be frightening for many athletes, and some will object to this request to search their souls. They might find it easy to lie to you and their peers, but it is difficult to lie to themselves.

Writing down goals accomplishes two things. First, these goals are indelibly imbedded in their subconscious. All of their physiological and psychological mechanisms are focused on achieving these goals. Second, if you know where your athletes want to go, you and the athletes can work together on this project. It is frustrating when a coach and athletes work at cross-purposes. You and your athletes *must* have identical goals.

Often, the athlete may write a goal that exceeds your expectations. I strongly advise you to take his or her affirmation to heart. There may be little tangible evidence that these goals can be attained, but if the athlete really believes in these goals — honor them. Several years ago, one of my runners wrote that he had a goal of becoming the Illinois state champion in the 400 meters. At the time, he was my fifth best quarter-miler. He also was recovering from a serious hip operation and was on crutches. I personally thought he was being unrealistic when he wrote this goal, but I kept my mouth shut. On the last weekend in May, he won the state championship in the 400 meters! When an athlete has goals written indelibly on paper and in his or her psyche — respect and acknowledge those goals. What the mind can conceive and believe, the body can achieve.

Visualize

Visualization is another powerful mental tool. Ask your athletes to visualize success. They should see themselves at an important competition; they should visualize the crowd and all of the circumstances related to this important competition. They should visualize themselves running, jumping, or throwing, and exceeding their best. They should internalize all of the physiological effects on their bodies as they go through this most important competition. This mental practice is not easy, but it is extremely valuable in the athlete's preparation for the conference and state meet. Athletes should also verbalize their various goals to themselves as often as they can. They should combine this with their visualization. This is the power of suggestion at its ultimate.

The power of suggestion is more powerful than you can imagine! As a neophyte coach, I was incorrectly convinced that hypnosis was the most effective method of demonstrating the power of mind over matter. I was wrong. The power of suggestion far surpasses anything that hypnosis could ever hope to accomplish. Under hypnosis, the control of the subconscious mind is given to someone else; you don't want that for your athletes. If a coach can help athletes convince themselves through suggestion that they are the best, they will become formidable competitors. The results obtained by hypnosis can be dramatic, but suggestion is more permanent, less dangerous, and much more effective over time.

Suggestology has become an exact science. An institute in Bulgaria established by Georgi Larzanov has developed a system of audio- and videotapes of a specific kind of music, coupled with repetitive positive verbal affirmations, that has produced some fantastic results in mental and physical endeavors. The wise and prudent application of the science of suggestology is the new frontier in athletic achievement.

Emphasize Discipline

Discipline is an important factor in developing a proper psychological basis for athletic success. The most successful athletes possess outstanding self-discipline. This admirable trait can be taught, but at some level, this most necessary characteristic must be intrinsic. No coach could or should attempt to monitor an athlete's personal affairs in order to guarantee that the athlete observes the kind of personal habits that might promulgate athletic success. The best approach is to teach youngsters the value of sacrifice and discipline and hope the athletes will be dedicated enough to accept this message.

Most young people possess a burning desire to succeed; often they haven't a clue to how this can be accomplished. It is your bounden duty to teach athletes the values that will enable them to reach their goals. Your athlete may be surrounded with an abundance of negative circumstances, but all of these factors can be negated with patient and careful instruction. Additionally, your positive attitude can often be contagious; an entire community can be affected by the success of your track and field program. If this happens, you no longer have to be concerned about negative feedback from the athlete's environment. When the school, parents, teachers, students, administration, and community are behind the track program, discipline becomes easier. Extrinsic discipline gradually becomes self-discipline, but you cannot do it alone.

Focus and Concentrate

Focus and concentration are extremely important mental skills that must be taught and developed in athletes. If athletes' attention to the task at hand — be it running, jumping, throwing, studying, or whatever — is scattered or distracted, they will invariably become less efficient. Insist that your athletes develop academic skills such as listening, good study habits, and the ability to relax under pressure; these skills will have a positive carryover value into track and field success. Athletes should be called upon every day to practice these mental skills. They should also be required to remember their splits or times, to focus on certain techniques, to listen to and internalize their workouts and drills, and to learn and understand the basic rationale of their training program in general. Eventually, they will come to understand that excellence in track and field is mostly a mental endeavor — that most great track and field athletes have been academically astute as well as physically gifted. After a few years under your program, athletes ought to be able to assist you in planning their training schedule and their competitive season's goals. They eventually become responsible for their own destiny.

KNOW YOUR CRAFT

You should know your craft as a coach. Athletes need to be confident that their coach is knowledgeable. Then, those intangible entities of belief and faith will make a positive impact on them. Don't attempt to fake this expertise; most athletes can spot a phony a mile away. If you are a new coach, read, study, and ask — but be careful that you do not deal with unscrupulous rival coaches who would jump at every chance to destroy your relationship with your team because of your temporary lack of expertise. Avoid these types at all costs. Do not be afraid to query world-class athletes; many of these people are decent sorts who will be flattered by your interest in their event. I have gained a tremendous amount of information from the likes of Brian Oldfield, Mal Whitfield, Brooks Johnson, Samson Kimobva, Willie Davenport, and the late Ira Murchison — just to name a few. If you persist in your quest for the truth, at some point in your career, you will be so knowledgeable, that your athlete's faith in you, will potentiate the effects of your training program.

PRACTICE GOOD PUBLIC RELATIONS

Become a people person. Public relations is more important than knowing how to coach. No coach ever won a championship alone. You need everybody on your side. Parents, teachers, relatives, the administration, and the community, should be made to feel that every victory is their victory. Enlist their expertise whenever it is offered. The coach usually carries a tremendous burden. If you are the typical "forgotten coach," you are running a bare-bones program. You have inherited a program with no assistants, no budget, no facilities, and no supplies; you need all the help you can get! If everyone is involved in your program, then everyone will understand and appreciate the difficulties you face. These people can help make your road to the top a reality. Without their help, a difficult job becomes almost impossible. With their help come positive feedback, financial assistance, various kinds of expertise, assistant coaches, community involvement, media coverage, fund raising, track officials, clerical help, and moral support. Let them share in your success.

TEACH MENTAL REHEARSAL

This mental skill is very similar to visualization. Most young children are born with this skill, but as we are "detrained" in our education, we lose this powerful mental mechanism. Some people have given this skill a negative connotation, characterizing it as daydreaming. Call it what you will, humankind's most creative geniuses were dreamers. Almost every scientific or sociological advancement was developed by a man or woman who dared to dream. Virtually every revolutionary track and field innovation came from the creative juices of an athlete who went against commonly held beliefs and dreamed or visualized a better way of doing things. Coincidentally, most of these people were athletes of free societies where a certain amount of deviation from the norm is accepted and admired. The fiberglass pole vault, the O' Brien shot-put technique, the Fosbury Flop, fartlek training, the development of the 400 meters from a middle-distance race into the longest dash, the jet-sprint relay pass, the first four-minute mile, the aerodynamic javelin, the 13-step stride pattern in 400 hurdles, the 60-foot triple jump, and the rotational shot-put technique — all were developed in countries where freedom is promulgated. Teach your athletes to dream.

Mental rehearsal can help your athletes prepare themselves for the tension-filled, high-pressure competitions that they will inevitably encounter. It is impossible to duplicate the actual pressures that athletes face at the state meet, conference championships, the NCAA finals, the Olympic trials, or the Olympic finals — but it can be a definite advantage for athletes to mentally rehearse the pressures of these important competitions. This skill can be developed through regular practice. Encourage your athletes to mentally rehearse or visualize execution of perfect technique while practicing or participating in the event during more relaxed situations. The more they visualize, the more proficient they will become when they are called upon to compete under more demanding circumstances. One word of caution however: Athletes should not be taught to fixate on winning, but only on the process of performing at an optimum level. If they can learn through mental rehearsal and concentration to be the best they can be, the winning will take care of itself. Consider what the apostle Paul had to say regarding the thought process: "Finally, brethren, whatsoever things that are true, whatsoever things that are honest, whatsoever things that are just, whatsoever things that are pure, whatsoever things that are lovely, whatsoever things that are of good report, if there be any virtue and if there be any praise, think on these things." Philippians 4:8.

Section 3

TALENT SEARCH

Many coaches don't enjoy the luxury of a junior high or elementary school feeder system. They must use every stratagem at their disposal to get people out for the team. This section explains how to do this more effectively by understanding and implementing basic statistics to accomplish this goal.

Several years ago, I attended a track clinic in Chicago and one of the featured speakers opened his presentation with this statement. "Coaches, before I begin my talk, I want to tell you how to make rabbit stew: Before you begin, you have to find a rabbit." You need talent; without athletic talent, you can't win. I have seen several absolutely brilliant coaches' programs go down the drain when the vicissitudes of urban life began to impact upon the talent pool in their community. In the early forties, urban high schools benefited from the migration of millions of people from the rural south to the urban north. Many of their descendants are now leaving these same urban areas and returning to the south; families who can afford it are moving to the suburbs or sending their youngsters to private schools. Those who remain are left to contend with criminal activity, that is, street gangs, drugs, and so on. The job of getting kids out for track and field has become much more difficult. I can remember when the city schools dominated the various state competitions. Things are different these days, but do not despair. There is still hope. You just have to become more creative in getting the talent out for your team.

STATISTICS AS AN AID IN YOUR SEARCH

When I was a neophyte coach, I did the usual things to get the athletes out. I put up signs all over the school advertising the first day of track tryouts. I had the details of the tryouts announced over the intercom for several days. For several years, I coached frosh-soph football and cross-country at the same time (I was young and foolish), so I could be in a position to persuade football players to run track. That strategy worked then, and it may work for you now. On the first day of tryouts, over one hundred boys came out for track. As the years passed and times changed, I noticed that my numbers were decreasing in spite of a winning program. Out of desperation, I began to visit the local elementary schools and became acquainted with the physical education instructors. I attended playground and park district track meets and organized an intramural track meet at my high school. These tactics helped somewhat, but I was still not getting the numbers I formerly enjoyed. According to statistical predictions based on a normal probability curve, as it related to my school's population of aproximately 1,000 boys, I should have attracted *at least* twenty-two gifted athletes to my squad.

Whenever I enroll in a difficult graduate course, I always attempt to justify the usefulness of this academic requirement, in order to motivate myself to meet the anticipated demands of the subject in question. Statistics was such a course. I found statistics to be an important tool in my quest to determine the number of talented athletes I could expect to be in my school's population. Knowledge of statistics also helped me to determine how to place people in the proper event and how to optimize their training once I got them there. Terms like *probability, standard deviation, reliability, correlation,* and *levels of confidence* are extremely useful concepts — if you know how to apply them. Once I brought it down from the ivory tower and simplified its use, statistics became an extremely practical tool in my quest to continue a winning program in spite of the formidable odds that are often encountered by the majority of urban coaches.

Some Basic Statistical Measures That Can Be Useful to Track Coaches

1. *Probability.* The statistical measure that determines the percentage of a given population that may be average, below average, or above average in traits, skills, and talent.

2. *Mean.* A measurement of central tendency, an average.

3. *Standard deviation (SD).* No test result will be the same every time; it will deviate from test to test, but only to one standard deviation. This will represent a minimal amount of points, plus or minus — the measure of variability. For example, your athletes' performance will inevitably vary during the season, but that difference should not change more than one standard deviation.

4. *Correlation.* Talent in one skill or test can often predict talent or ability in other unrelated skills or characteristics, for example, an exceptional vertical reach jump often predicts talent in the sprint events.

5. *Levels of confidence.* An .05 level of confidence means that 95% of the people tested will respond to a certain training method or system; 5% won't. An .01 level of confidence predicts that 99% of the people tested will respond to certain training modality; 1% won't.

6. *Validity.* The workout or training method you employ should be developing or effectuating the skill or trait that was expected by following said workout or training method.

7. *Reliability.* The workout or drill should produce basically the same result every time.

There are a multitude of other statistical measures, but these are the ones that I have found to be the most useful for coaching track. These concepts have helped me pick my team, place people in the correct events, and plan workouts. I touched upon these particular statistical terms because I will refer to them frequently throughout the course of this book.

Statistics can often be used to predict with some degree of accuracy the characteristics of a random sample of a certain population. By using the perameters of a bell-shaped curve, a coach who is familiar with its statistical measure can reasonably determine the nature of a given random population — namely the school where he or she works. The term *random* is used loosely in any coaching situation, but we have to assume that your school — or any public high school, — is a random sampling of young people in a given community. This is not always true, because your particular community may be biased by income, race, location, and other factors too numerous to mention, and these biases may be positive or negative. Let us assume we have a random sampling of students that make up this bell-shaped probability curve. If you are among the fortunate few who work in a special situation, then your probability curve may be skewed to the right, but most coaches probably work in situations that could be characterized as normal, average, or typical. Figure 3-1 represents a normal bell-shaped curve. The exact mid-point of this bell-shaped curve represents the

Figure 3–1 — Probability Curve

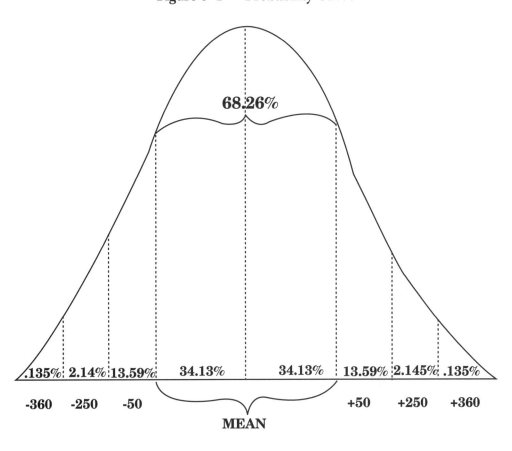

68.26%

.135% 2.14% 13.59% 34.13% 34.13% 13.59% 2.145% .135%

-360   -250   -50   +50   +250   +360

MEAN

arithmetical mean. To the right of this line is the part of the population that may show better-than-average athletic potential. The broken vertical lines are called standard deviations. The group within one standard deviation on each side of the mean represents over 68% of your school's male population. Most of your candidates for track will come from this group; they are your average people. Your gifted athletes will come from the last two standard deviations to the right. Theoretically speaking, 2.27% of your school's male population might be considered gifted and 13.59% might be somewhat talented. Therefore, based on a male population of 1,000, close to 150 boys should be out for track and 22 boys, plus or minus, could be talented. Of the 22, 1¹/₃ boy could be your future state champion. That hypothesis motivated me to engage in a relentless search for talent until the composition of the team represented the above figures. Is this attitude unrealistic? No indeed. I didn't always keep 150 boys on my squad, but I kept most of the 22. When I competed against the suburban schools, I always filled every event with quality athletes. I will be the first to tell you, getting athletes out wasn't easy. Coaching track, especially in the urban areas is a difficult, arduous and often thankless job at best. But it was the most rewarding job I ever had. Nevertheless, if you expect coaching track to be a cushy profession; seek another.

HOW TO CONDUCT YOUR SEARCH

Now that you have an idea how to determine the number of athletes you are hypothetically supposed to expect; let me now tell you how to get most of them on your squad:

1. Walk the halls between classes and give the students a personal invitation. Show your interest in them as individuals, but show no malice toward anyone who rejects your offer. Sometimes students will change their minds the next day. Tell them to bring a friend.

2. Visit the physical education classes on your free periods; observe the various games being played. The students with track talent are not difficult to identify even when playing other sports.

3. Ask the other members of the physical education department to spot potential track athletes for you. Give them credit for being talent scouts if the athlete does well later on.

4. Check every student's resting pulse rate. I discovered four excellent distance runners in one day with this method.

5. Keep track of athletes cut from other teams. Invite them to your squad.

6. Never cut a student from your team. Let them cut themselves.

7. Be encouraging to athletes of marginal ability. They often will blossom after a year or two of maturation.

8. Make your workouts fun. Others will be tempted to join in.

9. Keep a sharp eye out for tumblers, swimmers, weight-lifters, and bodybuilders; talent in those activities often correlate with some track event.

10. Find out who performed well on the school's physical fitness test. If these students had the drive or mental toughness to win the physical fitness test, they might also be excellent candidates for the track team.

Most affluent suburban and private elementary schools have interscholastic athletic programs; most of the poorer public school districts do not. Early involvement in an organized athletic situation gives a student a decided advantage in the developmental process. Certain physical skills and traits must be developed at the proper maturational level; if athletes from a poor school district have not accidentally impacted upon a skill or trait before entering high school, they are at a disadvantage compared with the average suburban freshman. The rural or urban student probably knows little or nothing about track and field upon entering high school. Most of these students are usually walk-ons. All is not lost, however; most underprivileged rural and urban youngsters are usually physically active, and many of them will come to you with skills developed by a dedicated physical education teacher, by an inspired playground or park district program, or from a community that encourages and rewards physical prowess. If this is your situation, you must find a way to uncover this plethora of raw talent — and find it quickly, because your potential athletes might be at least two years behind their suburban counterparts in formal training. The forgotten coach must develop an accurate and efficient system of determining the extent and kind of latent talent that may come to him or her. The statistical measure of correlation is the most important tool that can be exploited for this purpose. Experience has shown that several basic motor skills correlate with certain track and field events:

Basic motor skill or physical trait	*Correlated event*
1. Standing long jump	Sprints, long jump, triple jump
2. Vertical reach jump	Sprints, long jump, triple jump. high jump, 800 meters
3. 30 yard sprint — flying start	Short sprints — 60–100 meters
4. 60 yard sprint — flying start	Long sprints — 200–400 meters
5. Tumbling skills	Pole vault
6. Push press with barbell	Shot put or discus throw
7. Cross country talent	2 mile, mile, 800 meters
8. Pull-ups	Pole vault
9. Low resting pulse rate	2 mile, mile, 800 meters
10. Tall, fast, and flexible	Hurdles, long sprints

The correlations above are not etched in stone, but at least it shows a quick method of determining where to place talent temporarily. Your athletes should be retested periodically; training and maturation may modify these traits. Some athletes will not accept where you place them; for example, almost every male athlete wants to be a sprinter. So let them sprint. After a few unsuccessful and futile attempts in competition, they will come to you seeking another event.

The late coach Eddie Hurt of Morgan State University used a unique method of determining running talent. He timed every runner in the 400 meters. Those who won the 400 time trial were his quarter-milers; those who led in the first 200 meters became his sprinters, and the athletes who showed speed at the end of the race became his middle-distance runners. I took this approach one step further. I timed every candidate in every running event from the 30 meter sprint to the mile run. This endeavor would take about one week. Athletes love to be timed. I would often give the runners three attempts in the sprints and only one attempt at the longer races. By the end of the week, most of the team was prepared for workouts because of this strenuous five-day competition. I also used this week to teach starts, sprint drills, running form, tactics, pace judgment, proper warm-up, finishing technique, sportsmanship, and track etiquette. You will have an attentive and highly motivated audience; most youngsters want to make a good first impression. After this rather difficult week, a few of the runners will experience some muscular soreness. Refrain from any serious work for the next two weeks; this will give the team time to recover from any muscular trauma that may have occurred. Use this time to teach some additional technical aspects of running. It can also be an excellent opportunity to begin work on several of the field events. On Friday, let them play a game of their choice. Sacrilege? Not a chance — they will love this brief change of pace and look forward to this aspect of track and field. This type of activity can have a positive effect — athletically and socially.

PHYSICAL CHARACTERISTICS TO LOOK FOR

Find out what athletic activities each candidate participated in prior to entering high school. This information will give you valuable insight into the sources of their latent talent and skills. Much of their success will depend largely upon what inadvertent exposure to training they may have had while in elementary school or junior high. Scientific studies have shown that some physical traits must be developed before adolescence. A high school coach can only make a minimal impact on these physiological gifts. Listed below are several physical characteristics that the high school athlete must bring to you on the first day of practice. Then it becomes your job to discover and develop the talents and skills the student has brought to you.

1. Red (slow-twitch — endurance) muscle fibers. This is a hereditary trait, and their number and kind cannot be changed by training. Their cross-sectional girth and blood supply can be modified by training,

2. White (fast-twitch — speed) muscle fibers. This is also a hereditary characteristic, and their number and kind cannot be altered by training. Their cross-sectional girth can be hypertrophied; their blood supply can be enhanced. Some physiologists believe that class IIb white fibers can be converted to class IIa white fibers. This may not be a desired modification. Other scientists feel that training can cause hyperplasia (an increase in the number of muscle fibers).

3. Turnover or leg speed is largely developed before puberty. Training has a limited effect upon this skill.

4. Oxygen uptake, or the capacity of the body to absorb oxygen, is developed before puberty and is changed very little after that.

5. Coordination is developed mostly in early childhood. This is difficult to modify in high school. Difficult — but not impossible.

6. Muscular strength is a highly trainable characteristic in adolescence. According to the Bulgarian sports scientists, training for strength should begin as soon as the male hormone, testosterone begins to manifest itself in the athlete's body. Strength training should be closely supervised. Structural damage can be done to the athlete's bony framework, connective tissue, and musculature, if you are not careful.

7. Cardiac output is a highly trainable characteristic. The chronic physiological effects of distance running, especially interval running, are a significant increase in the size of the chambers of the heart, a greatly reduced resting pulse rate, a proliferation of vascular circulation, and a greatly improved anaerobic threshold. A knowledgeable coach can radically change a runner's physiology and athletic performance. A well-trained distance runner's heart and circulatory system can process oxygenated blood throughout the body with incredible efficiency. Oxygen uptake will improve somewhat, also.

8. Anaerobic endurance. Proper training can enable an athlete to adapt physiologically to the inevitable accumulation of lactic acid in the musculature caused by strenuous activity. Glycolysis (the breakdown of glycogen into lactic acid), and the diminution of phosphate reserves in the blood and liver can be neutralized through training. An experienced coach's expertise can contribute significantly to this process.

9. Track and field technique. Many adolescents enter high school with poor development in the basic skills of running, jumping, and throwing. An excellent athlete may be hidden beneath this manifestation of incorrect motor skills and body mechanics. This is another excellent opportunity for a coach to make a great impact upon an athlete's competitive effectiveness.

10. Flexibility. Range of motion is often lacking in today's athlete. This is another highly trainable characteristic; it can be a considerable challenge to the coach's expertise and patience.

Prospective athletes' untrained efforts are often not an accurate indication of their athletic potential. They might come to you without any of the above characteristics and perform very poorly initially. For this reason, I devoted some space to focusing on the substantial contribution coaches can make toward athletes' attainment of physical improvement by concentrating most of their attention on the ten factors above.

A final word of advice about this talent search: Walk the halls every chance you get. Observe each student's gait and stride. Observe their body types, skeletal structure, symmetry, muscular development, rhythm, posture, the bounce in their steps. Never let prospective athletes' personal opinion of their capabilities deter you from inviting them out for track. They are not the experts; you are. A young man who eventually ran 37.5 in the intermediate hurdles and 47.9 in the 400 meters told me that he was not fast. What did he know? I have been involved in athletics for almost four decades; something as nebulous as a student's persona or body language will often remind me of some world-class athlete, and the radar in my psyche becomes sensitized. I have discovered hundreds of outstanding candidates in that manner. I am frequently asked, "How did you know that I could run fast just by watching me walk down the hall?" I usually respond, "You remind me of _____." If you intend to coach track and field for any length of time, develop this instinct. It's a valuable skill and will contribute greatly to successful recruitment activity.

Section 4

FACILITIES
AND EQUIPMENT

Many coaches are assigned to positions and left to fend for themselves. They are alone. They are told to coach track and field without facilities, equipment, supplies, or support. They are given a meager budget, or none at all, and are expected to run a viable track and field program. Of course, the benign administration doesn't understand and no on else seems to care. If this is your situation, you have inherited mission impossible.

You *can* make a way out of no way. Facilities and equipment *are* available — if you know where to look. You can build a winning program if you know how to improvise and innovate. That's what this book is all about.

Several years ago, I was conversing with a veteran coach whose team began to perform quite creditably after two decades of subpar seasons. I was curious about his team's recent rise to power; I began to question him about his training methods and the kind of talent he was getting out. I incorrectly assumed these were the reasons for his success. His explanation? The school finally built him an indoor facility.

On another occasion, I asked a coach why his state champion did so well in his junior year and failed to place in his senior year He said his school was building a new all-weather track; it wasn't finished and there was no other 400 meter track in his district.

Many coaches in similar situations will probably think there is nothing wrong or strange about the above responses to these questions — that their solutions to their dilemmas were perfectly reasonable. It was clear that these coaches felt they could not do anything significant to improve their situations and there was no need to try. Both coaches were dead wrong in their lack of enterprise and attitude, when they made no attempt — or at best, a feeble attempt — to develop some kind of alternate plan to deal with their unfortunate situations. The sad thing about this was there were probably dozens of facilities around them; they just didn't look like facilities.

There are a number of excellent ways to deal with circumstances that at first glance seem to be impossible. Most third world countries are running American athletes into the ground with little or no modern facilities as we know them. They take what little they have and make the best of it. With a little innovation, you can optimize whatever situation you have inherited. This section covers some solutions to problems coaches may face if they happen to work in a situation that is less than ideal. Listed below are some of the alternative sites used in lieu of proper facilities.

NO INDOOR TRACK

1. *Train outside.* Tell your athletes why this is necessary for a successful outdoor season. Most athletes will not object if you suffer with them through this ordeal. Don't send them; join them. Have them wear scarves around their necks, skull caps, gloves, and extra socks to protect them from the cold. Keep the team moving for the entire workout. Move them inside immediately after the workout is finished. If the temperature drops below 10 degrees above zero, stay inside. Some dedicated athletes will insist on going out when the weather is below zero, but let that be their choice.

   In 36 years of coaching, my athletes never contracted a serious illness practicing in inclement weather; however, I contracted serious upper respiratory ailments twice. Standing around, holding a stopwatch in February is not good for your health, but somebody had to do it.

2. *Use the halls.* Take special care to prevent injury. The floor's surface is hard and the turns are sharp. Teach the runners how to negotiate through the halls safely. Most administrators will give you permission to use the halls and stairs if you can convince them that your people will not cause problems or get hurt. Send all spectators home. They can cause more trouble than you think.

   Running in the halls on the unforgiving surface can cause stress fractures and shin splints. Entertain any complaint about the slightest physical problem. An ounce of prevention is worth a ton of cure. Advise the athlete in question to stop running immediately and ice the injury. A thorough warm-up and warm-down, however, can prevent most injuries caused by hallway activity. Have the team wear extra socks or orthotics during practice; this may help to prevent shin splints.

   Divide your team according to event and ability. This keeps the traffic flow workable and will prevent unnecessary crowding while practicing. Assign group leaders or captains to help maintain an organized and orderly practice. Conduct team meetings before and after practice. Keep these meetings short and to the point; say positive things. Eliminate the negative; send them home in a good mood.

3. *Use the swimming pool if it is available.* Adelphi University is famous for developing a tremendous indoor program by the intelligent utilization of a swimming pool. You can conduct a tremendous workout in water. The team can run laps in the shallow end of the pool; they can hold on to the side and simulate running. You can extend a pole across the pool and the team can hold on and run in place. I have also improvised crude wet vests with life jackets and had the team run in the deep end of the pool. I have also used the swimming pool during the outdoor season to rehabilitate injured runners. After two weeks in the pool, the injuries were healed and the athletes in question ran faster than ever.

4. *Find an empty classroom or exercise room.* On some days, you can conduct an hour or so of calisthenics and aerobics. Be creative and you can keep their interest in this activity for several weeks. We also did sprint drills and partner resistance running, exercised with surgical tubing, and did plyometrics in this empty class room. The kids loved it! I found an abandoned exercise room in the basement; we climbed ropes and worked on the horizontal bars, parallel bars, and stall bars. We hopped, skipped, and did plyometric drills. We also worked on various medicine ball drills.

5. *If you have a weight room, take advantage of its possibilities.* Circuit train to maintain endurance. Power train for strength and speed. Train two to three times a week. Teach the Olympic lifts if you have the expertise. Use repetition clean-and-jerks to build stamina, power lift for strength. Specific routines for each of the track and field events will be covered in more detail in the event-specific sections later in this book.

6. *When the basketball team is playing an away game, use the gymnasium.* Do not get so involved in the basketball program that you end up escorting them to their away games; this is an opportunity to use the gym. If you don't prioritize the track program, who will?

7. *Use lunch rooms, gym balconies, auditoriums and school basements for track practice.* Yes, it's a shame that the urban or rural track program has to go to these extremes in order to survive and prevail, but your athletes can learn a valuable lesson that will help them in life — How to overcome adversity and how to make a way out of no way.

8. *You can also use the above facilities to develop the field event people.* When we did that, we went to indoor invitationals and often won most of the field events. If you use your imagination, there is always somewhere you can high jump, put the shot, long, and triple jump. You may not be in a position to do the full event all the time but there is always someplace you can set up certain drills. A field eventer can be trained in swimming pools, hallways, balconies, on stairs, or whatever. I am not talking about average performances either; I am talking about state-and national-caliber results!

NO OUTDOOR TRACK

I wrote the above heading just to attract your attention. You may not be blessed with a million-dollar, eight-lane, all-weather outdoor track, with all of its concomitant amenities, but when you begin your outdoor practice, the possibilities are endless. Most urban high schools do not have easy access to an outdoor track. If you do, consider yourself among the fortunate few. The nearest track may be several miles away. So walk — if it's safe. Walking is an excellent warm-up for track practice. Nearly all the accessible facilities that I used were cinder or dirt tracks; this soft surface is an advantage for most events — except the intermediate hurdles. The big invitationals, our conference meet, and the state championship are held on an all-weather surfaces. This is enough difference to compromise your hurdler's stride pattern. The solution to this problem is to take your hurdler to the nearest all-weather track on the weekends. There has to be one somewhere within a reasonable driving distance.

If there are no tracks nearby, then there are parks within walking distance. One of the parks I used was a veritable gold mine of possibilities. It had all kinds of hills, bridle paths, a large parking lot, and trees for marking distances. I borrowed a measuring wheel from the physics teacher and marked off 100s, 200s, 400s, and every distance I would need for interval training. If a park is not within walking distance, then there has to be a playground or vacant lot somewhere. If there are no available parks or playgrounds, you may have to use asphalt pavements and sidewalks as a last resort. I don't recommend that you do much sidewalk work, but if you have to, find a smooth surface. If a youngster falls on this unforgiving surface, you will be in big trouble. Be careful.

A track meet held in a gymnasium. All we needed were a few cones.

One of our training areas — a parking lot.

Another training area — a local park. We are discussing a workout with the distance runners.

Try to find a park if at all possible. The surface is soft and because this surface is kind to your legs and feet, injuries to your athletes' lower extremities will become history. Another advantage of a park is the panoramic view that you will have of the entire team. You can observe every event with little or no difficulty. Psychologically, the distances you have measured will appear shorter than those on a 400 meter track. The workouts will seem less difficult. If you can organize your markers strategically, practice can be easier to organize here than on a track. You will have to do a great deal of improvisation for your field eventers, but with a little creativity, it can be done. It is a great place for drills, however.

Your car can also be a tremendous training aid outdoors. Sometimes I use it for overspeed training by towing the runners. On other occasions, I may use the car for resistance training by pushing it. Be careful with these drills, because there is an element of danger in towing and pushing; make sure that your athletes are warmed up thoroughly prior to undertaking these drills. Make sure you practice in a safe, traffic-free area. Explain in careful detail what you want your team to do. Have them repeat what you said about this workout word for word. Assume nothing. If there is *any* possibility that an athlete is not safe doing these drills, don't do it. Properly executed, these drills can make dramatic improvements in your athletes' ability to run, jump, and throw.

We also used the nearby public housing project stairs and balconies as an indoor and outdoor training resource. (If you are not friendly with the local street gangs, don't try this. I happened to have a few gang members on my team and this gave us easy access through the community.) We did most of our hill training in these buildings in the winter. Fortunately, there were four sixteen-story buildings located within a three-block area about a mile from the school. We would run from the school to the buildings, run to the top floor of every building, and return to school. The sprinters would run every building once, and the distance runners would run every building twice. This extremely beneficial workout took less than one hour to complete, once the team was in reasonable physical condition.

EQUIPMENT

Most urban schools provide some sort of meager budget. One affluent high school's athletic expenditure might exceed that of an urban school system's entire athletic budget, but the fact remains, you have a budget. If you are not financially astute, you can still make it work. If you need additional funds, find a way to raise the money. Sell candy, sponsor a dance, put on a gym show, have a bake sale, appeal to the parents, install pop machines. Raise the money. I made over $2,000 every year by sponsoring a bodybuilding show. It was so successful that several schools began to copy this idea. The show became so popular that officials from the downtown office came to see one of my shows.

The bodybuilding show served two purposes. It gave my team a chance to get in some early season weight training, and it provided an opportunity for students to become involved in an exciting happening. Several participants in the show said this event prevented them from becoming dropouts. They looked forward to this event every year. You can never predict what might motivate a student to continue his or her education.

The proceeds from the show were not enough to pay for expensive track equipment like pole vault pits and such. The money basically paid for relatively inexpensive items such as hurdles, shot puts, tape measures, high jump cross bars, stretch hoses, relay batons, vaulting poles, and local transportation. The school paid for some entry fees, mats, uniforms and downstate expenses. The rest of the equipment was donated to us by suburban schools and nearby colleges and universities who were discarding old equipment and understood our situation. Most of the equipment they gave us was in mint condition; the remainder required very little effort or expertise to repair.

Essential Equipment and Supplies

You *must* have certain equipment and supplies in order to function effectively. When you raise your funds, or if the athletic budget is adequate, purchase or acquire these items for your equipment room:

1. *Uniforms.* When you order uniforms, get the best available. Uniforms made of cheap or inferior material will not last over the years, and will quickly begin to look trashy and ugly. Buying inferior uniforms will cost you more in the long run. Besides, athletes seem to run better in sharp uniforms.

2. *A high jump pit.* Granted, it can be a high-priced item, but the Fosbury Flop practiced on an unsafe landing area is not a good idea. If your principal will not cooperate with your budgetary demands, make a pit. Most furniture factories will donate foam rubber to public schools. Put the foam rubber in net bags and you can jump in relative safety. Store these bags in a safe place; foam rubber is flammable. I also used discarded bed springs that I found in a junk yard. I covered the springs (top and bottom) with tumbling mats; this made a fairly decent pit. I never used it to jump for height. It was basically a training aid. Various drills on these makeshift pits will enable your jumpers to compete on an equal basis with athletes who happened to be blessed with state-of-the-art equipment. However, the best of all worlds is to purchase an official high jump pit. Some companies will let you buy one on an installment plan. It is worth the trouble.

3. *Try to accumulate shots and disci over time.* Keep one or two in mint condition, so that it can pass inspection at the big meets. When you buy shots and disci, make sure they are all the same shape and size. You should however, have a few overweight and underweight implements on hand for training purposes.

   You can put the shot and discus throw anywhere. These are probably the easiest field events to improvise. Draw a 7-or 8-foot circle on a sidewalk or an asphalt pavement and throw the shot or discus into a park or vacant lot. Use the curb stone as a toe board. A curb is not your only option for a toe board however, you can make or buy one. These boards are usually not very expensive and are also relatively easy to make.

4. *You can make relay batons out of almost anything.* Never discard broken fiber glass poles; they make excellent batons. When they are cut to the proper length, these homemade batons are usually about the same weight and diameter as a commercially made baton. All you need is a saw.

5. *A decent set of hurdles can be made in the school's wood shop.* Most shop teachers will be willing to make this a class project. Students can also make the most of your weight benches, squat racks, high jump standards, jump boxes, and so forth.

6. *Weights.* When I began coaching track in the early 1960s, almost no public school in Chicago had a weight program. Most administrators were afraid of the possibility of liability due to an unreasonable and misguided fear of injury during weight training. In the 1960s, most urban coaches felt that weight training was counterproductive to a successful athletic program; since that time, the attitude in the city toward weight training has changed dramatically. Currently, every school has a weight program; I had to set up a weight program without any administrative support. I made most of the weight equipment; I had no other choice. A local junkyard dealer was kind enough to donate ten six-foot steel bars to our cause. I bought 600 pounds of secondhand barbell plates, added an additional number of various flywheels from the junkyard, and a crude but effective weight room was born.

7. *Get the best possible starting blocks available.* A good pair of starting blocks will last for several years. Paint them in your school colors to discourage theft.

8. *It is also not wise to compromise on pole vault equipment.* This is too hazardous an event to subject your athletes to substandard equipment. If you don't have the funds to purchase the best equipment, you may have to forgo this event temporarily; you could get an athlete seriously injured. However, all is not lost. There are several solutions to the pole vault dilemma: If you are close enough to a nearby suburb, you could cancel practice at times, take your vaulters to a school that has pole vault equipment, and do a really concentrated instructional session at this site. Whenever we had a home basketball game, our principal would often cancel track practice; I would use this occasion as an opportunity to work with the vaulters at a school that had a decent vaulting facility. The rest of the time, we would do drills in our gymnasium. I also persuaded a few of the vaulters to upgrade their skills by attending a vaulting camp in the summer. Or if they couldn't afford to attend a camp, I worked with the vaulters on a one-to-one basis during the summer at a nearby university or college. When school was in session, drills and frequent competition kept them sharp. Don't give up trying to raise money for the proper equipment; it may take a few years, but it can be done.

9. *Long jump in a safe pit.* The quickest way to lose an athlete to injury is to attempt a competitive type of jump in an unsafe landing area. The next best idea is to use the high jump pit to practice a few of the long

jump drills. These are basically simulated jumps, but it can prepare your jumpers for the real thing. If you don't have a decent long jump pit, take your jumpers (on the weekend), to the nearest track that has one.

Overcoming the Disadvantages

There are no disadvantages that cannot be overcome by an ambitious urban coach. A coach is limited only by creativity and enterprise. You can develop a comprehensive track and field program that can be on a par with that of the most affluent school. Until students become our most important resource, then the urban coach — or any coach faced with a similar situation — will have to continue to improvise and innovate to remain competitive. You will have to work far beyond the parameters of your job description, but if you let financial and logistical outrage impact upon your program, then you will be a part of the problem instead of a part of the solution. You are not alone in this dilemma; thousands of coaches in rural, urban, and some suburban areas are not competing on a level playing field. The solutions and innovations offered in this book will stimulate your creativity and imagination. Make a difference. It is up to you to make the playing field level.

Section 5

THE 100 METER DASH
The Ira Murchison Club

Some track runners are born with a large percentage of fast-twitch (class IIb) muscle fibers. This is a rare genetic trait, which endows an athlete with unbelievable leg speed and little or no muscular endurance. These people are usually world record holders at the 100 meters and under. They seldom run world-class times in the longer sprints. Ira Murchison, Houston McTear, and Bob Hayes are perfect examples of this kind of runner. This section explains how to recognize and train these unique individuals.

I can remember the first time I met Ira Murchison. Wendell Phillips High School was competing against Tilden High School at Tilden. I was a member of Tilden's track team. It was an indoor meet. The meet was held in the hallways after school was dismissed for the day. Fortunately, I was a middle-distance runner and I would not be competing against Ira. Ira's reputation as a sprinter preceded him, and I was looking forward to seeing him run the 60 yard dash. We had an outstanding sprinter on our squad who was undefeated that year; I incorrectly thought that this diminutive runner from Phillips was in deep trouble. I was in for a rude awakening! I have never, before or since, seen a sprinter to duplicate Ira Murchison's leg speed. He cleaned our runner's clock. Some track books claim that the fastest leg turnover on record is five strides per second; then Ira must hold that record.

Figure 5–1 — Ira Murchison, a former world record holder (100 meters, 1956) won an olympic gold medal in 1956 as a member of the 4 × 100 meter relay team. Ira ran the 100 meters in 10.1 seconds.

Ira Murchison came from a rich Chicago tradition of great sprinters. Some of his predecessors were Ralph Metcalfe from Tilden High School, Fritz Pollard from Senn High School, and Buddy Young, Jim Golliday, and Sundar Nix from Wendell Phillips High School. All of these men eventually became world-class sprinters. Ira went on to participate in the 1956 Olympics, and subsequently equaled the world's record in the 100 meter dash. Several Americans have dominated the sprints, but I dedicate this chapter to Ira, because he was the quintessential 100 meter runner. Ira turned in some respectable 200 meter times, but he was utterly fantastic in the shorter sprints. Ira was only 5'5" tall — very muscular, and his leg speed defied logic. He was a prototype of the classic short sprinter. In the history of track, several other runners had similar genetics — Barney Ewell, Eddie Conwell, Jim Golliday, Bob Hayes, Houston McTear, Ben Johnson, Gail Devers and Linford Christie, just to name a few.

TRAINING THE SPRINTER

In Section 1, I talked about muscle fiber types. There are a few genetically gifted athletes who have few or no slow-twitch fibers in their musculature. Endurance running of any kind is anathema to them. It is difficult for these people to extend their speed beyond 100 meters. Every characteristic about them is clear evidence that they have inherited an abundant supply of fast-twitch, class IIb, white muscle fibers and a paucity of slow-twitch, class I, red muscle fibers. These athletes excel on every test of power and speed — the standing long jump, the vertical reach jump, the power clean-and-snatch and the 30 yard sprint from the starting blocks. You don't need a muscle biopsy to determine that they are born to sprint; empirical observation tells you all you need to know. Ira Murchison was this kind of sprinter.

An athlete's physiological makeup also determines how his or her body will respond to exercise. This is true for every person on this planet. If a person is blessed with an abundance of white muscle fibers, endurance running is contraindicated. The lack of any significant amount of red muscle fibers indicates that endurance training of any kind is basically a waste of time and energy. Most of this athlete's training program should consist of a generous portion of speed work. Exercise science tells us that excessive endurance work will cause white muscles to atrophy and diminish sprinting speed. Why attempt to train in a manner that will contribute little or nothing to successful sprinting? Sprinters who have this genetic gift should rarely, if ever, engage in an aerobic endurance running program. They should sprint all year long.

This type of sprinter's psychological attitude toward training is characterized by an abiding distaste for anything that remotely resembles endurance running. The sprinter is happiest when given copious amounts of the kind of training that suits his or her personality. The latest research corroborates this approach to sprint training. You will not have to struggle to persuade this athlete to do speed work; That's all he or she wants to do.

When you give this athlete the kind of work his or her body best responds to, several physiological phenomena are manifest:

1. Muscle fibers will hypertrophy dramatically. White muscle fibers grow rapidly when subjected to a training program of low-volume, high-intensity exercise.

2. Ability on tests of power increases dramatically with proper training.

3. Aerobic ability will show very little improvement. The resting pulse rate of a world-class sprinter is usually higher than that of the general population.

4. Anaerobic endurance will increase somewhat with proper training. Occasionally, these people can run a decent 400 meters, but their performance in this event is mediocre compared to their times in the shorter sprints.

5. Thorough and careful warm-ups become extremely important. There is a very limited blood supply to white muscle fibers. It takes a long time to warm up these fibers, especially in cold weather. When white muscle fibers are examined under a microscope, there is visual evidence of a minimum of mitochondria (cells that absorb oxygen). Slow jogging will not adequately prepare this athlete for sprint competition. At some point in the warm-up, this athlete has to duplicate the speed encountered in competition.

6. An increase in muscular strength is accompanied by an increase in hypertrophy and muscular power. Sprinters respond easily to strength and power training.

7. Maintenance of flexibility is difficult, but not impossible. Rapid response to strength and power training may impact negatively on flexibility. Special attention to flexibility and stretching is necessary for the 100 meter specialist.

TALENT IDENTIFICATION

Outstanding sprinters are seldom found in the average school population. I have had the privilege of working with some exceptional sprinters in my career, but unfortunately, I have never had one of these genetic anomalies on my squad. Several have competed in the Chicago area; some of these athletes have gone on to distinguish themselves in national and world competition.

Because these people are so rare, they are not difficult to identify, but you identify them by their psychological and physiological characteristics and not by their somatotype. They come in a thousand different physical uniforms. Some are tall, some are short. Most are thickly muscled, a few are muscular and wiry. All have exceptional leg turnover, remarkable relative strength, and unusual muscular power. Most walk with a pronounced bounce or spring in their step.

Just because these athletes are gifted and rare, it does not mean that you have nothing to do. These gifts have to be developed. There are at least seventeen trainable characteristics that a knowledgeable coach must potentiate in order for this athlete to attain optimum velocity in the 100 meters. Talent is not enough.

A better trained, less gifted athlete can often defeat a gifted, but poorly trained sprinter. Listed below are some of the variables that must be developed in order for a sprinter to reach optimum potential:

1. *Muscular strength.* A sprint coach must have expertise in weight training or some sort of resistance exercises. Improper weight training can negatively affect a runner's speed. This is why some coaches with antediluvian attitudes still insist upon avoiding weight training as a viable training modality, but remember — Ben Johnson did not take steroids to improve his turnover or running technique. He took steroids (even though he didn't necessarily have to), to increase his muscular strength.

2. *Muscular power.* This trait is improved through plyometric exercises, for example, jumping and bounding with and without weights.

3. *Range of motion.* Flexibility exercises are an excellent way to prevent injury; they also increase range of motion, which will positively affect stride length with little, if any, negative effect on stride frequency or leg turnover.

4. *Reaction time.* With constant practice, this characteristic can be improved.

5. *Starts from the blocks.* This is self-evident. A poor start in the 100 meters is often disastrous.

6. *Rapid and smooth acceleration.* A good start without rapid acceleration must be avoided. This is a highly trainable, but often overlooked, skill. Starts, and a smooth transition to acceleration, take a long time to learn.

7. *Relaxation.* There is no championship running without proper relaxation. Speed cannot be forced; it must emanate from proper technique.

8. *The marriage of turnover with stride length.* You may have to shorten a runner's stride length to improve a sprinter's results. On the other hand, you may have to teach your sprinter just the opposite. This has to be determined by the coach and the athlete, via many hours of practice.

9. *Knee lift.* Is the sprinter's knee lift too high or too low? Work with your sprinter; practice and study films to determine the optimum knee lift required for championship sprinting. This is a highly individual matter, depending primarily upon the muscular development and structure of each sprinter.

10. *Arm action.* A strong and efficient arm action, properly coordinated with the legs, will help to prevent any extraneous body twisting and shoulder sway. The elimination of all wasted motion in the body will optimize the delivery of speed. The arms should be at a 90 degree angle. On the forward stroke, that angle decreases somewhat and on the backward stroke, the angle of the arms will increase a few degrees.

11. *Foot plant.* The touchdown of the foot must be directly below the runner's center of gravity — on the ball of the foot. The toes of the foot should be

facing in the direction of the run or turned slightly inward. The feet should never point outward; this puts the quadriceps in a very inefficient running position.

12. *Body lean and posture.* Most advocates of body mechanics frown on coaches who teach their runners to lean. Mechanically speaking, sprinters are not supposed to lean. Conversely, some coaches incorrectly overdo the emphasis on leaning. Both are wrong and both are right. If a sprinter has good posture and runs on the balls of his feet and if you draw an imaginary line of force from his plant foot through his center of gravity, there will be a *slight* deviation forward of this line from the vertical. Therefore, an almost imperceptible, but necessary, forward lean is manifest. This puts the body in a position so the gluteus maximus muscles (extensors of the hip) can deliver their greatest force. If this line were exactly vertical, the sprinter would have to run flat-footed and the contribution of the glutes to a powerful and effective running stride would be greatly compromised. (Incidentally, did you know that all great sprinters have well-developed gluteals)? However, I have seen some coaches teach their runners to lean forward so much that it causes the sprinter's torso to break at the waist. This puts the gluteus maximus in an untenable position, and the touchdown of the driving foot and leg is behind the center of gravity and cannot deliver optimum force. Leaning this far forward breaks all the laws of body mechanics.

13. *Hand position.* The hands should be open and relaxed. The thumb should be on top and remain on top throughout the arm action. The wrists must be relaxed also.

14. *Head position.* The head should be in a neutral position throughout the race. The runner might be able to see the rise and fall of the knees without looking down. Sprinters always look forward; any other head position will reduce speed.

15. *Recovery leg.* The recovery of the lower leg is an important aspect of the athlete's stride pattern. At the conclusion of each stride, when the support leg leaves the ground or surface, there is a rapid folding of the lower leg toward the thigh. The closer the gastrocnemius and the heel of the foot are brought to the rear of the gluteals and the upper thigh, the greater the efficiency of the recovery to the next stride and subsequent leg turnover. This is another application of the law of the conservation of rotary momentum mentioned in Section 1.

16. *Elimination of backward lean.* Whenever a runner leans backward, she is establishing a braking action. The runner is reducing speed.

17. *Anaerobic endurance.* A poorly trained sprinter will tie up in the last 20 meters of a 100 meter race. If a sprinter is fortunate enough to make it to the semifinals of an important competition, recovery ability will be so limited that properly trained but genetically inferior sprinters will keep a more talented competitor out of the finals. A poorly trained sprinter's fatigue will be so overwhelming that she might also be useless as a leg on a sprint relay.

Sprinters are born; however, there is a great deal that you can do to develop this potential. Without dedicated attention to a consistent work ethic, raw talent will not be enough to get a sprinter past the preliminaries of an important competition.

OPTIMAL USE OF AVAILABLE FACILITIES AND EQUIPMENT

Facilities and equipment — or the lack of them — do not significantly impact on the development of sprinters. Sprinters can train almost any place. Short halls, long halls, gym balconies, stairs, gymnasiums, swimming pools, parking lots, bridle paths, playgrounds, parks, basements, and empty class rooms can do the job. State, national, NCAA, international, and Olympic champions have come from similar situations. But if you can beg, buy, or borrow the ideal, then do so. Training with substandard facilities and equipment is always a compromise. All kids deserve the very best in facilities and equipment, but we cannot throw in the towel because we don't have it. Some day the powers that be will wake up and realize that our young people are our most valuable resource. Someday.

Try to limit sprint training on hard surfaces, but if this is all you have, careful attention to his shins, ankles and feet will pay great dividends in the long run. Sudden stops on these surfaces are contraindicated. Insist that sprinters wear the best of training shoes; have them wear extra socks or some kind of cushion or orthotic in their shoes. An ounce of prevention is worth a ton of cure.

TECHNICAL ASPECTS

The Sprinter's Start

Without a decent start, a sprinter's race may be over before it begins. The sprint start, more than any other phase of the race, has experienced constant change. Initially, sprinters did a standing start. Later it was the crouch start. When Jesse Owens won the 1936 Olympics, sprinters dug holes in the track to anchor their feet. Then various kinds of starting blocks and starting techniques were tried. Sprinters tried the bunch start, medium start, and elongated start. They crowded the line; they moved away from the line. In the set position, hips were held in a variety of positions. The most effective start should be based on the runner's body structure and leverage attained when the sprinter is in the set position.

On Your Mark

Proper body alignment is the key factor when the sprinter assumes the "on your marks" position. The thumb and fingers should be as close to the starting line as possible without touching it; the arms are 90 degrees from the shoulders to the ground. The knee of the front leg should be even with, or slightly behind the arms. The dominant leg is in the back block (this recommendation is not carved in stone). Sometimes it is best to experiment with this position; there are a number of variables that may determine whether the right leg or the left leg is placed in the front block. The feet are straight against the blocks without any toeing out. A slight toeing in is acceptable. The head is in a neutral position, the eyes are focused on the ground in front of the hands. Check this position every day until it is mastered.

Photo 5–1. The "on your marks" starting position.

Get Set

The "set" position is one in which the legs are straightened somewhat. The front leg is brought to an angle of 90 degrees and the back leg is at approximately 120 degrees. The angles of the legs can vary some depending on the relative leg strength of the individual. Of course, these positions and angles can be adjusted from time to time as the sprinter becomes accustomed to this rather uncomfortable stance. The head stays neutral (you should be able to draw a straight line

Photo 5–2. The "get set" starting position.

from the middle of the hip to the middle of the head). However, the hips are slightly higher than the head by several inches. The arms are shoulder width apart and the shoulders are ahead of the starting line. The eyes are focused on the ground a few inches in front of the starting line. The fingers are in the highest position that the sprinter can hold. A novice sprinter will experience great difficulty in holding this position for any length of time. Practice holding the "set" position for 20–30 seconds several times a day to build strength in the arms, hands and fingers. Consistent work on fingertip push-ups and a regular weight-training program will also help your sprinter learn to hold this stance easily. Last but not least, the feet are pressed firmly against the pedals of the starting blocks; the toes barely touch the ground.

Go!

When the starter's pistol is shot, there should be an explosive leg drive against the starting blocks. Strength and power are important here. Weight training is absolutely necessary to develop the kind of explosiveness required for an optimum start. If your sprinter's right leg is in the front block, then his *right* arm is thrust forward. An excellent drill to develop the correct arm action from the blocks is to place a relay baton in the sprinter's right hand and have him thrust his arm forward and release the baton. The baton should land several feet in front of the runner. The drive of the right foot lasts longer than that of the left foot, but there is more power generated by the left foot for a shorter period of time. The torso is driven forward and upward to a point where it is directly in a

Photo 5–3. The first stride from the "blocks."

line of force applied by the rapidly straightened right leg. An imaginary line of force could be drawn from the middle of the right leg through the center of mass and continue on through the middle of the still-neutral head position.

Acceleration

The next five strides are crucial. Each of these strides, in rapid succession, should increase gradually in length and in speed. The torso will gradually attain an erect posture by the fifth or sixth stride. There should be a deliberate effort to run out of the blocks and not chop the steps in doing so. There must be a smooth transition to full running form by the fifth or sixth stride. At this stage of the race, the sprinter endeavors to accelerate to her maximum speed which will be attained at about 70–80 meters. This is also the point at which most sprinters begin to decelerate — where relaxation, scrupulous attention to the technical aspects of running form, and anaerobic endurance become extremely important to the sprinter. Sprinters who are endowed with an abundance of class IIb, fast-twitch fibers tend to tie up in the last 20 meters. Proper training can modify this physiological manifestation.

The Finish

Sprinters who double as 200 meter runners usually experience fewer problems in the last 20 meters of the 100 meters. Their physiological and structural characteristics are slightly different from those of the 100 meter specialist. Generally, they have a greater supply of class IIa, fast-twitch muscle fibers, which give these sprinters an edge in the endurance department. Most of these people are taller, and usually attain top speed a little later in the 100 meter sprint. Sometimes this is enough to overcome a more muscular opponent. Both kinds of sprinters should be taught to maintain correct form, stride length, arm drive and time their lean for the finish line. All of these skills can be developed by consistent drill and practice.

Sprinting is a technique event. I disagree with coaches who feel championship sprinting is all talent. Before you decide to move a youngster into a longer event, try to eradicate some of the technical flaws the athlete brought with him. An untrained effort in sprinting does not always indicate his real talent. I am told that Jim Golliday competed in the mile run as a freshman. As he matured, his coach made him a sprinter. At Northwestern University, Jim was a world-class sprinter. Several years ago, a member of our school's football team came out for track to improve his speed for college football. He was overlooked by the college recruiters because he was considered too slow for Division I football. After several months of training, this athlete became a valuable member of our sprint relay team that eventually won the Chicago Public League championship. He went on to become a running back for the University of Illinois as a walk-on and was later drafted by a professional football team. This was not an isolated occurrence; it happens all the time.

In thirty-six years of coaching, I have never been fortunate enough to have four gifted sprinters to run the 400 or 800 meter relays. Most coaches consider themselves extremely lucky if they coach one gifted sprinter in their entire career. Freshman candidates may come to you with a number of serious physical limitations. With hard work, dedication, and close attention to the seventeen previously mentioned principles, many of these people can become decent sprinters. You will often have to manufacture most of your sprint corp from average athletes. With proper training and great baton passing, you can develop highly competitive sprinters and relay teams from limited talent.

Finally, all runners must be tested every season and sometimes during the season. An adolescent's body changes dramatically in four years. There may be a sprinter hidden beneath some clumsy, inept, soft, and often undeveloped teenager's untrained physique. Don't let some kid's initial efforts mislead you. You never know.

THE 100 METER TRAINING PROGRAM

To develop otimum sprinting ability, an athlete must gradually build strength and stamina to endure rigors of a competitive season. This is accomplished by the following cycles of periodization:

1. *The general preparation period.* The general preparation period is a four- to six-week period of general conditioning. This period may not look like the typical track workout. Have your runners literally do everything, that is, aerobics, gymnastic exercises, calisthenics, weight training,

Feb 12 –
March 9

games, swimming, plyometrics, rope jumping, hill or step running, and, of course, sprint drills and some sprinting at 80%–90% effort. The goal is to prepare the body in every possible way for the rigorous sprint competition that it will inevitably face later on in the season. I do not like to schedule meets during this period.

If you have a conference dual meet obligation, run this type of sprinter in the 200 or 300 yard dash. The body is not ready for the short sprints yet. The general preparation period lasts through the month of January.

2. *The specific preparation period.* This is another four-week period that covers the month of February. Now, the training program begins to look more like a typical track workout. We run repeat sprints of 100 and 200 meters, or back-to-back short sprints of 30–60 meters. Aproximately half of these sprints are done from the starting blocks. Plyometrics, rope jumping, and weight training become more intense; we still play games like basketball, volleyball, and soccer on Friday. Occasionally, we will also swim on Friday.

3. *The precompetitive period.* Some coaches might characterize this four-week period as a competitive period. I don't. This is the month of March — the most competitive part of the indoor season. If you peak for the indoor championships, that is one peak too many. Everything you do should be in preparation for the big meets in the latter part of May. If you happen to win the indoor conference meet, think of the psychological advantage you will have over the teams that peaked for this meet — but this competition should not be your major focus.

During this mesocycle, I like to conduct workouts that combine speed work with anaerobic conditioning. The 100 meter specialists will be given volume workouts, but I will not ask them to run anything over the 200 meters in training. They will run repeat 50s, 60s, 100s, 150s, and 200s. They will compete in sprints from the 50 yard dash to the 300 yard dash. Our weekly minicycle will consist of hard days followed by an easy day. We taper off on Friday for Saturday's meet. Some coaches train through the unimportant meets; others like to taper off. I prefer to taper off; recovery is just as important as training. Recovery from training may be more important than training.

We continue doing plyometrics and weight training, but the workouts are becoming more intense. The weight training is much heavier and the repetitions began to decrease; the rest period between sets increases. There is a greater possibility of injury during this time; close supervision of the weight room becomes extremely important. As a matter of fact, close supervision of the entire training program is mandatory because of the intense nature of the training program. Be careful.

After the conference meet or a meet of similar importance, I give the team four days off. I arrived at this arbitrary number from empirical observation. Whenever I gave the team four days off after a tough high-caliber competition, I never had to deal with soft tissue injuries. When an athlete undergoes the kind of intense effort that is required of him or her in a conference or state competition, there is usually some kind of microscopic damage to muscles, tendons, and ligaments. Sometimes this damage is so minor that it will not manifest itself until the outdoor season. Muscle pulls are the result of cumulative insults to the soft tissue over an extended period of time without proper recovery.

4. *The competitive period.* In the month of April, most coaches train outdoors and try to ignore the uncooperative weather. Distance runners can train outdoors almost all year regardless of the climate; sprinters cannot. If the temperature is below 50 degrees, you are asking for trouble with a sprinter. Coaches tell me that they have not had any serious injuries from training or competing in sprints in the cold weather. They are playing Russian roulette with their athletes' hamstrings. Have you ever noticed how sprinters from warm climates dominate the high school lists in the *Track and Field News* every year? It's the warm weather! Where is it warm in the colder climate? It is warm inside!

I talked to Ira Murchison at length about training inside during the early part of the outdoor season. We concurred that it is impossible and dangerous to do any kind of serious speed work in cold weather. As a neophyte coach with poor indoor facilities, I welcomed the opportunity to train outside immediately after the indoor season. What a mistake! The team was shivering and suffering in the cold weather doing workouts that were much too slow to be speed work.

There was no way to run fast without insulting your soft tissue. We tried wearing extra sweats, tights, nylon stockings, long underwear, and atomic balm; nothing worked to our satisfaction. Our only alternative was to run a lot of overdistance or reduce the intensity of our speed work. Then our speed work was not speed work. According to Eastern European research, we were not working the fast-twitch muscle fibers properly. We were suffering in the cold unnecessarily.

Much to the consternation of the janitorial staff and the administration, I kept the sprinters in the hallways until the weather became amenable to our soft tissue. When we embarked on our outdoor competition, we were injury-free and fast — even in cold weather. I was careful, however, not to yield to the temptation of running short sprinters in the 100 or 200 until the weather was more forgiving. We continued to run fast in training as we waited for the weather to change. There were usually several days in April when the weather would permit us to engage in sprint competition, or we could train outdoors, and we took advantage of these rare and unpredictable opportunities. But regardless of how warm the temperature becomes, insist that your sprinters wear tights and *two sweat suits* during their warm-ups.

Be careful not to cause your athletes to become overly concerned about injuries of any sort. Sometimes when an athlete is psychologically fixated on this possibility, certain negative seeds can be planted in his subconscious that ought not to be there. It is up to the coach to conduct the training program so that the possibility of injury is eliminated. The coach should bear the cross of concern alone.

The training during this cycle is very intense; the recovery time between repeats has to be longer. Whatever you do at this point begins to resemble actual competitive situations. Weight training is lighter and more explosive. You taper off earlier in the week for Saturday's competition. All out sprinting is required in preparation for the conference and state finals. With any luck, the weather will be much warmer, even hot — but still wear two sweat suits in your warm-ups. I learned this little precautionary measure from Dave Bethany, the head track coach at Texas Southern University.

5. *Peaking*. Rest, recover, and compete. Training is of minor importance during the closing weeks of the season; competition is the prime directive. You are mostly recovering from an important competition, or you are tapering for another important meet. You might, out of necessity, compete two or three times a week. Your sprinters might participate in three or four events at each meet. This includes preliminaries, semifinals, and finals. Pay close attention to their warm-ups and their ability to handle this amount of sprinting. Teach them how to conserve their energy through the preliminary heats. This is a crucial time in the season. Remember, if you have been fortunate enough to have a gifted sprinter on your squad, *handle with care*. You are dealing with a thoroughbred.

On the following pages, you'll find examples of a week's training program for each of the five mesocycles or training periods covered above. These training programs are merely guides; they are only suggestions and not exercise prescriptions to be assiduously adhered to. Each program will have to be modified depending on your situation and available talent:

Weekly training schedule for 100 meter sprinters during the general preparation period

Day	Duration (min)	Activity	Training details
Monday	15–20	Warm-up	800 meter jog, stretching Spint drills — high knees butt kicks, chop downs, etc.
	30	Agility exercises	Soccer
	10	Power	Easy plyometrics, hopping and jumping drills
Tuesday	15	Warm-up	Aerobic exercise, stretching and calisthenics
	30	Exercise continuum	Basketball game
	30	Strength	Weight training
Wednesday	15–20	Warm-up	Easy intervals and walking between each (100 meters)
	30	Agility exercises	Volleyball
	15	Power	Easy plyometrics

Day	Duration (min)	Activity	Training details
Thursday	15	Warm-up	1000 meter jog, stretching and sprint drills
	30	Agility and anaerobic endurance	Soccer
	30	Strength	Weight training
Friday	20	Warm-up	Easy intervals and calisthenics
	30–40	Relaxation and recovery	Swimming

The chart above represents a typical week of sprint training during the general preparatory period. This is a four- to six-week period that at first glance does not look much like the typical track workout. Don't let its appearance mislead you. This workout will accomplish just what it is designed to do — build a physiological foundation for the more difficult work ahead. Psychologically, this is fun. Good news travels fast — and recruitment of athletes becomes easier when students perceive that track and field is not all pain and drudgery. If a coach is reputed to be a dictatorial slave driver, prospective athletes will avoid him or her like a plague. Coaches can work their athletes as hard as they desire when athletes are convinced that hard work is fun. Perception is everything.

Weekly training for sprinters during the specific preparation period

Day	Duration (min)	Training Task	Training details
Monday	20	Warm-up	800 meter jog, calisthenics and stretching
	10	Sprint drills	High knees, butt kicks, chop downs, etc.
	30	Stair running	3 min. stairs, 3 min. jog, 3 min wind sprints. Repeat this cycle 3 times.
	5	Warm-down	800 meter jog, stretch, walk 800 meters
Tuesday	20	Warm-up	Easy interval running, 100 meter repeats, calisthenics and stretching
	10	Sprint drills	
	30	Baton passing, block starts	Walking, jogging and half-speed baton passing. Learning the "on your mark" and "set" positions
	10	Warm-down	800 meter jog, stretching

Day	Duration (min)	Activity	Training details
Wednesday	20	Warm-up	1600 meters fartlek calisthenics and stretching
	20	Sprint drills	High knees, butt kicks, chop downs, form runs, etc.
	30	Stair running	Same as Monday,
	10	Warm-down	jog 800 meters, stretching
Thursday	20	Warm-up	800 meters jog, calisthenics, and stretching
	10	Sprint drills	Same as Tuesday
	30	Relay baton drills, block starts	Nothing is at full speed; these drills are part of the learning process
	30	Weight training	High reps (10–15), low sets (1–3), light weights (60% of max)
Friday	20	Warm-up and sprint drills	Same as Monday
	50	Swimming, basketball or volleyball	
Saturday relay.		Competition. Run an overdistance event (300 meters) and a	

This is an example of another four-week cycle. The training activities are beginning to look more like a track workout. Near the end of the month of January, we begin to compete against other schools. The 100 meter sprinters are entered in races longer than their favorite distances for anaerobic reasons. Their speed will be challenged by their participation in sprint relays. In the next four-week cycle, they will begin to participate in shorter (55 meter) indoor sprints.

Weekly training schedule for the precompetitive period

Day	Duration (min)	Training task	Training details
Monday	20	Warm-up	800 meter jog, calisthenics and stretching
	10	Sprint drills	High knees, chop downs, 1, 2, 3s, overstrides, form runs
	30	Anaerobic speed	10–12 × 100 80%–90% effort, walk 100 meters between each*
	10	Warm-down	800 meter jog, stretch

Day	Duration (min)	Training task	Training details
Tuesday	20	Warm-up	400 meter jog, 4 × 100 meter interval strides, jog between each, stretch
	10	Sprint drills	Same as Monday
	30	Baton passing and starts	Establish passing zones for the 4 ×100 relay, 80% speed through the zone, 30 meters from the blocks
	30	Weight training	1 set 10 reps (upper body), 2 sets 10, lower body
	10	Warm-down	
Wednesday	20	Warm-up	Same as Monday
	10	Sprint drills	High knees, butt kick, over strides, skipping with high knees and chop downs
	30	Alactic sprinting	1 × 100, 1 × 90, 1 × 80, 1 × 70, 1 × 60, 1 × 50, 1 × 40, 1 × 30, 4 × 100 accelerations (80% – 90% effort)
	10	Warm-down	
Thursday	20	Warm-up	Same as Tuesday
	10	Sprint drills	Same as Tuesday
	30	Baton passing, block starts	4 × 200 passes at 90% effort, starts at 20 meters, 100% effort
	30	Weight training	4 sets, 5 reps
Friday	20	Warm-up	10 × 100 intervals, 50% speed, jog 100 in between each
	10	Sprint drills	Same as Monday
	30	Speed work	5 × 30, 2 sets, 5 × 60, 2 sets. 1 × 400 stride; rest 2 min between sets
Saturday		Competition.	

* A runner's best time divided by the percentage will give you the exact speed of a required run. For example: 11 secs. divided by 90 = 12.2!

The month of March is the most important part of our indoor season. We will train through dual meets and taper off for the big invitationals and the conference championship. Our indoor taper is usually just one day. We usually jog an 800 and stretch, run through a few sprint drills, and rehearse a few baton passes and starts on the day before our important meets. We have not reached our peak physical condition yet — nor do we intend to reach it. That is the reason this four week period is called a precompetitive period. Our ultimate peak occurs in the final two weeks of the outdoor season in May. However, most of our sprinters usually turn in outstanding efforts because of the excitement associated with most indoor competition.

Weekly training for sprinters during the competitive season

Day	Duration (min)	Training task	Training details
Monday	20	Warm-up	Jog 1600 meters, calisthenics and stretching
	10	Sprint drills	High knees, chop downs, form runs, etc.
	30	8 × 200 meters	Each 200 at 90% effort, walk a 200 in between
	10	Warm-down	Jog 800 meters, stretch
Tuesday	20	Warm-up	Jog 800 meters, 100 meter strides, jog 100 in between
	10	Sprint drills	Same as Monday
	30	16 × 100 meters	Use the first four 100s as a warm-up, the last 12 at 95% effort. Monitor every 100 to avoid leg problems
	30	Weight training	Heavy weights, lower reps, 4 sets, 5 reps
Wednesday	20	Warm-up	Jog 800 meters, walk 200 meters, jog 800 meters, calisthenics and stretching
	10	Sprint drills	Same as Monday
	30	Baton passing and starts	Work primarily through the passing zone
	10	Warm-down	Single-file jogging for 800 meters with baton passing
Thursday	20	Warm-up	Same as Tuesday
	10	Sprint drills	Same as Monday
	30	Stride frequency work	4 × 30 (2 sets), 4 × 60 (2 sets) Rest to recovery between sets
	30	Weight training	Light weights with speed reps, 8 – 10 reps per set
	10	Warm-down	
Friday	20	Warm-up	Same as Tuesday
	30	Rehabilitation	Relaxed water drills and swimming
Saturday		Competition.	

The previous cycle should be completed in the month of April. However, this and others can be arranged according to any schedule. These cycles can be lengthened or readjusted to accommodate the time when your conference or championship meet might occur. The above recommendation fits quite neatly with the Illinois High School Association's state final, which is usually held on the last Saturday in May. The above cycle, at first glance, looks like most track workouts, but there are a few subtle differences that have to be modified by that omnipresent problem: the *apparent* lack of facilities.

Coping with the Weather

April is a very difficult time of the track season in some locations. In Illinois, the weather is unpredictable, and may change in the middle of a workout or a track meet. You need a plan "B" ready at all times. Be ready to change your training program at any moment; be prepared to pull your sprinters out of an event at a relay carnival that you may be winning. I have seen the temperature drop 40 degrees in the middle of an important track meet in Chicago. Before the meet reached its conclusion, the stands looked like a hospital ward. Several outstanding sprinters' seasons were over; other potential state champions limped through the remainder of the season nursing injuries that refused to heal. A word to the wise is sufficient.

If your conference or league has a compulsory league schedule, you may have to compete in cold weather. If this is the case, run no race under the 400 meters. If you have to train outside, make this day your overdistance workout. You cannot — I repeat, you cannot and should not — attempt to do any speed work if the temperature is below 50 degrees. The times will be so slow that your training will deteriorate into an exercise in futility. Trying to do speed work in cold weather is a waste of time and manpower. If it is possible; train inside. Have you ever wondered why athletes from Texas, California, Florida and Louisiana dominate the sprints every year? Their climate permits these coaches to train fast whenever they want to. Coaches from the colder climates can train fast also — inside. Make friends with the engineer and the janitors, so you can train inside whenever you choose. It's worth the effort.

Call the weather bureau every morning. These people make fairly accurate forecasts. This will give you time to make an alternate plan before you go to a meet or practice. If I have to fulfill a meet obligation, I will move everybody to longer events. It is surprising how well some sprinters can run the 1600 and 3200 meter relays. Also, your middle-distance runners may not have to run more than one event on these occasions.

If possible, arrange to meet with your principal or your administrative staff and explain your philosophy with regard to running in cold weather. Make sure the emphasis is on the students' health and the expenses the school may incur if an athlete requires medical care. A sensible administrator will agree that discretion is the better part of valor.

Some coaches swear up and down that training and competing in cold weather are things that you can adjust to. Don't believe it. Some state that they have never had a serious leg problem due to running in cold weather. They advise that a more thorough warm-up will solve the problem. Don't believe that either. If you have been running your sprinters in cold weather, and they have not pulled a hamstring yet; chalk it up to pure dumb luck. Sometimes a pull in hot weather is the accumulation of numerous micro-tears that occurred in April. Running in cold weather is bad news! Ask Jim Golliday, one of the fastest sprinters I have ever seen. Jim Golliday ran a 9.1–100 yard dash in the early fifties, on a *cinder* track in shoes that no sprinter today would ever wear. Two watches caught him in 9.1; one watch caught him in 9.4 and that's the time he was given because no one believed a man could run that fast. At a subsequent competition, Jim pulled a hamstring so severely that he never ran in competition again. Jim Golliday's remarkable gift of speed was developed in the hallways of the Chicago public school system. His brief track career ended much too soon. His career ended at a midwestern university, where he probably trained and competed too often in cold weather.

The fifth and final period is the crucial cycle of the track season. I can only suggest the kinds of things that should be done in the final days of the season. You must assess each runner's readiness to compete individually. You must know who should train harder and who requires more recovery time. Who should continue to weight train and who should not? Whom should you push and whom you should leave alone? You will have to decide what and how many events your sprinters will compete in to sharpen them for the big picture. Take the time to learn all of the psychological and physiological idiosyncrasies of each athlete. Coaching is an art as well as a science. At this point in the season, you become more of an artist. The next four weeks of training — listed below — are, at best, a guide. You have to decide how to use it.

Weekly training schedule for sprinters during the peaking period

Day	Duration (min)	Training task	Training details
Monday	20	Warm-up	Jog 1200 meters, calisthenics and stretching
	30	Starts and baton work	Work the full 400 meter relay, work the 800 meter relay through the passing zone
	30	Weight training	Light weights done with speed, 2 – 3 sets
	10	Warm down	Jog while passing the baton
Tuesday	20	Warm-up	Jog 800, walk 800, stretching
	20	Sprint drills	High knees, butt kicks, chop downs, skipping with high knees, form runs
	20	Warm-down	Same as Monday
Wednesday	20	Warm up	Jog 1200, stretch
	20	Starts and baton work	Work through the passing zone, run one 400 meter relay
	10	Warm-down	Same as Monday

Day	Duration (min)	Training task	Training details
Thursday	20	Warm-up	
	10	Sprint drills	
	10	Warm-down	
Friday	20	Warm-up	
	30	Relaxed swimming	
Saturday	Competition.		

This is the lightest training period of the season, but the most important. Your athletes are in the best condition of their lives and will want to do more. Be certain to remind them to rest and recuperate at home. The temptation to engage in neighborhood recreational activities will be overwhelming. Some of your athletes will be seduced by their "friends" to engage in activities that will be counterproductive to optimum performance. Your dedicated people will not.

SPRINT TRAINING WITH LITTLE OR NO EQUIPMENT OR FACILITIES

It is possible to develop a sprinter anywhere. When I began coaching, most of the successful coaches in our area were very positive in regard to developing sprinters. The record books are full of world-class sprinters who trained under the worst conditions imaginable. State champions were developed in hallways, streets, and parking lots; in parks; on bridle paths and playgrounds. You use what is available. To be sure, some of these surfaces can cause damage to the soft tissue of the lower extremities. Exercise caution in the implementation of a training schedule. With careful planning, most injuries can be avoided.

Whenever I was assigned to a new school, I took a drive around the neighborhood to determine the kinds of surfaces that were available. I planned my workout program based on local terrain. Things that are not usually considered training areas became training areas. There was always something. Let's take a look at some of these atypical places:

Hallways or Corridors

Consider yourself fortunate if you inherit a hallway that runs in a rectangular or square shape and does not have a dead end. Most large schools usually have halls that are very close to being 200 meters or more around. This becomes your indoor track — if your principal will give permission to use it. When your athletes learn how to negotiate the turns safely and efficiently, some remarkable times can be registered. Some schools will have a 100 – 200 meter straightaway with no turns. No problem. Run repeat 200s, 100s, 80s, 60s, and so on. Run them back-to-back for anaerobic endurance. Walk back between repeats for speed work. Always plan for a 20–30 stopping distance. Nail your starting blocks to a piece of plywood, slap two small pieces of plywood together for a starting gun and you have everything you need to train sprinters indoors.

Training on a corridor's hard surface can cause several soft-tissue problems. Shin splints can be a significant injury often caused by the unforgiving surface of most school hallways. An ounce of prevention might be a ton of cure, If you have the sprinters wear two pairs of sweat socks in their running shoes or suggest they purchase orthotics, this problem can be eliminated or minimized. If the athletes cannot afford orthotics, have them insert foam rubber in their running shoes as a substitute. Stretching and flexing their shins against manual resistance can also help. Another preventive measure is to instruct your athletes to ice their shins after each practice session, even if they have not experienced any pain. Another excellent idea is to have the sprinters walk 200 meters on their heels each day prior to any serious training. It is also helpful to have the sprinters run clockwise around the halls occasionally. An often overlooked method of shin splint prevention is to instruct all your runners to *gradually* return to a walk after each run or sprint. Race walking seems to work the shins and the hamstrings. We often use race walking as a part of our warm-up. Its also fun; the sprinters love to race walk.

The Swimming Pool

A swimming pool is an excellent place to train sprinters. If they cannot swim, teach them. Many important drills will be conducted in deep water; however, a number of excellent drills and workouts can be done in shallow water. If you don't have a senior life saving certificate, stay away from water drills.

The best way to train in water is to use a wet vest. These unique floatation devices make it possible to stay upright in deep water and simulate running. If I had the money I would buy one for every member of the track team, but like everything else, that kind of money was not available. There are however, several inexpensive alternatives: (1) Put two life jackets on the runner (front and back), and the athlete will be able to float vertically and simulate running; (2) place a strong rope across the pool and have runners hold on and run in place; (3) have athletes hold on to the side of the pool and do a running motion in the water; and (4) run laps in the shallow water.

Running in water is great for rehabilitating injured runners, and is a viable substitute for a whirlpool bath. I find this innovation superior to a whirlpool; in addition to the rehabilitative factor, the athlete can maintain and even improve his or her physical condition by running in the water.

Gymnasiums

The bigger they are, the better they are. Some schools have gymnasiums that are large enough to accommodate track meets. Most of these are usually not available during the winter because of the school's basketball program. Sometimes it is possible to get a section of the gym for the track program. That section can be used mainly for field events, jogging, and sprint drills. The only time you can use it for a viable track workout is when the basketball team is playing an away game. If this is all you have, plan accordingly. Take a look at the basketball schedule and try to plan your track meet schedule so that you can have two days on a real track — one day at the track meet and one day when you have access to the gymnasium.

If the gymnasium is a small, auxiliary facility, you might get to use it every day. Such a place is ideal for the general and the specific preparation periods. Most of these kinds of facilities contain a variety of gymnastic equipment and mats. You should experience little difficulty in conducting drills, calisthenics, plyometrics, and basic conditioning in these places.

Cafeterias

Some high school cafeterias are large enough to accommodate track practice. On several occasions, we conducted a track meet in the cafeteria. If the tables can be moved, an indoor track meet is possible. If the tables cannot be moved, practice is possible.

Classrooms

When our head custodian was in a bad mood, the hallways "suddenly" became unavailable and the only place we could use was an empty classroom. How do you train in a classroom? You line up the runners in rows and run them in place. The sprinters run for 10–20 seconds, the quarter-milers for 50 seconds, the half-milers for two minutes. The distance runners should run 4–5 minutes in place, or go outside and run. Give each group two minutes rest between efforts. Not long after we had learned to work with this uncomfortable situation, the school hired a new head custodian who loved kids — especially track athletes. We could run anyplace we wanted. He even offered to help me coach. I welcomed his assistance. He even came to all the track meets and supported the team.

These were the indoor facilities, if you can call them that. Sprinters can be trained successfully almost anywhere. Let your imagination run wild. If you are fortunate enough to be blessed with a gifted sprinter, a state, district or sectional champion can emerge from some of these ostensibly difficult indoor situations. More in the next section on how to develop sprinters in a few atypical outdoor "facilities."

Track coaches who can boast of better situations might think that I was languishing under these circumstances. I was not. It was the most exciting time of my life. The creative juices were flowing at all times. Every problem became an opportunity.

A CLOSER LOOK AT THE 100 METER DASH

Distance coaches often break down the mile into splits in order to determine where the runner needs to change and improve a weakness in her race. The same thing can be done in the 100 meter dash. I learned of this approach to sprinting by standing around talking track trivia with some members of the University of Chicago Track Club. They related that Bobby Morrow (the 1956 100 and 200 meter Olympic champion) was allegedly the most perfectly trained sprinter who ever competed. Bobby could run several repeat 100 meter dashes and his footprints in a cinder track would be the same every time. I never forgot that lesson.

Most great sprinters have a weak phase in the 100 meters; Bobby Morrow had none. Bob Hayes had a lousy start and a tremendous finish. If Ralph Metcalfe had had a better start, Jesse Owens would have lost the 100 in the 1936 Olympics. Ira Murchison often faded in the last 20 meters of the 100 meters. Every phase of Bobby Morrow's race was honed to perfection. I used this approach to training and turned average sprinters into district champions. The 100 meters can be divided into five phases, and each phase must be timed in order to find out the sprinter's weakness:

Phase 1

Reaction time: It is extremely important that the coach use a starting gun in practice as much as possible. Do not depend on clapping your hands or hitting a locker or any other device or method, to substitute for the actual gun. Use whatever funds or budget you have and buy a starting gun and shells. You can use these alternate methods when your sprinters are learning how to start. When they have mastered the technique, use the gun. Teach the sprinter to focus his mind on the front leg in the set position and *not* on the sound of the gun. If the sprinter's mind focuses on the sound, there will be a fraction-of-a-second delay as the mind changes its focus to the movement of the front leg. Races have been won or lost by fractions of a second.

Phase 2

The start: Ira Murchison was the consummate starter. His technique was uniquely his. I would not recommend it for anyone else except those sprinters who are built like Ira. I saw Ira try to teach his start technique to a tall sprinter, and it didn't work. Ira was short in stature and very muscular, and he was very successful in crowding the starting line with a narrow foot spacing a la Jesse Owens. My advice is to try various techniques and foot spacing until you find the best method for your sprinter. The best technique is the one that permits your sprinter to reach top speed in the most efficient way possible. Experiment. One size does not fit all.

Sometimes a sprinter cannot be effective from the blocks because of a lack of muscular strength. The explosion from the blocks is a power move. Ben Johnson beat Carl Lewis from the blocks because he had the power to squat with 500 pounds. Weight training with heavy poundages is a must in training for a powerful start.

Acceleration from the Blocks

Armin Hary, the 1960 Olympic Games 100 meter champion had mastered the acceleration from the blocks in the first 20 meters so well that the officials thought he had false started. Upon review of films, they found that his start was a fair one, but his acceleration was the best they had ever seen. *Acceleration* is the operative word. The first five or six strides from the blocks should be a gradual but rapid increase in stride frequency and stride length. The torso should rise from the sprinter's crouch and gradually attain erect posture at the fifth or sixth stride — no sooner. If you turn your back on this activity, you should hear a rhythmical increase in the speed of the footsteps of the sprinter. This skill was perfected by Armin Hary. If you measure the steps for the first 20 meters, they should gradually increase in length. If they do not, it will have a negative effect on the next phase of the 100 meters.

Attainment of Maximum Speed

If the previous phase has been negotiated properly, this phase will be a smooth transition to maximum speed. Both of these phases can be developed by running short repeats of 30–60 meter sprints and acceleration drills that improve stride frequency. Uphill and downhill running (slight incline — about 10 degrees) is recommended to develop and improve this characteristic. Towing can also help, but the weather has to be warm and the conditions have to be as safe as possible.

Constantly experiment with stride frequency and stride length. Each sprinter has a genetic predisposition toward one or the other. Both have worked with my athletes. Sometimes I have changed neither. But you may have to change something if he has hit a plateau in results. Often a proper application of weight training and plyometrics can help. I have found that the quicker lifting with moderate to light weights is more effective in modifying stride frequency. I usually do plyometrics after I weight train. This exercise sequence was recommended to me by the Bulgarian strength coach, Angel Spassov.

The Finish

Most sprinters will attain maximum speed at about 80 meters. Many novice runners tend to decelerate after this. If they learn how to effectively relax and sprint at the same time, their momentum will carry them several strides beyond 80 meters. The best way to teach this skill is to reduce workout speed whenever you detect a lack of relaxation in their running form. Never let sprinters continue a run when tension impacts on their running form. If you are consistent about teaching this skill, your sprinters will learn to relax at maximum speed. Tension usually starts from the face down; if you stop it before it starts, you are quite a bit ahead of the game.

The anaerobic metabolism is taxed in the last 20 meters of the 100. The best way to develop the anaerobic capacity in a 100 meter specialist is by running back-to-back sprints. Occasionally, a few 150 meter sprints can help. When you impact upon the anaerobic system in practice, the body will adjust and adapt by producing an anaerobic reserve of adenosine triphosphate and creatine phosphate and other blood buffers to neutralize the accumulation of excess lactic acid in the body. After a month or so of this kind of training, the final 20 meters will be less of a problem.

The sprinters also must practice finishing skills. Place a finishing tape across the track and have the sprinter start at 70 meters and run through the tape. You will be surprised at the number of athletes who habitually slow down before the finish. Teach her to run 10 meters beyond the finish. She has to practice this skill throughout the season. Telling her to run through the tape will fall on deaf ears. This skill has to be practiced constantly. Running *through* the tape has to become a habit.

RESISTANCE TRAINING

Sprinters should engage in some form of resistance training. Many successful sprint coaches claim that their sprinters have never weight trained, but I submit that some kind of resistance training was done, whether the coach or the runner is willing to admit it or not. Many coaches and athletes still believe today that weight training will make their athletes musclebound and slow. An extremely successful sprint coach admitted to me that he never used weight training because he never needed it. What a lucky coach! He is not the first coach to tell me this. Back in the 1940s and 1950s almost no one weight trained, yet the quadriceps development of some of the sprinters of that era had to be seen to be believed. Even Ira Murchison's thigh development was so massive that he looked abnormal.

What is my point? My point is that many great sprinters inadvertently do something that contributes to their unusual development. I also contend that most coaches who inherit these great sprinters haven't a clue about how these gifts were developed.

Let's investigate the rationale with regard to some of our best sprinter's informal development:

1. Many of these people were football players. Pushing a blocking sled is resistance training, isn't it?

2. Some of the fastest runners in my neighborhood owned bicycles. Contrary to popular belief, riding a bicycle is not hazardous to running speed.

3. Most coaches do quite a bit of hill training.

4. Hershel Walker ran through plowed fields and mud as a training method

5. Almost all athletes have to run stairs from time to time.

6. I know several great sprinters who trained exclusively with stretch hoses.

7. The list is endless — there is towing, resistance running, parachutes, downhill running, heavy pants, weight vests.

If you are not knowledgeable about weight training, discretion would be the better part of valor. You can do much damage to the sprinter if you don't know what you are doing. Expertise in weight training can revolutionize your track program, but you must understand some basic rules in regard to weight training:

1. You are not developing a power lifter or a weight lifter; you are developing a faster runner. The sprinter next to your runner on the starting line couldn't care less about how much your runner can lift, and neither should you.

2. Your runner is not a bodybuilder. Hypertrophy is not your primary focus. Every pound of unnecessary body weight gained is an extra pound to carry.

3. Lifting maximum weights will put your runner in the emergency ward; you need ony 60%–70% of maximum to lift for best results, anyway.

4. Slow lifting is not sport specific. Your runner must lighten the weight and lift faster (with proper technique). No one learns to move fast by training slow. Specificity, please.

5. Always have runners stretch before and after they lift.

Covering the subject of resistance exercise requires volumes of books of encyclopedic proportions. This section was about sprinting, and I felt that resistance training should not be ignored. See Section 20 for more information on weight training, along with examples of specific exercises and basic workouts.

Being a voracious reader and student of the sport, I can guarantee that new ideas and training methods are being developed before the ink dries on this paper. My final advice to any coach is to continue to learn. There is no last word in track and field. Somewhere on this globe, some athlete, coach, or researcher has gone in a new direction and is developing sprinters by the dozens.

There are several compelling new innovations in sprint training that have crossed my desk in the last several months. I tried these methods on two college sprinters this summer. The results were remarkable. Space does not permit me to cover these important new concepts in detail, but I offer them briefly to perk your interest. If you want more information about these techniques, I invite you to contact me by "E" mail at EWallac603@aol.com

1. *The Louie Simmons hip and lower back machine.*

2. *Power Factor Training by Peter Sisco and John Little.* This is a system of partial movements with heavy weights that also contributes to improvement in sprinting speed, as does the apparatus above.

3. *Stabilizer Training.* Charles Poliquin (a Canadian strength coach) and Paul Chek have developed a system of training with a "Swiss" ball that forces an athlete to train in an unstable environment to develop and strengthen muscle stabilizers.

4. According to the latest physiological research, muscle growth is stimulated best at 50-60% of max.

5. *Time your sprinters every 10 meters.* You will be surprised where your sprinters lose speed.

Section 6

THE 200 METER DASH
Stanfield, Carr, and Smith

Classic 200 meter runners are usually athletes who do not register world record times in the shorter sprint events but are spectacular performers in the longer sprints. Their physiological makeup is different from that of 100 meter runners, and they must be trained differently. Often, these people are also world-class runners in the longest sprint, the 400 meters. Andy Stanfield, Henry Carr, and Tommy Smith were the best in the world in the 200 meter dash. Currently, Michael Johnson, with his unbelievable 19.33 world record in the 200 meters and his incredible Olympic 200 and 400 meter double, continues this legacy.

The classic 200 meter runner is quite different physically from the 100 meter specialist. He or she is different in somatotype (body structure), muscle type, and inherent physiology. Though they can turn in a commendable effort in a short sprint, most of these people seem to fare much better in the longer sprints. Much of this difference results from their greater physical stature; most of the great 200 meter runners are taller and thinner than the great 100 meter runners. My educated guess is that they possess a greater percentage of type IIa white muscle fibers (fast-twitch muscle fibers with a capacity for endurance) than do their 100 meter counterparts. This being the case, 200 meter sprinters can thrive on a more demanding work schedule and can be expected to run a respectable and often world-class 400 meters. A perfect example of this is the current men's world and Olympic champion in the 200 meters and 400 meters, Michael Johnson.

Of course, there have been some exceptions to the above description, but they are just that — exceptions to the rule. I have had the privilege of working with a few extraordinary 200 meter champions who were not tall, but none could be characterized as short in stature. However, these athletes possessed every trait common to the 200 meters but exceptional height. In the 1952 Olympics, the quintessential 200 meter runner appeared on the world scene — Andy Stanfield of Seton Hall University. Andy was a tall, long-striding, 200 meter specialist. He could run a decent 100 meters, but he dominated the 200 meters. He thrived on a demanding work schedule. Andy has been known to test his speed in the 800 meters. Henry Carr, Tommie Smith, and Michael Johnson were cut from the same cloth. These men were Olympic 200 meter champions (1964, 1968, and 1996) who could run world-class times in the 400 meters.

Because of the unique physiology (the ratio of class I, class IIa and class IIb muscle fibers) and biomechanics (bone structure and leverage) of each athlete that you coach, there are some 200 meter runners like Florence Griffith Joyner and Jesse Owens who will experience success at the 100 meters. These differences may explain why some sprinters can double in the 200 and the 100, and others cannot. I suggest you test your athlete periodically. You will eventually determine the nature of the sprinter's versatility.

TALENT IDENTIFICATION

Most talented 200 meter runners excel in the standing vertical jump and the standing long jump. These relatively simple tests can give you some insight into their muscular power and the nature and extent of their fast-twitch muscle fibers. The 60 yard dash from a flying start is helpful also, but the best indicator of talent in this event is the actual 200 meters. An untrained effort in the

200, however, can be misleading. This test is often modified by a certain level of maturation, year in school, and prior experience. If a performance in the flying 30 yard sprint is not very exciting, but a 60 yard dash with a flying start is impressive enough (6.5 seconds or better), the results of these tests can be a clue to the level of 200 meter sprinting talent. Occasionally, the results of the above tests may not indicate anything special, but as the season progresses, a runner's latent talent may become manifest. Trust your instincts, a great deal of coaching is still an art.

Talent in the 200 meters can be found in unusual places. Basketball guards and forwards, and football wide receivers and defensive backs, are often fertile ground for sprinting talent. Take a closer look at the swimming team; fast-twitch fibers in water can translate to fast-twitch fibers on dry land. Sometimes a dedicated baseball player can help your cause. I can remember when a member of our 4×200 relay team was also an infielder on the baseball team. After every practice, he ran from the baseball diamond to our practice site just to work on baton passes. He never missed an important track meet, and he played in every baseball game. That's dedication! When you want something badly enough, an athlete and coach can "make a way out of no way." Be flexible when an athlete wants to play another sport that may conflict with track and field. The record books are full of great track athletes who engaged in other sports that were not compatible with the track and field season. Don't look a gift horse in the mouth.

Quite unlike the 100 meter specialist, the 200 meter runner enjoys and thrives on overdistance training. Many of these athletes will voluntarily run cross-country and enjoy it. Some 200 meter runners can excel in cross-country, but excessive mileage in the fall is contraindicated. Most of this training should be fast intervals, fartlek (Swedish speed-play), and repetition running. Long, slow distance running is not the exercise prescription for sprinters.

TECHNICAL ASPECTS OF THE 200 METERS

The starting technique and position for the 200 is identical to the 100 meter start. Response to the starter's pistol is crucial, but an error in reaction time will not have the same impact on the outcome of the 200 as it does in the 100 meters.

The most important part of the 200 is how effectively the turn is negotiated. The proper execution of the turn can often determine the outcome of a race. The athlete has to deal with several mechanical realities. The first problem is the difficulty in generating speed on the turn. Centrifugal force is causing the runner to drift away from the inside border of the lane. This same force will also make it difficult to run on the balls of the feet. The sprinter has to lean in toward the center of the track while endeavoring to accelerate into the straightaway — and this must be done without tying up. If the sprinter does not generate speed before the straight, the race may be over. The turn cannot be used as an opportunity to rest; the 200 meter runner must stay even with the competition (or be slightly ahead), and paradoxically accomplish all of this in a smooth and relaxed manner. At this point, the race is half finished; the runner has another 100 meters in which to increase the stride pattern without overstriding. Physiologists claim that it is metabolically possible for a well-trained athlete to run at full speed for 300 meters. They further claim that the fatigue poisons, that is, lactic acid, adenosine diphosphate breakdown, and glycolysis will not accumulate sufficiently to have a deleterious effect in the 200 meters. This may be the theory, but in real life, in the last 40 meters of this race, something is happening to the body to cause considerable muscular discomfort. Proper training can ameliorate this condition, but it is never completely eliminated. This is why the tall athlete seems to have an advantage in the 200 — he can run the race with fewer strides. Fewer strides mean less fatigue. For example, a runner with a seven-foot stride will use about 86 strides in a 200 meter race: a sprinter with a six-foot stride will need 100 strides to negotiate the same distance. That's a 14-stride difference! Quick turnover can help a short sprinter in the 100 meters, but in the 200 the athlete needs more than that. That partially explains why tall sprinters built like Stanfield, Carr, and Smith often dominate this event.

There is another reason for their superiority in the furlong. I have no real scientific data on these people, but I will bet my last dollar that there is a vast physiological difference between the 100 meter and the 200 meter specialist. The 200 meter champion will have a greater percentage of class IIa fast-twitch, glycolytic fibers than the 100 meter specialist, so the blood flow to the muscles is more prolific because of a greater supply of oxygen-absorbing cells (mitrochondria) within the muscle fibers, and this contributes substantially to the runner's ability to endure the onset of fatigue. This type of muscle fiber can also withstand, and thrive upon, an anaerobic speed-endurance training program, which will subsequently further enhance the athlete's performance in the longer sprints. To summarize:

1. The 200 meter runner will leave the starting blocks using a starting technique that is a carbon copy of the 100 meter start.

2. In 5 strides, the sprinter will gradually attain an erect posture.

3. At 55 meters, the runner will begin to accelerate to maximum speed into the curve, staying as close as possible to the inside border of the lane. At this point, the sprinter will attempt the difficult task of maintaining maximum speed while relaxing.

4. If the turn was negotiated properly, momentum will bring the runner to approximately 160 meters before the body begins to experience any serious challenge to efficient running form.

5. If the anaerobic training program has been effective, or if the sprinter has been obliged to run an occasional 400 meters, the final 40 meters — and its concomitant accumulation of lactic acid in the musculature — may not negatively impact upon finishing speed. Instruct the 200 meter runner to drive the arms, lift the knees (almost waist high), maintain relaxation, and sprint 10 meters beyond the finish line.

Photo 6–1. Curve running in the 200 meters. Notice the body lean toward the inside of the track to counteract the pull of centrifugal force.

TRAINING CYCLES AND WORKOUT PROGRAMS

The 200 meter general preparation period is identical to the 100 meter sprinter's general preparation period. The goal is to build a foundation of strength, flexibility, skill, and anaerobic endurance so the body will respond favorably to the greater demands that it will inevitably encounter during the competitive season. Follow the exact general preparation program I suggested for the 100 meter candidate in Section 5.

The specific preparation period, however, is the time when several differences in the training programs of the 200 meter runner become manifest. The 200 meter runner is often required to compete, and is physiologically capable of competing, successfully in a greater number and variety of events than the 100 meter specialist. As a consequence, his or her specific preparation must contain a larger amount of anaerobic activities On any given day, this athlete may be required to run the 200 meters and the 4×100 relay, run the anchor on the 4×200, and run a leg on the 4×400 relay. On other occasions, I have had to ask this athlete to run an 800 meter leg on the 3200 meter relay and the 100 meters

Photo 6–2. This is where we often train — in a local park.

in the same meet! As I stated earlier in this section, many 200 meter runners can run a commendable 800 meters; it depends primarily on the ratio of class IIb and IIa fast-twitch fibers and the athlete's attitude toward the longer event.

During the specific preparation period, the 200 meter sprinter's training should become more anaerobic. The speed-endurance runs become longer and the shorter sprints are greater in number. If the anaerobic system of this athlete is stressed two to three times a week, the quantity aspect of his or her training is increased without compromising its quality.

Weekly training for sprinters during the specific preparation period

Day	Duration (min)	Training task	Training details
Monday	20	Warm-up	800 meter jog, calisthenics and stretching, 800 meter stride
	10	Sprint drills	High knees, butt kicks, chop downs, etc.
	30	Stair running	3 min stairs, 3 min jog, 3 min wind sprints. Repeat this cycle 3 times.
	5	Warm-down	800 meter jog, stretch, 800 meter stride, walk 800 meters

Day	Duration (min)	Training task	Training details
Tuesday	20	Warm-up	Easy interval running, 10 × 100 meter repeats, calisthenics and stretching
	10	Sprint drill	
	30	Baton passing, block starts	Walking, jogging, and half-speed baton passing, learning the "on your mark" and "set" positions
	10	Warm-down	800 meter jog, stretching
Wednesday	20	Warm-up	3200 meters fartlek, calisthenics and stretching
	20	Sprint drills	High knees, butt kicks, chop downs, form runs, etc.
	30	Stair running	Same as Monday
	10	Warm-down	Jog 800 meters, stretching
Thursday	20	Warm-up	800 meters jog, calisthenics and stretching
	10	Sprint drills	Same as Tuesday
	30	Relay baton drills, block starts	Nothing is at full speed; these drills are part of the learning process
	30	Weight training	High reps (10–15), low sets (1–3), light weights (60% of max)
Friday	20	Warm-up and sprint drills	Same as Monday
	50	Swimming, basketball, or volleyball	
Saturday		Competition. Run an overdistance event (300 meters) and a relay.	

The chart above represents one week of the four-week specific preparation cycle. The training activities are beginning to look like a typical track workout. Near the end of the month of January, we begin to compete against other schools. The 200 meter sprinter is entered in races longer than his favorite distances for anaerobic reasons. Leg speed is developed by participation in sprint relays. In the next four-week cycle, the sprinter will begin to compete in occasional short (55 meter), indoor sprints, but a major portion of the sprinter's running will be the anaerobic sprints like the 300 and 400 meters. I have often entered a 200 meter runner in the 600 and 800 meters if his anaerobic development is a major consideration. I like to win the indoor meets, but they will never take precedence over some of the long-range goals that the athlete and the coach have agreed upon. Indoor competition should never be an end in itself.

As the athlete's year begins to move toward the end of the indoor season, his workouts begin to become track-specific. The differences between the 200 meter training program and the 100 meter program are clearly evident; however, the workouts can be modified depending upon his individual genetics. There is a marked difference between a 200 meter runner who goes up to the 400 and the 200 meter runner who experiences difficulty negotiating the "longest sprint."

On the other hand, there are some sprinters who can do it all. The great Herb McKenley from Jamaica was a world-class 400 meter runner, who subsequently earned a silver medal in 100 meters *and* 400 meters in the 1952 Olympics. Go figure.

Weekly training schedule for 200 meters in the precompetitive period

Day	Duration (min)	Training task	Training details
Monday	20	Warm-up	800 meter jog, calisthenics and stretching, stride an 800
	10	Sprint drills	High knees, chop downs, 1,2,3s, overstrides, form runs
	30	Anaerobic speed	16×100, 80%–90% effort,* walk 100 meters between each
	10	Warm-down	800 meter jog, stretch
Tuesday	20	Warm-up	400 meter jog, 10×100 meter interval strides, jog between each, stretch
	10	Sprint drills	Same as Monday
	30	Baton passing and starts	Establish passing zones for the 4×200 relay, 80% speed through the zone,* 60 meters from the blocks
	30	Weight training	1 set 10 reps (upper body), 2 sets 10, lower body
	10	Warm-down	
Wednesday	20	Warm-up	Same as Monday
	10	Sprint drills	High knees, butt kicks, over-strides, skipping with high knees, and chop downs
	30	Anaerobic sprinting	8×200 or 10×150 (80% effort), 2 min recovery between each
	10	Warm-down	

Day	Duration (min)	Training task	Training details
Thursday	20	Warm-up	Same as Tuesday
	10	Sprint drills	Same as Tuesday
	30	Baton passing, block	4×200 passes at 90% effort, starts at 50 meters, 100% effort
	30	Weight training	4 sets – 5 reps
Friday	20	Warm-up	16×100 intervals, 50% speed, jog 100 in between each
	10	Sprint drills	Same as Monday
	30	Speed work	5×30, 2 sets; 5×60, 2 sets Rest 2 min between sets, 1×800 stride
Saturday		Competition	

* A runner's best time divided by the percentage will give you the exact speed of a required run. For example: 22 secs. divided by 90% = 24.4 secs.

The month of March is the most important part of our indoor season. But we will train through most dual meets and taper off for the big invitationals and the conference championship. Our indoor taper is usually just one day. Our routine is to jog 800 meters and stretch, run through a few sprint drills, and rehearse a few baton passes and starts on the day before our important meets. We have not reached our peak physical condition yet. This is one reason this four-week period is called a precompetitive period. We intend to have our ultimate peak occur in the final two weeks of the outdoor season in May; however, most of our sprinters will run outstanding efforts because of the excitement that is associated with championship indoor competition. Make a special effort to remain calm and attempt to be as low-key as possible.

Weekly training for 200 meter sprinters during the competitive season

Day	Duration (min)	Training task	Training details
Monday	20	Warm-up	Jog 1600 meters, calisthenics and stretching
	10	Sprint drills	High knees, chop downs, form runs, etc.
	30	8×200 meters	Each 200 at 90% effort, walk a 200 in between
	10	Warm-down	Jog 800 meters, stretch

Day	Duration (min)	Training task	Training details
Tuesday	20	Warm-up	Jog 800 meters, 8×100 meter strides, jog 100 in between
	10	Sprint drills	Same as Monday
	30	16×100 meters	Use the first four 100s as a warm-up, the last 12 at 95% effort. Monitor every 100 to avoid leg problems
	30	Weight training	Heavy weights, lower reps, 4 sets, 5 reps
Wednesday	20	Warm-up	Jog 800 meters, walk 200 meters, stride 800 meters, calisthenics and stretching
	10	Sprint drills	Same as Monday
	30	Baton passing and starts	Work primarily through the passing zone
	10	Warm-down	Single-file jogging for 800 meters with baton passing
Thursday	20	Warm up	Same as Tuesday
	10	Sprint drills	Same as Monday
	30	Stride frequency work	4×60 (2 sets), 4×80 (2 sets), rest to recovery between sets
	30	Weight training	Light weights with speed reps 8–10 reps per set
	10	Warm-down	Jog 800 meters and stretch
Friday	20	Warm-up	Same as Tuesday
	30	Rehabilitation	Relaxed water drills and swimming

Saturday   Competition.

The cycle above should be completed the last week in April; however, this and other cycles can be arranged according to your schedule. These cycles can be lengthened or readjusted to accommodate the day when your conference or championship meet might occur. The above recommendation fits quite neatly if a conference or state championship is scheduled for the last Saturday in May. This cycle, at first glance, looks like most track workouts, but a few subtle differences may need to be modified. For example, if a sprinter shows a lack of anaerobic endurance, Thursday's repeats could be a series of 150s or 300s instead of the 60s and 80s. This modification can be determined by the sprinter's performance in practice or a recent competition.

This training schedule can also be modified if you lack facilities. The facilities *are* there, and we'll look at them later in this section.

Photo 6–3. Sprint instruction in April.

I have heard from some of my friends in Texas and California that they have also experienced sudden temperature changes in the spring. The weather can be unpredictable in any climate, and may change in the middle of a workout or a track meet. You need a plan "B" ready at all times. Be ready to change your training program at any moment; be prepared to pull your sprinters out of an event at an important relay carnival that you may be in the process of winning. I have seen the temperature drop 40 degrees in the middle of a track meet in Chicago. I am aware that this identical warning was given in a previous chapter, but deserves repeating. I want to spare you that helpless feeling when your best sprinter grabs the back of her thigh and falls to the ground in pain, and you know that your sprinter may be out for the rest of the season

In Section 5, I advised coaches to train the sprinters inside if the weather is cold. If you have to run outside, run overdistance and wear two sweatsuits, tights, a warm hat, and other cold-weather paraphernalia. I have not experienced a serious injury since I adopted these precautions.

The fifth and final period is the crucial cycle of the track season. I can only suggest the kinds of things that should be done in the final days of the season. You must assess each runner's readiness to compete individually. You must know who should train harder and who requires more recovery time. You have to know your athletes physiologically, psychologically, and sociologically before you can really train them properly; successful coaching is holistic. Then you will be able to determine what and how many events the 200 meter sprinter will compete in to sharpen the runner for the big picture. Take the time to learn all of the psychological and physiological idiosyncrasies of each athlete. The next four weeks of training, in the schedule for the peaking period are a guide; it is up to you to decide how to use it.

Photo 6–4. Another cold day in the Midwest. I am deciding whether to run our sprinters in this weather or send them home.

Weekly training for 200 meter sprinters during the competitive season

Day	Duration (min)	Training task	Training details
Monday	20	Warm-up	Jog 1600 meters, sprint the last 200, calisthenics, etc.
	30	Starts and baton work	Work the full 400 meter relay, work the 800 meter relay through the passing zone
	30	Weight training	Light weights done with speed, 2–3 sets
	10	Warm-down	Jog 800 while passing the baton single file
Tuesday	20	Warm-up	Jog 800, walk 800, stride an 800, stretching
	20	Sprint drills	High knees, butt kicks, chop downs, skipping with high knees, form runs
	20	Warm-down	Same as Monday
Wednesday	20	Warm-up	Jog 1600, stretch
	20	Starts and baton work	Work through the passing zone, run two full 800 meter relays
	10	Warm-down	Same as Monday

Day	Duration (min)	Training task	Training details
Thursday	20	Warm-up	
	10	Sprint drills	
	10	Warm-down	
Friday	40	Warm-up and relaxed swimming	
Saturday		Competition.	

This is the lightest training period of the season, but the most important. Your athletes are in the best condition of their lives and will want to do more. Be certain to remind them of the importance of rest and recuperation during these final weeks. Remember that the temptation to engage in neighborhood recreational activities will be overwhelming, and that some of your athletes will engage in counterproductive activities. Remember also that your dedicated people will not.

200 METER TRAINING WITH LITTLE OR NO EQUIPMENT OR FACILITIES

If your situation is less than ideal, you will have to innovate. Keep in mind that champions have been developed in hallways, streets, and parking lots; in parks; on bridle paths and playgrounds. Use what is available. Exercise caution in your training schedule, since some of these surfaces can cause damage to the soft tissue of the lower extremities. With careful planning, most injuries can be avoided. Areas that are not usually thought of as training areas can become training areas; use what is available.

Hallways or Corridors

If you have that hallway that runs in a rectangle or square and does not have a dead end, this becomes your indoor track. Most large schools have halls that are very close to being 200 meters or more around. You have no problem, if your principal will give permission to use it. Even if the longest available hall is considerably less than 100 meters, not to worry. For example, if you run 4×55 meters back-to-back with a minimum of rest in between, your athletes will experience nearly the same physiological effects of a 200 meter sprint. Try to eliminate sudden decelerations and sharp turns in an attempt to negotiate corners; this type of activity could damage ligaments and soft tissue. Try running stairs in combination with a hall if the corridor is too short. Design the workout based on a certain time structure. I often ran one-, two-, or three-minute circuits depending on the time of the year and the runner's event. Sometimes we hopped up stairs for plyometrics; at other times we carried each other piggyback for resistance exercise. We also did wheelbarrow walking upstairs to develop the arm and chest muscles. The team loved these innovations.

Auditorium

Sometimes a school auditorium is an ideal place to train. I was assigned to a school that had a huge assembly hall. There was a gradual slope from the entrance down toward the stage. We did uphill and downhill running and we jumped from the stage for plyometrics; the shot-putters threw an indoor shot on the stage. We were careful to cover the stage with mats to protect the floor. On other days, the high jumpers did a three-step run up and worked on technique.

TRAINING OUTDOORS ON UNUSUAL SURFACES

Parks are ideal places to train 200 meter runners. If the park is large enough, you can measure any distance you want. What can be better than a 100 or 200 meter straightaway on the soft grass surface found in most parks? If you look hard enough, you can find hills of all kinds for resistance running or downhill slopes for overspeed training. We used the a car's odometer, or a measuring wheel borrowed from the physics teacher, to determine distances longer than 200 meters. Across the street, in another section of the park, was an unused bridle path. The surface was similar to a cinder track. We usually ran short sprints on this surface.

If a school playground was nearby, we had the additional advantage of playground equipment for resistance exercises. Most playgrounds are equipped with chinning and dipping bars for upper body exercises. There is also a great variety of resistance exercises that can be done on monkey bars and such.

If you have no other choice, train in the streets or a parking lot. Both have asphalt surfaces that are similar to some all weather tracks. Get permission from the local city government to barricade the street during your practice. Most municipalities will be glad to accommodate you. Mark your distances with cones or chalk.

I do not recommend training on a sidewalk. The surface is too hard and unforgiving. But if this is all you have, it can work on a limited basis. There were times when a light workout on the sidewalk was the most convenient way to train. Choose an area that has a smooth surface, but keep in mind that any protracted training on the sidewalk is death on the joints and shins. Find an alternative site as soon as possible!

A beach is an excellent place to train sprinters. If they cannot swim, teach them. Many important drills will be conducted in deep water; however, a number of excellent drills and workouts can also be done safely in shallow water. If you don't have a senior life saving certificate, stay away from water drills. Running in the sand is an excellent change of pace for the team. Running on a variety of surfaces can have a positive physiological and psychological effect on your runners. Training on the same track (if you have one), day after day, can be a boring affair, and could be a deterrent to any meaningful progress.

If a cinder track is within walking distance of your school, by all means use it. It may be archaic and in poor condition, but when your athletes set foot on an all-weather track, they will run like antelopes. One of my hurdlers improved from 14.9 to 13.9 seconds in one week when he switched to an all-weather track. Our best 800 meter runner went from a 1:59 half to a 1:52! You can keep your synthetic surfaces.

A synthetic track has one big advantage. Your intermediate hurdlers will experience great difficulty negotiating a stride pattern if they do not have access to an all-weather track. The intermediate hurdler must practice under conditions that will permit him to establish a proper stride pattern. It cannot be done on a run-down cinder track or any other alternative surface. A hurdler needs the real thing. Visit a state-of-the-art facility of a nearby university or suburb (get their permission), and get your hurdlers' stride pattern established. A hurdler won't get a correct stride pattern established on a meet day; there is just too much difference in surfaces. A good time to take your hurdlers to a synthetic track is on the weekends when you have no distractions. There will be more about this subject in Section 13.

Your 200 meter runners can train anywhere, and it will not negatively affect their development. They might be better off training on these diverse surfaces and conditions. If you have a really tough situation, your 200 meter sprinter might be better prepared than her more affluent counterpart. Running under these conditions can prepare the sprinter for the vicissitudes of the furlong beyond your wildest dreams. The world-class sprinter, the 1995 NCAA indoor 200 meter champion David Dopek, of DePaul University in Chicago, developed his skills by training in hallways and such. *Training champion sprinters under adverse conditions can be done*. It is being done.

THE IMPORTANCE OF SPRINT DRILLS

I devote a great deal of time to sprint drills throughout the track season. These drills are extremely important in the development of *every* runner. As athletes become proficient in these drills, their running technique will become fluid and efficient, and they will subsequently run faster — as matter of fact, much faster. Sprint drills also help in the warming-up process. I once watched Ivory Crockett, the great 100 meter runner from Southern Illinois University, do sprint drills for 20 minutes prior to his competition. Ivory Crockett never pulled a muscle. There is no substitute for sprint drills.

High Knees

Run with an exaggerated and rapid knee lift. There will be very little horizontal progress down the track. The emphasis is on knee lift and arm drive. This drill should be done for at least 50 meters.

Butt Kicks

Try to run forward as the heels kick the glutes. Endeavor to run on the toes. Forward progress is minimal; leg motion is rapid.

Photo 6–5. A good example of the "high knees" drill.

Chop Downs

This drill can be done while skipping or running. The knees are lifted waist high and the lower leg is extended and snapped down toward the track.

One, Two, Threes

Run 50 to 100 meters while emphasizing the knee lift of the left leg only. The next run will emphasize the knee lift of the right leg. Repeat several times.

Quick Steps

Run about ten relaxed steps on the toes, immediately followed by aproximately ten rapid knee lifts while on the toes. The movement is always forward. Repeat for 50–100 meters.

Form Runs

The form run is a 50–100 meter sprint with the emphasis on relaxed technique. Speed is at about 80% to 90% effort. Focus is on correct leg and arm action. This drill should be last in the warm-up; its primary purpose is to determine readiness to run at full speed.

Occasionally, we will do other drills, but we do those mentioned above almost all of the time. We can also be seen running backward, walking with a high knee action, or skipping with high knees, but we do these and other drills primarily in practice, depending upon our needs. For instance, the backward run seems to work the hamstrings. It closely resembles the backward run practiced by defensive backs. Some of the fastest men in the NFL are defensive backs. If you don't believe it, ask Deon Sanders. The value of this drill has not been scientifically investigated, but I will never forget when a defensive back ran away from Willie Gault and Herschel Walker in the Super Stars competition. Both of these men were world-class sprinters. That was proof enough for me.

Every track athlete — including distance runners, lifters, jumpers, shot putters and discus throwers — should do sprint drills. When these drills are included in your program, the effect will be immediate and dramatic. I have seen milers' and two-milers' times improve as much as 10–20 seconds in one week when sprint drills were included in their training regimen.

Section 7

THE 400 METER DASH
Rigor Mortis

The 400 meters is often referred to as the man killer of track. This race causes a buildup of lactic acid in the muscles that almost paralyzes the runner with pain. The untrained runner finds it impossible to continue at any reasonable speed. People who are familiar with track call this uncomfortable feeling "rigor mortis." This section tells the coach how to train the quarter-miler to cope with this omnipresent physiological phenomenon.

The 400 meter dash requires courage, determination, a high pain threshold, and an intelligent work ethic and speed. You have to admire these people. There is nothing in track and field like the 400 meter runner. There is no greater challenge than the last 80 — 100 meters in the 400 meters. The first time a novice sprinter experiences the onset of lactic acid and its attendant effects on the body, the athlete will often be overwhelmed by this painful phenomenon. I have seen this "rigor mortis" stop runners dead in their tracks and throw them to the ground! The "bear" has jumped on the runner's back. It took me several years of frustration as an athlete before I learned to negotiate those most difficult last 100 meters of the 400. A coach and a willing athlete working together can solve this problem in one season. The pain will always be there, but the helpless frustration of the final 45–50 meters in this challenging race can be conquered. The purpose of this section is to give you the various strategies in overcoming the physiological and psychological barriers that confront the athlete in this most difficult event. Another purpose of this section is to relate the personal anecdotes and experiences that were responsible for my sometimes unorthodox, but highly effective, approach to developing quarter-milers.

Most great quarter-milers can run a world-class 200 meters. The list is endless. Tommie Smith, Henry Carr, Michael Johnson, Herb McKenley, Lee Evans, and Larry James. Then there were others who came from the ranks of the great 800 meter runners. Mal Whitfield, Arthur Wint, Alberto Jauntorena from Cuba, and Rudolph Harbig, the great German 800 meter champion. Some quarter-milers were not known for anything but the 400 meters. George Rhoden, Ollie Matson, Marie-Jose Perec of France, Otis Davis, and Vincent Matthews are a few quarter-mile specialists, but all these athletes could run a 21-second (plus or minus) 200 meter dash. Sprint speed is a definite requirement for success in the "longest sprint."

The genetic profile of these athletes can run the gamut. Empirical observation tells me that the quarter-miler would possess the following hereditary traits:

1. A high percentage of anaerobic fast-twitch (class IIa), muscle fibers.

2. Average or better height.

3. Intelligence.

4. A high capacity for intense speed work.

5. A high pain threshold.

6. Muscular flexibility.

In addition to the above, the following characteristics must be developed:

1. The ability to relax while running at near top speed.

2. Vast reserves of creatine phosphate and other blood buffers to neutralize the onset of lactic acid.

3. The capacity to focus or concentrate on the task at hand.

4. Pace judgment.

The athlete will also need an excellent work ethic. I am not sure whether this is a hereditary or a learned characteristic, but it has to be there. The right kind of work ethic can be the most important trait of all; I have seen sheer grit and desire transcend a multitude of genetic limitations. The prime directive in this event is unparalleled dedication and determination.

TALENT IDENTIFICATION

You can find talent for this event in several places. Quarter-mile talent might be right under your nose. It can be found on the track team. It can come from misplaced hurdlers, sprinters, and jumpers. Many of your younger athletes have matured over the summer, and their bodies have changed. The basketball and football teams are loaded with potential quarter-milers. Otis Davis (1960 Olympic champion), was a basketball player and Ollie Matson (1952 bronze medalist), was a football player. Quarter-milers can come from the ranks of swimming, soccer, volleyball and of course, the school's physical education classes. One of my state champions was brought to me by our school's guidance counselor. It pays to network with your faculty. On another occasion, a student brought his friend to practice to meet me; this athlete ran a 46.5 in college and eventually became a Division I All-American.

It is much easier to find an exceptional quarter-miler than a talented 100 meter runner. Very few people have a high percentages of class IIb fast-twitch muscle fibers. A great 100 meter candidate is a rare bird. Most people seem to have a mix of various types of muscle fibers. Most track candidates will be 400, 800, 1,600, and 3,200 meter runners. Athletes with a mix of various types of muscle fibers have always been the foundation of my teams.

Quarter-milers can be the foundation of your team. Quarter-milers can score points in just about every event in your running program — and everything they run will contribute to their development. I can remember a state champion in the 400 who was timed at 9:42 in the 3,200 meter run during the indoor season. Another quarter-miler blew away the competition when he ran the anchor leg on the 4×100 relay. Quarter-milers are probably the most versatile runners in track and field! The late Eddie Hurt of Morgan State University, who coached George Rhoden (1952 Olympic champion) and a plethora of other Jamaican quarter-milers, held only one tryout for his sprinters. He timed everybody in the 400. The winners became his quarter-milers. Those who were in front early in the race became his 100 and 200 sprinters. Those who came on strong at the end became his 800 and 1600 meter runners. I am a bit more comprehensive in choosing and placing athletes, but Coach Hurt's system worked for him.

TECHNICAL ASPECTS

Starting skills for the 400 are identical to those taught to the 100 and 200 competitors. The action from the starting blocks might not be as explosive, but the movement into full running stride has to be effective. Quarter-milers cannot donate yards or meters to the rest of the field. They have to gain a lead the hard way — they have to earn it. Some quarter-milers might use the standing start, and occasionally I will permit this — temporarily. When they approach 50 seconds in the 400, I put them in starting blocks.

There are several approaches to running a successful 400 meters:

1. Some coaches advocate an even-paced effort. They divide the race into four 100 meter segments. The athlete is instructed to run each segment at the same speed. A 50-second quarter-miler will run each 100 meters in 12.5 seconds.

2. Run a positive split. The quarter-miler is taught to run the first 200 faster than the second 200 meters. Herb McKenley often ran the first 200 under 21 seconds and ran the second 200 in 25 seconds. This method was successfully used by many world class quarter-milers in the 1950s and 1960s. This suicidal approach to the 400 is taught by many coaches today, but I don't like it. Rigor mortis is a quarter-miler's constant companion, but aggravating the situation by accumulating more lactic acid than is necessary is not a good idea.

3. Run a negative split. According to my empirical observation, it is possible with this method for the quarter-miler to experience the onset of lactic acid much later in the race. The result is a more economical distribution of effort: The athlete attempts to run the first 200 about one second slower than the second 200 meters. According to a recent report in the *Track Coach's Quarterly*, most of the world records from the 400 meters to the marathon were achieved by competitors who ran a negative split. The accumulation of lactic acid and its impact on the muscular system still occur, but most runners seem to manage the final 100 meters of the 400 or the final mile of the marathon with less difficulty. This method gets my unequivocal support.

4. Run the race as a unit. The athlete is told to run the first curve as fast and relaxed as possible. Try to freewheel (maintain speed with minimum effort) on the backstretch and accelerate into the turn. Come out of the turn and finish the final 80–100 meters with the energy that remains. This method is advocated by many coaches, and will work well with most quarter-milers. One of my best quarter-milers used this popular technique to win the state championship. The key to success with this method is the skill of the runner in negotiating a relaxed run on the backstretch. Speed cannot be compromised in this segment of the race, or all is lost. This is an extremely difficult skill to learn. Runners who can grasp this perplexing concept will consistently turn in outstanding results in the 400 meters.

5. Some runners will never run a decent 400 until they are taught to run the 400 in the following rather unorthodox manner: Have the athletes cruise the entire first turn or the first 100 meters in approximately 2–3 seconds slower than their goal pace. They then run the remaining 300 meters all-out. A 50-second quarter-miler will run the opening 100 meters in 14 seconds and finish the final 300 meters in 35–36 seconds. Rigor mortis will be experienced, but much later in the race. I have been criticized by track purists whenever one of my runners employs this unusual method, but they can't argue with the results we get. Some of these athletes improved their times as much as four seconds in one week when they used this unorthodox method.

PHYSIOLOGICAL CONSIDERATIONS FOR THE 400 METERS

I mentioned earlier that creatine phosphate and certain other blood buffers can modify the onset of lactic acid and other fatigue poisons. A certain kind of training is required to accumulate reserves of these important chemicals in the liver and bloodstream. That training is anaerobic speed work. Hoover Wright (the 1952 Olympic coach) and Dave Bethany of Texas Southern University like their athletes to run 600s and 500s in the precompetitive season. Lou Hartzog, formerly of Southern Illinois University, and Bud Winter (Tommie Smith's coach) had their men run repeat 200s and 100s. Jim Bush, the great UCLA sprint coach, advocated an eclectic training system that included all of the above, with the addition of 300s and 150s. There are many roads that lead to Rome.

Which system is best? Sometimes when a neophyte track coach is confronted with an amalgam of training methods, confusion and trepidation may set in. Not to worry. Remember the virtues of variety. Well, here it is. Lets take a look at the physiology of these ostensibly diverse training systems as they relate to the above workouts.

First, the training effects of 4×600, 5×500, 8×200 or 16×100 are about the same. The total distance is almost identical. The extent and nature of the aerobic effect will depend upon how much rest the runner gets between repetitions. Decrease the rest between the 200s and 100s, and the runner's body will experience an anaerobic response similar to 500 and 600 meter workouts. Increase the rest periods and you have a speed workout. These workouts, and others like these, can be manipulated to fit the athlete's needs. You can crescendo the workout. If this is the case, the final 100 or 200 can be run faster than the initial portion of the repetition to teach acceleration skills and a stronger finishing kick. You can also run these repeats at an even pace to teach pace work. You can even run repeat 50 and 60 meter sprints and get an anaerobic effect if they are run back-to-back with little or no rest in between. If you are emphasizing speed, increase the rest period between repetitions. A walk-back equal to the distance run, is the usual exercise prescription for speed work. Some coaches may prefer to take a pulse count between repeat 600s and 500s. The pulse should return to 100–120 beats per minute for recovery. However, counting pulse rates may not be practical if you do not have assistant coaches. If taking a runner's pulse is not expedient, talk to your runners during the workout to determine how each individual is responding to the training session. Some of your people may need longer rest periods, and others may have to discontinue the workout. Trust your judgment; remember that coaching is an art as well as a science. Be prepared to change your workout at any time.

How to Overcome Rigor Mortis

Most trained runners have no difficulty in running a fast 300 meters. It is in the final 80–100 meters of the quarter-mile that their bodies seem to shut down. The onset of lactic acid and other fatigue poisons in the muscles and bloodstream creates a feeling of total muscular helplessness that has to be experienced to be understood. It may take an athlete several years to solve this problem alone; however, a knowledgeable coach and a willing athlete can overcome it in several months:

Solution 1. Run overdistance workouts to improve their anaerobic endurance. Most athletes will respond to a steady diet of 600s, 500s, and an occasional 800 meter run in practice. If a quarter-miler continues to have trouble with the final 100 meters, I will have the athlete run the 800 meters in competition.

Solution 2. Try the 50-second run. This unorthodox workout serves two purposes: (1) It will teach an athlete to adjust to rigor mortis, and (2) it can be done anywhere. You don't need a track for this workout. If the quarter-miler's goal is to run a 50-second 400 meters, I have the athlete run 200 meters in 25 seconds. The runner continues running until 50 seconds have elapsed. I place a marker at the point where the 50-second run was accomplished. After a complete recovery, the runner attempts to reach that same spot two more times. If the athlete cannot, then the workout is repeated after two days of easy workouts. When the runner can reach the designated point three consecutive times in the same workout, the marker is moved up 10 yards for the next scheduled "stress" workout. This process is continued until the quarter-miler can run three 50-second 400s in the same workout. If this difficult task can be accomplished, the athlete will be capable of running faster than 50 seconds in competition.

Solution 3. Run four 100s back-to-back. This can be done on the straightaway or around the track. Give runners enough time to slow down between each 100 and gather themselves to run the next 100. Run each 100 in 12.5 seconds if your goal is a 50-second 400. Repeat each set of four 100s three to four times.

Solution 4. Run 16×100s in 12.5. If this has been successfully completed, then add 50 meters to the 100s in the next hard workout, and run 10×150s in 18.75. In the next hard workout, run 8×200 in 25 seconds. Have the athlete walk back the same distance that was run. If this workout has been successfully completed, add 50 meters to the next workout. You are basically maintaining the same pace and decreasing the repetitions, but total distance covered in the workout remains the same. Eventually the quarter-miler will be running 4×400 in 50 seconds. This procedure will take about eight to ten of these sessions. This type of workout should be initiated about the middle of the precompetitive season, and should be finalized a week before the important meets are scheduled.

Photo 7–1. Relaxed finishing technique in the 400 meters. This runner (my oldest son), is a prototype of a typical (tall and lean) quarter-miler.

Solution 5. Mark the last 100 meters of the 400 with lines that are 5, 6, 7, and 8 feet apart starting with lane one. If your school has a track, each lane will have markings with progressively longer distances. Time the quarter-miler for 300 meters at his or her goal pace. A 48-second quarter-miler will run the 300 in 36 seconds. If the athlete has a 6-foot stride, she must move to lane two and hit every line in lane two while running the final 100 meters. Repeat this drill three to four times. This workout can be done in a park, playground, bridle path, or parking lot if a track is not available.

All of these workouts should start in the middle of the precompetitive season. Plan to culminate these kinds of "stress" workouts just prior to the peaking period or cycle. You don't need any special surface for these workouts. You can do them anywhere. Pack a few cones in your car and you are ready. These solutions to the "rig" problem may be unorthodox, but they may be the only way some of your runners can learn. I related these workouts to a rival coach and his 4×400 relay team ran one of the best high school times in the nation.

TRAINING PROGRAM FOR THE 400 METER

The charts on the following pages will not contain these special workouts. Just insert them during the precompetitive period, and endeavor to finalize them when you initiate your peaking period. Notice also that the general preparation and the specific preparation period are not included for the 400 meter runner. They are basically the same as the 100 and 200 meter runners' training schedules.

Weekly training schedule for 400 meter runner in the pre competitive period

Day	Duration (min)	Training task	Training details
Monday	20	Warm-up	1600 meter stride, calisthenics and stretching, stride an 800
	10	Sprint drills	High knees, chop downs, 1,2,3s, overstrides, form runs
	30	Anaerobic speed	4×500, 80%–90% effort, walk 500 meters between each
	10	Warm-down	800 meter jog, stretch
Tuesday	20	Warm-up	1600 meter jog, 10×150 meter interval strides, jog between each, stretch
	10	Sprint drills	Same as Monday
	30	Baton passing and starts	Establish passing zones for the 4×400 relay, 80% speed through the zone, 60 meters from the blocks
	30	Weight training	1 set 10 reps (upper body), 2 sets 10, lower body
	10	Warm-down	
Wednesday	20	Warm-up	Same as Monday
	10	Sprint drills	High knees, butt kicks, overstrides, skipping with high knees, and chop downs
	30	Anaerobic sprinting	8×200 or 10×150 (80% effort), 2 min recovery between
	10	Warm-down	
Thursday	20	Warm-up	Same as Tuesday
	10	Sprint drills	Same as Tuesday
	30	Baton passing, block	4×400 passes at 90% effort, starts at 50 meters, 100% effort
	30	Weight training	4 sets, 5 reps
Friday	20	Warm-up	16×100 intervals, 50% speed, jog 100 in between each
	10	Sprint drills	Same as Monday
	30	Speed work	5×60, 2 sets, 5×60, 2 sets. Rest 2 min between sets, 1×800 stride
Saturday		Competition.	

* A runner's best time divided by the percentage will give you the exact speed of a required run. For example: 60 secs. divided by 90% = 66.6 secs.

The month of March is the most important part of our indoor season, but we will train through most dual meets and taper off for the big invitationals and the conference championship. Our indoor taper is usually just one day. Our routine is to jog and stretch, run through a few sprint drills, and rehearse a few baton passes and starts on the day before our important meets. We have not reached our peak physical condition yet — nor do we intend to reach it. If runners peak too often or too soon, they might not be able to rise to the occasion when you really want them to. Our ultimate peak is planned to occur in the final two weeks of the outdoor season in May. However, most of our quarter-milers usually turn in outstanding times because of the excitement generated during indoor competition. This a good time to determine who will perform best when the pressure is on. This kind of situation can give a coach great insight into each quarter-miler's character when the chips are down. The athletes are expected to be excited, but the coach must endeavor to be calm and composed at this time and observe each quarter-miler's response to competition.

Weekly training for 400 meter runners during the competitive season

Day	Duration (min)	Training task	Training details
Monday	20	Warm-up	Jog 1600 meters, calisthenics and stretching
	10	Sprint drills	High knees, chop downs, form runs, etc.
	30	3–4 × 600 meters	Each 600 at 90% effort, walk a 600 in between
	10	Warm-down	Jog 800 meters, stretch
Tuesday	20	Warm-up	Jog 800 meters, 16 × 100 meter strides, jog 100 in between
	10	Sprint drills	Same as Monday
	30	16 × 100 meters	Use the first four 100s as a warm-up, the last 12 at 95% effort. Monitor every 100 to avoid leg problems
	30	Weight training	Heavy weights, lower reps, 4 sets, 5 reps
Wednesday	20	Warm-up	Jog 1600 meters, walk 200 meters, stride 800 meters, calisthenics and stretching
	10	Sprint drills	Same as Monday
	30	Baton passing and starts	Work primarily through the passing zone
	10	Warm-down	Single file jogging for 800 meters with baton passing

Day	Duration (min)	Training task	Training details
Thursday	20	Warm-up	Same as Tuesday
	10	Sprint drills	Same as Monday
	30	Stride frequency work	4×150 (2 sets), 4×50 (2 sets), Rest to recovery between sets
	30	Weight training	Light weights with speed reps, 8–10 reps per set
	10	Warm-down	Jog 800 meters and stretch
Friday	20	Warm-up	Same as Tuesday
	30	Rehabilitation	Relaxed water drills and swimming

Saturday   Competition.

The above cycle should be completed the last week in April. However, this and other cycles can be modified according to your schedule. These cycles can be lengthened or readjusted to accommodate the day when your conference or championship meet might occur. The above recommendation fits quite neatly for a conference or state championship scheduled for the last Saturday in May. At first glance, it looks like a typical track workout, but there are a few subtle differences that can be altered. For example, if a sprinter shows a lack of anaerobic endurance, Thursday's repeats could be a series of 200s or 300s instead of the 150s and 50s. This modification can be determined by the quarter-miler's performance in practice or competition.

When you know the weather is unpredictable and may change in the middle of a workout or a track meet, you need an alternate plan. Be ready to change your training program at any moment; be prepared to move your quarter-milers to a longer event at a relay carnival or a dual meet. Preventing a serious injury is more important than winning a meet. I have seen the temperature drop 40 degrees in the middle of an important track meet in Illinois. (Yes, this is the identical warning I offered in previous chapters; it deserves repeating.) You may have to make a drastic move if the temperature makes a sudden and extreme downward shift in the middle of a meet.

It's your choice — lose a team or lose a meet. I know of a coach who put his team back on the bus and went home. A month later, his team won the state championship. The team that won the meet was through for the season due to a multitude of injuries. Why hurt athletes unnecessarily? Train your quarter-milers inside if the weather is inclement. If you have to run outside because of your situation, run overdistance and dress in the appropriate gear. Quarter-milers do not usually experience hamstring pulls as often as their 100 meter and 200 meter team mates, but its better to be safe than sorry.

The fifth and final period is the most crucial cycle of the track season. You will have to assess each runner's readiness to compete. You must know who should train harder and who requires more recovery time. You have to decide who should continue to weight train and who should not — whom you should push and whom you should leave alone. You will have to determine what and how many events the quarter-milers will compete in to sharpen them for the important competitions. Take the time to learn how your athletes respond to various kinds of competitive situations. At this point in the season, you become a scientist, psychologist, surrogate parent, and psychiatrist. The next four weeks of training are the most difficult of the season. Modify the schedule that I suggest based on the weather, personnel, and your situation.

Weekly training schedule for quarter-milers during the peaking period

Day	Duration (min)	Training task	Training details
Monday	20	Warm-up	Jog 1600 meters, sprint the last 200, calisthenics, etc.
	30	Starts and baton work	Work the full 1600 meter relay, work the full 800 meter relay
	30	Weight training	Light weights done with speed, 2–3 sets
	10	Warm-down	Jog 800 while passing the baton single-file
Tuesday	20	Warm-up	Jog 1600, walk 800, stride an 800, stretching
	20	Sprint drills	High knees, butt kicks, chop downs, skipping with high knees, form runs
	20	Warm-down	Same as Monday
Wednesday	20	Warm-up	Jog 1600, stretch
	20	Starts and baton work	Work through the passing zone, run two full 1600 meter relays
	10	Warm-down	Same as Monday
Thursday	20	Warm-up	
	10	Sprint drills	
	10	Warm-down	
Friday	40	Warm-up and relaxed swimming	
Saturday		Competition.	

The training schedule is very light during this period, but this is the most important cycle of the season. This is basically four weeks of doing little or nothing. Because your athletes are in the best condition of their lives, they will be tempted to do more. Remind them of the importance of rest and recuperation during these final weeks. Try not to let them be seduced by their "friends" to engage in activities that can have a negative impact on their performance. Have you ever had a runner on your team show up at a meet with a leg in a cast? I have.

400 METER TRAINING WITH LITTLE OR NO EQUIPMENT OR FACILITIES

It is possible to develop a quarter-miler anywhere. As usual, you will have to innovate. Some surfaces can cause damage to the soft tissue of the lower limbs, exercise caution with your training schedule and most injuries can be avoided. Every playground, every park, every "facility" that you used with the 100 and 200 meter runners can be exploited by the quarter-miler. Measure your distances, terrains and areas and go to work. Wherever you can train a 100 and 200 meter runner — a quarter-miler can train there with equal success.

You may have to spend time explaining to some of your neophyte runners how a properly marked and maintained track looks. To reinforce this information, have your veteran runners talk to the team. Young people need to hear from their peers about what to expect. They may be able to communicate certain ideas to one another that you may have taken for granted. Try to arrive early for your first indoor and outdoor competitions. Walk around the track with your team and explain the lane markings, passing zones, and such. Show them the long jump, triple jump area, shot put, and high jump area. If you are given a program or schedule, share this information with the team. Some of the members of your team have never seen a state-of-the-art 400 meter track. This may be the first time most of your athletes have participated in a track meet.

Teach your team track etiquette. Emphasize the importance of showing up on time for a race. Explain that being prepared and ready for a race will improve their chances of success in competition. They need to know that silence is expected when the "gun is up." They should be told to bring all problems with the officials to the coach or a responsible adult. Any minor difficulties should be handled by the team manager. Finally, teach the team the most important rule of all: Sportsmanship is more important than anything. Win with class, lose with class.

Section 8

THE 800 METERS
Mal Whitfield and Company

Mal Whitfield was the quintessential 800 meter runner. The 1948 and 1952 Olympic champion dominated the middle distances for almost ten years. His running form was the most flawless in the history of track and field. Fortunately, form is teachable. The 800 meter runner must also possess a generous combination of sprint speed and aerobic endurance. Physiological preparation has to include every training method in existence. Every system of the body is called upon to operate at its maximum in this most demanding event. Most 800 meter competitors either come up to this event from the 400 or come down from the 1600 meters. Mal Whitfield did neither; he was an 800 meter specialist.

The 800 meter run, also referred to as the half mile, is a unique event. It is too long a race to be characterized as a sprint and too short to be a distance race. A candidate for this event must bring sprint speed and an ample supply of aerobic and anaerobic endurance to the starting line. The 800 is not a sprint, nor is it a distance race; it is both. Lactic acid will accumulate in the muscles more gradually than in the 400 meters, but this fatigue poison will last for a longer period of time. In the final 200 meters, the half-miler has to ignore this painful trauma and somehow marshal the remainder of a rapidly diminishing supply of energy for a final and painful sprint to the finish. Without a highly developed sense of pace judgment, the onset of fatigue poisons will occur too early in the race and frustrate this final burst of speed.

The 800 meter runner is difficult to identify by body type and stature. There have been great tall half-milers, great half-milers who were not tall, thin half-milers, and muscular half-milers. They come in a myriad of physical uniforms. Champions in this event can come from every athletic endeavor: Some have come from the ranks of the great milers and others have been world-class 400 meter runners.

Because half-milers come from every somatotype and physical description, no one seems to agree on the best way to train a half-miler. Some half-milers seem to thrive on an extensive speed program. Some were developed via a distance-oriented system. Others attained world-class status from a more eclectic approach to training. Does this event and the best way to deal with it confuse most coaches? You can bet your last money that it does.

There have also been a number of 800 meter specialists. John Woodruff the 1936 Olympic half-mile champion, Tom Courtney the great half-miler from Fordham University, Arnie Sowell of Pitt University, and Dave Wottle, the 1972 Olympic 800 meter champion, were never world-class in any other track event. But if there ever was a quintessential half-miler, it was Mal Whitfield, the 1948 and 1952 Olympic champion in the 800 meters. Mal's running technique was so smooth and efficient that he was often accused of not trying. I saw him break six world records in one meet. He was trying, but it just didn't look like it. One writer aptly stated, "Mal Whitfield doesn't run; he flows."

Mal Whitfield could run a world-class 400 meters, but never dominated the event. He also made a brief attempt to become a miler near the twilight of his career and didn't dominate that event either. He was born to run the half and was invincible in this event for almost a decade. Though several runners of the modern era have eclipsed his records, no one ran the 800 meters better than Mal Whitfield.

TALENT IDENTIFICATION

One of the first outstanding runners I ever coached was a half-miler. Initially, I was desperately trying to make this athlete into a quarter-miler and was failing at it. In an effort to build his anaerobic endurance, I entered him in an 800 meter race. Lord have mercy! He annihilated the competition. The rest is history. He won two state championships in high school and subsequently won two successive NCAA Division I 800 meters titles at the University of Tennessee.

An absolute requirement for the 800 meters is the ability to sprint (many world-class 800 meter runners were former quarter-milers). On one occasion, I needed candidates for the 4×800 relay, so I held a time trial for the event. Everybody on the team was invited. When the dust cleared, only one half-miler made the relay team. Quarter-milers and hurdlers dominated the time trial. One quarter-miler and a 110 meter hurdler ran well under two minutes the first time they ran the 800 meters. We never lost a 4×800 meter relay that season. Go figure.

You may have half-mile talent right under your nose. Invite basketball and soccer forwards, football wide receivers, swimmers, and members of the cross-country team to try the 800 meters. Peter Snell, the 1960 and 1964 Olympic champion, and Tom Courtney, the 1956 Olympic champion, were built like weight lifters. John Woodruff and Alberto Juantoreno were big enough to play defensive end on the Chicago Bears. Sebastian Coe and Rick Wolhuter were small in build and stature. These athletes only had one thing in common; they were all world-class half-milers. There is another seemingly unrelated correlation among 800 meter runners; most of these athletes can execute a respectable high jump. Several half-milers I coached could high jump over six feet. It makes sense to take closer look at some of your average high jumpers. Half-mile talent can also run in families. Several members of the same family were state champions in Illinois.

A half-miler has to love to run anything and everything. As you work to develop this athlete, you can implement all kinds of training modalities. I mentioned earlier that most sprinters don't want to do anything but sprint. This attitude cannot be true of 800 meter runners. Half-milers may have to run long distances, fartlek, interval training, repetition sprinting, tempo runs, and over-distance repeats. Success in this event requires work and plenty of it. Talent is necessary, but a work ethic is just as important as genetics in the half mile. I have seen sprinters perform commendably on a perfunctory work schedule. No decent half-miler can ever expect to do anything respectable in this event without paying his or her dues.

Half-mile talent can come from the ranks of hurdlers, sprinters, and jumpers. Retest the runners every year; many of your younger athletes will mature over the summer and their bodies may manifest major physical changes. The basketball team and football team are loaded with potential half-milers, along with athletes from the ranks of swimming, soccer, volleyball, and, of course, the school's physical education classes. When these athletes join your squad, don't expect an immediate manifestation of middle-distance talent. It takes about two or three weeks for an athlete from another sport to adjust to the physiological demands of the 800 meters. If the unrelated sport has developed the cardiovascular system, the athlete can realize 800 meter potential in less than a month. One of our outstanding half-milers swam the 500 meters; in three weeks, this athlete became the anchor on the 4×800 relay team. A month later, he captured the city championship in the half mile. This youngster ran no cross-country and did not compete in track until the middle of March. The cardiovascular training gained from swimming was excellent preparation for the 800 meters. Once this athlete's musculature adjusted to running, I had a champion half-miler.

SOME PROBLEMS AND SOME SOLUTIONS

Championship track and field is difficult to achieve under the best of circumstances. The mission of this book is to assure the coach who has inherited an ostensibly impossible situation that he or she is not alone. There are probably more of us out there than you realize. Sometimes hard work and improvisation are not enough. I have been told and am sure some of you have been told by your administration, "THERE IS NO INDOOR TRACK PROGRAM IN THIS SCHOOL!" The administration often expects the coach to build a winning program with no outdoor facilities, no budget, no equipment, and — last but not least — no indoor program. A winning track program without an indoor track schedule? Successful track and field without an indoor program has to be an oxymoron.

I have been there. Some administrators have no idea what it takes to build a winning program. But there is more than one way to skin a cat. You might get by with developing a sprinter on a limited program but the problem is a bit more difficult to solve with a middle-distance runner. These athletes require a longer period of time to reach their potential. A lack of a viable indoor program complicates an already perplexing situation. Listed below are some solutions to this frustrating dilemma:

1. Encourage everyone on your team to participate in a fall and winter sport. Wrestling, basketball, and swimming will build a tremendous foundation for your track people. In the fall, every track athlete should run cross-country, or play football, volleyball, or soccer.

2. Get your team involved in a park district or playground program. Most parks have a variety of physical activities available for your athlete.

3. Gymnastics, tumbling, dancing, or weight training can be of value. One of my best hurdlers (13.8 over the 110 meter high hurdles) participated in ballet. Ballet is a fantastic preseason activity for runners and hurdlers.

4. Have some of the team members join an outside track club. Become one of the coaches. This recommendation is perfectly legal and it affords your athletes an opportunity to compete during the indoor season. Once you start your season, they cannot continue to compete for the club, but they can rejoin the club in the summer.

5. If none of the above suggestions is suitable, write a training schedule for your runners, and periodically confer with them about their progress. Middle-distance runners can train outside almost every day of the year if they are dedicated. I did not require them to run if the temperature was below 10 degrees Fahrenheit. It was their choice — and most runners chose to run every day in spite of the severe and often unpredictable midwestern weather.

6. If it is financially possible, your middle-distance runner can join the local health club or YMCA or boys and girls club. Most of these organizations have facilities that can accommodate a runner's training requirements during the general and specific preparation periods. Your middle-distance runner must be active all year. If your runner reports to you at the beginning of the outdoor season in good physical condition, you are ahead of the game. You won't have to start from square one every year. Be careful of overtraining, however. Every athlete needs *some* time away from intensive training. Rest and restoration are extremely important. Schedule one or two weeks rest at the end of each season. Half-milers should be encouraged to take a short vacation from track and field to "recharge their batteries."

HOW TO RUN THE 800 METERS

Success in the 800 meters requires a unique combination of speed, endurance, pace judgment, and racing tactics. The 800 is long enough to tax a runner's cardiovascular system and short enough to place optimal demands on leg speed. If an error is made in pace judgment, the race will be over before it starts. In the first 200 meters, there is a mad scramble for position because this race is not run in lanes after the first turn. If the runner is not alert, legs and arms can get tangled and the athlete will be thrown off stride. The half-miler has the additional problem of avoiding getting boxed between runners. During this initial chaos, the athlete must maintain a relaxed stride and not lose a sense of pace. The runner must also endeavor to be in a good position at the 600 meters and conserve enough energy to launch a decent finishing kick in the final 200 meters. No other race in track requires this many mental and physical adjustments so quickly.

Most half-milers use a standing start. There is a tendency among athletes to take the standing start for granted. The standing start must be practiced as diligently as the crouch start. I have seen 800 meter races won and lost because of poor starting technique. Use the following guidelines:

1. The dominant leg should be forward.

2. The arms should be hanging in a relaxed position and the body should be bent at the waist before the command "Go to your marks." Lift the non dominant arm forward and bent at 90 degrees. I have seen runners stumble over the starting line before the gun was shot. Such an action will result in a disqualification.

3. When the starting pistol is fired, the half-miler should quickly drive from the bent-over starting position to the proper erect running posture in about four strides.

A runner who is vastly superior to the competition or does not have great finishing sprint should move immediately to the lead and endeavor to control the race from the front. Half-milers with superior sprinting ability will usually position themselves 5–10 meters behind the leaders until the final 200 meters. Any distance further back may be difficult to make up in the latter stages of the race. The following runner cannot give up too many meters early in the race and must stay in contact with the front runners. At 600 meters, the runner has to be within one to two strides of the leaders. The half-miler must begin to accelerate into the final turn and pass the leaders down the final straight. All this must be done while paying strict attention to pace. Front runners usually run a positive split, and runners who depend on their sprinting ability in the final 200 usually run a negative split. I mentioned in Section 7 that pace is important to a quarter-miler. Some quarter-milers can make a mistake in pace judgment and manage to win somehow. Poor pace judgment in the half mile is disastrous. If pace is misjudged in the first 400 meters, the race is virtually over for that poor soul. A champion half-miler has to know what the pace is for every 200 meters. Some may know their pace for every 100 meters. Half-milers have to be aware of where they are every step of the way. During the precompetitive and competitive phases of training, the half-miler trains on two basic kinds of pace schedules. One is called "date" pace and the other is called "goal" pace. Date pace is the particular pace that the coach and the athlete have decided that can be negotiated in the early stages of interval training. This pace is slower than the athlete's predetermined 800 meter goal. This kind of training is done with an emphasis on quantity. With goal pace, workouts are run at a pace that is equal to or faster than the pace the athlete has determined as a late-season goal. The runner's repeat 400s, 300s and 200s are run with an emphasis on quality and not quantity.

Quantity and *quality* are relative terms. When I am designing a workout with quantity in mind, the total mileage of the interval training is approximately two miles in distance. This means that an 800 meter workout will consist of 8×400, 16×200, 10×300 or 32×100 or an infinite combination of these suggested workouts. Each of these workouts totals about two miles, plus or minus a few meters. These repeats are run at date pace with an equivalent distance jogged in between. As we approach the latter part of the competitive period, we will reduce the number of repeats and increase the speed to goal pace. A good formula to follow is the suggestion learned at a Camp Olympia clinic conducted by Dr. Tom Rosandich several years ago. I have used this helpful mnemonic device for most of my coaching career. The acronym DIRTY can help coaches and athletes organize an interval or repetition workout. This system eliminates all of the confusion related to planning an interval training schedule:

D = Distance. The distance to be covered i.e., 400s, 300s, 200s, etc.
I   = Interval of rest. How long you rest between each repeat. This depends on the nature of the workout, time of year, and what you are trying to achieve physiologically on a given day.

R = Repetitions. The number of repetitions are determined by the time of year, the athlete's physical condition and whether this is a quality or quantity training session.

T = Time. How fast each repetition or repeat should be.

Y = You. What do you do between repeats? Does the athlete walk, stand or jog between each repetition?

SOME BASIC EXERCISE PHYSIOLOGY

When I was a neophyte coach, I sought out knowledgeable coaches for advice. Many of these people were quite helpful and others were vague and evasive. That's the chance you have to take in your search for Truth. I once asked a successful middle-distance coach how he trained his athletes. He told me that he used physiology and walked away. I stood there with my hat in my hand and a question mark above my head. How cruel.

Like most coaches, I took chemistry, physics, anatomy, and physiology in pursuit of a college degree. The instructors never told us how to put all those formulas and lab experiments to practical use. "Just take my course and pass my exams," they said. How cruel.

Now I finally know how to apply this stuff in a practical way. After years of separating the wheat from the chaff, I can tell you what you need to know without all the scientific terminology that the PhDs use to confuse practically everybody:

1. *Long runs* (10–15 miles), primarily affect the vascular system. Six to eight weeks of this kind of training will cause the capillaries to increase in number and the veins and arteries to increase in size. The blood flow to the musculature will increase via this enhanced circulatory system. An increased blood flow means that more oxygen will be delivered to the various systems of the body. More oxygen — more aerobic endurance. The efficiency and size of the heart are also affected, but long runs contribute mostly to the development of the vascular part of the circulatory system. Leg speed, however, is negatively affected by long runs. Don't expect to sprint effectively or jump high after eight weeks of nothing but long runs. You can't have your cake and eat it too. That's why Arthur Lydiard (Peter Snell's coach) and Percy Cerutty, the great Australian middle-distance coach, included fartlek (speed play) in their training programs during this preparatory period. Never totally eliminate speed work from your training program.

2. *Tempo running* (2–6 miles). These are timed runs — a compromise between long runs and speedwork. Basically, they are neither; however, an athlete can race at 800 meters and run commendable times after using this method. Cardiovascular development is compromised somewhat but aerobic and anaerobic endurance is maintained. Some great half-milers never run beyond 6–8 miles. I think this approach will depend on the type of half-miler you are coaching. Usually, the quarter-miler who comes up to the 800 will not thrive on a distance-oriented training program. This is as far as they need to run.

3. *Fartlek* (Swedish speed play). Fartlek is a method of training that was used quite successfully by two world-class Swedish middle-distance runners in 1944. Gunder Hagg and Arne Anderson ran the amazing times in the mile of 4:01.4 and 4:01.6! It took ten years before Roger Bannister of Great Britain did any better than this. Fartlek was later used by Arthur Lydiard of New Zealand and Percy Cerutty of Australia to develop several sub-four-minute milers. Fartlek is an extremely effective system of training. *Fartlek* means, literally, to play at speed. It is a combination of sprinting, striding, jogging, running uphill and downhill; the tempo of running is changed while a certain distance is covered. True fartlek is run on a time basis. Usually, the athlete runs continuously for 30 minutes to an hour. During that time, 5 to 10 miles may be negotiated. Physiologists characterize this kind of training as the exercise continuum; every system of the body is affected by fartlek. With fartlek, a runner can positively affect aerobic endurance, anaerobic endurance, speed endurance, and sprinting speed. In addition to all of the foregoing, most athletes can enjoy the freedom of expression and creativity that is engendered by the fartlek system. Fartlek is a near-perfect system of training, but it has to be combined with other training modalities in order to develop the complete runner.

An excellent modification of fartlek is a method of training I invented and named "organized" fartlek. I usually determined a specific distance (3–4 miles to a certain destination and 3–4 miles back) to be covered. In the city, it was often a particular landmark; for example, Soldier Field, McCormick Place, or a nearby stadium. You can use any convenient landmark in your town or city. I usually gave a few basic instructions to the captains of the team: Run one easy mile, 4–8×400s, another easy mile, 16×100 meters, one more easy mile, and run the remainder of the distance doing what ever the captains decided. All distances were approximations except the destination and the return to school. This is not fartlek in the classic sense of the word, but it was perfect for our situation. We used various modifications of "organized" fartlek throughout the season.

When you introduce this kind of workout, certain safety measures are in order. Give your younger and least experienced runners a head start. If you start all your runners at the same time, you will be waiting forever for everybody to return. When your more experienced runners pass the weaker athletes, instruct them to continue running. At some point, the stronger runner will be returning from the scheduled destination. When the younger runners see the more experienced runners returning, they must turn around and head for the point of origin. If you have planned this properly, everyone will finish the run at the same time.

This procedure serves several important purposes:

a. All runners are running at their own level of ability.

b. At some point during the run, everyone is running in a group.

c. This type of practice can turn into a friendly competition.

d. The younger runners often try to get to the starting point ahead of the more experienced runners.

e. This workout is fun.

4. *Interval training.* Interval training was scientifically codified by two German physiologists in 1936. Coaches and athletes were probably using a crude form of this training system before this, but this pair of brilliant PhDs developed interval running into a highly organized and productive system of training. Simply put, interval training consists of running repeats of a certain distance (400, 300, or 200) and taking a timed rest period after each effort. This interval of rest is one to two minutes. The runner's pulse has to return to 120 beats per minute during this rest period. If the pulse does not return to 120 in one to two minutes, the previous run was too fast or too long. Interval training can be used to tailor a workout to each athlete's ability. Speed, volume, rest, and intensity of the workout are easily adjusted for the strongest or weakest runner on your squad.

Interval training's basic physiological purpose is to improve cardiac efficiency. A six- to eight-week period with an emphasis on interval training should result in a marked increase in the minute volume of the heart and concomitant decrease in the athlete's resting heart rate. Other physiological manifestations will be increased capillarization and improved oxygen uptake. The athlete's pace judgment will be improved. The runner's speed will also be positively affected. However, the most significant physiological modification will be the capacity of the heart to deliver oxygenated blood to the muscles. Aerobic endurance is the desired outcome of interval training. Interval training is usually 100–400 meter repeats done a little more slowly than race pace (date pace).

5. *Repetition training.* This method of training is often confused with interval training. There is usually a designated distance run followed by an interval of rest. To the casual observer, this method looks like interval training. There are some significant differences, however. The distances covered are longer (400–1600 meters) and the emphasis is on speed (goal pace) and anaerobic endurance. The rest periods (five to seven minutes), between repeats have to be longer; they are also fewer in number. I once observed Lowell Paul, a member of the world-class University of Chicago Track Club's 4×800 relay team, run 2×400 in a workout and go home. His workout was over for the day. Each 400 was run in 49 seconds.

Repetition training is usually done near the end of the competitive period and in the beginning of the peaking period. During the competitive period, the emphasis is on quantity, and as the athlete approaches the peaking period, the focus changes to quality. Therefore, the half-miler may for example, run 6–8×400 in April at race pace, and run 2–4×400 in May, faster than pace. The distances, times, number of repeats, and rest periods can be manipulated to suit the athlete's physiological needs on a given day. These physiological requirements are determined by the runner's performance in competition.

Occasionally, pyramids can be a part of repetition training. A pyramid workout is a workout where each successive repetition is decreased in distance. The pace can remain the same or increase in speed as the distance becomes shorter. The total distance of this workout is 2400 meters. A half-miler might be required to run 2×600, 2×400, and 2×200. During the final weeks of the season, this workout can be reduced in volume and increased in speed. The half-miler would run 1×600, 1×400, 1×200. Each repetition would be faster than race pace. This kind of workout can add variety to your training program. When workouts are faster than race pace, you will develop anaerobic endurance plus speed. Again, this will depend on how fast each repeat is run and the length of the rest period between repeats. The first workout is intended for the competitive period. The latter is a peaking period workout.

6. *Repetition sprinting.* Sprinting should be an integral part of every runner's training program all year long. You don't have to do much of this, but you must do some. Repeat 50s, 60s, or 100s should be the steady diet for the middle-distance runner. Leg turnover can be maintained if the half-miler does a few additional sprints after an anaerobic or aerobic training session. A few (about 7), repeat sprints 2–3 times per week will pay off when your half-miler is within 100 meters of the finish line in a close race.

The most effective way to implement speed work is to walk back between repeats. Speed work should be done at least with 80% to 90% effort. Emphasize proper technique and relaxed running form. The distance run should be 30–100 meters.

7. *Hill training.* Arthur Lydiard and Percy Cerutty were staunch advocates of hill training. Hill training is an effective lead into repetition running and speed work. Whenever I was assigned to a school, I searched the neighborhood for a hill; I always found one. Any kind of hill will do; if you cannot find a hill, run stadium stairs. If you cannot find stadium stairs, run the stairs of a local apartment building. At one school we used the stairs of a local housing project. At another school, we found a truck delivery ramp. At another, it was a nearby sloping street pavement. There is a hill somewhere. I once entertained the idea of using the stairs at Sears Tower!

Hill training should be done immediately preceding the precompetitive period. However, we did some hill or stair running later on in the track season. It could be just the thing to stimulate your team during the competitive period. Most experts recommend steep hills during the early season, and hills with a minimal incline during the competitive period. Some coaches often prescribe a specific degree of incline for the hill. We looked for two variables — steep and not steep. Basically, we used what was available. So did Lydiard and Cerutty. A final word of caution: Hill training is a severe form of exercise. Two hill sessions a week are enough.

PACE JUDGMENT IN THE 800 METERS

Pace judgment in the half mile is crucial. Half-milers have to know where they are during the race. Sometimes, a quarter-miler can survive an error in pace judgment in the 400. Poor pace judgment in the 800 is disastrous. Earlier in this section, I briefly touched on the importance of pace. I discussed negative and positive splits. I also stated that most world records in the middle distances were attained with a negative split. In the past, the practice was to run a positive split. For example, a 1:58 half miler would run 58 seconds for the first 400 and finish with 60 seconds for the final 400 meters. A negative split for the same race would be 60 seconds for the first 400 and a 58 second 400 meters.

The easiest way to figure out splits for your runners is to purchase an Oregon pace rule. This device is usually advertised in the *Track and Field Market Place* — a catalogue published by *Track and Field News* in Los Altos, California. You can figure out the splits for every middle-distance runner on your team within a few minutes with this device. Another excellent training aid for the coach is the *Smith Encyclopedia of Individual Computerized Track Workouts*. This book has catalogued every interval or repetition workout possible, and can also, along with hundreds of other valuable books and videos, be purchased from the *Track and Field Marketplace*.

It is also a good idea to have the more experienced runners plan their own splits. Athletes often perform better when they are given some responsibility for their training and competition. When runners write their own splits, they are also more likely to remember them. Occasionally, a runner will set a goal that you never dreamed of — and achieve it!

TRAINING CYCLES AND WORKOUT SCHEDULES

Half-milers should train all year, if it is possible. They don't have to do track workouts, but they should at least be physically active all the time. If you can motivate them to run during the off season, try to put as much variety in their running program as possible. Make every effort to design a summer program that will be an enjoyable experience.

Summer Program

The middle-distance runners' summer program should emphasize long-distance running, but speed work should never be abandoned. The schedule below is intended for an experienced athlete; it is too difficult for a novice. It will take four years of consistent training for most youngsters to build up to this kind of schedule.

Summer training schedule for middle-distance runners

Day	Duration (min)	Training task	Training details
Monday	20	Warm-up	Jog 800 meters, stretch
	60–65	10 mile run	Cover each mile in 6–7 mins
Tuesday	20	Warm-up	Jog 1600 meters, stretch
	30–40	Fartlek	"Organized fartlek"
Wednesday	20	Warm-up	Jog 800 meters, stretch
		10 mile run	Same as Monday

Day	Duration (min)	Training task	Training details
Thursday	20	Warm-up	Jog 1600 meters
	40–50	Soccer	Game is played nonstop for 40–50 min.
Friday	20	Warm-up	Jog 800 meters, sprint drills
	35–40	6 mile run	Tempo Run
Saturday	20	Warm-up	Jog 800 meters, stretch
	90	12–15 mile run	6–8 min per mile

This training schedule is designed basically for runners who plan to run cross-country in the fall. Many 800 meter runners can be exceptional cross-country competitors. The weekly mileage is considerable, but I know coaches who require their athletes to do more than this. There are also many successful programs that thrive on much less work. This schedule is merely a guide — not a mandate. I abandoned a heavier work load because a few of the runners complained of minor soft tissue injuries. This reduced program got the job done without any damage to the lower extremities. On most days, our workouts are completed before an hour has elapsed — a small price to pay for competitive success. They have 23 hours left to enjoy their summer vacation!

Please be reminded that none of the newer runners were required to follow the above program. I am also careful not to upgrade the workout schedule in speed or volume if an athlete was making progress on much less training. An athlete should not be moved to a heavier program before it is necessary. If an easier training schedule is getting the job done, a premature increase in mileage can be counterproductive. Sometimes more is not better. In Hindu philosophy, this is called "the law of least effort."

This schedule begins approximately four weeks after our last outdoor competition. Our graduating seniors often join us in this program in preparation for their college or university training schedules. Many of the athletes who are currently enrolled in colleges or universities also join us in this summer program. Their involvement in our summer program was an inspiration to the younger kids. It is important for the younger athletes to realize that going to college is an attainable goal. I also encouraged the older athletes to counsel our underclassmen on the virtues of scholastic endeavors in their quest for higher education. I have never failed to get a runner in college who really wanted to go. Some never ran a step for the college they enrolled in, but most earned a college degree. Incidentally, the majority of your athletes will not be fortunate enough to earn a full athletic scholarship, but if you work at it, nearly all of your athletes can be accepted into some institution of higher learning. If the athlete makes an honest effort academically and athletically, the coach should do every thing possible to help student athletes to continue their education. Practically every student can matriculate somewhere, regardless of ACT or SAT scores, or athletic ability. If they cannot be accepted at a regular four-year institution, try a junior college or a trade school. Your student athletes should be encouraged to continue their education if they sincerely want to. I feel that this effort is a part of a track coach's job description.

Cross-Country

During September, some of the half-mile candidates will participate in a variety of fall sports in lieu of cross-country. This is as it should be on the secondary school level. They should be permitted to enjoy soccer, tennis, or football if that is their choice. Adolescence is a time to explore options. I have also known several world-class half-milers who were never great cross-country runners. However, they should be encouraged to train with the cross-country team, if they are not involved in a fall sport. Middle-distance runners will find it impossible to realize their potential if they are not involved in some sort of physical activity during the fall.

Cross-country training schedule for middle-distance runners

Day	Duration (min)	Training task	Training details
Monday	20	Warm-up	1600 meter jog, stretch and sprint drills
	60–70	10–12 mile run	6–7 min per mile
Tuesday	20	Warm-up	1200 meter jog, calisthenics and stretching
	40–50	12×400 or 6×800	Each 400 is run at date pace in September and goal pace in October
	10	Warm-down	1600 meter jog, stretch
Wednesday	20	Warm-up	1600 meter jog, stretch
	60–70	8–10 mile run	7–8 min per mile
Thursday	40–50	Fartlek	"Organized fartlek"
Friday	20	Warm-up	1600 meter jog, stretch
	30–40	16×100	Speed work at goal pace
	10	Warm-down	10 min jog, stretch
Saturday	Competition.		

This is a typical midseason week of cross-country training. We run intervals on Tuesday and fartlek on Thursday early in the season. Near the end of the season, we run 800 (6), or mile repeats (3–4) on Tuesday at goal pace and interval 400s on Thursday at date pace. Of course, you can assume that we don't do the same workouts every week. This schedule is merely a guide.

After the cross-country season, there is a long break of about six weeks. Our state organization does not permit any official track practice. If your runner does absolutely nothing from the last week in November to the second week in January, detraining will set in. Most of the hard work during the summer and cross-country season will be negated. Everybody needs a break from training, however, and that is probably why our state organization enforces a no-practice rule until the middle of January. A few weeks of rest and restoration can be great therapy for athlete and coach; we need to get away from it all and recharge our batteries. But after this brief vacation, most of our runners are looking for something to do. Those who are so inclined should get involved in another sport that has an aerobic component. Most of our people find their way to wrestling, swimming, or basketball. Others may play volleyball or get involved in some outside running club. Some continue to run on their own. I reiterate: Sitting around doing nothing for almost two months is counterproductive to championship middle-distance running.

When the team reports for practice around January 15, I expect everyone to be in reasonable physical condition. The remainder of the team will report to practice in March after their respective winter sports have ended. When they report for practice, I will gradually introduce them to the phase of conditioning that we are currently working on. If anyone reports for practice out of shape, I will modify the workload, but no mercy is granted. Common sense will determine how much training is required of each athlete. The poorly conditioned athlete's response to training is monitored closely. The last thing I want to do is injure an athlete.

Standard Periodization Program

Our periodization cycle for January is the general preparation period. We follow basically the same type of training that was recommended for sprinters with three basic differences:

1. The emphasis is on long-distance running prior to the recreational aspect of the workout.

2. Middle-distance runners are encouraged to run outside in the winter months. Running long distances in the halls is too monotonous and the hard surface can cause damage to the legs and lower back. Running outside is the safest way to go, and the pace is too slow to cause any soft-tissue damage.

3. On some days, their recreation will be in the form of fartlek. The recreation days are usually Monday, Wednesday, and Friday. This four- to six-week period is a time when several students who were undecided about track are often attracted to the sport because of all the fun we are having. Within several weeks, they are hooked on track and field.

Training program for half-milers during the general preparation period

Day	Duration (min)	Training task	Training details
Monday	20	Warm-up	800 meter jog., stretch, sprint drills
	30	Fartlek	One mile easy, 4×400, jog 400 between, 16×100, return to school
	30	Soccer or basketball	Games are played without rest periods or time outs
Tuesday	20	Warm-up	1600 jog, stretch, sprint drills
	40	Circuit training	Rope jumping, gymnastic work on rings, parallel and horizontal bars, aerobics
Wednesday	20	Warm-up	800 jog, stretch, sprint drills
	40–50	8 mile run	6–7 mins per mile
Thursday	20	Warm-up	1200 meter jog, stretch
	40	Basketball	Full court, nonstop
Friday	20	Warm-up	Water aerobics
	40	Swimming	Recreation swim; the major purpose is to relax tired muscles
Saturday	30	Relaxed recovery run	4 miles easy

The general preparation period for most programs should begin in January. Competition is several weeks away and there is no real rush to train specifically for track and field. The purpose of this four-week period is to continue to build a foundation for the harder work to come. When we subsequently embark upon an intense interval and repetition running program, their aerobic, anaerobic, and muscular systems will respond favorably to the demands of these physiological challenges.

In February, competition is initiated and the specific preparation period begins. The specific preparation period is characterized by a gradual transition to date pace interval training and twice a week hill training. Speed work is never totally abandoned; sprint drills and a generous dose of repetition sprints are a ubiquitous ingredient in our training program. Brooks Johnson, the author of the book *The Winning Edge*, stated unequivocally that coaches make a big mistake when they neglect speed work during early season training. I believe. Dennis Watts, the author of the book *The Complete Middle Distance Runner*, states that only 33.3% of a half-miler's training should consist of aerobic training; 66.6% should be anaerobic running. It is easy to conclude from that observation that most world-class 800 meter runners are genetically endowed with an abundance of fast-twitch class II glycolytic muscle fibers and a smaller percentage of slow-twitch class I muscle fibers. Therefore, it would be a mistake to neglect sprinting or speed-endurance training during any part of the track season. However, I would also be careful to maintain an aerobic base with the inclusion of at least two long runs during the week. Since we are not peaking at this time, we train through the meets. The following schedule represents a typical training week for the month of February:

Specific preparation period training schedule for 800 meter runners

Day	Duration (min)	Training task	Training details
Monday	30	Warm-up	Jog 3200 meters, calisthenics, stretch, sprint drills
	40	6–8 × 400	Each 400 slightly slower than pace, 90 sec rest between each
Tuesday	20	Warm-up	Same as Monday except jog1600 meters
	40	Three minutes × stairs	Run stairs for 3 mins jog 3 mins, 3 mins wind sprints, repeat for 4 sets
Wednesday	20	Warm-up	Jog 800, stretch and calisthenics, sprint drills
	50–60	6–8 mile run	6–7 min per mile
Thursday	20	Warm-up	Same as Tuesday
	40	Hill training	Same as Tuesday
Friday	20	Warm up	Same as Wednesday
	50–60	6–8 mile run	7–8 mins per mile
	15–20	7 × 100	90% effort
Saturday		Competition or a "stress" workout to simulate meet conditions.*	

*A stress workout is a method that is used to prepare an athlete for actual meet conditions in lieu of actual competition.

Competition is an integral part of the training process. There are times when a scheduled meet has been cancelled and the coach may feel that the stress of competition is necessary. Over the years, I have developed several methods to simulate meet conditions without running the actual race. A logical solution would be to run a time trial. It is difficult for an athlete to summon the psychological and physiological juices necessary for a meaningful time trial. The disappointment of a cancelled or postponed meet may render some athletes incapable of turning in a viable time trial. The following stress workouts can be used as a substitute for actual competition:

1. *The two minute run.* The half-miler is asked to run as fast as possible for two minutes. Place a cone or marker at the distance the athlete has negotiated in two minutes. Call out the splits at every 200 meters. Shout every second after the runner passes the 600 meter mark. Repeat this effort two additional times. Give the runner full recovery between attempts. If the runner can reach the initial mark on every attempt, move the marker an extra 10 meters for the next stress workout.

2. *Have the half-miler run back-to-back 400s or 200s at goal pace.* Tell the athlete the time of the distance run and immediately run the next 400 or 200. An 800 meter runner will run 2×400 or 4×200 in three sets. The rest between sets will be to full recovery to simulate meet conditions.

3. *Run a 600 meters at race pace.* Rest long enough to tell the athlete the time of the distance run. Sprint the final 200. Repeat this effort for two or three sets.

The kind of stress workout you decide upon will have to be determined by the athlete's physiological needs. If the athlete needs endurance, run longer repeats. If speed is the required trait, run 100s, 200s, or a 50-second run. The nature and extent of the workout often will depend upon the collaboration of coach and athlete. I have given you a few guidelines and parameters, but in the final analysis, the decision is yours.

All of the above workouts can be conducted on most surfaces or terrain. All you need is a tape measure, a measuring wheel, and cones. Find a corridor, lunch room, park, playground, an empty parking lot, bridle path, or open field, and you are in business. Percy Cerutty, the great Australian middle-distance coach, seldom used a track in his training program and yet developed four world record holders. One of his runners, Herb Elliot, the 1960 Olympic champion in the 1500 meters, was never defeated in the 1500 meters or the mile run. Who needs a track?

Be aware that characterizing the next training period as precompetitive is misleading. This cycle occurs during March — the most competitive part of the indoor season. However, you are still pointing toward the outdoor season and most coaches do not peak their athletes at this time. Your half-milers will run commendable times because indoor track is a very exciting part of the track season. One of our half-milers ran the best indoor time in the nation at the 1969 Chicago Public indoor championships, and he did not peak for the meet. The training that we did during the "precompetitive" cycle was sufficient. Successful track and field is just as much mental as it is physical.

Weekly training schedule for half-milers in the precompetitive period

Day	Duration (min)	Training task	Training details
Monday	20	Warm-up	1600 meter stride, calisthenics and stretching, stride an 800
	10	Sprint drills	High knees, chop downs, 1,2,3s, overstrides, form runs
	40	Anaerobic speed	16×200, 80%–90% effort,* jog 200 meters between
	10	Warm-down	1600 meter stride, stretch
Tuesday	30	Warm-up	3200 meter run, 10×100 meter strides, jog between, stretch
	10	Sprint drills	Same as Monday
	30	Baton passing	Establish passing zones for the 4×400 relay, 80% speed through the zone,* 10×60 meters
	30	Weight training	1 set 10 reps (upper body), 2 sets 10, lower body
	10	Warm-down	1600 meter stride
Wednesday	20	Warm-up	Same as Monday
	10	Sprint drills	High knees, butt kick, overstrides, skipping with high knees and chop downs
	30	Anaerobic sprinting	8×400 or 10×300 (date pace), 2 min recovery between
	10	Warm-down	
Thursday	20	Warm-up	Same as Tuesday
	10	Sprint drills	Same as Tuesday
	30	Baton passing	4×400 passes at goal pace, 10×50 meters, 90% effort
	30	Weight training	4 sets, 5 reps
Friday	20	Warm-up	16×100 intervals, 50% speed, jog 100 in between
	10	Sprint drills	Same as Monday
	30	Speed work	5×50, 2 sets, 5×100, 2 sets, rest 2 min between sets, 1×800 stride
Saturday			Competition. Run 6–8 miles after the meet to maintain aerobic conditioning.

* A runner's best time divided by the percentage will give you the exact speed of a required run. For example: 22 secs. divided by 90% = 24.4 secs.

Weekly training for half-milers during the competitive season

Day	Duration (min)	Training task	Training details
Monday	20	Warm-up	Stride 3200 meters, calisthenics and stretching
	10	Sprint drills	High knees, chop downs, form runs, etc.
	30	8 × 400 meters	Each 400 at goal pace, walk a 400 in between
	10	Warm-down	Stride 1600 meters, stretch
Tuesday	20	Warm-up	Stride 1600 meters, 16 × 100 strides, jog 100 in between
	10	Sprint drills	Same as Monday
	30	16 × 200 meters	Use the first two 200s as a warm-up, the last 14 at 95% effort.
	30	Weight training	Heavy weights, lower reps, 4 sets, 5 reps
Wednesday	20	Warm-up	Stride 1600 meters, walk 200 meters, stride 1200 meters, calisthenics and stretching
	10	Sprint drills	Same as Monday
	30	Fartlek	"Organized" fartlek in a local park
	10	Warm-down	Stride 1600 meters
Thursday	20	Warm-up	Stride 3200 meters, stretch
	10	Sprint drills	Same as Monday
	30	Stride frequency work	8 × 150 (2 sets), 8 × 100 (2 sets)
	30	Weight training	Light weights with speed reps, 8–10 reps per set
	10	Warm-down	Stride 1600 meters and stretch
Friday	20	Warm-up	Same as Tuesday
	30	Rehabilitation	Relaxed water drills and swimming

Saturday   Competition. Run a relaxed 6–8 miles after the meet.

The above cycle should be completed the last week in April. Most of these cycles can be readjusted to accommodate your conference or championship meet obligations. This training schedule will fit a conference or state championship scheduled for the last weekend in May. The cycle above can be modified and applied to your unique situation and personnel. For example, if a half-miler shows a lack of anaerobic endurance, Thursday's repeats could be a series of 600s or 800s instead of 150s and 100s. This modification can be determined by the athlete's performance in practice or a recent competition.

This training schedule can also be adjusted for your "facilities." The beautiful thing about the schedule is that it can be adapted to almost any situation. However, there is one minor problem associated with never practicing on a regulation 400 meter track — pace judgment. Some athletes may experience difficulty with this important aspect of middle-distance running. If this is the case, find a nearby track and devote a few weekends to working exclusively on repeat 400s and 200s. Usually, some local college or high school will permit you to share their facility. If this is not the case, practice on Sunday when no one is there.

April is a difficult time of the track season for sprinters, but it poses no problem for middle-distance runners. Middle-distance runners can train in complete safety in any kind of weather. It is next to impossible to pull a muscle training for or running the half mile. However, you still need be to diligent about warming up and wearing the proper attire. There is no need to be careless. I said that an injury was *next to impossible* — but anything can happen in track and field, and it often does. Use the bad weather as an opportunity to discover something new about your team; move all the sprinters to a middle-distance race. Some sprinters and hurdlers will run a better 800 meters than most people can imagine. On one occasion, a coach from a local high school entered a 47-second quarter-miler in the two-mile run. I thought the coach was nuts. The boy ran 9:35! On another occasion, I converted an inferior distance medley relay team to a superior one by using sprinters and hurdlers. When these athletes returned to their regular events, they ran faster and were injury free.

The peaking period is the critical cycle of the track season. At this point, you and the athletes must assess their readiness to compete. Together, you must decide who should train harder and who should not; who should continue to weight train and who should not; who should be pushed and who should be left alone; what and how many events the half-milers will compete in to sharpen for the big picture. It will also be necessary to learn all of the emotional and physiological idiosyncrasies of each athlete. The training schedule here is only a guide.

Weekly training for half-milers during the peaking period

Day	Duration (min)	Training task	Training details
Monday	20	Warm-up	Jog 1600 meters, sprint the last 200, calisthenics, etc.
	30	2–3 stress runs	2–3×, a 2-min. run, or 3×600 at date pace and 3×200 at 90% effort
	30	Weight training	Light weights done with speed, 2-3 sets
	10	Warm-down	Jog 800 while passing the baton single file (visual pass)

Day	Duration (min)	Training task	Training details
Tuesday	20	Warm-up	Jog 1600, walk 800, stride a 1600, stretch
	20	Sprint drills	High knees, butt kicks, chop downs, skipping with high knees, form runs
	30	Fartlek	"Organized" fartlek
	20	Warm-down	Same as Monday
Wednesday	20	Warm-up	Jog 1600, stretch
	30	Anaerobic speed work	10×200 at 80% effort, jog a 200 in between
	10	Warm-down	Same as Monday
Thursday	20	Warm-up	
	40	Long run	5-mile run
	10	Warm-down	Jog 1600 meters
Friday	40	Warm-up and relaxed swimming	
Saturday		Competition. Run 5–6 miles after the meet and stretch.	

HALF-MILE TRAINING UNDER DIFFICULT CONDITIONS

Middle-distance runners can train anywhere and everywhere. Middle-distance runners can train in all kinds of weather and on any type of terrain. This may explain why the Midwest has produced its share of world-class middle-distance runners. Our "playing field" if you will, is on the same level as everyone else's. There are no circumstances and situations that can be considered a deterrent to good middle-distance development. Peter Snell trained on pavements; Herb Elliot trained in the sand; Roger Bannister trained on a cinder track; Kip Keino trained on unpaved roads; and Gunder Hagg trained in the snow. Great middle-distance runners have trained on whatever was available. If there are no hills; use stairs, truck ramps, or streets that are on an incline. Or run in the sand or plowed fields as a substitute for hills. But remember that sprinting should always be done in warm weather or indoors. Half-milers can pull hamstrings too.

Insist that each athlete dress warmly for outdoor practice. Make sure they wear a cap, a scarf, extra socks, tights, and two sweat suits. Keep the runners inside if the temperature drops below 10 degrees Fahrenheit. Some athletes may choose to run in colder temperatures at their own risk; make sure that their parents are informed of this choice. If the athletes can afford vitamin C tablets, encourage them to take at least 500 milligrams per day to prevent colds. Most doctors do not recommend vitamin supplements, but it worked for us. Respiratory ailments can wreak havoc on an athlete's training program. There are several kinds of food supplements and herbs that can improve an athlete's performance, but discuss use of those with the runner's parents. You may be accused of practicing medicine without a license.

HOW TO USE COMPETITION TO DEVELOP RUNNERS

Early season competition should not be an end in itself. It should be a means to an end. The team should be made to understand this philosophy. Enter the half-milers in the 3200 or 1600 meter run to improve their endurance. If lack of leg speed seems to be the problem, enter the runner in the 400 or 200 meters. If they need pace work, enter them primarily in the 800 meters and the 4×800 relay. Use competition to accomplish whatever goal the athlete and coach have decided upon. Some leagues have an obligatory dual meet schedule that may compromise your training schedule. It is difficult to train if the team has to compete more than once a week. Most of your workout time will be spent recovering from competition. In spite of these difficulties, this kind of schedule can be used to develop athletes. If a team has sufficient depth, athletes can improve by being placed in events for developmental purposes as a prime directive.

800 METER RUNNING FORM

Since the half-mile is a cross between a sprint and a distance event, a certain adjustment in running form is in order. A runner has to run this event almost at top speed without compromising relaxation. Brooks Johnson, the author of the book *The Winning Edge*, characterizes this technique as "cruise" speed. Cruise speed, simply put, is that speed a runner can negotiate easily and efficiently that is close to his or her maximum speed. The greater your maximum speed, the faster your cruise speed. Increased maximum speed equals increased cruise speed. This is one of the reasons why Johnson believes that all runners should never neglect sprint training.

The ability to relax is another important aspect of attaining optimum cruise speed. I have often recommended that sprinters run an occasional half mile in order to learn how to relax while running fast. You cannot run an acceptable 800 meters without relaxing. I mentioned Mal Whitfield's running technique earlier in this section; it was so smooth that it seemed to be effortless. Mal was not born with this skill; he worked at relaxation throughout his athletic career. This is also the "law of least effort." Tension begins with the facial muscles. Whenever the pain of fatigue begins, most neophyte runners manifest this pain by frowning and scowling. If it is not kept under control, the tension that begins in the facial muscles will gradually spread over the entire body. When this occurs, relaxed running is ended and speed is compromised. Control your facial muscles and tension won't spread to the rest of the body.

You cannot force speed. Speed must flow from an effortless running technique. All animals run with this relaxed speed, but somehow we humans seem to feel that clenched teeth and hands and tight muscles will increase speed. Percy Cerutty studied the movement of horses and taught it to his runners.

Photo 8–1. An excellent example of arm action and running technique in the 800 meters. This athlete maintains good running form in spite of the obvious fatigue he is experiencing.

Many coaches thought he was nuts. I thought he was a genius. Coach Cerutty taught his runners to lightly pinch the thumb and forefinger together when running at top speed. The arms were not held rigidly at 90 degrees but were moved from about 120 degrees on the backswing to less than 90 degrees on the forward motion. On the forward swing of the arms, the arms moved toward the midline of the body but never crossed it.

Percy Cerutty insisted that the torso should rise and fall with each stride. All breathing should come from the diaphragm; this kind of breathing causes the torso to rise and fall. The knee lift is less pronounced in the middle distances, but an athlete would be able to see the knees without moving the head from its neutral position. The half-miler lands on the outside edge of the ball of the foot and rotates to the big toe. The dominant leg and the dominant arm have a longer

stroke than the nondominant leg and arm, but there is no shoulder rotation —
causing the athlete to run with an uneven rhythm. Most athletes are trained to
run similar to the horse that is taught to trot. The natural gait of a horse is to
gallop. And so it is with a human being. This "gallop" is not obvious to the
untrained observer but it is there in many athletes. Most athletes have a dominant side and their running style will manifest this trait.

This technique may seem little different from what is commonly taught, but
it is very effective. If your athletes experience difficulty learning this method,
don't force it on them; an athlete's body structure may lend itself to another running style. However, those who can master this style will improve their speed
beyond their wildest dreams. The best approach is to watch each athlete run and
determine if this technique can be applied to the running form. You will be surprised how many athletes are doing a modified version of this style naturally.

I have studied films and videos of the running technique of hundreds of athletes and many of them ran with an undeniable lilt. I noticed that many world-
class runners had an uneven beat in their stride pattern. However, there have
been many notable exceptions to this rule. Jesse Owens, Michael Johnson, Willie
Gault, Jackie Joyner Kersee, Wilma Rudolph, and Carl Lewis seemed to run
with an even stride pattern. Roger Bannister, Bob Hayes, Ralph Metcalfe, and
Herb Elliot ran with an uneven rhythm. Probably each runner's unique body
structure determined the running style. The best advice is to observe the athlete; teach a technique that seems most natural to the runner and still obeys the
laws of body mechanics.

FINAL OBSERVATIONS

The 800 meter run is an event without an identity; it is too long to be characterized as a sprint, but it requires an abundance of leg speed. It is too short to
be a distance race, and yet many of its participants and record holders come
from the ranks of the great milers. Seldom, if ever, does an athlete specialize in
the half mile. As a consequence, the training programs for the 800 meters are
usually an amalgam of alactic, anaerobic, and aerobic training. Most great half-
milers move up to the half from the 400 meters or come down to the half from
the 1600 meters, and they often bring with them the training methods from
these events. There is often little consensus on the best training methods for the
800 meters. For this reason, I think the world record for the 800 has plenty of
room for improvement. Someday a gifted half-mile specialist will appear on the
middle-distance scene, train exclusively for the 800 meters, and run a sub 1:40
half mile. I am certain that in the not-too-distant future, a gifted athlete will run
a 50-second first 400, combined with an easy 49 second 400, and negotiate a 1:39
half mile. That doesn't sound too difficult — does it? Just about every track and
field barrier has been broken; its just a matter of time before the 800 record will
become what it ought to be. I am aware that I have gone out on a limb with the
above prediction, but I feel strongly that this record has to go. There are no limitations when you believe. A woman can run 1:53.28. If a man can run the mile
under 3:50, triple jump 60 feet and high hump 8 feet, then the sky is the limit.

Photo 8–2. A chamption half-miler using the Percy Cerutty running technique en route to the Illinois State Championship. His right foot has landed on the outside edge and his left arm and hand are in perfect harmony with this action.

Section 9

THE MILE RUN
America's Dilemma

The mile run is the glamor event of track and field. Most track events are over too soon or last too long to hold the average spectator's interest. Most people have some idea of how far a mile is — and how difficult it is to run one in four minutes or less. It is the ultimate test of anaerobic and aerobic endurance. Success in this event has been attained by using an amalgam of training methods from marathon running to fartlek and interval training. Over the last 100 years, American athletes have performed commendably in this event. Some have managed to set world records, but only one American has won the metric mile in the Olympic games. Mel Sheppard captured a gold medal in 1908. No other United States citizen has been able to match that effort. That is America's dilemma.

The mile run. To the track and field aficionado, this race is the ultimate running event. It has all the ingredients that make most athletic events exciting. The mile lasts long enough to create suspense and drama. It is short enough not to bore spectators. It is the supreme test of endurance and speed. Everyone can understand the distance to be covered. People unfamiliar with track and field appreciate the significance of the four-minute-mile. There have been numerous great American milers, from Glen Cunningham to Wes Santee to Jim Ryun to Steve Scott. Great milers have been the glamor boys of track and field. The national anthem is often played just before the mile run is held. When Roger Bannister ran the first sub-four-minute mile the whole world stood up and cheered. Sadly, in all the years of the modern Olympic games, only one American has won a gold medal in this event. Mel Sheppard won the metric mile (1500 meters) in the 1908 Olympics and no American has won it since.

Some experts reason that there is a difference in the physical requirements for the mile run and the metric mile. The only difference in the two races is a matter of aproximately 135 yards. Athletes from Great Britain and Ireland compete regularly in the mile run and they seem to fare quite well in its metric equivalent. It is the American miler that fails to rise to the occasion at the Olympic games. Why? The American milers compete too much and too often — and the Europeans and the Africans don't.

By the time most of our milers have finished a grueling NCAA schedule where they are called upon to double, triple, and quadruple for alma mater, they are too pooped to pop. And when our postgraduate milers have finished the European circuit, they are finished, too. You can't run a sub-four-minute mile week after week and expect to rise to the occasion at the most difficult competition of all — the Olympic games. Sprinters can run world-class times every week and thrive on that schedule. Middle-distance runners cannot. This happened to several world-class American milers, and all of them failed to win a medal at the Olympic games. Lasse Viren of Finland seldom competed in world-class competition until the Olympics. He won the 5,000 and 10,000 meters at two Olympics in world record times. The Finn was accused of blood doping and drug use. He was found not guilty. His only "crime" was the uncommon use of common sense. There must be a lesson in there somewhere.

American coaches know better, but their jobs are at stake and they want to keep them. To make matters worse, most of the other teams are loaded with overage foreign athletes on full scholarships while young American athletes often do without. It takes time to develop middle-distance runners and college and university coaches have to win *now*. They don't have time to develop some high school athlete who may take years to mature into a world class athlete. When an occasional prep phenom manages to get an athletic scholarship, some coaches run these kids to death before they graduate. Fortunately, many coaches bring our young athletes through a sensible program. If we had more coaches like that, we would not be in a survival mode with our middle-distance runners. America is in a heap of trouble on a world-class level from the 1500 meters to the marathon.

TALENT IDENTIFICATION

Milers often know that they are milers. Whenever I have a tryout for the mile, most of the gifted candidates know up front that they will excel in this event. Often the gossip around school precedes the athlete. These kids were beating their classmates in endurance races in elementary school and everybody knew this. These athletes love to run long distances and often avoid sprinting like a plague. Their friends think they are nuts.

Great milers have two physiological characteristics in common. Most world-class middle-distance and distance runners seem to enjoy these characteristics — an inordinately high oxygen uptake and an extremely low resting pulse rate. The trait that separates a 1500 meter champion from a 10,000 meter champion is leg speed. Almost all great milers can turn in a commendable 800 meters. Some world-class milers are also remarkably swift in the 400 meters. Jim Ryun, the 1964 Olympic silver medalist in the 1500 meters and former world record holder in the mile, could run a sub-47-second 400 meters. Many coaches often put their slowest athletes in the mile run. This is a mistake.

Before we proceed any further in our discussion of the mile run, the term *oxygen uptake* must be understood. Oxygen uptake is the capacity of the body to absorb oxygen. An untrained candidate for the middle distances may breathe in copious quantities of oxygen, but the body has to absorb a certain percentage of this oxygen for effective aerobic endurance. World-class milers can absorb over 75% of the oxygen they inhale. Oxygen uptake (VO2 max), can be improved through aerobic training but according to the book *Sports Talent,* written by Robert Arnot and Charles Gaines, a large portion of this trait has to be acquired before puberty. Arnot and Gaines also state that VO2 max is mostly a genetic predisposition and training can add only 30% to the equation. Simply stated, an athlete brings most of his or her oxygen uptake talent to the coach before any formal training ever begins. Leg speed, coordination, and strength training should also be embarked upon prior to puberty. If training for these physical traits is delayed until adolescence, an athlete's potential is severely limited.

Most middle-distance candidates can manifest a significant improvement in their resting pulse rate after embarking on a long-distance running program. I have known runners whose pulse rate decreased 10–15 beats per minute after an eight-week program of distance running. An extraordinary low resting pulse rate is also a genetic trait. On several occasions, I have recruited cross-country runners based on nothing but a low resting pulse rate. On their first attempt in the two-mile run, they beat everyone on our cross-country team.

There is a high correlation between a high oxygen uptake, a low resting pulse rate, and successful middle-distance running. The best middle-distance runner I ever coached had a resting pulse rate of 45 beats per minute. Test every runner's resting pulse rate. There are several other physiological factors common to world-class middle-distance runners. Proper training after puberty can make a significant impact upon these characteristics:

1. Cardiac output or the ability of the heart to deliver oxygen to the body. Interval training positively modifies this factor

2. An increase of ATP, CP, and other blood buffers in the blood stream and the liver. Repetition training has the most profound effect on this characteristic.

3. The enhancement of respiratory permeability.

4. Capillarization and an improvement of the efficiency of the vascular system. Long-distance running is responsible for the development of respiration (item 3), and a marked increase in the vascular system.

5. Good running mechanics. Correct technique can significantly delay the onset of fatigue during training and competition.

The intelligent combination of the above factors will improve oxygen uptake and lower the athlete's resting pulse rate. However, Gaines and Arnot seem to feel that repeat 800s improves oxygen uptake better than any other training modality. I spent a few moments with Samson Kimobva, NCAA 10,000 meter champion from Washington State University, and he enthusiastically proclaimed that repeat 800s was largely responsible for his running prowess.

Most milers are tall and slender, but this body type is not an absolute requirement. A few excellent runners were less than average in height. The mix of muscle fiber types may be of greater significance than stature. An educated guess is that an equal percentage of fast-twitch (class IIa) and slow-twitch (class I) muscle fibers, are present in these athletes. If this is the case, it correlates with the ratio of speed and endurance qualities required for success in this event. Most experts also recommend that the training for the mile be equally divided between speed-endurance and aerobic-endurance training.

Successful middle-distance running cannot be reduced to mere physiology and physical stature; there are other more intangible factors — motivation, desire, attitude. Several years ago, I took seven of my top cross-country runners to a physiology lab to be tested. They were tested for cardiac output, blood lactate, anaerobic threshold, and oxygen uptake. After the test results were examined, I asked the physiologist to tell me which runner had the best physiology. The best runner on the team had the sixth worst test results among the seven. The second best runner had the worst physiology of all. I asked the physiologist to explain this contradiction. He stated that these two runners had a stronger desire to win than the rest of the team. Research has shown that the winner of a middle-distance race often experiences more physical distress than the losers. There is a lesson to be learned somewhere in that statement.

TALENT SEARCH

The mile run may be popular with the general public, but this is not the case in most disadvantaged communities in America. Some coaches from these communities reflect this attitude when they put their rejects in the mile and the two-mile run. Sprinting is the big deal in the ghetto, and suburban and rural athletes seem to dominate this event most of the time. The attitude of the coach can exacerbate the lack of popularity of the mile and the two-mile — especially the two-mile. Coaches can also enhance the popularity of the mile by their attitude. There is just as much talent for this event in the inner cities as in the suburbs and rural areas. The mile and two-mile were so popular in the schools where I coached that sprinters often volunteered to run these events in dual meets. The reason for this unusual behavior was that our middle-distance runners were just as important to us as the rest of the team. I was excited about the middle distances and the runners knew it.

Where can you find milers? I have often attended other sports events primarily to look for athletes who were indefatigable. I have seen basketball and soccer players who seemed never to tire during a game. I have also seen evidence of this trait in swimmers and football players. I was also always on the prowl for talent in the physical education classes. I had the physical education staff doing detective work for me. As I mentioned earlier, I check pulse rates. I checked the pulse rate of every student in the school. And of course, most of the members of the cross-country team were recruited for the middle-distances. I left no stone unturned.

HOW TO RUN THE MILE

The traditional method for starting the mile is the standing start. The race starts from a stagger or alleys. The runner must stay in the assigned alley until the first turn is completed. There is usually a frantic jockeying for the inside lane, but early positioning is not as crucial as it is in the half mile. An error at this point in the race is not the end of the world. The most important thing in the mile is to establish the correct pace for the first lap. For as long as I can remember, the "experts" advocated an even pace. Theoretically, a sub-four-minute miler was advised to run every lap in aproximately 60 seconds each. In real life, the first lap was usually run in 58 seconds; the second in 60; the third in 62, and the final lap in 59. Over the last decade, some rather bizarre splits have been turned in for sub-four-minute miles. Filbert Bayi from Tanzania ran 50 seconds for the first lap of a 3:51 mile. Jim Ryun used to follow the pack for three laps and sprint the last lap in 52–53 seconds. Herb Elliot usually ran his mile from the front from the beginning to the end of the race. Noureddine Morcelli of Algeria does whatever he wants to do. The latest research tells us that the best tactic physiologically is to run a negative split, in which the runner will run the first half of the race slightly slower than the last half. It is no great catastrophe, then, if you are a few meters behind the leaders after the first 400 meters of the mile run. When tactics of the mile run are discussed, you have to keep in mind that this strategy will differ somewhat from the tactics of the metric mile (1500 meters), but the differences are not significant; the world record in both events is usually held by the same person. The time differential between the events is about 18 seconds. If there are any differences between these events, the NCAA has negated that problem; they have replaced the mile with the 1500 meters.

In most competitions there is a timer giving splits at each 400. If the runner can't hear the lap times, there is usually a large electronic device near the finish line so that all the competitors can easily see the splits. If it is permitted, most coaches usually station themselves near the 400 meter mark and shout lap times. A coach in our league gave his runners splits for every 200 meters. The coach ran from one side of the track to the other throughout the race. At the end of the race the coach was as tired as the runners.

If pace work is practiced often enough during the season, most runners will soon get the feel of the race and not need to rely on the coach for splits. I often timed athletes in practice during interval training and asked them to tell me how fast they ran each interval. Sooner or later most of my middle-distance runners knew their pace within tenths of a second. It is extremely important for milers to know their splits and to have a kinesthetic feeling of their pace. Often, coaches are not permitted to be at trackside in big meets. If a middle-distance runner has not learned this skill, all may be lost. I have seen coaches blow whistles, or wave towels and such from the stands to help the runner stay on pace. That's how important pace judgment is.

After the milers have positioned themselves within striking distance of the leaders, they will have plenty of time to get into the rhythm of the race and think about pace. By this time, the runners are well into the second lap. Every effort should be made to relax and maintain contact with the leaders. The runners with superior sprinting speed usually follow and wait for the final 400 meters to make their move. The runners with questionable sprinting speed often run from the front in an effort to negate the sprinting speed of the competitors. The best tactic for these athletes is to make an effort to speed up on the third 400. This is usually the place in the mile where most milers are trying to conserve energy for the final sprint. The runners with inferior sprinting speed cannot afford this luxury; they should make a serious surge at this point. The superior sprinter has to maintain "contact" with the leaders, or a finishing kick will be useless. Contact is an imaginary line between the following runners and the runners in the lead. The distance depends upon the following runner's sprinting ability. On the average, the distance is about 10 meters.

The length of the finishing sprint depends upon the leg speed of the miler. Runners with great speed can wait until the final 200 meters to launch their sprint. If a competitor is not gifted with sprinting ability, the finishing kick may have to be initiated much earlier in the race. Kip Keino, the great Kenyan middle-distance runner, often began his sprint with 600 meters to go. I once instructed a runner to start his kick at the 800 meters. Everybody thought I was nuts, except the athlete; it was the only way this runner could win. Everyone in the race had better sprinting ability than this particular runner; he had to risk this unusual tactic. By the time the rest of the field realized what he was doing, the race was over. No risk, no reward.

Successful middle-distance competition is similar to a game of chess — especially in the mile. The mile is long enough for the spectators to appreciate the various maneuvers of each runner and short enough to maintain interest, making this event popular with the general public. The mile is the ultimate test of speed, strength, strategy, stamina, and skill. The drama in this event is easily understood by the average spectator. This is a race where talent is a requirement, but without sacrifice and conscientious endeavor, talent is never enough. This is what middle-distance running is all about.

Photo 9–1. An outstanding middle-distance runner demonstrating exemplary running form. He has an erect and relaxed posture. His arm action is similar to that taught by Igloi.

TECHNICAL ASPECTS

A relaxed running technique is an absolute requirement in middle-distance running. All of the great milers have developed their own unique style that permitted efficient running. There are as many techniques as there are runners. It is a mistake to force any particular style on your runners. The best idea is to observe your athletes and teach them the style that best fits their personality, physique, and body structure. There are five basic running styles that most of your runners will fit into. I have studied hundreds of films of world-class middle-distance runners and these five running styles will fit just about any runner you coach:

1. *The Igloi style.* The arms are held low and swing across the body. The back-and-forth motion of the arms is minimal. The body is erect, the foot plant is ball-heel-ball. The head is in a relaxed neutral position; you can see the knees lift in your peripheral vision. The arm and leg stroke is an even beat rhythm. This style was taught by Mahali Igloi, the great Hungarian middle-distance coach. Jim Ryun and Wes Santee used this technique.

2. *The Percy Cerutty style.* I discussed this style in the previous chapter. Basically, the runner runs with an uneven swing of the arms. The dominant arm and leg have a longer stroke than the other arm and leg. The dominant wrist and hand rotates and pushes back with the palm down, and returns to the forward position with the thumb on top. The other wrist and hand does not turn; the thumb stays in the top position. The entire running form involves movement of the torso and head. Everything moves. The touchdown of the foot is on the outside edge near the little toe. The push-off is from the big toe. The runner appears to gallop slightly. This is an uninhibited type of running technique. You will be surprised how many of your runners will adapt to this unusual style. Herb Elliot and Roger Bannister used this technique.

3. *The American style.* The arm is bent at a 90 degree angle. On the back swing the arm opens slightly to more than 90 degrees. As the arm swings forward, the arm closes to slightly less than 90 degrees. On the forward swing of the arm, the hand rises to a position that is a little lower than shoulder height. On the back swing, the hand moves slightly beyond the hip. The thumb is on top at all times. The foot touches down on the ball of the foot and drops to the heel slightly and pushes off from the toes; knee lift is minimal. I call this the "American" style. Mary Decker Slaney of the United States uses this technique.

4. *The Lydiard style.* This technique was taught by Arthur Lydiard, the great New Zealand distance coach. The only difference between this running form and the American style is how the arms are carried. The arms are almost straight on the forward and backward stroke. There is a slight bend in the arms. Everything else about this style is similar to the American technique.

5. *The athlete's own individual style.* Some athletes, you should leave alone. There may be no particular style that they fit into. If they are moving economically and efficiently, don't change anything. If it ain't broke, don't fix it.

I devoted this much space to running form because without good technique there cannot be good middle-distance running. I knew a coach who claimed that the effect of correct running form on an athlete's performance was negligible. I prevailed upon him to permit me to work with his middle-distance runners for one day. After *one day* of technique work, his runners improved an average of 15 seconds in the mile in the next meet.

TRAINING CYCLES AND WORKOUT PROGRAMS

Our middle-distance runners followed basically the same summer, cross-country, general preparation, and specific preparation periods as the half-milers. There were a few minor exceptions to this rule. Some of the more mature milers and two-milers would run as much as 60–70 miles a week during these earlier periods of training. They also ran 15 miles *every Saturday*. In their senior year, some of the milers would run twice a day, but there was no pressure from the coach to do this; I merely suggested that this additional running would be a good idea. Most of the time, these early morning runs were strictly voluntary and at the athlete's request. The morning runs were usually 2–4 miles at a 6-minute-per-mile pace. The morning runs were held on Monday, Wednesday, and Friday. The majority of the middle-distance runners were not invited to do twice-a-day workouts, but they joined in anyway. The main reason for such an unprecedented desire for additional work was that I taught most of the older runners the value of these early morning runs — the tremendous contribution to their cardiovascular fitness. They also saw the great improvement that the upperclassmen had enjoyed the previous year. They felt that the runners who requested the early morning runs were getting extra physiological benefits from this additional work. They also felt that they were missing something. They were right. Knowledge is power.

The runners who are involved in the early morning runs should be monitored closely. Some of the younger athletes may not be physically ready for this additional work. Their resting pulse rates must be checked every day. If they are falling victim to minor injuries and colds, discontinue these runs immediately. It may be a case of too much too soon. The runners who can handle this extra work will thrive on it. When you embark upon the final weeks of the outdoor season, back off these two-a-day workouts. Rest, recuperation, and restoration are more important than anything during the month of May.

Since the preparatory periods for the milers are similar to those of the half-milers, with the exception of the extra mileage on Saturday, I will only submit the last three periods of training:

Weekly training for milers during the precompetitive period

Day	Duration (min)	Training task	Training details
Monday	20	Warm-up	1600 meter stride, calisthenics and stretching, stride a 1600

Day	Duration (min)	Training task	Training details
	10	Sprint drills	High knees, chop downs, quick steps 1,2,3s, butt kicks, form runs
	40	Interval running	8–12 × 400 date pace 1–2 min jog between
	10	Warm-down	1600 meter stride, stretch
Tuesday	30	Warm-up	3200 meter run, 10 × 100 meter stride
	10	Sprint drills	High knees, 1,2,3s, form runs
	20	Baton passing	Work on passing technique for the 4 × 800 relay
	30	Warm-down	3 mile run, walk 800 meter
	30	Weight training	1 set × 10 reps upper and lower body
Wednesday	20	Warm-up	Same as Monday
	60	Aerobic running	10 mile run
	5	Warm-down	800 meter walk
Thursday	20	Warm-up	Same as Tuesday
	10	Sprint drills	Same as Tuesday
	40	Interval training	10–12 × 300, jog 200 meters between
	10	Warm-down	Walk and jog 1600 meters
	30	Weight training	1 set × 10 upper and lower body
Friday	20	Warm-up	Same as Monday
	30	Fartlek	Easy running with surges of 100 meter sprints
	10	Warm-down	Walk and jog 1600 meters
Saturday	90	Aerobic running or competition	10–15 mile run (6 min per mile) or run the 3200 and 800 meters if there is a meet

If there is competition on Saturday, the miler should take an easy run on Sunday just to loosen up. If the competition was especially difficult, switch the interval training to Tuesday and Thursday so the runner can recover. If the competition was not difficult, follow a program similar to the one above. Keep in mind that in this cycle, training is more important than competition. Use the competition as a means to develop your runners. If the milers need more endurance work, run them in the 3200 and 1600 instead of the 3200 and the 800.

The next period of training is the competitive period of training. Several changes in the training program begin to be manifest. Speed is the prime directive. Interval training gradually evolves into repetition training. There is more quality in the program, but the distance base is maintained whenever possible. For those who can handle it, continue the morning runs. During this cycle, competition is just as important as training. Each week's training program is based on the results of the previous weekend's meet:

Weekly training for milers during the competitive period

Day	Duration (min)	Training task	Training details
Monday	20	Warm-up	Stride 3200 meters, calisthenics and stretching
	10	Sprint drills	High knees, butt kicks, chop downs, form runs, etc.
	50	6 × 800 meters	Each 800 at goal pace, rest until pulse returns to 120 beats/minute
	10	Warm-down	Stride 800 meters, walk 800 meters
Tuesday	10	Warm-up	Stride 800 meters, calisthenics and stretching
	60	Long run	10 mile run — 6 mins/mile
	10	Warm-down	Walk 800 meters, stretch
Wednesday	10	Warm-up	Stride 1600 meters, calisthenics and stretching
	30	Fartlek	"Organized" fartlek, cover 5 miles
	10	Warm-down	Jog 800, walk 800, stretch
Thursday	20	Warm-up	Stride 1600, calisthenics and stretch
	10	Sprint drills	Same as Monday
	30	8 × 400	Goal pace, rest 2 minutes between 400s
Friday	20	Warm-up	Stride 800, walk 800 meters, calisthenics and stretching
	10	Sprint drills	High knees, quick steps, chop downs
	30	Stride 3200 7 × 80 meters	7 mins/mile 90% effort
	10	Warm-down	Jog 800 meters, walk 800 meters

Saturday   Competition.   Run 8 easy miles after the meet.

The fifth and final period is the peaking cycle. The major focus during these last four weeks is competition, rest, and restoration. An occasional "stress" work-out is scheduled to simulate meet conditions and to work on the athletes' weaknesses, if there are any. The stress workouts for a miler are the four-minute run or 16 × 100 meters at goal pace. The 100s are run back-to-back with no rest between 100's. These workouts are done in 2–3 sets. The rest between sets is to full recovery.

Weekly training schedule for milers during the peaking period

Day	Duration (min)	Training task	Training details
Monday	20	Warm-up	Jog 1600 meters, sprint the final 200, calisthenics and stretch
	30	2–3 "stress runs"	2–3 × a 4-minute run or 16 × 100 at date pace, 3 sets
	15	Heavy bar work	Chins and dips on playground equipment, 1 set × 15
	10	Warm-down	Jog 800, walk 800, and stretch
Tuesday	20	Warm-up	Jog 800, calisthenics and stretch
	60	Aerobic maintenance	10 mile run, 7 min/mile
	15	Speed work	7 × 60 — 90% effort
	10	Warm-down	Walk 800 meters, stretch
Wednesday	10	Warm-up	Jog 1600, stretch
	10	Sprint drills	High knees, chop downs, form runs
	30	8 × 400	Run each 400 faster than goal pace, rest to recovery between
	15	Bar work	Chins and dips, 1 set, 10 reps
	10	Warm-down	Jog 800, walk 800
Thursday	20	Warm-up	Same as Monday
	40	Fartlek	Easy "organized" fartlek
	10	Warm-down	Jog 1600 meters, stretch
Friday	20	Warm-up	Same as Tuesday
	15	Speed work	7 × 70 meter sprints — 90% effort
	30	Restoration	Relaxed swimming

Saturday   Competition. Compete in the 1600 and the 4 × 400 relay. Run 8 miles after the meet.

The morning runs are discontinued during this cycle. Occasionally I will prescribe a 5–6 mile run on Sunday to prepare the body for Monday's speed work. I monitor the miler's pulse rate closely to determine if the athlete has recovered from Saturday's competition. Most of the middle-distance runners are required to keep a daily chart of their pulse rate to determine if their recovery from practice or competition is complete. We are not training through the competition at this time. We hold our practices in a variety of locations: Interval or repetition work is on a "borrowed" 400 meter track; fartlek, in a nearby park; our long runs in a park or on the lake front. We try to change training sites as much as possible for the sake of variety. Try to keep your runners away from concrete sidewalks; this surface can cause serious damage to soft tissue. There is always somewhere to run safely. Most great middle-distance runners have trained on every kind of surface you can think of.

CONCLUDING REMARKS

Middle-distance runners cannot compete on a high level as often as sprinters. I have seen world-class milers run sub-four-minute miles week after week prior to the Olympic games Everyone seems to expect these runners to continue this world-class effort through the Olympics. It can't be done. It hasn't been done. It won't be done. These runners are human beings — not machines. One great American miler ran a sub-four-minute mile on 14 consecutive weekends; he was never heard from after that. Another ran 10 sub-four-minute miles (some were under 3:50) prior to the Olympics and didn't even place in the final. When are we going to learn? Foreign athletes come to America and are trained by some of our best coaches; they return to their respective countries and run circles around our middle-distance runners in world-class competition. When they run for their country they do not race indiscriminately; every competition has a developmental purpose. Our athletes compete until their endocrine reserves are depleted of epinephrine and testosterone. The circulatory system must be loaded with the catabolic substance, cortisol. In plain English, they are worn out. After this ordeal, they are expected to produce on a world-class level. What happened to common sense? We have great training methods and coaches in America, but somewhere along the way we take leave of our senses. Competition prior to the Olympics ought to be a means to an end, and not an end in itself. When we learn that lesson we will dominate the middle-distances in world-class competition. If we continue down the same insane path that we have always traveled, we will get the same results — nothing.

Section 10

THE TWO MILE RUN
Sixteen Blocks to Go

Most people can't fully appreciate what a good two mile race means. To help the uninitiated understand the kind of dedicated training and effort required to run a two mile (3200 meters) in nine minutes or less, I have to communicate how great an achievement this has to be. When I introduce my two-miler to a gathering of parents or students, I tell them that this runner is capable of running sixteen city blocks in nine minutes. Then they understand.

Several years ago, I was one of the speakers at our school's athletic banquet. The basketball coach spoke about his team and everybody in the place understood what he was talking about. Basketball is an activity that gets unbelievable media coverage and the sport needs no explanation. The basketball coach finished his talk and took his seat. You could tell by the response of the audience that he had communicated. The basketball team got a standing ovation even though they didn't do diddly that season. No one at the banquet seemed to know much about track; I suspected they knew even less about the two-mile run, and it was my turn to speak. One of the outstanding members of our track team ran the two miles, and he beat everybody that year but the future world-class runner, Craig Virgin. He was a fantastic distance runner, and I wanted everyone at the banquet to appreciate that fact. Experience has taught me that times and distances mean little to people who are unfamiliar with track and field. I had to think of something that would communicate that this runner's athletic achievements were meaningful.

Years of media indifference toward track and field has caused the average person to be oblivious of the various nuances of times and distances. I needed to communicate something that the audience could relate to without insulting their intelligence. I told them that this runner was the best two-miler I had ever coached. I said he could run sixteen city blocks in 9 minutes and 11 seconds! The crowd went wild. He received a standing ovation that made the basketball team's "ovation" seem like a whisper. They understood. Everyone there could relate to the sixteen blocks concept and the significance of how short a time it took to run this distance. They understood that this was an outstanding athletic endeavor. I had communicated.

In the two-mile, an assiduous work ethic and sheer determination are more important than anything. An athlete must, of course, have talent to excel in the 3200 meters, but if a runner is not willing to work, all the talent in the world is useless in this event. Two-milers must love to run. Fortunately, most of the distance runners I have had the privilege to coach seemed to enjoy running long distances. As a matter of fact, many of my ex-runners are still competing in road races and marathons. A few years ago, I happened to turn on the television and saw several of my former two-milers participating in the Chicago marathon. I was proud of them.

The two-mile run is not an event that is often contested on a world-class level; it is basically a high school race. Three races on the collegiate level come close to the physical requirements of the two-mile run: the 3000 meters, the 5000 meters and the 10,000 meters. The training methods for all of the above events are identical. A well-trained distance runner can be competitive in any race from the 800 meters to the marathon. A cursory look at the history of middle-distance running offers clear evidence that the great ones could do it all.

Emil Zatopeck from Czechoslovakia won the 5000, 10,000, and the marathon in the 1952 Olympics. Lasse Viren of Finland nearly accomplished the same feat in 1976. Then, of course, there are the renowned African runners like Kip Keino, Henry Rono, Wilson Kiprigut, Samson Kimobwa, and Ismael Kirui of Kenya; Filbert Bayi of Tanzania; Noredine Morecelli of Algeria; Mahammad Gamoudi and Said Aquita of Morocco; Abebe Bakila and Momo Wolde of Ethiopia and Junxia Wang of China — just to name a few. They have dominated every race from the 800 meters to the marathon during the last decade. Several Americans have also conducted themselves very well in these events on a world-class level: Frank Shorter, Steve Prefontaine, and Billy Mills (the 1964 Olympic champion in the 10,000 meters) could run world-class times from the 1500 meters to the marathon. Many world-class milers have also run commendable two-mile and 5000 meter times; because of their ability to perform on a world class level in a wide range of distances, I began to develop an approach to training that embraced an eclectic approach toward preparing distance runners for running and racing.

TALENT IDENTIFICATION

Sprint speed is necessary in every event on the track program, but in distance races like the two-mile, 5000, and 10,000 meters, oxygen uptake, capillarization, and cardiac output are the physiological qualities in the greatest demand for success. It takes arduous and exhausting aerobic and anaerobic training to optimize these attributes. Hard work over a long period of time is an absolute requirement if an athlete expects to be competitive in the long distances. Proper training can make an enormous contribution to an athlete's competitive ability. Heredity is still important in any track event; regardless of the erroneous notion that is often promulgated — that any distance runner who is willing to work can excel in the two-mile — the great ones must be gifted. An athlete may run 100 miles per week on a two-a-day program for several years and never run under 10 minutes in the two-mile run. On the other hand, a physiologically gifted youngster will approach the nine-minute mark with half this training time. The best way to make rabbit stew is to find a rabbit.

Most of my exceptional two-milers have come to me with certain physiological and psychological gifts. They have all had a decent amount of leg speed but more important, they have had bodies that respond readily to the tremendous work load necessary to excel in the long distances. They also have a high pain threshold and a love and sheer joy for the challenge of running long distances. If athletes are not willing to put in long hours of strenuous work and beg for more, then this is not the event for them.

As I stated earlier, two-milers seem to be about average in sprinting ability and are often reluctant to be timed in any event shorter than the 800 meters. They know that they are not sprinters. The elementary school physical education teachers are often surprised when these athletes excel in track and field in high school, because the ability to run long distances isn't always tested at the elementary school level. Somehow these athletes have instinctively known they could excel at long-distance running when they came to me.

Distance runners may come in all shapes and sizes. You cannot identify them by stature or somatotype. They are also not usually superstars in the so-called major sports. These sports place great emphasis on fast-twitch muscle ability, that is, sprinting and jumping. Distance runners often come from the ranks of soccer, wrestling, long-distance swimming, or cross-country. Distance runners can be small in stature and are also often not very muscular. Long-distance running is not compatible with muscular hypertrophy. Look for the kid who does not tire easily when your physical education department administers its physical fitness test. Check every student's resting pulse rate. There has to be someone in your school's population with distance running talent. You just have to look hard enough.

Most distance runners also seem to be better than average in intelligence. To become a capable distance runner, an athlete has to play mind games in order not to give into the massive amount of fatigue and pain that is experienced in practice and competition enroute to championship distance running. It also takes a sharp mind to remember lap times and racing tactics while competing. Schools with the highest academic standards often have the best distance programs. One of the most outstanding distance runners I ever coached had an ACT composite score of 32. A few years ago, our conference 1600 and 3200 meter champion earned an *academic scholarship* to a prestigious Ivy League university.

TECHNICAL ASPECTS

The oxygen requirements for the two-mile are aproximately 20% anaerobic and 80% aerobic. These requirements indicate that a large percentage of aerobic training will contribute to competitive success in this event. The best performers in the long distances probably are genetically predisposed to a generous supply of red, slow-twitch muscle fibers. These fibers contain an abundance of mitrochondria (cells that absorb oxygen). Therefore, most of the training for the two-mile should be aimed at increasing the runner's anaerobic threshold — the capacity to run long distances at a faster and faster pace, and still continue to function within the parameters of aerobic metabolism.

TRAINING CYCLES AND WORKOUT PROGRAMS

Again, sprint training is a minor consideration in preparing for competition in the longer distances, but it *is* a necessary consideration. Sprint training should be included in a distance runner's training program at least twice a week during each periodization cycle.

Summer Program

You may recognize that most of these two-mile workouts are basically slight modifications of a miler's training program. Their training schedules are so similar that milers and two-milers will often train together.

Weekly summer running program for distance runners

Day	Duration (min)	Training task	Training details
Monday	20	Warm-up	800 meter jog, stretch
	90	Long run	15 mile run
	10	Warm-down	800 meter walk
Tuesday	20	Warm-up	800 meter jog, stretch
	10	Sprint drills	High knees, chop downs
	40	Fartlek	"Organized" fartlek
	10	Warm-down	800 meter walk
Wednesday	20	Warm-up	Same as Monday
	75	Long run	12 mile run
	10	Short sprints	50 meters $\times$ 7
	10	Warm-down	Walk 800
Thursday	20	Warm-up	Jog 800 meters, stretch
	38	Tempo run	6 mile run
	10	Warm-down	1600 meter walk
Friday	20	Warm-up	Jog 800, stretch
	63	Long run	A very easy 9 mile run
	10	Speed work	7×60 meter sprints
Saturday	20	Warm-up	Jog 400, stretch
	90	Long run	15 mile run
	10	Warm-down	800 meter walk

The summer training program for distance runners usually emphasizes aerobic training . We try to train in relationship to the percentage of white to red fibers that the athlete ostensibly has. This running program is also based on, but not identical to, an aerobic running program advocated by Arthur Lydiard, the great New Zealand middle-distance coach. Be aware that fartlek and the small amount of sprinting included in this schedule will help the athlete retain leg speed. The retention of leg speed will improve the athlete's "cruise" speed. As a result, we can have the best of both worlds: enhanced aerobic capacity in addition to the maintenance of sprinting speed. During this phase of training, some of our distance runners have participated in road races and on rare occasions, in a marathon. One of our runners ran a 2 hour, 35 minute marathon and played basketball immediately after the race. Our summer program is very effective in developing aerobic endurance.

Cross-Country

The next period is the cross-country season. From September to November, there is no significant difference in the two-miler's training and the program that I recommended for middle-distance runners. We are all working for the same goal

— excellence in cross-country running. However, permit me to relate some of the experiences that have affected us during cross-country competition. The standard racing tactic in cross-country competition is group running. In our situation, we have found this approach to be patently ineffective. The differences in talent and dedication have been so vast on our squad that we have found it necessary to run in three or more groups. The runners of similar ability and training background run in their respective groups. At one time, our best distance runner (14:45 for 3 miles) ran with the leaders of the race. Four runners (15:30 for 3 miles) ran as a group, and the final two (16:00 for 3 miles) ran together. We have never had a team with the kind of talent and total commitment that was necessary to run as a tight seven-runner pack. I tried to do that in the past and somebody always seemed to suffer because of it. This approach has worked best for us.

The cross-country season ends in early November. We usually take a one- or two-week break and resume long-distance running for about four more weeks. This long-distance running schedule gradually evolves into the general preparation and specific preparation periods. These two cycles are almost identical (with the exception of a few extra miles), to the general and specific preparation periods of the middle-distance runners.

Standard Program

The two-milers and milers may train on the same schedule at this time. They will also take turns running each other's events during the indoor track season. This is a time to experiment based on the athletes' competitive strengths and weaknesses. The training emphasis gradually begins to become more specialized as we embark upon the precompetitive period, but the distance runners who seem to require more speed work will continue to train with the middle-distance runners. Check the training chart for the precompetitive period.

Weekly training for the distance runners
during the precompetitive period

Day	Duration (min)	Training task	Training details
Monday	20	Warm-up	Jog 800 meters. stretch
	60	Long run	10 mile run
	10	Warm-down	Walk 800 meters, stretch
Tuesday	20	Warm-up	Run 1600 meters, stretch
	10	Sprint drills	High knees, form runs,
	50–60	Interval training	12×400 at date pace, jog 400 meters between
	10	Warm-down	Walk 800 meters, stretch
Wednesday	20	Warm-up	Jog 800 meters, stretch
	70	Long run	10 mile run (easy pace)

Day	Duration (min)	Training task	Training details
Thursday	20	Warm-up	Jog 1600 meters, stretch
	10	Sprint drills	Same as Tuesday
		Interval training	12×300 date pace, jog 100 meters between
Friday	20	Warm-up	Jog 800 meters, stretch
	50	Long run	8 mile run, 6 min/mile
	15	Speed work	7×100, walk 100 between
Saturday	20	Warm-up	Jog 800 meters, stretch
	90	Long run	15 mile run

Some of the more accomplished runners will start running two-a-day workouts during this period. These are morning runs, and are usually scheduled for Monday, Wednesday, and Friday. They are easy runs of about 3–4 miles covered at a 6–7-minute-per-mile pace. I didn't require these twice-a-day workouts earlier in the year, I saved them for this period. I have occasionally had the team run two-a-day workouts during the cross-country season, but this is not a regular procedure. When I schedule these extra workouts, I am careful not to overtrain these young athletes. I don't want their enthusiasm for running to end at the high school level. I am always mindful of the "too much, too soon" syndrome. If any of our runners show any signs of overtraining — staleness, sickness, or diminishing performance — I discontinue the extra training immediately.

The next cycle is the competitive period. This cycle usually begins in the month of April. The distance runners no longer train through the competition. They should enjoy a day or so of tapering off prior to competition. During this cycle, your choice of events for the two-miler should be made based mainly on the runner's developmental needs. If the distance runners require more speed work, enter them in the 800 meters and the 4×400 relay. If endurance and pace work seem to be the major consideration, enter the athletes in longer races. At this point in the season, the purpose of competition is to prepare the runner for the more important meets later in the season. See the following weekly training schedule for the competitive period.

Weekly training schedule for distance runners during the competitive period

Day	Duration (min)	Training task	Training details
Monday	20	Warm-up	Jog 800 meters, stretch
	55	Long run	10 mile run
	10	Warm-down	800 meter walk, stretch
Tuesday	20	Warm-up	Stride 1600 meters, stretch
	10	Sprint drills	High knees, form runs, etc.

Day	Duration (min)	Training task	Training details
	40	Repetition training	5 × 800, goal pace, rest until recovery between
	10	Warm-down	Jog 1600 meters, stretch
Wednesday	20	Warm-up	Jog 800 meters, stretch
	90	Long run	12 miles, 7 min/mile
	10	Warm-down	Walk 800, stretch
Thursday	20	Warm-up	Stride 1600, stretch
	10	Sprint drills	High knees, 1, 2, 3s, chop downs, form runs
	40	Repetition running	8 × 400 faster than goal pace, rest to recovery between
	10	Warm-down	Jog 1600 meters, stretch
Friday	20	Warm-up	Jog 800 meters stretch
	50	Fartlek	6 miles with occasional 100 meter surges
	10–15	Speed work	7 × 50 meters, walk back between
	10	Warm-down	Walk 800 meters, stretch
Saturday	Competition. Run the 3200 and the 1600.		

Run 6 miles after the meet to warm down. If leg speed is a problem, an athlete can substitute the 800 meters for the 1600. If some of your runners are tired, limit their competition to one event. Try to win meets if possible, but not at the expense of the athletes' preparation for the important meets in May. If you intend to have the distance runners compete in more than one event in May, prepare them for it. Determine if the runners can handle this much competition prior to the conference, sectional, and state competitions.

I haven't said much in regard to weight training for distance runners. A distance runner's training program is so full that it is difficult to find time for weight training. Hill training and stair running are about all the resistance work they do for the lower extremities; a set or two of chins and parallel bar dips for the upper body will do the job. I have seldom required distance runners to follow an extensive weight program. Considering all the miles of running that they do, enough is enough.

The fifth and final period is the peaking cycle. This four-week cycle leads up the most important competition of the year. Everything the runner has done in training has been in preparation for these final meets. The most important factors at this time are competition, rest, and restoration. The best approach physically during these last few weeks is to put training on the back burner. The athlete's physical and psychological condition should be monitored closely. For the most part, competition should be used to get the runners sharpened for the final meets. An occasional "stress" workout may also be necessary to eliminate a few weaknesses in the athletes' competitive fitness profile. The chart on page 158 gives a weekly schedule for the peaking period.

Weekly training schedule for distance runners during the peaking period

Day	Duration (min)	Training task	Training details
Monday	20	Warm-up	Jog 800 meters, stretch
	55	Long run	10 mile run
	10	Warm-down	800 meter walk, stretch
Tuesday	20	Warm-up	Stride 1600 meters, stretch
	10	Sprint drills	High knees, chop downs, quick steps. 1, 2, 3s, form runs
	30	"Stress" runs	2–3×4 minute runs or 2–3×16 100s run back-to-back at race pace, rest to recovery between sets
Wednesday	20	Warm-up	Jog 800 meters, stretch
	60	Long run	8 miles at 7 mins/mile
	10	Warm-down	Walk 800 meters, stretch
Thursday	20	Warm-up	Stride 1600 meters, stretch
	10	Sprint drills	Same as Tuesday
	30	Repetition training	8×400 faster than goal pace, rest 2–3 mins between
	20	Warm-down	Jog 1600 meters, stretch
Friday	20	Warm-up	Same as Thursday
	30	Tempo run	5 miles at 6 min/mile
	10	Sprint training	7×70 meters, walk 70 meters between
	10	Warm-down	800 meter walk, stretch
Saturday			Competition. Jog and stride 6 miles after the meet.

RUNNING TECHNIQUE, PACE, AND RACING TACTICS

The two-miler's running form is similar to the middle-distance running style. The only difference is that the distance runner's arms may be held slightly lower. The foot plant is essentially the same as that of most middle-distance runners, but many excellent distance runners have been known to run flat-footed. The torso is erect, and breathing should come from the diaphragm. When distance runners learn to breathe in this manner, their times will improve dramatically. Relaxed running form and proper breathing are two keys to successful distance running.

Knowledge of correct pace is also essential for effective distance running. Correct pace was so important to the great Finnish distance runner, Paavo Nurmi, that he carried a stopwatch when he competed. He totally ignored the other runners and raced against the clock. Paavo Nurmi completely dominated middle-distance and distance running in the early 1920s. In those days an even-paced race was the recommended method of successful distance running; however, many of today's experts are advocating a negative split. According to the 1994 fall issue of the periodical, *Track Coach*, most of the modern world records in middle- and long-distance running have been set by athletes who ran the last half of a race faster than the first half.

Distance runners should work on pace judgment until they know it in their sleep. Lap times are usually called in most competitions, but most well-trained distance runners know where they are every minute of every race. This is one of the many virtues of interval training. After several months of interval training, a distance runner should have developed a kinesthetic sense of pace. To help develop this skill, I ask the distance runners to calculate their splits, and we usually discuss these lap times the day before the meet. They should have these splits stamped into their memory so that at some point during the season correct pace will become an automatic skill. I reiterate: Correct pace judgment is absolutely essential for effective distance running.

HOW TO TRAIN FOR THE TWO MILE
UNDER DIFFICULT CONDITIONS

Distance runners must cover plenty of miles. They can cover these miles on any available surface — except sidewalks. We use what we can find — asphalt streets, playgrounds, parks, sand, hills, cemeteries, whatever. If the athletes use the streets for their long runs, try to take a route where automobile traffic is at a minimum. Have them wear bright clothing so they can be seen easily. They should be taught to work together in order to protect each other from traffic and other hazards. With the team, go over in detail all of the possible hazards and how to prevent them. Choose the safest route possible. If this is not feasible, have the team run near the sidewalk on the grassy area near the street. Get permission to do this kind of running from the administration and the parents, or you may be held liable for any accidents that might occur. If you get a thumbs-down on running in the street, have the team walk or drive to the nearest park or playground for their long runs. If you are in a rural area, run the roads; but take plenty of precaution there also. Traffic is not as heavy as it is in the cities, but there is still an occasional vehicle.

Interval training and repetition work can be done almost anywhere. Borrow a measuring wheel from the physics department to measure distances. If you don't have a measuring wheel, use your car and calculate distances with your car's odometer. If you have neither of these devices, walk and estimate the distances. Measure how long your stride is and figure how many of your strides will make a 400, 800, a mile, or whatever you choose. You don't always need to know the exact distances. Have your team run on a time basis or do a "stress" work-out. Just determine the length of time (e.g., 30 minutes) you want them to run and measure how far they can run in 30 minutes.

Very few world-class distance runners train on a track. Where do you think the great African and European distance runners train? Anywhere they can. You are under no handicap when it comes to training distance runners; everybody is on a level playing field. If you brainstorm, you will find an adequate place to train. The biggest challenge to a coach's creativity is not the distance events; it is the field events. Many areas and countries haven't figured out how to solve that problem yet. I have never seen a world-class African shot-putter or pole-vaulter. This is where a lack of facilities and equipment can be a real challenge to a coach's creativity. We will deal with the problems associated with coaching the field events later in this book.

Section 11

THE RELAYS
Teamwork Around the Track

To win any relay race, you must train four runners to work in harmony with one another. A coach has to solve the following problems: (1) the placement of each runner, (2) the personality of each athlete, (3) the kind of baton pass to use, (4) who is the best curve runner, (5) who has the best start, (6) who has the best finish, (7) who has the most speed, (8) who has the least amount of speed, (9) the height of each runner, and (10) who runs the best under pressure. When coaches can solve these and other problems, they can often teach four average runners with flawless baton passes to triumph over four runners with superior speed and mediocre baton skills.

The most exciting running events in track and field are the relays. I will always remember when Chicago hosted the *Daily News* Relays at the Chicago Stadium. This was the time (about 40 years ago) when track and field meant something in America. There was a major indoor meet on television every weekend; a televised track meet these days is as rare as a chicken with teeth. College and university relays were the highlight of these meets. What made the 1955 *Daily News* Relays doubly exciting for me was being invited to participate as a member of a winning mile relay team. On that occasion, I had the opportunity and memorable pleasure to observe world-class athletes up close and personal. It was one of the greatest thrills I have ever experienced.

I have participated in, or coached, every conceivable type of relay. Each relay has its own unique qualities and physical demands. Baton passing and its technique is the essence of the sprint relays. In the distance relays, the baton pass is not as significant, but you cannot hand a baton to an athlete without giving some sort of instruction. Too many things can go wrong. All of the runners on the relay team must know what they are doing — even in the distance relays. Precious yards can be lost in any relay race if the baton exchange between runners is not negotiated properly.

In this section, I will cover every relay and the type of baton pass necessary for optimum results. Every relay has its special characteristics and technical idiosyncrasies; therefore, the mechanics for each relay can be different. Listed below are the relays and their various categories:

1. The sprint relays — 4×100, 4×200, and 4×400 meters
2. Middle distance relays — 4×800 and 4×1600 meters
3. Sprint medley relays — 400, 200, 200, 800; and 100, 100, 200, 400 meters
4. Distance medley relays — 800, 400, 1200, 1600; and 1600, 1200, 1600, 3200 meters

Several relays are not run around a track: shuttle relays, field event relays, and other unconventional events that might be held at a relay carnival. Since a baton is not used for most of these relays, I will not deal with them in this section.

Various kinds of baton techniques have been advocated in the four categories listed above. When your athletes learn the necessary methods for each, they will be prepared to run any relay in any competition.

SPRINT RELAYS

Relays are the only events in track and field that require teamwork. Four athletes must work together in harmony to achieve optimum results. It is possible to have four superior sprinters on a 4×100 relay team and lose because of poor technique. I have seen relay teams at all levels of competition — with average sprinters — defeat teams that were loaded with world-class sprinters. I have also seen world-class relay teams drop the baton, pass out the zone, and, in general, get disqualified due to poor technique.

The most difficult relay to negotiate is the 4×100 relay. One mistake and the race is over. You can make up for a blunder in the longer relays, but things happen too fast in the 400 meter relay to permit the slightest hint of an error. A sprint relay can be lost for over 80 reasons, but skillful baton passing can negate all of them. Actually, in well-executed relay races. the whole can be greater than the parts. You can add all the best times of each individual runner and a brilliantly orchestrated relay team's time can be considerably faster than that total. For example, if every member of the relay is capable of a 10 second 100 meters, the final time should not be 40 seconds; with superior baton passes the time could be 37.0! Nobody has ever run 37.0, but that is because teams with the talent to do so have never had flawless baton passing.

Effective baton passing is difficult to master — especially in the sprint relays. There are several reasons for this unhappy state of affairs:

1. Sprint relays are negotiated with a "blind" pass. This means that the exchange of the baton is made without the outgoing runner looking back.

2. The baton has to be passed at top speed.

3. The baton pass must be made within a 20 meter passing zone. A baton passed outside the zone will result in a disqualification.

4. The choice and placement of personnel can be a problem. The decision of who runs first, second, third, or anchor can make a significant difference in the outcome of a relay race.

5. Strategy, and the proper use of the 10 meter international or "free" zone, is also crucial in the outcome of a sprint relay.

6. There cannot be any distraction or lack of concentration during the execution of a baton exchange.

The "Blind" Pass

The technique or style of the blind pass has undergone a myriad of changes in the last several years. Most current relay teams use either an upsweep or the overhand type of pass; there is no consensus on which technique is best. For more than ten years, most American teams favored the overhand or "jet sprint" relay pass popularized by Bud Winter, the former sprint coach at San Jose State University. Most European teams use the underhanded pass advocated by Stan Wright, the 1972 American Olympic sprint coach. Let's look at the virtues and disadvantages of both methods.

Advantages of the Overhand Method

1. There is more "free space" between the incoming and outgoing runners. This means the baton pass can be completed without the runners' getting

Photo 11–1. The overhand passing drill for the sprint relays.

Photo 11–2. The underhand passing drill for the sprint relays.

too close to each other. The result is less chance of the athletes' interfering with each other's leg movement and a decreased possibility of a collision between runners.

2. Both runners can make the pass at arm's length. Theoretically, each runner can save one step because of this extended reach.

3. The position of the outgoing runner's hands seems to prevent the dropping of the baton. I have never had a baton dropped using this pass.

Disadvantages

1. The incoming runners tend to raise the arm above shoulder height prior to the pass. This slows the speed of the incoming runner.

2. The outgoing runner's arm should be parallel to the ground prior to receiving the baton. It is difficult to run at top speed with an arm held this high.

3. The outgoing runner's torso often remains in a bent position too long prior to the pass. This position interferes with optimum speed during the exchange.

Advantages of the Underhand Pass

1. The pass can be made without remaining in a bent position.

2. The relay baton is usually exchanged without the incoming runner's raising the arm above shoulder level.

3. It is easier to complete this pass at full speed.

Disadvantages

1. There is less free space between the runners. The athletes have to be closer together in order to complete the pass. Each runner has to run an extra step to make the baton exchange.

2. The possibility of a collision between runners is greater because of diminished free space.

3. The baton is easier to drop because of the hand position of the outgoing runner. The fingers are pointed toward the ground. Make the slightest fumble and all is lost.

The method that you use for the baton pass is "six in one hand and a half a dozen in the other." Take your pick. I switched to the overhand method in 1970 because it seemed safer. If either method is taught correctly, your team will run fast times, but it is easy to deviate from the correct form with the overhand method — especially with the arms. Most athletes want to raise the arm above the shoulder prior to the pass because it looks spectacular. This action can compromise a good baton pass. I have often been tempted to go back to the underhand method because of this indiscretion.

Photo 11–3. Correct waiting position for the number-two and number-four runners in the sprint relays. The number-three runner will face in the opposite direction.

Photo 11–4. An excellent baton pass made during the pressure of competition. The pass is from the number-one runner to the number-two runner. The outgoing runner has his receiving (left) arm parallel to the ground. This is a near-perfect hand position for receiving the baton.

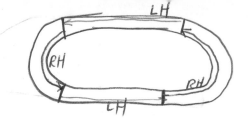

Choosing and Arranging the Relay Team

Picking the members of a relay team seems like an easy task. Nothing could be further from the truth. Just pick the four best sprinters — right? Wrong. A less talented athlete might be a better relay team member for some reason; for example, some people seem to run faster with a baton in hand. Most important, all four members of the relay team should trust and believe in one another. This attitude will definitely have a positive impact on their performance. You will have to experiment to see what promotes chemistry among them.

Often an excellent sprinter will have poor hands and will constantly drop the baton. You have three choices in this case: (1) Be patient and work with the runner and hope for improvement; (2) put the athlete first on the relay so that receiving the baton is not a factor; or (3) try someone else. You will be forced to do all three at some point in your career. If coaching track were easy, everybody would do it.

After you have picked the four members of your 4×100 relay, you must decide who runs in what order. The typical recommendation is to have your best sprinter run the anchor leg, the next-best sprinter run first, and the slowest athlete run second. Simple? Nope; there is more to it than that. Another approach is to put the most reliable starter first. Have the best sprinter run second (because of the long straightaway); the best curve runner should take the third position, and the second-best sprinter ought to run anchor. This approach will work well if your second and third runners have the best hands on the team. These runners will have to pass and receive the baton. If they cannot, some other arrangement may work better. You also have to consider the height of each runner. A tall sprinter will often experience difficulty passing the baton to a shorter runner. The personalities of the runners are also extremely important; some athletes run better when they are in the lead and others are more effective from behind. In addition to all these considerations, runners two and four must learn to receive and run with the baton in the left hand. An infinite number of possibilities will lead to a successful relay combination. I've only scratched the surface. Coaching track is an art as well as a science.

To summarize: Runner one will run with the baton in the right hand and will run near the left border of the lane. Runner two will receive the baton in the left hand and will run near the right border of the lane. Runner three will receive the baton in the right hand and run near the left border of the lane, and the anchor will receive the baton in the left hand and run near the right border of the lane. At no point in the relay will any runner on the relay team change hands with the baton. Runners two and four will face the inside of the track prior to leaving their prearranged marks and runner three will face the outside of the track and follow the same procedure as runners two and four.

How to Calculate Perfect Baton Passing

Successful baton passing means that the baton never slows down during the race. If all the runners were invisible, the baton would appear to move at the same speed through out the relay. A perfect baton pass is difficult to detect; it

©1998 by Parker Publishing Company, Inc.

Figure 11-1

A DIAGRAM OF THE 400 METER PASSING ZONE

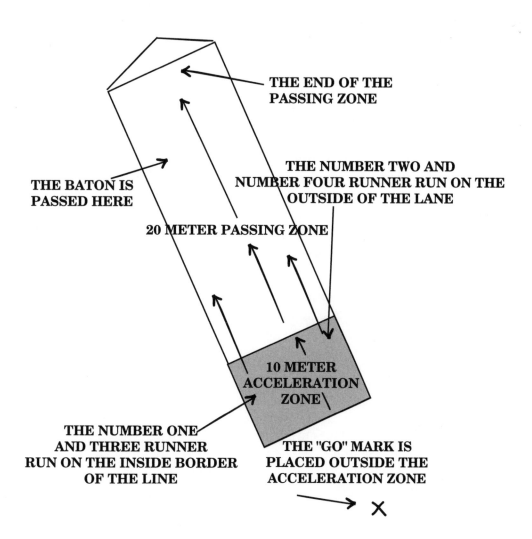

THE END OF THE PASSING ZONE

THE NUMBER TWO AND NUMBER FOUR RUNNER RUN ON THE OUTSIDE OF THE LANE

THE BATON IS PASSED HERE

20 METER PASSING ZONE

10 METER ACCELERATION ZONE

THE NUMBER ONE AND THREE RUNNER RUN ON THE INSIDE BORDER OF THE LINE

THE "GO" MARK IS PLACED OUTSIDE THE ACCELERATION ZONE

should be part of the running motion. A spectator should not be able to easily see when it happened. A perfect pass can be negotiated with the application of dedicated practice and simple calculation.

To help the outgoing runner and the incoming runner execute a perfect pass, measure 20 feet between a prearranged marker and the "go" line. Place the prearranged marker outside the 10 meter international zone, and the "go" line at the beginning of the international zone. Have the incoming runner approach this marker at top speed. When the foot of the incoming runner is above (but not touching) the established marker, the outgoing runner leaves the "go" mark at full speed. Always practice this drill at full speed with no effort on the part of either runner to compensate for the other athlete. If the incoming runner cannot catch the outgoing runner, the marks are too far apart. If the incoming runner catches the outgoing runner before entering the passing zone, the distance between the marks is too short. Several 50-minute practice sessions should be enough time to establish the two marks. Measure these distances with a fiber glass or steel tape measure or count foot-steps and record the length. Try to practice on a surface that is similar to the one you will be competing on. When we didn't have a track, we used an asphalt parking lot. We also set up cones to simulate the distances of the 20 meter passing zone and 10 meter international zone.

To Verbal or Not to Verbal

Many successful relay teams use a verbal signal to tell the outgoing runner when to receive the baton. You can hear various signals shouted in the passing zone. I have heard, "go," "hike," "hoy," "hand," "stick," and "reach" — the list is endless. Some teams use two verbals. Other teams count a certain number of arm pumps to determine when to pass the baton. Yet other teams compete successfully without any marks or verbals. Several years ago, we abandoned all verbals. We went to a third mark. After calculating our marks outside the international zone, our relay teams established another mark within the passing zone to receive the baton. The outgoing runner knew the exact moment when the baton was to be exchanged in the passing zone. This method took a tremendous amount of practice to perfect, but gave us some of our best exchanges. The team was never distracted when other teams shouted verbal commands.

RELAY STRATEGY

Most relay teams have only one or two superior runners. If this is the case, then it is best that these athletes carry the baton longer than the rest of the team. Simply stated — these runners should receive the baton earlier in the zone and pass it later in the subsequent zone — to the slower runners. If this is done correctly, runners two and four will run nearly 120 meters and runners one and three will run less than 100 meters. This being the case, the best sprinters should run second and anchor on the 4×100 relay.

The 800 meter relay (4×200) passing technique and strategy is similar to the 400 meter relay baton exchange. Some coaches teach a visual pass for this relay because of the greater fatigue experienced by the incoming runner, but if the athlete is in good physical condition, a blind pass is also the best technique for the 800 meter relay. However, I usually recommend a minor adjustment in the prearranged markings because of the fatigue factor. At the first practice session, each outgoing runner is instructed to measure 15 feet (instead of 20 feet) between markers. I ask the runners to simulate the speed of a tiring 200 meter run to determine if their markers need to be shortened or lengthened. After this drill has been completed successfully, I have the relay team run a full 4×400 relay with 400 meter markings. Immediately after this effort, the team will quickly establish the 4×200 markings and run another 4×100 relay. The physical distress felt on the second run will simulate the fatigue experienced in the 800 meter relay. If the baton passes are not satisfactory, repeat this drill or run the full 800 relay on the next scheduled speed workout.

When Things Go Wrong

Things can go awry in practice until the baton technique is perfected. They will never get corrected until all members understand they must run all relay practices at full speed. The runners must not adjust speed to make the baton pass happen. You will never know who is at fault or if the measurements are correct if all the passes through the zone are not executed at full speed.

If there is a mistake in baton technique, the incoming runner should never run over one stride with the arm reaching forward, but instead bring the arm back in running position to catch the outgoing runner. You will be surprised that, for some reason, most runners will slow down immediately prior to the baton pass. Teach the incoming runner to increase speed when entering the passing zone. The passing zone has to be worked consistently until that tendency is eliminated. The outgoing runner should never decrease speed in practice. If the exchange is not successful, adjust the marks for the next drill. If the incoming runner has difficultly making the pass in competition, have the outgoing runner hold the receiving hand rearward until the pass is made. If all else fails, the incoming runner will have to shout the verbal command "Wait!" If your relay team has to go through any of the above adjustments in competition, they will lose valuable yards, but at least the team won't be disqualified.

The Visual Pass

Every relay race from the 4×400 and longer should be executed with a visual pass. I have tried to use a blind pass in the 4×400 relay and lived to regret it. Too much can go wrong in a longer relay with a blind pass. I have seen a few college and university relay teams use this pass in the 4×400 relay, and it scares me every time. I can remember when I ran a lead-off leg on the mile relay and the outgoing runner pulled that on me and almost blew the relay. I was so overcome with rigor mortis that I couldn't see his hand. That faux pas cost us a 10 meter lead. Fortunately, the anchor man saved the race for us. I have seen too many batons fumbled or dropped in the mile relay because of an attempt to save a few tenths of a second with a blind pass. The visual pass is the way to go in the longer relays.

The responsibility for correct execution of the visual pass depends primarily upon the skills and alertness of the outgoing runner. Every member of the relay team must face the inside of the track prior to receiving the baton. The baton is received with the left hand and immediately switched to the right hand. The possibility of a collision with an opposing runner is greatly reduced when the runner's back is toward the athletes in the outside lanes and facing those in the inside lanes. All the members of the 4×400 relay team run with the baton in their right hands.

Since the incoming runner has run 400 meters and is obviously very tired, it is the job of the outgoing runner to determine the condition of the incoming runner and endeavor to match that runner's speed as the baton is passed. The outgoing runner must present a palms-up position of the left hand and literally *take the baton* from the approaching runner. The best way to match the speed of the incoming runner is to begin moving when the approaching athlete is approximately 10 meters from the outgoing teammate. The outgoing runner attempts to coordinate with the speed of the approaching teammate by facing forward and accelerating for about five strides and subsequently reaching back with the left hand. The outgoing runner "looks" the baton into the left hand and immediately switches the baton to the right hand. With consistent practice, the outgoing runner can receive the baton smoothly enough to attain sufficient speed at the exchange without losing ground. The baton should never slow down when it is passed. The incoming runner must make every effort to finish strongly and run through the zone, but the burden of the responsibility for an effective baton exchange in the longer relays belongs to the outgoing runner. After a tough 400 meters, it is almost impossible for the incoming runner to contribute much to the baton exchange.

The mechanics of the visual pass are relatively simple to learn, but this technique must be practiced as diligently as the more difficult-to-master blind baton pass. This maneuver should be rehearsed until a correct and effective baton exchange becomes automatic. I have seen some funny baton exchanges when an athlete becomes excited in competition and abandons proper technique. When the baton exchange is practiced on a consistent basis, your mile relay team will execute correct technique regardless of the situation.

The visual pass should be used in every race longer than the 4×200 relay, but everyone on the team should be taught both the blind and visual techniques. You never know when a runner will be called upon to compete as a last-minute substitute on an unexpected relay. Sprinters and middle-distance competitors may be called upon to use both baton techniques in the same meet. Sometimes blind and visual baton passes may be used in the same race. Be prepared.

Everyone on the team should be involved in baton drills. You may be forced to substitute a runner when you least expect it. Cut broomsticks, discarded plumbing pipes, broken fiber glass poles, floor hockey sticks, and various plastic rods, and use them for relay batons. Give one to every member of the team at practice. Try to give the official batons to the sprint relay teams so they can become accustomed to the feel, size, and weight of the correct equipment. Remember specificity?

In an effort to get every-one on the team familiar with handling a baton, we often warm-up and warm-down with them. Sometimes an entire practice is conducted with everyone carrying relay batons.

STEPS IN LEARNING CORRECT TECHNIQUE

We begin by teaching the baton pass standing still. Line up the relay teams in single file. Make sure that the sprint relay teams do all practices and drills together and in the correct order. After they have learned the correct technique standing still, have the various teams walk single-file and pass the baton. Then jog single-file and pass the baton. Involve every member of the team in these drills. This means that a team of 80 runners will have 20 relay teams practicing at the same time. Repeat these drills until they are perfected. All of these drills can also be used as a part of the team's warm-up. This routine may take several days.

After they have learned the above drills, spread the team out in single file about 30 meters apart. Pass the baton by running at half speed. When this drill looks adequate, increase the speed. Then try a 200 meter relay (4×50) at full speed. At this point, the athletes who use the visual pass will outrun those who use the blind pass. It will take a considerable period of time for the blind pass to be perfected. Be patient.

When the single-file passes have improved, work the baton passes around the track at half-speed and work up to full-speed passes. Once the team has perfected these drills and established their marks, work the passing zone at full speed. However, it is extremely difficult and probably impossible to improve baton technique by running nothing but full relays at top speed. After a few all-out attempts, the athletes will be too fatigued to continue. Modify somewhat to get the optimum value out of a relay workout. I often instruct the 4×100 relay team to jog or walk 50 meters and accelerate the final 50 meters into the zone and execute the baton exchange . After a few corrections, the team repeats this procedure for the remainder of practice. We often rehearse this drill as many as 12–16 times. Baton practice often becomes a sprint workout of $12–16 \times 50$ meter sprints through the passing zone. That way, we kill two birds with one stone. We also incorporate these baton practices into workouts when we work on other relays. On some days, we jog or walk 100 meters and sprint 100 meters into a 4×200 relay baton pass. Occasionally, we run 200s into a 4×400 meter baton exchange for a speed-endurance workout. The quality and volume of these training sessions is often determined by the cycle we are operating in at the time. This same procedure is also used for the distance relays. The distance runners frequently do repeat 400s and 800s and work visual exchanges through the passing zone. Our athletes love these relay workouts.

MEDLEY RELAYS

Medley relays present a different sort of baton passing problem. Some of these events may require a variety of passing techniques and markings for each runner in the relay. Some relay meets may have several types of medley relays and then the next week, another meet will have a different mixture of medley relays on the schedule. These competitions can be somewhat troublesome to prepare for.

1. The 800 meter or sprint medley. This particular relay is on the regular order of events in our girls' state meet. Since this is a regularly contested event, it can be easily prepared for throughout the track season. The order of the runners are 100–100–200–400. The baton exchanges in this event are not too complicated. There is nothing new to be learned. All three baton exchanges are blind passes. I have seen some teams use a visual pass on the final leg of the 800 medley, but this is not recommended.

The best strategy to use in this race is to lengthen the run of the second 100 leg and give the baton to the 200 meter runner deep into the passing zone. The 200 meter runner returns the favor to the 400 meter leg by giving the baton to the quarter-miler deep into the final passing zone. If this strategy is handled correctly, the quarter-miler will run considerably less than 400 meters.

2. Another popular sprint medley relay (mile medley), is usually arranged 400–200–200–800. This relay is a mixture of two blind passes and one visual pass. The quarter-miler runs with the baton in the right hand and gives the baton to the first 200 meter runner with a visual pass. Fatigue is a constant companion in the 400 meters (remember rigor mortis), and of course, the responsibility for a successful completion of this pass depends upon the skill and alertness of the outgoing runner. This runner receives the baton in the left hand and gives the baton to the next 200 meter runner's right hand with a blind pass. The 800 meter runner takes the final exchange with the left hand. This final pass is also a blind pass. The best strategy in this race is for the first 200 runner to receive the baton early in the passing zone, thereby shortening the distance the quarter-miler has to run — and the second 200 meter runner should pass the baton deep into the final passing zone to decrease the distance that the half-miler has to run. In this event, the 200 meter sprinters should run their part of the relay as far as it is legally possible.

3. The distance medley relay — 800–400–1200–1600. All of the distance medley relay runners use a visual pass. On several occasions, our team was invited to a meet that was organized to accommodate schools that have large distance running programs. In addition to the distance medley relay, they included a relay in the program that had no official name. I named it the long-distance medley — 1600–800–2400–3200. We used most of our best middle-distance runners in the distance medley and this relay was next. Most of our middle-distance runners were still recovering from the previous relay. I had to improvise. I had our 800 meter runner lead off the relay; a hurdler ran second, our second-best miler ran third, and our best 3200 meter runner ran anchor. We finished second. I considered that makeshift relay team's effort a major accomplishment.

Developing successful relay teams can add another positive dimension to your program that will increase participation, motivation, and enthusiasm. Relays can help you discover talent that may have been overlooked. It is also theoretically possible to win the conference, sectional, and state championships by finishing first in all the relay events, Our boys' state meet program has four relays: 4×800, 4×400, 4×200, and 4×100. The girls have five. If you don't have any individual stars on your team, it makes sense to spend a considerable amount of time working on relays. Being involved in a well-executed relay effort generates excitement and satisfaction for coaches and athletes alike, especially when the final race on the program — and my favorite event — is the mile relay. I think it was Yogi Berra who said, "It's not over until the fat lady sings," but the track meet's not over until the mile relay's been run!

DEVELOPING RELAY TEAMS WITHOUT FACILITIES

Earlier in this section, I mentioned that it is relatively easy to get enough relay batons to accommodate a team of 80 runners. All you need is a saw and a little enterprise. We also purchased about a dozen "official" batons for the sprint relay teams. Relay batons are an inexpensive item; even an extremely limited budget can afford these. The biggest problem confronting a track coach is finding the proper facilities to practice baton exchanges. At one time, the nearest all-weather track to our school was about three miles away, so we often walked or jogged to this site. At other times, we practiced in parks, bridle paths, parking lots, school corridors, and playgrounds located in or near our school.

We don't need a perfect situation during the learning process. We practice at our school most of the time. Later on, when we want to get the feel of the real thing, we go to an all-weather track. If we use a parking lot or school corridors, I simulate the passing zones with chalk or adhesive tape. When we practice on grass or dirt areas, we mark our passing zones with cones. After we establish our marks and eliminated most of our technical mistakes, we go to the nearest all-weather track to perfect our baton exchanges.

Some of our practice sites may seem primitive, but our athletes are so accustomed to training on these surfaces that we've never felt deprived. When we were in the learning stages, these alternative sites were the most convenient areas available. Since no other teams used these locations we didn't have to share space with anyone.

There are times when the relay teams needed to work through the actual lanes and passing zones. Most of the tracks we use are centrally located, and they were extremely crowded on certain days. Frequently, public, parochial, private, and suburban schools, plus a few colleges and universities are sharing the facility. It is difficult to find a lane to run in. When you have 30–40 runners working on baton passes, you need space.

The most efficient way to negotiate a relay practice on a crowded track is to do all the warm-ups on the infield. After our warm-up, we assemble the runners in the middle of the infield and assign everyone to a lane and their respective passing zones, When the track seems to be clear of runners, our athletes are instructed to go to their positions on the track. After we complete three to four baton exchanges, the relay teams immediately leave the track and jog to the middle of the infield for further instruction. Their mistakes, if any, are corrected and the relay teams are sent back to their original positions when the track is relatively clear of runners. We are able to work 32 sprinters at a time by using this method.

While the sprinters are working on baton exchanges, send your middle-distance runners on a long run. When they return, the sprinters should be warming down. If time permits, you can work 32 or more middle-distance runners on their visual passes. With this system, it is possible for one coach to train an entire track team at the same time. It is also possible, with the cooperation of the athletes, for a coach (with no assistants), to train runners, jumpers, relay teams, and weight lifters, shot putters, and discus throwers simultaneously. The logistics are covered in Section 22 devoted to that subject. It is an enterprise that will tax every ounce of your creative energy and organizational skills. But there is nothing that can equal the sense of satisfaction that you experience when you accomplish this ostensibly impossible task.

Section 12

THE HIGH HURDLES
The Legacy of
Willie Davenport

The hurdler with the best technique I have ever seen was 1968 Olympic Champion, Willie Davenport. He may not remember when he honored this writer with some valuable information on how to train for the 110 meter hurdles, but I will be eternally grateful for his advice. After you read this section, you will know the reason for my gratitude. Many thanks, Mr. Davenport. You are a class act.

The University of Chicago Track Club, under the leadership of the venerable coach Ted Haydon (now deceased), was a mecca of track and field. All you had to do was show up on any Saturday during the indoor track season and observe. It was possible to meet hundreds of world-class athletes. The University of Chicago was also a fount of knowledge for track and field; all you had to do was ask.

I often sat for hours and just watched and enjoyed the multitude of world-class athletes who competed there. The University of Chicago's indoor fieldhouse was the best track and field classroom in the world. I watched Willie Davenport and other world-class athletes compete in the high and low hurdles. I studied his flawless technique over the high hurdles, and was compelled to inquire why his form was so perfect. I have observed a number of world-class hurdlers, but in my opinion, Willie Davenport had the best hurdle technique in the history of track and field. There have been hurdlers who eclipsed his records, but no one ran better. When he finished his last event at the University of Chicago Holiday Meet in December of 1969, I asked him a litany of technical questions about hurdling.

Willie was kind enough to sit and talk to me about hurdle technique for as long as I wanted to ask questions. Thanks to that fruitful conversation, my hurdle expertise took a quantum leap forward.

TALENT IDENTIFICATION

The ideal hurdler should be an intelligent, tall, flexible, well-coordinated, and courageous sprinter. Consider yourself blessed if that kind of athlete crosses your path one or two times in your coaching career. A great sprinter is a rare bird, but a great hurdler is even more difficult to find. The great challenge of coaching is to develop decent hurdlers when they don't have all of those six characteristics.

You will have to use every coaching skill available until that rare specimen, the perfect hurdling prototype, appears. Most of the time, you will have to work with hurdlers who are lacking in some of the above characteristics. You can work wonders with an average candidate. You can improve a hurdler's flexibility and coordination. You might persuade a youngster to be courageous and *maybe* a lack of height can be over looked; a few great hurdlers were not tall. The only characteristic that cannot be ignored is sprinting speed. The great ones have been fast: Former world record holder, Renaldo Nehemiah could run world-class times in all the sprints. World champion Greg Foster was the NCAA champion in the 200 meters, and Harrison Dillard, the 1952 Olympic champion in the high hurdles, won the 100 meters in the 1948 Olympics. Willie Davenport ran the 100 yard dash in 9.4 seconds. Every conference and state champion hurdler I have ever coached was an excellent sprinter.

Most of the hurdlers you recruit from other sports will be basketball or football players in the skill positions. But don't stop there — you may find a few potential hurdlers in your physical education classes. On one occasion, several students were hanging around after school and asked to try the event. After a few preliminary instructions, I was surprised to see some of these youngsters negotiating the high hurdles in decent form. One joined our squad and eventually placed in the state meet. You never know.

It is a good idea to teach everyone on the track team to hurdle. This approach can be excellent insurance for your team at a relay meet. You can substitute anyone on the team in the shuttle hurdle relays if someone happens to be injured. High hurdling is also a tremendous training aid; it can improve stride length, knee lift, and leg power. It is also a great change-of-pace workout for middle-distance runners. One of our graduates became one of the best 3000 meter steeplechase runners at his college because of his involvement in some of our hurdle practices.

HOW TO TRAIN AND DEVELOP HURDLERS

We worked every member of our team on the mechanics and techniques of this event at the beginning of practice immediately following the warm-up. Athletes seem to learn complicated physical skills easier when they are fresh.

Hurdlers should begin their skill development during the general preparation period. Though an occasional candidate will learn how to hurdle in one training session, others may take longer to learn the technique. Don't give up on an athlete who has difficulty learning the event. It took one youngster three years to learn the event. He eventually ran 13.8 in the 110 meter hurdles.

Learning to Hurdle

There are several excellent ways to teach hurdling. If one method does not work, try another. You can also use a combination of methods. Each athlete may respond differently to a particular teaching approach. One rule must be followed regardless of the method you use. "Practice does not make perfect — perfect practice makes perfect." Never let an incorrect technique get implanted into an athlete's nervous system. Nothing is more difficult than trying to break an established bad habit. Stop the athlete immediately and correct the fault or faults before it is too late. I can remember when a runner became impatient and went ahead and taught himself to hurdle incorrectly; it took almost four years to eliminate all the technical flaws he accumulated in one day. Another hurdler attended a track and field camp and reported to practice with a plethora of bad habits. It set her back one year. Be careful of suspect track and field camps. Some camps can be marvelous and others can be a nightmare.

Three Basic Ways to Teach Hurdling

1. The "trail leg" method. Try to establish the athlete's lead leg (the leg that goes over the hurdle first) and trail leg (the leg that clears the hurdle last). Have the athlete jump a low hurdle or a hurdle trainer several times and watch which leg the potential hurdler chooses as the lead leg. Also, have the athlete kick a soccer ball several times and see which leg does most of the kicking. Finally, stand behind each runner and gently push the athlete; the leg the athlete uses to step forward to maintain balance could be the lead leg. The leg that the candidate has favored most often during these tests is usually the lead leg.

Instruct all of the athletes who favored the left leg to stand in front of, and to the left side of, the hurdle. Those who preferred the right leg should stand to the right of the hurdle. Walk each runner to the side of the hurdle and clear the hurdle with the trail leg only. The lead leg will pass to the side and slightly beyond the hurdle. Repeat this drill until every runner can execute a correct trail leg movement. A correct trail leg is pulled through with the knee lifted under the armpit and swung into the direction of travel. The arm on the side of the trail leg is pulled back and around the leg into a running position.

After the walking trail leg drill is learned, work on this same drill at a jog. Have the runner progressively lift the lead leg higher as the speed is increased (I usually place an empty cardboard box near the hurdle on the lead leg side to make the athlete lift the lead leg). When the runner succeeds in negotiating one hurdle, I add two more.

The next step is to walk the runner over the middle of the hurdle. If this drill is successfully completed, I gradually increase the speed to a full run. When the runner can run one hurdle, I add two more. When the athlete is capable of running the low hurdles, I gradually increase the height of the hurdles.

I seldom work over more than three hurdles during the learning phase. It is easier to make corrections and eliminate bad habits in this manner. The athlete can be stopped before any serious technical faults are learned.

2. The "sticks and bricks" method. Find 18 bricks and three sticks or three high jump cross bars. Lay two bricks on the flat side about three feet apart and place the sticks on the bricks. Make one flight of three hurdles about eight yards apart. Run the hurdle candidates over these obstacles. Place the bricks on their ends and repeat this drill. Continue this drill until the bricks are stacked three high on their ends. Move the "hurdles" further and further apart as you raise the height of the bricks. Emphasize a high knee action as the athletes practice this drill.

3. The Wilbur Ross method. One of the best books on hurdle technique is the *Hurdler's Bible*, written by Wilbur Ross. I often use his method of teaching hurdle technique when certain training aids are not available. All you need are a few hurdles. When I work with beginning hurdlers, I often tape the tops of the hurdles with foam rubber or towels to prevent injury to the runner's lower extremities.

The athlete extends the hands in front of the body about waist high, then runs with a high knee action and attempts to bring the knees as high as the hands while moving towards the hurdle. When the runner steps over the hurdle with a high knee action, the arms are kept in front of the body as the hurdle is cleared. Repeat this drill several times. Once this skill is mastered, try it with three hurdles. After this drill is mastered, have the hurdler run with high knees toward the hurdles at 70% speed. Gradually increase the speed of the drill. It is best to try the Wilbur Ross drill after the athletes have learned drills 1 and 2.

Start all the above drills with low hurdles about eight yards apart and gradually move them apart as the athlete's skill improves. When they have learned how to run the low hurdles, gradually raise the barriers to 39 inches.

IMPROVING HURDLE EFFICIENCY

High hurdling is a 110 meter sprint that is interrupted by ten 42 inch barriers (39 inches in high school competition) and 33 inches for women. Most lay people think and state incorrectly that athletes "jump" hurdles. Nothing could be further from the truth. Athletes *run* hurdles. The hurdler should have the mind-set that the 110 meter hurdles is a sprint race with three relatively longer steps every ten yards. This is what Willie Davenport appeared to do. How you execute those three longer steps will determine the success or failure in hurdle competition. The more a hurdler is forced to deviate from the sprinting action, the more the ten barriers will negatively impact on the hurdler's speed. Your mission is to exploit the laws of basic physics and body mechanics in an attempt to avoid the deleterious effect that the ten hurdles may have on sprinting speed. How well these factors are met will determine the eventual outcome of the hurdler's prowess.

The athlete's starting position is determined by the lead leg. The lead leg is usually in the back position of the starting blocks. This is assuming that the hurdler will take eight running steps to the first hurdle. If the hurdler takes seven steps to the first hurdle, then the leg positions are reversed. Most hurdlers will take eight steps to the first hurdle; the hurdler of the future might take seven.

When the hurdler accelerates from the starting blocks, a compromise in sprinting technique is necessary. Sprinters reach the erect running position in five strides; a hurdler must become erect in four. This gives the hurdler four additional strides to prepare for hurdle clearance. How effectively this technique is accomplished may determine the outcome of the race.

Upon approaching the hurdle, the lead knee is lifted waist height and the lower leg is extended and immediately snapped down. The trail leg is pulled through the armpit and back into running position. Most hurdlers take off about 6–7 feet in front of the hurdle and land 3–4 feet beyond the hurdle. If the hurdler is tall, the center of gravity of the body is raised only slightly. A short hurdler must raise the body's center of gravity much higher than the taller hurdler to clear the barrier — this will compromise forward momentum. A tall hurdler has an obvious advantage when it comes to efficient hurdle clearance. To compensate for this modification of running form, the short hurdler has to lean forward more during the hurdle clearance. This is another adaptation that may have a negative impact on the hurdler's forward progress.

The hurdler's shoulders and body must remain square prior to, during and after clearing the hurdle. The body cannot be torqued at any point during the

Figure 12-1

HIGH HURDLE TAKEOFF

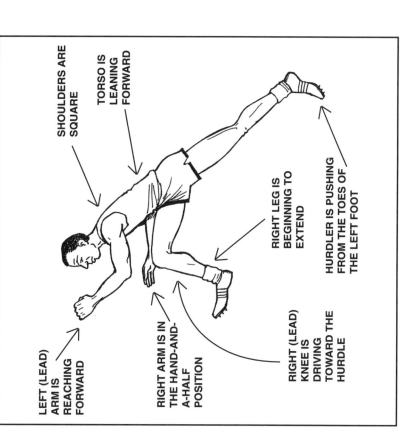

SHOULDERS ARE SQUARE

TORSO IS LEANING FORWARD

LEFT (LEAD) ARM IS REACHING FORWARD

RIGHT ARM IS IN THE HAND-AND-A-HALF POSITION

RIGHT (LEAD) KNEE IS DRIVING TOWARD THE HURDLE

RIGHT LEG IS BEGINNING TO EXTEND

HURDLER IS PUSHING FROM THE TOES OF THE LEFT FOOT

Figure 12-2

HIGH HURDLE TECHNIQUE

TRAIL ARM IS PULLED AROUND LEFT KNEE AND INTO RUNNING POSITION

THE TRAIL LEG (LEFT) KNEE IS HIGH AND MOVING INTO A SPRINTING POSITION IN FRONT OF THE BODY

TORSO IS NEARLY ERECT

THE LEFT FOOT IS STILL EVERTED, BUT IS BEGINNING TO TURN TO THE FRONT

RUNNER HAS CLEARED THE HURDLE, HEAD AND EYES ARE FACING FORWARD

LEAD ARM IS DRIVING FORWARD

LEAD (RIGHT) LEG IS SNAPPED DOWN

HURDLER LANDS ON THE BALL OF THE FOOT

race. When the lead foot touches the ground, the torso must return to running position in preparation for the next hurdle. The arms and legs must also be in correct alignment in order to run an effective 10 yard sprint to the next hurdle. Any modification from normal sprinting form caused by hurdle clearance has to be corrected when the hurdler has landed en route to subsequent hurdles.

A hurdler must be observed from every angle for possible technical indiscretions: From the front, you can look for and eliminate any rising and falling of the head. The arm action and the movement of the trail leg can also be easily observed from this position. From the side, you can critique the movement of the lead leg (it should never be locked), and how effectively it is "snapped" down. The running form between the hurdles should also be observed from the side. Check for any deviation from proper running form from the rear. From this vantage point, you can look for any twisting of the torso and "lateral drift" over the hurdle (lateral drift causes the hurdler to drift to the right or left over the hurdle after leaving the ground).

Do not inundate a hurdler with every fault you see. This approach will only confuse the athlete. Focus on one problem at a time and solve it before moving to another. You will often find that if you solve one major technical fault, several others will be remedied at the same time. You will also discover that most hurdling flaws can be corrected by adhering to Newton's third law of motion: "For every action there is an opposite and equal reaction." The following examples illustrate how this particular law affects good hurdling technique:

1. If a hurdler's torso is twisted to the left *after* the athlete clears the hurdle, then it must have been twisted to the right *prior* to clearing the hurdle.
2. To make the lead snap *down* faster, *raise* the torso faster.
3. If you want the trail leg to come *forward* faster, pull the lead arm *backward* with more force.
4. Initiate all leaning of the torso toward the hurdle *before* the takeoff and straighten the body *after* the lead foot touches the ground.

HURDLE DRILLS

Early in my coaching career, I discovered that correct drills were the key to improving hurdle technique. All the verbalization in the world will not have the same impact on a hurdler's improvement as a well-chosen drill. The trick is picking the right drill.

Trail leg drills

1. Sit on the floor in the hurdle position, pull the trail leg through and the lead arm back. Do several repetitions.
2. Place both hands against a wall; place a hurdle near the trail leg. Pull the trail leg through. Keep the knee high as you pull through.

Photo 12–1. Beautiful technique over the 110 meter hurdles. The shoulders are square, the trail leg is being pulled through and the lead leg is straight but not locked.

3. Line up a flight of three to five hurdles. Place the hurdles about 7–8 feet apart. Run by the hurdles using a trail leg action. Only the trail leg goes over the hurdle. This is a difficult drill to learn but it is worth the trouble.

Lead leg drills

1. Sit on the floor in a hurdle position. Reach forward with the lead arm and bend the torso at the same time. *Do not* reach for the toe of the lead foot.

2. Place a hurdle against a wall. Kick the lead leg above the hurdle and simultaneously bend at the waist. Incorporate the lead arm and trail arm action in this drill.

3. Line up a flight of three to five hurdles. Place the hurdles about 7–8 feet apart. Run by the hurdle clearing the barrier with the lead leg.

Photo 12–2. Hurdler has successfully cleared the barrier. The trail knee is pulled through under the armpit; shoulders are square. The eyes are focused on the next hurdle.

The Seventh Hurdle Problem

Several coaches have approached me with this "seventh hurdle" dilemma. Most young hurdlers seem to struggle and lose their form after clearing the seventh hurdle. They were expecting some esoteric and complicated solution to this situation; the solution to this problem was to put their hurdlers on the 4×400 relay. The stamina developed by running the 400 meters put an end to the seventh hurdle dilemma. Every good hurdler I ever coached was able to run a decent 400 meters. You may have heard of other methods to improve a hurdler's stamina — and I have, too — but this was the best solution for the athletes in our program.

If your mile relay team is loaded with talent, and if the hurdler cannot help this relay, try the " Nehemiah" method to develop hurdle endurance. Renaldo

Photo 12–3. The hurdle stretch exercise. This exercise is part of the hurdler's warm-up.

Nehemiah's high school coach had him run 100 hurdles in practice. The idea is to count every hurdle that is negotiated in a day's practice. For example, 20×5 hurdles = 100! I was never able to get a hurdler to finish that type of workout, but that was the goal. The most any of our hurdlers could do was 65, but this was all they needed. After several sessions of this type of practice, none of these runners faltered at the seventh hurdle.

Learning to Do Three Steps

All 110 meter hurdlers (100 meters for women), have to run three steps between hurdles. In this case, one size fits all. Most neophyte hurdlers experience great difficulty in making three steps and conversely, most older hurdlers overrun these same hurdles because as they mature and develop, the distance between hurdles seems too short. The runners have to adjust.

The easiest way to teach the rhythm of the three steps is to shorten the distance between the hurdles during the early learning stages of the event. Put the hurdles 8–9 yards apart — depending on the stride pattern of a young hurdler — and gradually lengthen the distance (10 yards for men and 8.5 meters for women) to the official measurements. Teach neophyte hurdlers to take a big first step from the hurdle in order to successfully make the obligatory three steps between the hurdles. When these athletes mature and become stronger, reduce the length of the first step.

FLEXIBILITY AND THE HIGH HURDLER

The high hurdler's limbs must be more flexible than those of any runner on the track team. After the rest of the team has finished their regular warm-up and stretching, the hurdler must do a battery of special stretching exercises:

1. Place the heel of the lead leg on the top of the hurdle, lean forward and grasp the hurdle with both hands. Hold this position for 20–30 seconds. Repeat this exercise with the other leg.

2. Place the trail leg on the hurdle and bend toward the ground. Touch the ground with both hands. Hold this position for 20–30 seconds. Repeat this exercise with the other leg.

3. Place both hands against a wall or fence. Swing the lead leg across the body as high as possible in both directions for several repetitions. Repeat this exercise with the trail leg.

After these special exercises have been completed, the hurdler should join the sprinters and do a few speed drills. Immediately following the sprint drills, run through a series of lead leg and trail leg drills with the hurdles. High hurdlers often require at least 20–30 minutes of warming up before they are ready to run hurdles in practice or competition.

TRAINING SCHEDULES AND WORKOUT PROGRAMS

The hurdle training schedules are similar to the periodization schedules that were offered in the earlier sections of this book. Volume training programs will be the norm during the winter months and they will gradually be replaced by workouts of a more intense nature later in the season. But remember that indoor hurdling does not contribute much to the hurdler's stamina. Most of the competition in the high hurdles is contested at distances that are 70 yards or less. It is imperative that the hurdlers endeavor to develop stamina for the longer outdoor 110 meter hurdle event by competing in the 400 meter run or the 4×400 relay. It is important to develop stamina during the indoor season or it may be too little and too late in April. I said this before, but it is was worth repeating.

The general preparation period for hurdlers is similar to the general preparation period for sprinters. Refer to the schedule recommended for sprinters in Section 5. The only modification to the sprint schedule is the inclusion of various hurdle drills. Since high hurdling is difficult to learn and master, introduce the drills related to this event as early as possible.

You will find that most hurdlers have an excellent work ethic and will want to practice hurdle technique after the warm-down. Make sure you are present to monitor the nature and length of this activity. They can pick up some funny techniques when you are not looking. Bad habits, once acquired, are almost impossible to break.

Weekly training schedule for hurdlers
during the specific preparation period

Day	Duration (min)	Training task	Training details
Monday	20	Warm-up	800 meter jog, calisthenics and stretching
	10	Sprint drills	High knees, butt kicks, chop downs, etc.
	10	Hurdle drills	Trail leg and lead leg drills
	20	Stair running	3 min stairs, 3 min jog, 3 min wind sprints, repeat this cycle 2 times
	5	Warm-down	800 meter jog, stretch, walk 800 meters
Tuesday	20	Warm-up	Easy interval running, 100 meter repeats, calisthenics and stretching
	10	Sprint drills	High knees, chop downs, 1, 2, 3s
	10	Hurdle drills	Same as Monday
	30	Technique work	45 hurdles, 15×3 hurdles, walk back between
	10	Warm-down	800 meter jog, stretching
Wednesday	20	Warm-up	1200 meters fartlek, stretch
	10	Sprint drills	Same as Monday
	10	Hurdle drills	Same as Monday
	20	Stair running	Same as Monday
	10	Warm-down	800 meter jog, walk 800 meters
Thursday	20	Warm-up	1600 meter jog, calisthenics and stretching
	10	Sprint drills	Same as Tuesday
	30	Technique work	50 hurdles, 10×5 hurdles, walk back between
	10	Warm-down	Jog 800 meters, stretch
Friday	10	Warm-up	800 meter jog, calisthenics and stretching
	20	Hurdle drills	Wall drills, lead leg and trail leg drills
	10	Technique work	3×5 hurdles full speed, rest 5 mins. between sets
Saturday			Competition. Run the 400 meters or the 4×400 relay in addition to the hurdle events

This is a four-week cycle beginning in February. The technique learned during this period should be adequate to prepare the athlete for indoor hurdle competition. Some of your more gifted athletes will perform exceptionally well in spite of their limited exposure to the event. Encourage the athletes who are experiencing difficulty in negotiating the high hurdles to "hang in there." Assure the hurdle candidates that they can adjust to this difficult event in a few weeks if they persevere.

The next cycle is the precompetitive period. This four-week period occurs during the most important weeks of the indoor season. We usually train through this part of the season with a minor tapering off a few days before the indoor conference championship scheduled for the last week in March. Quantity and volume are the prime directives at this time. We will not, nor do we intend to, peak during the precompetitive cycle, but we have always performed well in spite of this philosophy.

Weekly training schedule for high hurdlers during the precompetitive period

Day	Duration (min)	Training task	Training details
Monday	20	Warm-up	800 meter jog, calisthenics and stretching
	10	Sprint drills	High knees, chop downs, form runs, overstrides, quick steps
	10	Hurdle drills	Trail leg and lead leg drills over hurdles × 20
	30	Technique work	15 × 5 hurdles. walk back between
	10	Warm-down	800 meter jog, stretch
Tuesday	20	Warm-up	800 meter jog, 800 meters of interval 100s at 70% speed
	10	Hurdle drills	Wall drills, lead leg and trail leg drills
	30	Technique work	15 × 3 hurdles, jog back between
	10	Warm-down	Jog 800 meters, stretch
Wednesday	20	Warm-up	Same as Monday
	10	Sprint drills	Same as Monday
	10	Hurdle drills	Same as Monday
	30	Technique work	20 × first hurdle (on time)
	10	Warm-down	Jog 1600 meters, stretch
Thursday	20	Warm-up	Jog 1200 meters, sprint the last 100 meters, stretch
	15	Hurdle drills	Trail leg × 20, lead leg × 20, wall and hurdle drills
	30	Hurdle technique	10 × 6 hurdles, walk back
	10	Warm-down	Jog 400 meters, walk a 400

Day	Duration (min)	Training task	Training details
Friday	20	Warm-up	Jog 1200 meters, stride a 400 and stretch
	10	Sprint drills	High knees, chop downs, 1, 2, 3s, butt kicks
	10	Hurdle drills	Trail and lead leg drills over hurdles
	20	Technique work	3×7 hurdles, walk back between
	10	Warm-down	Walk 800, stretch

Saturday. Competition. Run hurdle events and a leg on the 4×400 relay or the 400 meters.

At the conclusion of the indoor season, you will have to assess the physical fitness of your team. Some of your athletes may need a brief rest following the stress that accompanies a strenuous indoor campaign. Other athletes can embark upon the outdoor season without a break in training. Whatever the case, "active rest" might be the most appropriate exercise prescription for most of your athletes. Active rest is basically a recreational period between seasons to help an athlete maintain a certain level of fitness while recovering from the rigors of a highly competitive indoor season.

The mission of the following training schedule is to initiate a four-week period of intensive speed and quality training. The goal of this program is to sharpen the athlete for the important competitions in the last three weeks of May. April is a difficult time of the year for most athletes in America. The weather is often unpredictable and in certain climates this can visit havoc on an athlete's physical condition. The following workout assumes that the weather will be decent for the most part, but you will have to be flexible enough to modify the program when a wind approaches from the north.

These workouts are not etched in stone. When Mother Nature frowns upon your situation, have an alternate plan ready. I suggest that you also have two plans for meets — one for good weather and another for the often inevitable hostile conditions most coaches have learned to expect. You may have to keep your hurdlers and sprinters on the team bus. Remember, your commitment is to your athletes, not to the meet director:

Weekly training for hurdlers during the competitive season

Day	Duration (min)	Training task	Training details
Monday	20	Warm-up	Jog 800 meters, calisthenics
	10	Sprint drills	High knees, 1, 2, 3s, chop downs, etc.
	10	Hurdle drills	Trail leg and lead leg drills (hurdles are 7 ft. apart)
	30	Interval hurdling	2×5 hurdles in seven sets
	10	Warm-down	Walk 800 meters, stretch

Day	Duration (min)	Training task	Training details
Tuesday	20	Warm-up	Jog 1200 meters, 100 meter strides, jog 100 in between, stretch
	10	Hurdle drills	Wall and hurdle drills
	30	Technique work	15×3 hurdles, 95% effort
	10	Warm-down	Jog 800 meters, stretch
Wednesday	20	Warm-up	Jog 800 meters, stretch
	10	Sprint drills	Same as Monday
	10	Hurdle drills	Wall drills
	30	Hurdle starts	Work to the first hurdle 15–20 times
	10	Warm-down	Jog 800, walk 800, stretch
Thursday	20	Warm-up	Jog 800 meters, stretch, jog a 800
	20	Hurdle drills	Trail leg and lead leg drills, wall and hurdle drills
	30	Speed work	Baton passes with the 4×100 and 4×400 relay teams
	10	Warm-down	Jog 800, walk 400, stretch
Friday	20	Warm-up	Jog 1200 meters, walk 400, stretch
	10	Sprint drills	Same as Monday
	10	Hurdle drills	Same as Tuesday
	20	Technique work	$2–3 \times 7$ hurdles, 5 min rest between, walk 800 meters
Saturday	Competition.		

Let's hope that, up to this point, things have gone according to your plans. During the next four weeks, your team will rest and compete. Workouts and training assume a secondary role. The major purpose of training during this period is restoration from a previous competition. If it is at all possible, you might schedule a stress workout early in the week, but allow plenty of time for recovery for Saturday's competition. This is a time for you to take a closer look at the fitness and health of each athlete. Some may need more rest than others. The following schedule is merely a guide. Let common sense govern your decisions. You have to become an artist again.

Weekly training schedule for hurdlers during the peaking period

Day	Duration (min)	Training task	Training details
Monday	20	Warm-up	Jog 1200 meters, calisthenics and stretching
	10	Sprint drills	High knees, 1, 2, 3s, chop downs, form runs
	30	Technique work	15×3 hurdles, walk back between
	10	Warm-down	Jog 800, walk 800, stretch
Tuesday	20	Warm-up	Jog 1600 meters, calisthenics and stretch
	20	Hurdle drills	Trail and lead leg drills
	10	Warm-down	Jog 400 meters, walk 400 meters
Wednesday	20	Warm-up	Jog 800 meters, stride 800 meters, stretch
	10	Sprint drills	Same as Monday
	10	Hurdle drills	Wall drills
	30	Hurdle technique	5×7 hurdles, 95% effort, rest to recovery between sets
	10	Warm-down	Jog 800, walk 400, stretch
Thursday	20	Warm-up	Jog 800, stride 400, calisthenics and stretch
	10	Sprint drills	High knees, chop downs, butt kicks, form runs
	30	Hurdle drills	Wall drills, drills on the side of the hurdles, starts to the first hurdle
	10	Warm-down	Jog 800, walk 800, stretch
Friday	20	Warm-up	Jog 800, stride 800, stretch
	10	Sprint drills	Same as Monday
	20	Hurdle drills	Lead leg and trail leg drill to the side of the hurdles
	20	Technique work	3×8 hurdles, 95% effort, rest to recovery between
	10	Warm-down	Jog 800, walk 400, stretch
Saturday			Competition. 110 meter highs, 4×100 relay, 4×400 relay.

The training schedule above contains the kind of peaking workouts that usually lead up to a major competition. There is just enough work to keep the body sharp and prepare the athlete for the next meet — not total rest, but an emphasis on recovery. If a hurdler seems to need more work — give it — but monitor the athlete's physical readiness closely. You don't want to leave the hurdler's best race at practice. Take resting pulse rates on a regular basis and ask each athlete for subjective information regarding his or her physical well-being. Look for subtle signs of fitness or lack of fitness. Do not be afraid to take a day off from practice if the team looks flat. Occasionally, go for an easy swim if rehabilitation seems necessary.

HURDLE TRAINING WITH LITTLE OR NO EQUIPMENT OR FACILITIES

Since hurdling is a technical event, it is imperative to train periodically with the proper facilities and equipment. When your athletes become proficient and skilled in the 110 meter hurdles, spend some time perfecting their technique at a local all-weather facility. There are probably several near your community. Call the local athletic director for permission to use their facility; most of these people will be glad to accommodate you. I often use the weekends for these work-outs, and bring only the hurdlers and relay teams so I can focus on their training needs. The rest of the time, we trained on our school grounds.

When I first took a coaching job, we didn't have a track or any hurdle equipment. We put sticks across chairs and we used "sticks and bricks." Soon after that, I asked the wood shop teacher to make us a few hurdles. He was glad to oblige. I bought ten hurdles with money we raised from a physique show, and we never looked back after that. A few years later, a friend from a local suburban high school bought a new set of hurdles and gave us their old set. A few screws and a little paint, and these hurdles looked as good as new.

Outdoor Surfaces

Some of the surfaces located near our school did not provide us with the proper traction, so we had to reduce the distance between the hurdles slightly. I often set the hurdles about 2–3 feet shorter than the official distance. This modification never seemed to bother our athletes in competition. I found that establishing the rhythm between the hurdles was more important than anything during the developmental stages. However, when we trained on asphalt or concrete, we found that the hurdlers could easily negotiate the official 10 yard distance between the hurdles. We had to be extremely careful about soft-tissue damage when using the sidewalk; the team ran on this surface only when we scheduled our easier workouts.

When we used cinder, grass, or dirt, the hurdles were placed closer together. Very few of our hurdlers could run the hurdles at the regular 10 yard distance on these surfaces. Training in this manner may seem counter-productive for championship hurdling, but some of the best hurdlers in the state came from this situation. The athletes never seemed to be negatively affected by these modifications.

Hallways and Corridors

During the indoor season, we trained in the halls. I tried to find an area that would not interfere with the rest of the team. We ran two flights of three to five hurdles most of the time. Since the majority of the indoor hurdle events were 55 meters, there was no need to run over more than five hurdles. As a matter of fact, our athletes seldom ran more than five hurdles outdoors. If we needed more stamina, they would run in sets of three to five hurdles back to back. That kind of workout built all the endurance we needed for outdoor competition.

Our hurdlers never seemed to suffer from any serious injuries training on these makeshift surfaces. In 36 years of coaching, we never had one serious case of shin splints or stress fractures due to hurdling on hard surfaces. The leg and foot exercises we advocated for sprinters in an earlier section prevented the onset of soft-tissue injuries to our hurdler's lower extremities.

Gymnasiums

One of the best places to train a hurdler indoors is in the gymnasium. This surface can absorb the shock to lower extremities. Whenever the gym was available, we used it.

Most gymnasiums can accommodate at least three hurdles. If we were forced to use a smaller gymnasium, I always found a way to set up three hurdles. We often ran hurdle workouts from one corner of the gym to the other.

There is always a place to train hurdlers. I have used cafeterias, gym balconies, auditoriums, and empty classrooms. I have used empty boxes, sticks across chairs, and high jump standards. The athletes found this variety of "facilities" and equipment exciting and interesting. We were never bored.

A CLOSER LOOK AT THE 110 METER HURDLES

The high hurdle race starts with the lead leg in the back of the blocks. At the sound of the gun, the hurdler drives out of the blocks and rises to full running form by the fourth stride. By the eighth stride, the hurdler literally "attacks" the first hurdle. The lead knee must be high and the lead foot must extend quickly and immediately snap down. The hurdler's attention is focused on the first hurdle. The trail leg is pulled through with the knee brought as high as possible under the armpit. The trail leg is swung forward and into the line of travel. The hurdler takes off approximately 7 feet in front of the hurdle and lands about 4 feet beyond the hurdle.

When the lead foot touches down, I teach the athlete to think in terms of a 10 yard dash to the next barrier (actually the distance is more like 20–21 feet). The hurdler must think of negotiating one hurdle at a time. It is counterproductive to think beyond the next hurdle to be cleared.

There is also a tendency for the torso to twist as the hurdler fatigues. Every effort should be made to keep the shoulders square throughout the race. Any incorrect action of lead arm can cause the torso to twist. As the lead arm extends forward on takeoff, it should not reach for the toe of the lead foot. This will cause the body to torque. If the body twists *before* takeoff, it has to twist in the *opposite* direction upon landing after clearing the hurdle (Newton's third law of motion). This twisting motion can become more of a problem with each ensuing hurdle.

Most hurdlers begin to tire at the seventh hurdle. Technique and form are often compromised and it becomes more difficult to maintain a rhythmic stride pattern. The two most crucial places to time your hurdler are at the first and seventh hurdle. Most hurdling problems occur at these critical stages in the race. If the athlete is in reasonable condition, speed at the first and seventh hurdle can determine the outcome of the race. If you time your athletes to the first hurdle and seventh on a regular basis and put them on the 4×400 relay team, most of their hurdling problems will be solved.

As the race progresses, the hurdler must not be distracted by the opponents. All of the athlete's attention should be focused on the next barrier. This focus should be so complete that the flailing arms of an opponent in the next lane will not disturb your hurdler. However, you should prepare your hurdler prior to the competition in regard to the lead arm of the opponent in the next lanes. Basically, if the opponent's lead arm is next to your runner, your athlete has to be prepared to deal with a swinging arm from that lane. To be forewarned is to be forearmed.

After the last hurdle is cleared, there is the all important 15 yard finishing sprint. This skill must be practiced regularly. I have seen hurdle races won and lost in the last few yards. The lean at the tape can also be miscalculated; the timing of this finishing skill takes quite a bit of time to develop.

Hurdle Efficiency

I chose Willie Davenport as a model hurdler for several reasons — his impeccable technique and his ability to perform under pressure, and his willingness to share knowledge with a perfect stranger. There have been hurdlers who have exceeded his best time (13.2), but no one has been more efficient than Willie Davenport in hurdle clearance. Willie Davenport's best 100 yard dash was 9.4 seconds. I calculated that he could probably run 110 meters (without hurdles), in approximately 11.3 seconds. Therefore, hurdle clearance for the entire race cost him less than two seconds. You can use this formula to determine the effectiveness of your runner's hurdle technique.

CONCLUDING REMARKS

Hurdlers can be the most versatile and valuable members on your track team. They can be highly competitive in almost all of the track and field events. This explains why most of America's decathlon and heptathlon champions often come from the ranks of great hurdlers. Hurdlers have also been world-class performers in several events outside their specialty. Dan O'Brien, the 1996 Olympic decathlon champion, is a world-class 110 meter hurdler. Gail Devers is a world-class competitor in the 100 meter dash and the 100 meter hurdles. Jackie Joyner Kersee, the world record holder in the heptathlon, is a world-class hurdler. The list is endless. Hurdlers have singlehandedly won conference and national championships. Because of their versatility, hurdlers are the consummate athletes.

Section 13

THE INTERMEDIATE HURDLES
Moses and the Promised Land

Intermediate hurdlers have struggled with the step pattern of the 400 meter hurdles for several decades. Some used a 15-step pattern; others tried 14 and switched to 15 near the end of the race. Olympic champion John Aki-Bua from Uganda tried 13 and switched to 14. Then, a young upstart from a little Division III college (Morehouse), known more for academics than athletics, did the impossible and negotiated 13 steps between all ten hurdles. This athlete dominated the 400 meter hurdles for eight years. His name is Edwin Moses. Training techniques and physical conditioning for this event are covered in this section.

The intermediate hurdles were a complicated event until Edwin Moses (the 1976 and the 1984 Olympic champion), appeared on the international scene and revolutionized the event. Edwin Moses competed for Morehouse College in Atlanta, Georgia which was known for everything but track and field.

His approach to the 400 meter hurdles simplified the event and solved all kinds of problems related to the stride pattern between the hurdles. The stride pattern between the high hurdles has never been an issue. Everyone does three steps in between the hurdles. But when world-class runners competed in the intermediate hurdles, there was no such consensus. Some ran 15 all the way. Others tried 14 and changed to 15. A few tried 13 to the curve, switched to 14, and finished with 15 strides. There were all kinds of stride patterns — until Edwin Moses ran a 13-step stride pattern. As simple as this concept was, no one ever ran 13 all the way. As it is with all revolutionary concepts, no one beat Edwin Moses until they accepted his idea. Until someone finally discovered that Edwin was right, this genius of the intermediate hurdles ran over 100 consecutive races without a loss. His undefeated streak spanned 10 years.

Morehouse College is an unlikely place for a world-class hurdler to stage a revolution in track and field. This all-black institution is known primarily for the development of great scholars and Nobel prize winners. This is the school that turns out African-American intellects by the thousands. The great civil rights leader, Dr. Martin Luther King, Jr., was one of its many renowned graduates. Edwin Moses enrolled at Morehouse and majored in physics. He was not, by any stretch of the imagination, a jock. Edwin was no prep track phenom; he was an intellect. His track coach, though competent, was primarily a man of the cloth. There are a number of historically black colleges and universities that are famous for producing great track stars — Tennessee State University, Texas Southern, Grambling, Florida A and M, Tuskeegee Institute, Morgan State, Southern University, and North Carolina Central University. All of these schools have developed world-class athletes in track and field, but Morehouse never had. This was the most unlikely place for a revolution in the intermediate hurdles to take place.

How did this happen? Until the advent of the Eastern Europeans, most track and field techniques were based on tradition more than science. Then someone came along and broke with tradition and set the track and field world upside down. The records fell and everyone wondered why they didn't think of such a logical solution to a particular problem. Since Morehouse College had no track tradition, all Edwin Moses had was science to rely upon. Apparently science was enough. Why not 13 steps between each hurdle? So what if no one had done it before!

Didn't Parry O' Brien, Brian Oldfield, Dick Fosbury, Valeri Brumel, Aubrey Dooley, and Roger Bannister turn their backs on tradition? Track and field has

Photo 13–1. A potential intermediate hurdler practicing his technique on a sidewalk near the school.

not been the same. From these people came innovative techniques that revolutionized the shot put, high jump, pole vaulting, and middle-distance running. Like Edwin Moses, these people walked — or if you will, ran — to the beat of a different drummer.

Running 13 steps between the barriers was the next logical innovation in intermediate hurdling. Any improvement in this event had to go the way of a longer stride. They had gone as far as possible with the amalgam of 15-, 14-, and 13-step stride pattern. Why not 13 all the way? When you mix the strides, you have to clear each hurdle with a different lead leg, which inevitably complicates matters. With 13 all the way, a hurdler can use the same lead leg every time. Simple calculation could have proven that most intermediate hurdlers had a stride length that could accommodate a 13-step stride pattern. Subtract 11 feet for takeoff and landing from 35 meters or 114' 10" (the distance between hurdles), and you have approximately 103' 10" left. Divide 103' 10" by 13 and your stride should be approximately 2.42 meters. Translate that to feet and you need aproximately a 7' 10" stride pattern. A mature runner over 6' 2" in height should be able to hold a stride pattern of that length all the way to the last hurdle. The problem is going to be a little more difficult when a hurdler of the future uses a 12-step stride pattern. Now you are back to alternating lead legs over each hurdle. But 12 strides between the hurdles has to be the next logical step in the development of this event. For those who want to go this route, their stride length would have to be aproximately 8' 6". There must be an intermediate hurdler out there somewhere who can run that stride pattern. If this is the case, the 46-second intermediate hurdles will be just a matter of time.

TALENT IDENTIFICATION

Most high school coaches usually convert their 110 meter hurdlers to the intermediate hurdles. This is relatively easy to do because the high school event is only 300 meters. There is a world of difference between the high school event and the collegiate 400 meter hurdles. Those extra 100 meters place an extraordinary challenge on an athlete's metabolism. For that reason, it is difficult to compare the training for 300 meter hurdles to that of the 400 meter hurdles. The 400 meters *without hurdles* is called "the man-killer of track"; can you imagine how exhausting it is to run the 400 meters *with hurdles*?

Occasionally, a prep 110 meter hurdler will double as a 300 meter hurdler but seldom runs the 400 meter hurdles in college. Conversely, world-class 400 meter hurdlers can conduct themselves quite well in 110 meter hurdles, but it is extremely difficult to be world-class in both. You have to specialize.

Edwin Moses ran 13.6 in the 110 meter hurdles, 1:48 in the 800 meters and 45.6 in the 400 meters. That range of abilities lends itself to an outstanding 400 meter hurdles. For that reason a 400 meter hurdler needs endurance similar to that of a half-miler. Most of the mature candidates for the 400 meter hurdles should come from the ranks of athletes who can double in the 400 and 800 meters.

Though there have been intermediate hurdlers who were short in stature, better than average height is a definite asset in this event. The fewer strides an athlete takes between the hurdles, the better the result. And a taller athlete can master this more efficient stride pattern much easier than a shorter hurdler.

The best place to recruit intermediate hurdlers is from your track team. After you have assessed the various talents of the athletes you have, move the runners whose characteristics fit the "job description" to the intermediate hurdles.

TECHNICAL ASPECTS

Try to identify intermediate hurdlers as soon as possible. Then teach the candidates to hurdle with either leg from the beginning. This tactic will pay great dividends later on. As a matter of fact, athletes who learn to alternate will avoid problems as they mature. I have seen some athletes' stride pattern change in the middle of the year. Runners may switch from 17 to 16 to 15 within a season. When they switch from 17 to 16, they will have to alternate. You might as well teach the hurdlers to alternate from the beginning and save yourself a headache. In the future, some gifted hurdler may need to run 12 strides and should be ready to alternate when it becomes necessary.

It is also very important to have an idea of the stride pattern of your prospective intermediate hurdlers from the beginning. Listed below are measurements of the average stride patterns of the typical intermediate hurdlers that you may encounter. If you know their stride length, the hurdlers can count the number of steps between each hurdle and be relatively certain of this even before they make their first attempt:

Strides between hurdles	Strides to first hurdle	Approximate stride length
12	19	8′ 6″
13	20	7′ 10″
14	21	7′ 5″
15	22	6′ 11″
16	23	6′ 6″
17	24	6′ 3″

How to Establish a Stride Pattern

1. Some athletes count every step between the hurdles until a rhythm is established. After the hurdler has become experienced in the intermediates, the counting can be discontinued. Some hurdlers may not be able to count in this manner. They may still stall at the hurdles. Stalling or stutter-stepping at the hurdle can be a fate worse than death. If this habit is learned, there is no successful intermediate hurdling. What may be in order is another system of counting.

2. Another way to count is to divide the steps by two and count in two groups so that the numbers will be in single digits. A hurdler who has a 15-step pattern would count 7, followed by a count of 8 steps. This method seems to prevent stalling at the hurdle because it is easier to teach athletes to attack the hurdle in the last 8 steps.

3. Counting every time the trail leg foot touches down is another excellent way to establish a stride pattern. In this case, a 15 stride athlete will count 8 steps starting with the trail leg, count *only* the trail leg, and think "kick" as the lead leg attacks the hurdle. It may be easier for some athletes to establish a rhythm with this system.

4. Some athletes never count steps. If they can set a stride pattern without counting, let them. It happens occasionally.

5. Hurdlers who have an even stride pattern must alternate. They usually don't have to count steps either, but they must be taught how to judge when they are the correct distance from the hurdle to properly negotiate clearance. One way to teach this skill is to set the hurdles anywhere around the track to train alternators to judge when to clear the hurdle regardless of the spacing. After they have learned to do this, teach them to anticipate which hurdle will require a left lead leg clearance, and which will require a right lead leg.

6. Some hurdlers will change their stride pattern on the curve. We tried to eliminate this problem, and it wouldn't go away. Some of our hurdlers would start out with 15 steps and change to 16 on the curve. Subconsciously, they were easing up for the last part of the race, and would not accelerate into the turn. If this is the case, the hurdlers must

take 16 steps over two consecutive hurdles so they can finish the race on the preferred lead leg. If this procedure is followed, the hurdler will take only one hurdle with the nondominant lead leg.

The best of all worlds is to teach your intermediate hurdlers to alternate lead legs. You never know when a strong wind will come from the north and interfere with the stride pattern. On several occasions, the meet director accidentally put the hurdles on the wrong line, and all the hurdlers' steps were off but ours. Teach your kids to alternate.

Teaching hurdlers to alternate is not too difficult, since they are often the most well-coordinated athletes on the track team. Take them through the same drills outlined in the beginning of section 12. This learning process will take a little longer with the nondominant leg, especially if they are learning this skill after hurdling for several years. The best approach is to spend more time hurdling with the nondominant leg. We actually designated days when we did all our hurdling with the nondominant leg.

During the indoor season, have hurdlers compete in a few meets using the unfamiliar technique. They may feel awkward for a while, but the frustration of learning this new skill will be worth it in the long run.

7. Always remember, hurdlers using an *even stride pattern* to the first hurdle must have the *lead foot* in the *back* position in the starting blocks, and using an *odd number* of strides will put the *trail leg* in the *back*. There will also be times when you can disregard counting steps to the first hurdle. Just have them try the lead foot in the back block; if that doesn't work, reverse the foot placement and try it again.

Intermediate Hurdle Technique

Intermediate hurdlers may not have to make an appreciable modification in their running form to clear the barriers. Since the hurdles are only 3 feet in height, tall hurdlers can literally step over the hurdle with very little alteration in running form. This does not mean hurdle technique can be ignored. Efficient hurdle clearance can greatly reduce any unnecessary expenditure of energy during the race. Efficient hurdle clearance means that the intermediate hurdler should raise the center of gravity slightly with only an insignificant deviation from an erect running posture. The biggest modification of the normal running form is that the lead swings wide to maintain balance. The trail leg knee should also be brought high under the armpit as the runner negotiates the hurdle.

TRAINING PROGRAMS

The intermediate hurdler's training year begins with the cross country season. The physiological parameters of most intermediate hurdlers is an amalgam between a 400 and 800 meter runner; endurance and stamina training is an absolute requirement for this demanding event. The intermediate hurdler can often train and participate as a viable member of your cross-country team, using workouts identical to those recommended for the 800 meter runner.

The cross-country season usually ends in early November, and your intermediate hurdlers should spend the remainder of this month and most of December in a rather informal period of "active" rest. They should spend this time participating in various recreational activities. Some recommended ones are volleyball, basketball, soccer, weight training, gymnastics, and swimming. These activities will prevent physiological detraining that could occur by doing little or nothing of a physical nature. The physiological, psychological and emotional value of this training period will help hurdlers recharge their batteries and still maintain a reasonable level of fitness.

The middle of January is the official beginning of our indoor track season. At this point, most of the track team has embarked upon the general preparation period. The general preparation period for intermediate hurdlers is similar to the general preparation period recommended for 800 meter runners. The only difference is the inclusion of various hurdling drills. These are basically the same drills suggested for 110 meter hurdlers.

Some of your intermediate hurdlers will be 110 meter hurdler specialists. If this is the case, the focus of the training program will be on training for the shorter event. Since the high school intermediate hurdles are shorter in distance, and therefore less demanding than the 400 meter hurdles, the athlete should follow the 110 meter hurdle training schedule with certain minor modifications.

A 110 meter hurdler who doubles as a 300 meter hurdler should devote approximately half the time working on the step pattern of the longer event. The hurdle form learned by a high hurdler has an excellent carryover value to the 300 meter hurdles. Most world-class high hurdlers were outstanding 300 meter hurdlers in high school; however, very few of these athletes doubled in the two hurdle events in college. I have seen an occasional athlete run both hurdle events in college, but almost never in Division I competition. The physical demands of the 400 meter hurdles are so severe that most athletes usually specialize in the longer event.

The specific preparation period beginning in February is when the intermediate hurdler begins to specialize. Your intermediate hurdler will participate in a variety of events during the indoor season, but this participation is designed to prepare for outdoor competition. In our area, there is no intermediate hurdle competition indoors. Specific preparation for the 300 and 400 hurdles has to be done in practice.

Weekly training schedule for intermediate hurdlers for the specific preparation period

Day	Duration (min)	Training task	Training details
Monday	20	Warm-up	1600 meter jog, calisthenics and stretching
	10	Sprint drills	High knees, 1, 2, 3s, chop downs
	10	Hurdle drills	Trail leg and lead leg drills

Day	Duration (min)	Training task	Training details
	20	Stair running	3 min stairs, 3 min jog, 3 min wind sprints
	10	Intermediate	Work on steps to the first hurdle
		Hurdle drill	(45 meters)
	5	Warm-down	Walk 800 meters, stretch
Tuesday	20	Warm-up	Easy interval running 100 meter strides, calisthenics, stretching
	10	Sprint drills	Same as Monday
	10	Hurdle drills	Trail leg and lead leg drills with the nondominant leg
	30	Technique work	50 hurdles 25×2 (35 meters apart), walk between
	10	Warm-down	800 meter jog and stretch
Wednesday	20	Warm-up	1600 meters fartlek, stretch
	10	Sprint drills	High knees, chop downs, quick step
	10	Hurdle drills	High knees and trail leg drills (alternating)
	20	Stair running	Same as Monday
	10	Warm-down	800 meter jog, 800 meter walk
Thursday	20	Warm-up	800 meter jog. 800 meter wind sprints, calisthenics and stretching
	10	Sprint drills	Same as Wednesday
	30	Technique work	50 hurdles, place the hurdles various distances apart (for lead leg judgment)
	10	Warm-down	Walk 800 meters, stretch
Friday	10	Warm-up	800 meter jog, stretch
	20	Hurdle drills	Wall drills, lead leg and trail leg
	10	Technique work	3×5 high hurdles, 90% speed, rest 5 mins between sets

Saturday   Competition. Run the 55 meter high hurdles. Run the 800 meter run.

This is a four-week cycle beginning in February. The intermediate hurdlers have no choice; they have to compete in the high hurdles. The only experience they have with the intermediate hurdles will be in practice. The early involvement with the techniques of this event during the week will keep them acquainted with the step pattern of the intermediates. We work with only two or three hurdles, because most of our hurdling is done in the school corridors. This truncated hurdle practice can adequately prepare the athlete's stride pattern for the outdoor hurdles.

The next cycle is the pre-competitive period. Our intermediate hurdlers have to prepare for the indoor conference championship that has only the 55 meter high hurdles on the program. Continue to divide training time between both types of hurdles in preparation for the outdoor season.

Most talented intermediate hurdlers can hold their own against the high hurdle specialist. On the high school level, some of the better high hurdlers often win important championships in both hurdles. One notable example, Greg Foster, Olympic silver medalist and world champion in the 110 meter high hurdles, was the Illinois state champion in the 300 meter hurdles. By the same token, Rodney Milburn, the 1972 Olympic champion in the 110 meter high hurdles, was the Golden West champion in the intermediate hurdles. Your hurdlers will not experience a great deal of difficulty competing in both events on the high school level.

Weekly training schedule for intermediate hurdlers
during the precompetitive period

Day	Duration (min)	Training task	Training details
Monday	20	Warm-up	1600 meter jog, calisthenics and stretching
	10	Sprint drills	High knees, chop downs, form runs
	10	Hurdle drills	Trail leg and lead leg drills over high and intermediate hurdles
	30	Technique work	15×5 hurdles. walk back between, 15×3 intermediate hurdles
	10	Warm-down	800 meter walk, stretch
Tuesday	20	Warm-up	800 meter jog, 800 meter wind sprints calisthenics and stretch
	10	Hurdle drills	Wall drills, lead leg and trail leg
	30	Technique work	15×3 hurdles (intermediates) jog back between
	10	Warm-down	Walk 800 meters, stretch
Wednesday	20	Warm-down	Jog 1200 meters, stretch
	10	Sprint drills	High knees, chop downs, form runs

Day	Duration (min)	Training task	Training details
	10	Hurdle drills	Work the nondominant leg (intermediate hurdles)
	30	Technique work	20 × first hurdle
	10	Warm-down	Jog 800, walk 800, stretch
Thursday	20	Warm-up	Jog 800 meters, 800 meter wind sprints
	10	Hurdle drills	Trail leg × 20, lead leg × 20, alternate lead leg
	30	Technique work	20 × 3 hurdles (intermediates)
	10	Warm-down	Walk 800, stretch
Friday	20	Warm-up	Jog 800, stride 800, walk 800, stretch
	10	Sprint drills	High knees, 1,2,3s, form runs
	10	Hurdle drills	Trail leg and lead leg drills (nondominant leg)
	20	Technique work	3 × 7 high hurdles, walk back between
	10	Warm-down	Walk 800, stretch
Saturday	Competition.		Run high hurdles and the 600 meter run or the 4 × 400 relay.

This workout represents the culmination of the indoor season. Give the intermediate hurdlers a week of "active" rest; take a vacation from hurdling. After this brief recreational period, try to find a nearby all-weather track to work on stride patterns. A few sessions will help to establish the necessary rhythm between the intermediate hurdles. Check the weather report in the morning. It is best to establish the stride pattern on a warm day, and next to impossible to do it in cold weather.

During the early part of April, try to capitalize on the warm-weather days. However, prepare the team for any sudden change in weather. Any day that the temperature is above 60 degrees has to be a speed work day. The competitive period schedule on the next page is merely a guide. Take advantage of whatever day is warm enough to permit speed work.

You may have noticed that weight training is not listed in the workouts. Weight training is an integral part of our program; see Section 20. We do most of our weight training or resistance work after our track work is completed. The athletes return to school for workouts or we will do heavy gymnastics or resistance training with surgical tubing at the track. If we have a track meet on Saturday, our last resistance workout is on Wednesday. Occasionally, we will do several unique free-hand exercises that are just as effective as weight training. More about this later in Section 20.

Weekly training for intermediate hurdlers during the competitive period

Day	Duration (min)	Training task	Training details
Monday	20	Warm-up	Jog 1600 meters, calisthenics, stretch
	10	Sprint drills	High knees, 1, 2, 3s, chop downs, etc.
	15	Hurdle drills	Trail leg and lead leg drills (the hurdles are 7 ft. apart), repeat with opposite leg
	30	Interval hurdling	2×4 hurdles, 4 sets from the blocks and 4 sets from the curve to the finish
	10	Warm-down	Jog 800 meters, walk 800 meters, stretch
Tuesday	20	Warm-up	Jog 800 meters, 800 meters wind sprints
	10	Hurdle drills	Wall drills, alternate legs
	30	Technique work	16×3 hurdles (8× with left lead leg and 8× with right lead leg)
	10	Warm-down	Jog 800 meters, stretch
Wednesday	20	Warm-up	Jog 1600 meters, calisthenics, stretch
	10	Sprint drills	Same as Monday
	10	Hurdle drills	Trail leg and lead leg drills, hurdles 7 ft. apart
	30	Technique work	Starts to first hurdle 30 times
	10	Warm-down	Jog 800 meters, walk 800 meters, stretch
Thursday	20	Warm-up	Jog 1600 meters. calisthenics, stretch
	10	Sprint drills	Same as Tuesday
	30	Speed work	Train with the quarter-milers
	10	Warm-down	1600 meters, stretch
Friday	20	Warm-up	Jog 800 meters,10×100 meters, stretch
	10	Sprint drills	High knees, chop downs, form runs
	10	Hurdle drills	Wall drills
	20	Technique work	Set 5 intermediate hurdles at arbitrary distances (judgment drill)
	10	Warm-down	Walk 800 meters, stretch
Saturday		Competition.	High hurdles, intermediate hurdles, run a leg on the mile relay.

Establishing the correct stride pattern in the intermediate hurdles is the most important goal at this time. During this cycle, your hurdlers should be in excellent running condition. Assess this by their earlier performances in the 4×400 relay. If your hurdlers are fit, the stride pattern between the hurdles can finally be determined without being affected by overwhelming fatigue. Intermediate hurdlers should know at this point in the season if the stride pattern is 15 all the way, or at what point in the race that pattern will change. Those who alternate should decide which takeoff leg to use before the race. When they develop consistency of the stride pattern, they can focus better on the race.

Some of your younger hurdlers may still be struggling with their steps. This is to be expected. The adolescent growth spurt will continue to affect the stride pattern. I have seen young hurdlers change stride patterns almost every week. This is another reason you should teach these youngsters to alternate at the beginning of the season.

The next cycle is the peaking period. This is the period that you try to tie together all the loose ends in the hurdler's technical problems. As mentioned earlier in this section, the athlete's performance in the 200 meters, 400 meters, and 800 meters can often reveal the hurdler's readiness for competition. Use this information to determine the nature of your hurdler's training program for the weeks leading up to the conference championships and beyond.

Weekly training schedule for intermediate hurdlers during the peaking period

Day	Duration (min)	Training task	Training details
Monday	20	Warm-up	Jog 1200 meters, calisthenics and stretching
	10	Sprint drills	High knees, 1, 2, 3s, form runs
	30	Technique work	$5 \times$ first 4, $5 \times$ second four (intermediates)
	10	Warm-down	Jog 800, walk 800, stretch
Tuesday	20	Warm-up	Jog 1200 meters, stride 200 meters, stretch
	10	Hurdle drills	Trail and lead leg drills over hurdles
	10	Warm-down	Jog 400 meters, walk 800 meters, stretch
Wednesday	20	Warm-up	Jog 1600 meters, calisthenics and stretch
	10	Sprint drills	Same as Monday
	10	Hurdle drills	Wall drills, trail leg and lead leg drills (hurdles)
	30	Technique work	5×1 hurdle, 5×7 hurdles, 95% effort, rest to recovery between sets
	10	Warm-down	Jog 800, walk 800, stretch

Day	Duration (min)	Training task	Training details
Thursday	20	Warm-up	Jog 800, stride 800, stretch
	10	Hurdle drills	Drills to the side of the hurdle (trail and lead leg)
	20	Technique work	7×1 hurdle
	10	Warm-down	Jog 400, walk 800, stretch
Friday	20	Warm-up	Jog 800, stretch
	20	Sprint and hurdle drills	Same as Monday
	20	Technique work	$2 \times$ first 4 hurdles, $2 \times$ last 4 hurdles, rest to recovery between
	10	Warm-down	Jog 800, walk 400 meters, stretch

Saturday   Competition.   Intermediate hurdles, 4×400 relay.

None of the preceding workouts consists of running a full flight of hurdles. Usually, there is no real purpose in attempting the entire event in practice. There are often too many problems to be attacked to make this enterprise practical. Workouts are more effective when you look at segments of an intermediate hurdles race and make immediate corrections. Most hurdlers find it difficult to negotiate an entire flight correctly in practice more than once or twice. If there are several technical flaws, there is often not enough energy left to repeat the exercise. It is far better to run through segments of the race and correct the stride patterns and hurdle technique when the athlete is fresh. Constant and repetitive work on the rhythm and technique of the intermediates is the best approach in this most crucial cycle.

It is also especially important to critique the hurdler's performance in competition. You can observe any major weaknesses and flaws in the athlete's technique under the pressure of competition. Then, the nature and extent of the next week's workout can be based upon your analysis of the hurdler's technique.

Your hurdlers' level of fitness should not be a major concern during this part of the season. All of the training that occurred in the previous cycles should have prepared them for this peaking period. The prime directive in the final weeks of the season should be rest, restoration, and competition.

INTERMEDIATE HURDLING WITH LITTLE OR NO EQUIPMENT OR FACILITIES

After establishing the athletes' stride pattern at your training site, you should spend some time training with the proper facilities and equipment. Running in parking lots and makeshift running areas is acceptable and convenient during the developmental stages, but the best way to get your athlete ready for competition in the intermediate hurdles is on an all-weather 400 meter track. The transition from a parking lot, playground, or a cinder track is too much of an adjustment for even the best of athletes. Their stride pattern will invariably be inaccurate. One or two sessions on an all-weather track is the best preparation for competition on an all-weather track. (I am assuming that your conference, sectional, regional, and state meets are held on an all-weather track). If you have prepared your athletes properly, you will probably clear up their stride pattern problems in one or two workouts. You may have to give up a few weekends to accomplish this task, but the effort is worth it.

Find a track; most athletic directors will be willing to give you permission to use their facilities. Someone, somewhere, has to have one within reasonable driving distance. You may have to drive a few miles to find it, but you won't have to do this more than one or two times. Once the rhythm of the athlete's stride pattern is established, you probably won't need to borrow an all-weather facility for the rest of the season. You can solve the remainder of your hurdlers' technical problems in competition or at your "facility."

Section 14

THE HIGH JUMP
The Cow Jumped
Over the Moon

The cow in the Mother Goose nursery rhyme must have used all the latest training methods to make such a remarkable high jump. Human beings, in an effort to defy the omnipresent pull of gravity, have fallen short of this fabulous achievement, but we are getting closer. Modern training methods — plyometrics, periodization, and weight training — have made the seven-foot high jump a common occurrence. A Cuban high jumper has had the temerity to jump eight feet. This section will be devoted to developing a champion high jumper. The cow's record may be in jeopardy.

It was pure fiction, but that unbelievable high jump by the cow in the Mother Goose nursery rhyme was approximately 240,000 miles. Superman was also capable of a remarkable high jump; the man of steel leaped over tall buildings in a single bound. The best jump by a human being was a magnificent 8 feet by Javier Sotomayor of Cuba. I have no idea how the cow trained, but I am willing to bet that a jump of that magnitude was accomplished by doing plenty of plyometrics and weight training.

The high jump has gone through several technical changes since the first Olympics were held in 1896. All of these efforts were adopted to manipulate the body's center of gravity in the most effective manner to achieve bar clearance. High jump technique has undergone the following changes since 1896:

1. *The scissors.* The leg nearest the bar is kicked upward and the takeoff leg is lifted as the jumper clears the bar in an upright position.

2. *The eastern cutoff.* This style of high jumping was a modified scissors with a forward layout. This technique has to be seen to be believed. The female olympic champion Iolanda Balas was using this unusual technique as late as 1961.

3. *The western roll.* The outside leg is kicked upward and the plant foot or takeoff leg is the inside leg. The jumper clears the bar with a side layout.

4. *The straddle roll.* This jump is similar to the western roll, but the jumper clears the bar face downward.

5. *The Fosbury Flop.* The leg nearest to the bar is kicked upward and the plant foot is the outside foot. The jumper clears the bar with the back to the bar. For several years, a few high jumpers stubbornly continued to use the straddle technique, but I have not seen anyone use the straddle jump in twenty years. Every jumper in the 1996 Olympics used the Fosbury Flop.

Several years ago, I attended a track clinic at the University of Wisconsin. Geoffrey Dyson, the author of the book *The Mechanics of Athletics,* spoke on the subject of the high jump for four days. He stated that high jumpers have not fully exploited the potential of the eastern cutoff or the straddle roll. Before these two techniques could be perfected, Dick Fosbury appeared on the scene in 1968 and revolutionized high jump technique. The high jump has not been the same since that time.

The high jump is all about the manipulation of a jumper's center of gravity. Most of the earlier techniques were an attempt to manipulate the center of gravity over the bar. The Fosbury Flop technique does this better than any method that preceded it. If the jumper can time the backward arch properly it *may* be possible for the jumper's center of gravity to pass beneath the cross bar.

Most Floppers can approach the bar at a much greater speed. It is more difficult to do this with previous techniques. This greater speed also made it possible to attain the incredible clearances that have become commonplace in recent years. According to Geoffrey Dyson, someone might have jumped 8 feet using the eastern or the straddle but we will never know, since no one uses these techniques anymore.

Another advantage of the Flop technique is the virtual elimination of "eccentric thrust." The earlier high jump methods made it difficult to jump without offsetting the body's center of gravity. Upon takeoff, most jumpers found it necessary to lean away from the center of gravity in order to negotiate bar clearance. The great Russian high jumper, Valeri Brummel (using the straddle technique), seemed to reduce this technical flaw to a minimum, but it was still there. With the Fosbury Flop, the takeoff foot is directly below the center of gravity. When the takeoff foot is directly below the center of gravity, a more efficient delivery of force can be manifest by the takeoff leg.

The Fosbury Flop is relatively easy to learn. For most athletes, it takes several seasons to perfect the eastern and straddle rolls. A reasonably coordinated athlete can learn the Fosbury Flop in one training session. I have seen members of our track team observe the high jumpers practicing and before long everybody who wanted to try was doing a crude version of the Flop technique. The technique is easy to learn, but like any discipline, perfection does not come easily. However, because we didn't have a decent high jump pit, our jumpers would arrive at a meet early, practice the technique prior to competition, and subsequently win the event. Their form had a lot to be desired, but this never could have happened with any other style of high jumping.

Before the Fosbury became popular, the high jump was a relatively inexpensive event. All you needed was an area of dirt covered with sawdust (outdoors) or several gymnastics mats indoors. Now you need a $1,000 Port-A-Pit. The new technique cannot be used on a regular gym mat because of the backward landing that is a part of the Fosbury Flop. If you do not have access to a commercially made landing pit, then it becomes necessary to innovate or create a viable alternative. However, in the meantime try to raise funds in order to purchase a pit. A regular, commercially made pit is much safer, and the jumper can concentrate on jumping and not have to be concerned with the possibility of injury to the neck or spine. Later in this section, I will describe a few creative ways to develop a high jumper safely until the real thing arrives.

TALENT IDENTIFICATION

The best place to look for high jumpers is at a basketball game. Sit and watch the pregame warm-up, and you will see more high jump talent than you can imagine. At the 1977 Illinois State championship, Gail Olson won with a jump of 7' 2". The runner-up, Tyke Peacock jumped 7' 0". Both of these athletes were basketball players. Several basketball players joined our team in April of their senior year. Two of these athletes jumped 6' 8" before the end of the season.

It is also possible to find a high jumper by administrating a reach jump test. This is a quick and easy way to discover high jump talent. Have the prospective jumpers reach as high as possible and make a mark on a wall with a piece of chalk. Ask the candidates to jump upward (from a stand) and make another mark with the chalk. Measure the distance between the two marks. If an athlete's measurement is over 24 inches, this *may* indicate talent for the high jump. The correlation between a standing vertical jump and an actual high jump is not perfect, but this test can help you expedite your high jump tryouts.

Occasionally, your coaching instincts will lead you to invite a few youngsters who have demonstrated no tangible physical traits that would indicate high jump talent to try the event. Go with your gut reaction.

Once you have the candidate's vertical jump measurement, it is possible to predict (within a few inches), how the individual will do in the actual high jump. Let's assume that a jumper is 6 feet tall (tall athletes have an advantage in this event), and has a vertical jump of 3 feet:

The jumper's height divided by 2 = 3 feet + 3 foot vertical = 6 feet + technique (4 inches) = 6' 4" + weight training and plyometrics (4") = 6' 8" + run-up (2") = 6' 10". Some jumpers will do better than this formula predicts and some will do slightly worse. There are various intangibles that can modify a jumper's results (work ethic, belief system, attitude, etc.) No one has been able to accurately measure these factors.

TECHNICAL ASPECTS

There is a "unified theory," if you will, for all jumping events. The most important part of all jumping events is the run-up prior to the jump. Without a well-calculated and properly executed run-up, there cannot be championship jumping. The run-up for all jumping events has to be practiced until some consistency in the stride pattern becomes second nature. This leaves the jumper's mind free to concentrate on the jump itself.

The least complicated way to establish the run-up is to remove the crossbar, run through the steps, and execute a scissors jump into the pit. Try 3 steps, then 5, 7, 9, and finally, 11 steps (see Figure 14-1 on page 218). Initially, try a scissors jump with and without the crossbar. The angle of the approach should be at approximately a 20–40 degree angle to the bar. By doing a scissors jump, your jumper can concentrate on the run up and not be concerned about bar clearance. Work on the run-up so that steps 11–7 are preparatory and under control. From step 7, your jumper begins to attack the bar. The last 5 steps, the athlete begins to curve away from the bar. This is often referred as the "J" approach. Some jumpers may prefer an even number of steps and start their counting with the kickup leg or inside foot. Others start counting their steps with the plant or outside foot. We found that counting the outside (plant) foot was easier.

To make sure that we are on the same page, please visualize that we are talking about a jumper who approaches the crossbar from the right and plants with the left foot at the takeoff.

Our first session in establishing steps begins with the jumper's touching the bar at arm's length and shoulder height, and running away from the bar for the

Figure 14-1

MEASURING STEPS FOR THE HIGH JUMP

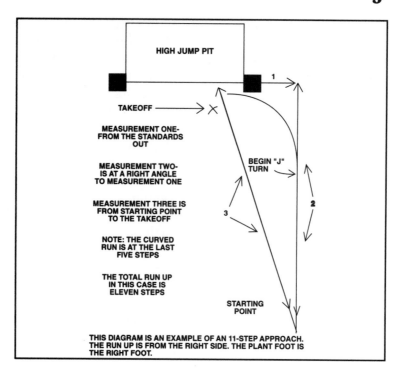

HIGH JUMP PIT

TAKEOFF ⟶ ✕

1

MEASUREMENT ONE-
FROM THE STANDARDS
OUT

MEASUREMENT TWO-
IS AT A RIGHT ANGLE
TO MEASUREMENT ONE

BEGIN "J"
TURN

MEASUREMENT THREE IS
FROM STARTING POINT
TO THE TAKEOFF

2

NOTE: THE CURVED
RUN IS AT THE LAST
FIVE STEPS

3

THE TOTAL RUN UP
IN THIS CASE IS
ELEVEN STEPS

STARTING
POINT

THIS DIAGRAM IS AN EXAMPLE OF AN 11-STEP APPROACH.
THE RUN UP IS FROM THE RIGHT SIDE. THE PLANT FOOT IS
THE RIGHT FOOT.

Figure 14-2

HIGH JUMP —
FINAL STEP

HEAD IS BACK
AND UP

BOTH ARMS ARE
DRIVEN DOWN
AND
SUBSEQUENTLY
FORWARD AND
UPWARD TO INCREASE
GROUND FORCE

FINAL STEP IS
AHEAD OF
THE CENTER OF
GRAVITY AND ON
THE LEFT HEEL

RIGHT KNEE WILL
DRIVE UP AND AWAY
FROM THE
CROSSBAR WHEN
THE CENTER OF
GRAVITY MOVES
OVER THE LEFT
FOOT

Figure 14-3

HIGH JUMP —
TAKEOFF

THE RIGHT
ARM IS
DRIVING UP
AND TOWARD
THE
CROSSBAR.
THIS WILL
RAISE THE
JUMPER'S
CENTER OF
GRAVITY

HEAD AND
EYES ARE UP

THE RIGHT
KNEE IS
LIFTED UP
AND AWAY
FROM THE
BAR

NOTE: SOME
JUMPERS WILL
"BLOCK" WITH
BOTH ARMS.
THIS JUMPER
HAS NOT

THE JUMPER
IS PUSHING
UPWARD WITH
THE TOES OF
THE LEFT
FOOT

THE JUMPER'S
CENTER OF
GRAVITY IS
DIRECTLY ABOVE
THE LEFT (TAKE
OFF) LEG. THIS
ELIMINATES
ECCENTRIC
THRUST

prearranged 11 steps. Mark the spot where the 11th step was made. Have the jumper run toward the pit and jump into the pit without a crossbar in place. Repeat this exercise until the jumper feels confident with the stride pattern. Have the jumper take an easy scissors jump with this stride pattern to further determine the accuracy of the run up.

Once the stride pattern is established, the next step is to measure the distance of the run-up:

1. Measure the distance from the right high jump standard to a distance that is perpendicular to the beginning mark of the jumper's run-up.

2. Measure the distance from the above mark to the beginning mark.

3. Measure the angle (hypotenuse) from the right edge of the high jump standard to the established beginning mark.

4. Record all three measurements for future reference.

This is not all there is to establishing the run-up. This stride pattern should be practiced every day. This is the only way the jumper can become consistent in the run up. There is no optimum jump without an effective run-up.

5. Place marks from 3, 5, and 7 steps from the crossbar.

6. Place a mark at the takeoff point.

These additional marks cannot be used in competition, but during the learning process, these marks are excellent training aids. Start training for the "J" at 3 steps from the bar. Then move back to the 5-step point and go through the run-up again. When the 5-step run-up is relatively smooth, move back to 7 steps. Continue this process until the full 11-step approach is learned. This learning process may take several weeks before you are satisfied with its effectiveness. Jumpers often need reinforcement of these drills during the season. You may have to repeat the whole process several hundred times before these skills become a part of the jumper's motor pathways. As your jumper becomes stronger during the season, it may also be necessary to adjust the marks from time to time.

Teaching Bar Clearance

Some athletes can observe an accomplished jumper and immediately execute a decent Fosbury technique. This is a rare occurrence, but you can eliminate a number of problems if you try this tactic before teaching the event. However, most of your high jump candidates will have to learn the Fosbury through several drills:

1. Have the jumpers execute the scissors jump into the pit or mat without a crossbar from a 3-step approach. Gradually teach the candidates to land in the pit on their backs.

2. From the scissors jump technique, ask the candidates to drive the lead knee away from the mat and land perpendicular to the mat. The jumpers must endeavor to land on their backs and not their hips.

3. Stand the jumpers on a 3-foot box with their backs to mat or pit. Have the candidates jump backward into the pit. Continue this drill until most of the jumpers feel comfortable landing on their backs.

4. Try to combine the 3-step run-up with the back layout. Add the crossbar when this drill looks good.

5. When the 3-step run up is executed to your satisfaction, gradually move the jumper back to the 5, 7, 9, and finally, the full 11-step run-up. This learning process may take several weeks.

6. Some jumpers will experience difficulty in learning an efficient back layout. Instruct the jumpers to look over their right shoulder's and attempt to see the heels (briefly), of their feet before they land in the pit. Another teaching cue is to tell the jumpers to look at the back wall before they land in the pit.

If you don't have a decent landing pit, pile up tumbling mats until they are high enough to provide a safe landing. Other alternatives are bed springs covered with mats or bags of foam rubber. If you have access to a swimming pool, have your athletes jump backward into the swimming pool. Never jump for height if you don't have a safe landing area. Working on bar clearance with a 3-step approach is about a far as you can safely go with tumbling mats.

The Flop Technique

After the drills are learned, we need to work on the attainment of an optimum high jump. The 11-step run-up should be initiated with the takeoff (outside) leg. The initial 4 steps are a gradual buildup into the final 7 steps. At this point, the jumper accelerates into the final 5-step "J" turn. As the turn is executed, the jumper leans away from the bar to control the centrifugal force generated. At the penultimate (next to last) step, and the longest step, the center of gravity of the body is lowered (action) in preparation for the drive off the ground. On the last step, the heel of the takeoff foot strikes the ground *ahead* of the center of gravity. When the jumper drives upward, the center of gravity should be directly above the foot for the explosive effort off the ground (reaction). The foot and the knee of the takeoff leg should be in perfect alignment for the most effective delivery of power. The knee of the inside leg is driven waist high and away from the cross bar. The centrifugal force from the "J" motion, and the knee action along the bar (action), will cause the body to rotate counterclockwise as the jumper leaves the ground. The energy developed by the run and the plant of the takeoff foot will cause the upper part of the body to forward rotate around the center of gravity. Therefore, the jumper should make every effort to drive vertically. There should be no attempt to lean toward the crossbar. When the center of gravity is at the height of the crossbar, the body should be arched into a layout and subsequently rotate around the center of gravity of the vertical axis. When the hips clear the crossbar, the legs and head are lifted in preparation for landing in the pit.

Arm Action in the Fosbury Flop

The Fosbury Flop has two styles of arm action:

1. *The double-arm thrust*. This technique is borrowed from the straddle roll. Every straddler used a double-arm thrust. The idea behind this technique is based on the physical law of ground force — the greater the force driven downward (action) with a jumper's arms, the greater the resultant force upward (reaction). Most "power" jumpers use this technique because the double-arm thrust may impact negatively on the speed of the run-up but can add to the power aspect of the takeoff.

Though most jumpers feel that the double-arm action is not a natural technique, body mechanics seem to refute this notion. If you ask anyone to attempt a standing long jump or a standing vertical jump, most people will negotiate these jumps with a double-arm thrust. The difficulty that most athletes experience in executing a double-arm thrust is from a one leg jump. This does not seem to come naturally to most jumpers.

After the double-arm thrust is learned, there is often a diminution of speed at takeoff. This can be a definite handicap to a "speed" flopper. Conversely, a double-arm thrust can be a definite asset to the power jumper. The decision to become a speed or power jumper will depend primarily upon the ratio of speed to strength of the jumper in question. There is also a question of personal preference. Some jumpers will adjust to one of these techniques more easily and you can go with the flow.

If your jumper is a power jumper and prefers to use the double-arm thrust on takeoff, then a weight-training program is extremely important for this athlete. Weight training is important for either style of jumping, but it is a prime directive for the power jumper.

2. The speed jumper approaches the crossbar at a faster rate of speed and the transition from the run-up to vertical lift is much quicker. This transition is quicker because the jumper does not usually employ a double arm thrust upon leaving the ground. The arm nearest the bar is merely lifted upward thereby causing the body's center of gravity to be displaced upward toward the inside arm.

We have tried both techniques and found that most of our athletes seemed to prefer the speed technique. This method of jumping appears to be more natural to most athletes. It is also interesting to note that Dick Fosbury, the originator of this technique, did not use a double-arm thrust .

TRAINING PHILOSOPHY

I mentioned earlier that most of our jumpers were basketball players. Some of them were able to clear 6 feet with very little practice. I am always amazed at the jumping prowess of many of the great professional basketball players. I have often wondered what Michael Jordan or Spud Webb could do in the high jump. Early in my coaching career, I noticed that many of our jumpers seemed to have more spring in their legs immediately following the basketball season. Though

Photo 14–1. An exceptional backward arch over the high jump bar. The jumper's knees are spread and turned outward. Her eyes are focused to the rear.

these athletes registered higher marks later on in the track season, their vertical jumping ability never changed appreciably. Most of their improvement was due to better technique. Something was happening on the basketball court that was contributing to their jumping ability, and I had to find out what it was.

I sat through several basketball games and marked down the number of times a basketball player jumped vertically. I was amazed to discover that most of these athletes took a maximal jump over 100 times in each game. I am certain we never jumped that many times in track practice. Some high jumpers think they are working hard when they jump 25 times in practice.

TRAINING PROGRAMS

During the general preparation period, we increased our total jumps — counting plyometrics, games, and drills — to over 100 jumps. The trick was to make these drills as interesting as a basketball game. Some of our drills looked a lot like basketball practice. We even encouraged our jumpers to play basketball and volleyball as a part of our practice sessions. I am aware that many track coaches discourage track athletes from playing basketball for fear of injury. We felt the benefits from this activity could be manifest without injury if closely supervised. When we felt injury was probable, we stepped in immediately. We thought that if an athlete became accustomed to playing basketball, the possibility of an injury could be eliminated. This approach practically eliminated youngsters sneaking behind our backs playing basketball. They often got their fill during track practice.

The general preparation period for high jumpers is basically the same training program we advocated for sprinters and hurdlers. However, the majority of our high jumpers were participating on the varsity basketball team. Their formal training for the high jump didn't officially start until late March. If these athletes are on your track team for four years, it doesn't take long to get them in shape for high jump competition. They won't forget techniques they learned during their freshman and sophomore years.

The jumpers who are not basketball players begin to specialize on high jump technique during the specific preparation period. Jumping for maximum height is reserved for competition. It is our intention to deliberately avoid peaking our athletes too early in the season. Most of our training is quantity as opposed to quality. The same approach is advocated in our weight program. The reps (10–20), and volume (3–4 sets) are high and the weights are relatively light. The various drills total at least 100 jumps.

Weekly training schedule for high jumpers during the specific preparation period

Day	Duration (min)	Training task	Training details
Monday	20	Warm-up	800 meter jog, stretch
	10	Sprint drills	High knees, 1, 2, 3s, chop downs
	20	Easy plyometrics	Rope jumping, dot drills, standing triple jump, box jumping, reverse dunk (volleyball)
	30	Weight training	Lower body, 4×12 reps
	5	Warm-down	Jog 400, walk 400, stretch
Tuesday	20	Warm-up	Jog 800, stretch
	10	Sprint drills	High knees, butt kicks, high knee skipping, form runs
	10	Jump drills	Hopping 40 meters, single and double leg, back overs from a 2 ft box
	30	Technique work	7 jumps 3-step approach, 7 jumps 5 steps, and 7 jumps 7-step approach
	20	Weight training	Upper body, 3 sets 12 reps
	5	Warm-down	Jog 400, walk 400, stretch

Day	Duration (min)	Training task	Training details
Wednesday	20	Warm-up	Jog 800, stretch
	30	Games	Basketball or volleyball
	20	Weight training	Lower body, 3 sets 10 reps
	5	Warm-down	Jog 400, walk 400
Thursday	20	Warm-up	Jog 800, stretch
	10	Sprint drills	Same as Monday
	30	Technique work	3 jumps, 3-step approach, 3 jumps 5-step approach, 3 jumps at 7 steps
	15	Weight training	Upper body, 3 sets 10 reps
	5	Warm-down	Jog 400, walk 400, stretch
Friday	20	Warm-up	Jog 800, stretch
	10	Sprint drills	Same as Tuesday
	20	Plyometrics	Box jumping, double and single leg Reverse dunk $\times 7$
	5	Warm-down	Jog 400, stretch

Saturday Competition.

There is no jumping for height (in practice), during the specific preparation period. The jumper's technical problems have to be eliminated before all-out jumping is permitted. The focus at this time is on technique. We spend several minutes after the jumping drills discussing jumping technique and the weight-training program that follows. This gives us the necessary 20 minutes' rest between the jump workout and the weight-training program. The Bulgarian strength coach, Angel Spassov, recommended that 20 minutes should elapse between a track workout and a subsequent weight-training program in order for the athlete's testosterone level to return to normal. We have never regretted following this advice.

The next schedule (the precompetitive period) represents the kind of training that is recommended for the most competitive part of the indoor season. We do not intend to build to a peak performance at this time, but most of our jumpers perform quite well in spite of this approach. During this period, several basketball players have joined the squad and will participate in some of these important meets. Their technique is a little crude, but this is to be expected. As I implied earlier, their vertical jumping ability is in good shape because of their basketball training. A few weeks of intensive technique work, and they will be ready.

Weekly training schedule for high jumpers during the precompetitive period

Day	Duration (min)	Training task	Training details
Monday	20	Warm-up	Jog 800 meters, stretch
	10	Sprint drills	High knees, high knee skipping, chop downs, form runs
	20	Plyometrics	Box jumping, one and two leg bounding (three boxes), depth jumping and stuff a basketball $\times 20$
	10	Technique work	Dunk a volleyball, 11-step approach
	30	Weight training	Lower body, 4 sets, 8 reps
	5	Warm-down	Jog 400, stretch
Tuesday	20	Warm-up	Jog 800 meters, stretch
	10	Sprint drills	High knees, chop downs, 1, 2, 3s
	30	Technique Work	High jump — 3 , 5, 7, 9, 11 step run up $\times 3$ (last 3 jumps 3' below max)
	15	Weight training	Upper body, 3 sets, 8 reps
	5	Warm-down	Jog 400, stretch
Wednesday	20	Warm-up	Jog 400, stretch
	10	Sprint drills	Same as Monday
	30	Games	Basketball or volleyball
	5	Warm-down	Jog 400, stretch
Thursday	20	Warm-up	400 meter jog, stretch
	10	Sprint drills	7×10 meter sprints (90% effort)
	30	Technique work	7, 9, 11 step run-up to starting height ($\times 3$), back overs $\times 7$
	20	Weight training	Lower body, 2 sets $\times 8$ reps
	5	Warm-down	400 meter jog, stretch
Friday	20	Warm-up	400 jog, stretch
	10	Sprint drills	Same as Tuesday
	10	Plyometrics	Box jumping, single leg — 3 boxes $\times 3$, depth jumping, dunk a volleyball $\times 7$
	5	Warm-down	Jog 400 meters, stretch
Saturday		Competition.	

Several things in the schedule above may puzzle a few coaches. One is the inclusion of volleyball and basketball as part of the training program. As you know, I commented on the positive effects that basketball had on the jumping ability of our jumpers. We felt that we should not look a gift horse in the mouth. Since basketball players, and to a lesser degree, volleyball players jump a lot during their respective activities, then why not incorporate these games into our training program? Why not have fun while we develop our skills? Basketball is a big deal in our community, and most track athletes will sneak around and play this game behind our backs, so we felt it was best that we exploit this passion. By making games a part of our training program, we reduced the possibility of their picking up an injury by participating in an unfamiliar activity. When basketball was a forbidden activity, some runners and jumpers would invariably get injured playing a pickup game in the playgrounds. After we endorsed the sport as a viable part of our program, the incidence of basketball-related injuries was greatly reduced.

You will also notice that we use drills that involve dunking a basketball (or volleyball.) When we began to use these drills, the jumper's run-up to the crossbar improved immediately. For some reason, the rhythm of the run-up *and* take-off was learned more easily when we did this.

Your girls will not be able to dunk a volleyball. Have them attempt to touch the net or rim of the basket. Notice also that we do not practice all-out jumping. Most of our jumping is several inches below maximum. We found that the jumpers could lose their explosiveness if they did too many full-technique jumps in practice. We also did not jump more than twice a week. Any more than this, and we found that the jumpers seemed to be flat in competition. A generous prescription of plyometric drills and weight training did the job for us.

The competitive period begins in April. If the temperature is cold, stay inside. It is literally impossible to conduct a high jump practice when the elements are working against you. However, call the weather bureau and take advantage of the warm days (we considered 60 degrees a warm day). Completely disregard your planned schedule and jump outside when the opportunity presents itself. Paradoxically, competition in the high jump during cold weather does not seem to bother high jumpers. I have seen high jumpers compete in weather so cold that I had to wear an overcoat. But we were cautious and had them jump in sweat suits to keep warm. Most of the athletes jumped quite well under these circumstances. At the slightest hint of a problem, we had the jumpers withdraw from the competition. An ounce of prevention is better than a *ton* of cure!

Weekly training schedule for high jumpers during the competitive period

Day	Duration (min)	Training task	Training details
Monday	20	Warm-up	800 meter jog, stretch
	10	Sprint drills	High knees, high knee skipping, form runs, figure 8 runs*

Day	Duration (min)	Training task	Training details
	30	Jump drills	Box jumping, volleyball dunk, depth jumping, back overs
	5	Warm-down	Jog 400 meters, stretch
Tuesday	20	Warm-up	Jog 800 meters, stretch
	10	Sprint drills	High knees, 1, 2, 3s, chop downs, form runs
	30	Technique work	7, 9, 11 step approach (2 at 7 and 9) seven jumps at 3" under max
	30	Weight training	Lower body, 4 sets, 5 reps, 2 sets of jumping squats $\times$ 10 reps
	5	Warm-down	Jog 400 meters, stretch
Wednesday	20	Warm-up	Jog 800 meters, stretch
	10	Sprint drills	Same as Monday
	30	Plyometrics	Box jumping, 18" — single leg (3 boxes $\times$ 7), depth jumping and dunk a basketball, 11-step approach and dunk $\times$ 7
	15	Weight training	Upper body, 3 sets, 8 reps
	5	Warm-down	Jog 400, stretch
Thursday	20	Warm-up	Jog 800, stretch
	10	Sprint drills	10×50 form runs
	30	Technique work	Figure 8 drill — 10 jumps with full run up 6" below max*, back overs $\times$ 10
	15	Weight training	Lower body, 60% of max
	5	Warm-down	Jog 400, stretch
Thursday	20	Warm-up	Jog 800, stretch
	10	Sprint drills	Same as Monday
	30	Games	Basketball, volleyball, or work with the long jumpers or triple jumpers
	5	Warm-down	Jog 400, stretch
Friday	20	Warm-up	Jog 800, stretch
	10	Sprint drills	7×50 meter form runs
	15	Plyometrics	Box jumping $\times$ 5, 11-step dunk with a volleyball $\times$ 5, back overs $\times$ 5
	5	Warm-down	Jog 400, stretch

Saturday   Competition.

*A figure 8 drill is an 11-step run that is curved on the last 7 steps, is practiced on a gym floor, and mimics the curved run to the crossbar. The curved run is continuous and resembles a figure 8. We usually do this drill for 10 repetitions.

The jumpers' workouts are shorter and the weight training is heavier with lower repetitions. The intensity is greater and the duration of the workouts for the most part is decreased. The number of full-technique jumps is negligible on Thursday. We jumped at 90% effort (about 3" below their best competitive jump) on Tuesday.

Try to determine from the jumpers' workouts when your athletes are in the groove. Count the number of attempts your jumpers need before their energy begins to decline. When you calculate the number of jumps it takes before this happens, you can make sure your jumper is relatively fresh when the bar reaches your jumpers' maximum height in competition. Keeping a record of your athletes' best efforts, and the number of attempts taken to reach this level, can also be valuable information for future competitions.

The next training period is the peaking cycle. This cycle is designed to prepare your jumpers for the most important competitions of the year. At this point in the season, it is difficult to plan workouts too far in advance, but I suggest you do it anyway. It is better to plan your schedule ahead of time and modify it later. No workout can be carved in stone. Workouts may be subject to change at a moment's notice during this part of the season. The major emphasis however, should be on quality (not quantity), rest, and restoration.

Weekly training schedule for high jumpers during the peaking period

Day	Duration (min)	Training task	Training details
Monday	20	Warm-up	800 meter jog, stretch
	10	Sprint drills	High knees, high knee skipping
	30	Plyometrics	Box drills, single leg, depth jumping and dunk a basketball × 10, 11-step run-up and dunk a volleyball × 10
	5	Warm-down	Jog 400 meters, stretch
Tuesday	20	Warm-up	800 meter jog, stretch
	10	Sprint drills	Form runs 10 × 50 meters
	40	Technique work	2 jumps at 3 steps, 2 at 5, 2 at 7, 2 at 9, and 7 at 11. Work to 2" below max
	20	Weight training	Lower body, 6 sets, 3 reps, 70% of max (explosive sets), jumping squats 2 × 10, 55 lbs.
	5	Warm-down	Jog 400, stretch

Day	Duration (min)	Training task	Training details
Wednesday	20	Warm-up	Jog 800 meters, stretch
	10	Sprint drills	Same as Monday
	30	Plyometrics	Box jumping, bounding over high hurdles (both feet), depth jumping 11-step run-up and dunk, back overs
	15	Weight training	Upper body, 4 sets, 5 reps
	5	Warm-down	Jog 400, stretch
Thursday	20	Warm-up	Jog 800 meters, stretch
	10	Sprint drills	Same as Tuesday
	30	Technique work	11-step run-up scissors into pit $\times$ 10 — work up to 6" below max, 7 jumps at that height, $10 \times$ backovers
Friday	20	Warm-up	Jog 800 meters, stretch
	10	Sprint drills	High knees, high knee skip, chop downs, figure 8s
	15	Plyometrics	Box jumping, depth jumping
	5	Warm-down	400 meter jog, stretch
Saturday		Competition.	

HIGH JUMP TRAINING UNDER DIFFICULT CONDITIONS

If you don't have a regulation high jump pit — get one. Raise the funds. Appeal to the administration, sell candy, put on a fund-raising activity, buy a used pit from the more fortunate school districts and repair it. It may take several seasons before you can order a regulation pit, but once you have one, it can last a considerable amount of time if you take care of it. Get a pit somehow. High jump training is much easier when you have the proper equipment.

High jump standards and crossbars are much less of a problem. It doesn't take much skill to fashion these pieces of equipment in a wood shop. Buy a rubber hose or a clothesline and tie weights to each end; you will have the best crossbar available for training purposes. This type of crossbar will merely sag when your jumper hits it.

While you are waiting for the "official" pit to arrive, you can do several things to develop an excellent high jumper. The high jump is divided into three main phases, and if you don't have the proper equipment, you may have to work on these phases separately in preparation for competition:

1. The run-up. Work on the steps or the run-up in a gymnasium. You can do this by doing plenty of figure 8s and 11-step volleyball dunks. If your jumpers do these drills on a regular basis, their run-up to the bar will become automatic. Another drill is to do plenty of scissors jumps on a regular gym mat after the obligatory 11-step run-up.

2. Bar clearance. Pile gym mats at least 2–3 feet high and work on back overs. Have your jumpers stand with their backs to the bar and jump backward over the crossbar. You can also have the jumpers take a 3-step approach and execute the Fosbury technique at low heights. After a few sessions, your jumpers will become accustomed to landing on their backs.

Take your jumpers to the swimming pool and stretch a rope across the pool in the shallow water. Have the jumpers do a back layout over the rope. Most young people love this drill and you find it difficult to keep the nonjumpers from joining in.

3. The landing. Go to the local junk yard or furniture store and get a few bed springs and foam rubber. Most businesses will be glad to give you what you need. Place the gym mats above and below the bed springs and you will have a decent landing area. Your high jumpers can work on their landing techniques from a 5- to 7-step run up. Do not attempt an all-out jump; it is too dangerous. The jumpers will have to be very conservative in their attempts. They have to be constantly aware of a safe landing. You can, however, simulate the full jump and prepare the athletes to handle themselves relatively well in competition. Let the parents and the administration know exactly what you are doing. Liability can be a problem. Get their permission.

Plan to arrive at the meets early and run your jumpers through the entire technique before the beginning of the meet. Don't attempt an all-out jump. Use this time as an opportunity to practice the full Fosbury technique. Save some energy for the actual competition. After several meets, you will have an accomplished high jumper. Some of our jumpers have jumped well over 6 feet (6' 2"–6' 9") using this procedure.

CONCLUDING REMARKS

High jump equipment is not impossible to purchase. Every track program, regardless of financial situation, should have an official pit. You may be able to improvise with most of the track events without great difficulty and be competitive, but it is to your advantage to get the state-of-the-art equipment in this case. I have worked with makeshift high jump equipment, and I have worked with an official pit. The official equipment is much, much, much, better, more effective, and safer. If you don't have an official pit, get one by hook or crook. In the meantime, imagine, improvise, and innovate.

Section 15

THE LONG JUMP
White-Fiber
Athletes Can Jump

It has often been incorrectly stated that white boys can't jump. Championship long jumping has absolutely nothing to do with the color of the skin; it has everything to do with the color of the muscle fibers. If an athlete has been genetically endowed with an abundance of class IIb, fast-twitch white muscle fibers — and is willing to work and develop this gift — an extraordinary long jump will be the result.

When an average citizen is asked to name great Olympic long jumpers several names are usually mentioned: Jesse Owens (1936), Carl Lewis (1984–1996), Bob Beamon (1968), and maybe Ralph Boston (1960). These men achieved fame for long jumping because something unusual happened when they made their best jumps. Jesse Owens is remembered because he won four gold medals in Hitler's face in the 1936 Olympics. Carl Lewis' name became synonymous with track and field for over a decade. Bob Beamon almost jumped out of the pit in the 1968 Olympics when he made the remarkable effort of 29' 2" and smashed the world record to smithereens. Ralph Boston made his athletic statement when he broke Jesse Owens's record of 26' 8" that stood unchallenged for 25 years. Mike Powell has broken Bob Beamon's remarkable record, but he has languished in the shadow of Carl Lewis's phenomenal achievements.

TALENT IDENTIFICATION

Long jumpers usually come from the ranks of great sprinters. Those jumpers who are not known as *great* sprinters are no slouches, however, when it comes to running the 100 or 200 meters. Sprint speed is an absolute requirement for success in this event. Send your turtles somewhere else.

After you have found athletes who have demonstrated adequate sprinting speed, test this group on the standing long jump and the vertical jump. If your candidate does well on these tests you may have an excellent long jump prospect. After you have narrowed the athletes down to a workable number, test them on the regular long jump. None of these tests has a one-to-one correlation with the long jump, but the data are close enough to guarantee that someone in this group who scored high on all the recommended tests will be your long jumper.

If you don't have an indoor long jump pit, then have your athletes test their ability by long jumping into a high jump pit. If an official long jump or high jump pit isn't available, this doesn't mean that your jumpers do no long jump training. They can practice dozens of drills on mats and boxes prior to their initial competition. The fun of this situation is the surprise performances that you will discover at the first meet. These drills will prepare your jumpers so well you will not be able to contain the excitement that will come with some of their efforts. The long jump is such a natural event that many of your athletes will jump like polished jumpers in their first competition. Properly executed drills on alternate equipment can do this for your long jumpers.

All of the previously mentioned tests are designed to identify the presence of white (type IIa and IIb) muscle fibers. It is not the color of the athlete's skin that makes a champion jumper; it is the color of the muscle fibers. Every ethnic group on this planet has somebody with an abundance of white muscle fibers. A plethora of jumpers of African descent dominating this event in the last decade means absolutely nothing. Research has proven that anybody with the right combination of white (fast-twitch), fibers can be a long jumper. Several Caucasian long jumpers have been champions in the long jump. Ter-Ovarnesyan of the USSR set a world record in 1967, and Lynn Davies of England won a gold medal in the 1964 Olympics. But it takes years of serious endeavor to become a world-class long jumper, and if it were easy, everybody would do it.

FINDING LONG JUMPERS

Attend football, basketball, volleyball, and soccer games. If you look hard enough you will find several prospects from these athletic contests. Get the results of the school's physical fitness tests. Walk through physical education classes and look for the students who routinely dunk a basketball. Look at each student's muscular development. Most track coaches instinctively "know" a good prospect when they see one. Encourage every kid with decent speed to try the event. Leave no stone unturned.

TECHNICAL ASPECTS

Several years ago, I attended a track clinic and one of the featured speakers was coach Tom Tellez. Tellez is Carl Lewis's coach and his topic was "coaching long jumpers." His talk lasted one hour and he spent 55 minutes discussing the run up. He spent 5 minutes discussing the technique of the hitch kick and hang techniques. After his talk, I asked him why he spent so little time on the these techniques? His response was brief and succinct. He said, *"There is no championship jumping without a great run-up."* He is right.

How many times have fantastic jumps been made that were negated by a scratch or a foul at the board? It is reputed that Carl Lewis jumped over 30 feet in the long jump but fouled by a fraction of an inch at the long jump board. The run-up is also important when speed at the board determines over 90% of the effectiveness of the long jump. The technique in air contributes only a fraction to the ultimate outcome of the long jump. This is why great long jumpers must have world-class speed.

Establishing a Consistent Run-Up

I have seen excellent jumpers foul on all three of their preliminary jumps. Establishing a consistent stride pattern to the board is not easy. There are several methods of establishing a stride pattern and most of these will be covered in this section. Unlike the high jump, most of our jumpers have success with an even-numbered stride pattern. When we used an odd-numbered stride pattern, our first stride was counted as "zero" and then we proceeded with an even-numbered count. With an even-numbered stride pattern, we take our first stride with the foot that will take the *penultimate* step. With an odd-numbered stride pattern, our first stride will be with the takeoff foot. The following procedure is the way we established our (18-step) stride pattern:

1. Without using the long jump board, run an 18-step stride pattern on the track or whatever surface you are using for a track. Count the steps and have someone make a mark at the 18th step.

2. Record the distance with a tape measure and transfer this measurement to the long jump runway.

3. Without looking at the long jump board, run the 18 measured steps. Adjust the marks and measurements after each effort.

4. The jumper must count the 18 steps by counting in groups of 6, and attack the board in the final 6 steps (without looking at the board). Looking at the long jump board interferes with the jumper's speed and stride pattern. Most jumpers will constantly make subconscious adjustments and experience great difficulty in establishing a consistent stride pattern.

5. Some jumpers may want to use another method of counting their steps. I have coached athletes who counted steps from 1 to 18; some have counted only their takeoff leg (9), and others didn't count any steps, but depended on their rhythm. There are an infinite number of ways to count steps. Go with whatever works. The goal is to hit the board consistently without looking at it.

6. Make a mark where the last 4 steps begin. This is the coach's mark. The jumpers should not see this mark. They will know they are there because they are counting the steps. There should be a gathering for the takeoff at this point.

7. The jumper's center of gravity is lowered on the next to last (penultimate) step in preparation for the takeoff. The penultimate step is slightly longer than the last step.

8. Your jumpers should practice their steps every day. It takes a considerable amount of time to perfect this part of the long jump. It is also important to note that the stride pattern may change slightly from meet to meet. Several factors will modify your jumpers' step pattern. Your jumpers' physical and emotional state will vary from meet to meet. The surface of the runway may be different. Be prepared to make minor changes in your jumpers' measurements at each competition.

9. Take your jumpers to the site of your championship meet to get them accustomed to the facilities. This will give your athletes a tremendous advantage later on.

10. Your jumpers will want to look at the takeoff board during their run-up. Athletes have a tendency to modify their step pattern when they do this. Spend a lot of time working on this aspect of the long jump.

Figure 15-1

LONG JUMP TAKEOFF

HEAD IS UP
EYES FORWARD

RIGHT KNEE
DRIVING HIGH
AND TOWARD
THE LONG
JUMP PIT

TORSO IS
ERECT

COMPLETE
EXTENSION OF
THE LEFT LEG

Figure 15-2

LONG JUMP — HANG STYLE

HEAD IS BACK
AND UP

BOTH ARMS WILL BE
ROTATED BACKWARD,
OVERHEAD, AND
FORWARD PRIOR TO
LANDING IN THE PIT

TORSO IS
ARCHED

FEET AND LEGS
ARE HELD BACK
IN PREPARATION
FOR LANDING

LEGS ARE EXTENDED
FORWARD BEFORE
LANDING
INTO THE PIT

Figure 15-3

LONG JUMP — HITCH KICK

THE OBJECTIVE OF THE
ARM SWING AND RUNNING-
IN-AIR MOTION IS TO
PREVENT THE LEGS FROM
DROPPING PREMATURELY
BEFORE LANDING INTO
THE PIT

BOTH ARMS ARE
WINDMILLING TO
COUNTERACT
FORWARD
ROTATION OF
THE BODY

TORSO IS
ERECT

RIGHT LEG IS
SWINGING BACK
AND WILL COME
FORWARD
PRIOR TO
LANDING IN THE
PIT

LEFT LEG
(TAKEOFF LEG) IS
FORWARD AND
PULLED BACK
PRIOR TO
LANDING INTO
THE PIT

How to Adjust Steps

When your jumpers are in the learning stages, some funny things will happen to their step pattern. Some will be over or beyond the board. Some will hit the board with the wrong foot and others will be behind the board. Your jumper's step pattern may change during the competition. The most frustrating thing in all of the jumping events is correcting the stride pattern at a competition. To make matters worse, the official may be closing down the runway for competition. Listed below are some solutions to your athlete's dilemma.

1. If your jumper is behind the board; this is the best of all worlds. If your jumper is a few inches behind the board, don't worry — after jumpers loosen up and take their first jump, most of them will be on the board. If your jumpers are *more than a foot* behind the board, divide the error by half, move their mark forward by that number, and continue to do run throughs Most of them will be on the board by the first jump.

2. If your jumpers' steps are beyond the board, double the distance of the error and move them back. For example, if a jumper is a foot beyond the board, move the athlete's mark back 2 feet.

3. When your jumpers' steps are on the board, have them take a few practice jumps. The last 4 steps will change slightly when the athlete takes a few preliminary jumps. Be prepared to make another adjustment. Expect your jumpers' stride pattern to change during the competition. As they get warmer, some will go over the board. When fatigue sets in, they will be behind the board. Also expect jumps 2–4 to be over the board and jumps 5–6 to be behind the board. If this is so, refer to solutions 1 and 2 above.

4. If your jumper's steps are erratic, the problem may be at the beginning of the run-up. The solution to this problem may be found by examining the first two steps of the run-up. Take a close look at those steps and measure them before each run-up. You will probably discover that these initial steps are a different length each time. Measure the first two steps and have the jumper touch these marks before every run through. This approach solves most of your jumpers' inconsistent run-up problems.

5. As your jumpers mature and get stronger, their step patterns will change. Be ready to help them adjust their steps when this happens.

6. Start your jumpers with an 18-step pattern. The rhythm (6-6-6), is easier to learn and the distance run is best for most jumpers. Because of the difference in size and stride pattern, every jumper on your squad will have a different measurement for the run-up. On an average, most female jumpers will have a shorter (about 110 feet) run-up. Most males will run about 130 feet. An 18 stride pattern will be perfect for most of your jumpers. Some of your jumpers may request a longer or shorter run-up. Experiment and see if it fits. World-class jumpers usually have run-ups of 20–24 strides.

Photo 15–1. This is an excellent example of the "hitch kick" style of a long jumping. Notice the perfect coordination of this athlete's arms and legs while in flight.

7. Your jumper should "attack" the board in the last 4–6 steps. Speed at the board is imperative for a successful long jump. Your long jumper should accelerate on the runway and hit the takeoff board at optimum speed. There is a gather, or a change of rhythm, in the last 4 steps *and* a lowering of the jumper's center of gravity on the penultimate step, but it is not done at the expense of speed at the takeoff board.

JUMPING TECHNIQUE

Jesse Owens used the "sail" technique. He basically ran as fast as he could and jumped. Most of your candidates can jump in this manner naturally without any instruction. Jesse Owens might have jumped much further than the 26' 8" with better technique and modern training methods. The main reason he jumped that remarkable distance was because of his speed down the runway. You really don't have to teach this style, and almost none of today's world-class jumpers use sail techinique because of its mechanical inefficiency. When a jumper is airborne, the body has a tendency to rotate forward in the air, causing the feet to drop prematurely. The sail technique does nothing to prevent this tendency.

The hitch kick and hang techniques prevent the jumper's body from rotating forward in the air by the swinging of the arms and legs to counteract this forward rotation. This force is called *nutation*. Both of these techniques are used by most world-class jumpers The most popular style of long jumping and, paradoxically, the most difficult to learn, is the hitch kick. In theory, jumpers can achieve similar results with either technique. Though the hang style is easier to learn, the timing of the jump is difficult to achieve. Conversely, once the hitch kick style is learned, timing is less of a problem.

Learning to Hitch Kick

The hitch kick technique is basically running or bicycling in the air after the takeoff is initiated. The swinging action of the arms and legs prevents the forward rotation of the body. If forward rotation is arrested, the jumper's feet and legs will not drop prematurely.

1. Have prospective jumpers lie on their backs and do an inverted bicycle motion with the legs. Tell the candidates to bicycle the legs three times and stop. Repeat this exercise several times. Repeat the bicycling action while hanging from a horizontal bar or rings.

2. Stand the athletes on a box, have two athletes hold the candidates under the armpits. While being held aloft, the jumpers step from the box, swinging the legs in a bicycling motion. They are then lowered gently to the long jump pit or a gym mat. Repeat this exercise several times.

3. Instruct your jumpers to run three steps to a box and jump from the box while attempting to bicycle the legs three times before landing. Tell them to land on their feet.

4. Bring the jumpers to the swimming pool. Have them (if they can swim), run off the diving board while executing the hitch kick motion.

5. Place an incline box at the edge of the pit. Have the jumpers take a 6-step run-up while executing the hitch kick motion.

6. Try the hitch kick style from a full run-up.

It may take the athletes several weeks to learn the hitch kick. If observable progress isn't being made during this time, consider switching to the hang technique.

Learning the Hang Technique

1. Stand the jumpers at the edge of the pit or a mat. Have the athletes jump from the box while arching the back into a hang technique. Instruct them to hold this position briefly and land on their feet.

2. Try the same movement without a box, swing both legs forward and sit *gently* in the sand or on mats.

3. Try the hang technique from the diving board.

4. Do the hang technique from a 6-, 12-, and 18-step run-up

5. If you have a commercially made high jump pit, do a run-up to a box and land into the pit. This drill can be done with either technique.

6. Regardless of the technique your jumpers use, the left leg (of a right-footed jumper) should be driven with a high knee action toward the pit.

Some jumpers will learn the hang technique in one day, but it takes considerable experience to perfect the timing of when to come out of the hang prior to landing in the pit. This aspect of the jump can lend itself to considerable inconsistency. If your jumpers come out of the hang position prematurely, they will rotate forward, and this will have a negative effect on their landing.

Into the Pit

When Jesse Owens won the long jump in the 1936 Olympics, his run-up, technique in air, and landing left much to be desired. He probably could have added a foot or more to his jump with better technique. Even the great Bob Beamon could have jumped further had he perfected his landing technique. He actually jumped forward after landing in the pit. If an athlete can jump forward after landing, some of the momentum of the jump is aborted. Most modern jumpers are taught to land with their hips as low as possible in the pit to exploit the trajectory of the center of gravity. Some jumpers even land into the pit and literally slide on their hips. Jumpers must practice this all-important skill. A proper landing can add nearly a foot to an athlete's long jump.

The landing should initially be practiced from a short run-up. There should also be an attempt to turn the body prior to the landing so the jumper can land perpendicular to the pit. After this technique is learned from a short run-up, gradually move the jumper to a full runway. This learning process may take several training sessions. It may take some jumpers several months to learn this technique.

PLYOMETRICS AND BOX DRILLS

An important aspect of all jumping is plyometrics and box jumping. I touched on the importance of these drills in previous sections, but I want to cover this training principle in detail. Plyometrics drills consist of leaping, jumping, and bounding with and without equipment. Actually, every participant in track and field can benefit from these drills. The theory behind these drills is that these explosive movements will stimulate the fast-twitch muscles. As in all training techniques, plyometrics should be gradually introduced into an athlete's training program. A sudden immersion in these drills may cause serious injury to the soft tissue. The drills should increase in intensity near the end of the season, but handle with care. The boxes you make can vary in height; 18" is recommended for most drills, but, you will need a few boxes 2–3 feet in height. We also used

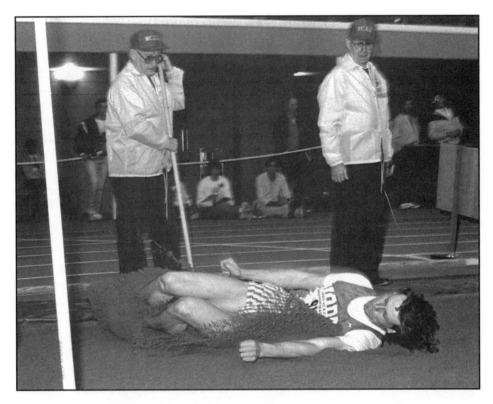

Photo 15–2. A long jumper using his center of gravity to optimum advantage by landing as low as possible in the long jump pit.

chairs, auditorium stages, and stadium stairs. A milder form of plyometrics can be done without any special equipment and is recommended for early season practices. Hopping, leaping, and rope jumping are good introductions to plyometrics during early season workouts. An excellent book devoted to this subject is *Plyometric Training,* by Fred Hatfield and Michael Yessis.

Jumping with light weights (45–50 pounds), can also be a tremendous training aid. The jury is out on the effectiveness of very heavy weights (lifted slowly), on jumping ability. A great deal of Soviet research that corroborates the value of explosive weight training. Jump training is all about power, and the formula for power is strength $\times$ speed. Be advised, however, that explosive lifting (though extremely effective), can visit trauma on muscles, ligaments, and tendons. Make sure your jumpers are thoroughly warmed up before each weight-training or plyometric session.

Most jumpers can handle some pretty impressive poundages in their lifts. I have a videotape of Mike Conley (the former world record holder in the triple jump), power cleaning over 300 pounds. The infamous Canadian sprinter, Ben Johnson, could squat with 500 pounds. Our approach to weight training is to lift the heaviest weights during the competitive season and emphasize lighter and more explosive lifting during the peaking period.

TRAINING PROGRAMS

The general preparation period for long jumpers is basically the same as those recommended for sprinters and high jumpers. I have stated earlier in this book that most of the members of the track team follow a similar general preparation period. We want to build a foundation for the more difficult training that will follow. If there is no general preparation period, most athletes will not be able to handle the high-intensity training that is necessary during the final weeks of competition. There is not a lot of difference between the specific preparation periods for high jumpers and for long jumpers. On the surface, their training programs may seem similar. Both disciplines require a great deal of bounding, plyometrics and explosive weight training. But most long jumpers are also sprinters and this proclivity will be reflected in their workouts during the specific preparation period.

Weekly training schedule for long jumpers during the specific preparation period

Day	Duration (min)	Training task	Training details
Monday	20	Warm-up	800 meter jog, stretch
	10	Sprint drills	High knees, 1, 2, 3s, form runs
	30	Sprint training	Work with the sprinters
	20	Easy plyometrics	Rope jumping, hopping 50 meters $\times$ 7
	5	Warm-down	Jog 400 meters, stretch
Tuesday	20	Warm-up	Jog 600 meters, stretch
	10	Sprint drills	High knees, form runs
	30	Technique work	Runway work, 6, 12, and 18 steps, pop-ups into a pit or on mats from 6 steps
	30	Weight training	Lower body, 3 sets, 12 reps, jumping squats
	5	Warm-down	Jog 400 meters, stretch
Wednesday	20	Warm-up	Jog 800 meters, stretch
	10	Sprint drills	High knees, 1, 2, 3s, chop downs, high knee skipping
	30	Plyometrics	Hopping, dot drills, rope jumping, easy box jumping
	15	Weight training	Upper body, 2 sets, 12 reps
	5	Warm-down	Jog 400 meters, stretch
Thursday	20	Warm-up	Jog 800 meters, stretch
	10	Sprint drills	Same as Monday
	30	Technique work	Runway work, 6, 12, 18 steps, pop-ups from 6 steps, work on landings

Day	Duration (min)	Training task	Training details
	20	Weight training	Lower body, light weights, 2 sets×15
	5	Warm-down	Jog 400 meters, stretch
Friday	20	Warm-up	Jog 400 meters, stretch
	10	Sprint drills	Same as Tuesday
	20	Technique work	Full runways×7
	15	Plyometrics	Hopping 4×50 meters, box jumping
	10	Weight training	Upper body, 2 sets×15
	5	Warm-down	Jog 400 meters, stretch
Saturday		Competition.	

During February, the long jumper's training is not very intense. We are building a foundation of techniques and plyometrics. Our weight training is with relatively light poundages. You have to be very cautious about soft-tissue damage when your athletes embark upon a long jump program. Make haste slowly. Long jumping is an extremely explosive activity; your athlete's introduction to plyometrics, sprint training, and weight training must be gradual and prudent.

The precompetitive period is characterized by a gradual increase in quality and decrease in volume. Every factor in training becomes more intense; weight training is heavier, sprinting is faster, and plyometrics are more difficult. This is also the most competitive part of the indoor season.

Weekly training schedule for long jumpers during the precompetitive period

Day	Duration (min)	Training task	Training details
Monday	20	Warm-up	800 meter jog, stretch
	10	Sprint drills	High knees, 1, 2, 3s, form runs
	30	Sprint training	Baton passing with the sprint relay team or work on 10 runways
	5	Warm-down	Jog 400 meters, stretch
Tuesday	20	Warm-up	800 meter jog, stretch
	10	Sprint drills	High knees, butt kicks, 1, 2, 3s
	30	Technique work	Full run-throughs×7, 7×pop-ups from a 6-step run up, 7×all-out effort
	30	Weight training	Lower body, 4 sets, 8 reps

Day	Duration (min)	Training task	Training details
Wednesday	20	Warm-up	Jog 1000 meters, stretch
	10	Sprint drills	High knees, chop downs, form runs
	30	Jump drills	Run-ups (18 steps), box jumping, depth jumping, pop-up from boxes
	20	Weight training	Upper body, 3 sets, 8 reps
	5	Warm-down	Jog 400 meters, stretch
Thursday	20	Warm-up	Jog 600 meters, stride 200 meters, stretch
	10	Sprint drills	Same as Monday
	30	Games	Basketball or volleyball
	20	Weight training	Lower body, 2 sets 12 reps (easy)
Friday	20	Warm-up	600 meter jog, stretch
	10	Sprint drills	Same as Tuesday
	10	Technique	Run-throughs (7)
	15	Plyometrics	Box jumping, depth jumping
	15	Weight training	2 sets, 10 reps, light weights
	5	Warm-down	Jog 400 , stretch
Saturday	Competition.		

Our athletes seem to jump better when we limit their all-out jumps with a full run-up to one day a week (Tuesday). We also schedule Monday as a relatively easy day. This gives our jumpers an extra day of recovery from Saturday's competition. Another wrinkle in our training schedule is the brief but intense workout on Friday. Jumpers seem to do better in competition when the musculature and nervous system are stressed (briefly) to near maximum the day before the meet. I have not specified a certain number of jumps, but our plyometric drills last only 15 minutes on Friday. This will be about 20–30 jumps. I learned this approach from a Romanian sprint coach. When our jumpers used this technique, they began to improve markedly in subsequent competitions.

The next phase is the competitive period. This occurs during the month of April and the erratic weather can be a problem for athletes in explosive events like the long jump. You must pay close attention to your jumpers' physical condition. Cold weather can play havoc with the soft tissue of your athletes' lower extremities. I have no problem in discontinuing practice or withdrawing a jumper from competition. This is a time when the jumping pits are cold and unforgiving, and injury could be distinct possibility. Teach your athletes to check the facility before they jump — but take advantage of every warm day. No workout is written in stone. If the weather is warm, take advantage of the situation; it may be cold the next day. Check the weather report every morning. If the weather forecast is disagreeable, practice inside.

The training emphasis during this period continues to be even more intense. The plyometric drills are more difficult, weight training is heavier, and sprinting is faster (when the weather permits). Your jumpers will not peak during this period for two reasons. One reason is the inclement weather will impact on their performance, and the other is that it takes time to adapt to the rise in training intensity.

Weekly training schedule for long jumpers during the competitive period

Day	Duration (min)	Training task	Training details
Monday	20	Warm-up	800 meter jog, stretch
	10	Sprint drills	High knees, chop downs, skipping
	30	Plyometrics	Box jumping (one leg), depth jumping, jumping over hurdles (both feet)
	30	Weight training	Lower body, 5 sets, 5 reps, jumping squats with light weights
	5	Warm-down	400 jog, stretch
Tuesday	20	Warm-up	Jog 600 meters, stride 200 meters, stretch
	10	Sprint drills	High knees, quick steps, form runs
	40	Technique work	Run-throughs, $10 \times$ full runways, 10 all-out jumps, work on landing skills
	15	Weight training	Upper body, 3 sets, 6 reps
	5	Warm-down	Jog 400 meters, stretch
Wednesday	20	Warm-up	Jog 400, stride 4×100, stretch
	10	Sprint drills	Same as Monday
	30	Technique work	3, 6-step run-up with pop-ups from boxes and inclined plane
	5	Warm-down	Jog 400, stretch
Thursday	20	Warm-up	10×100 strides, stretch
	10	Sprint drills	Same as Tuesday
	30	Technique work	$10 \times$ runway
	20	Weight training	Light weights, 3 sets, 10 reps
	5	Warm-down	Jog 400, stretch
Friday	20	Warm-up	Jog 400, stride 400, stretch
	10	Sprint drills	High knees, form runs, 3 run-ups
	20	Plyometrics	Box drills, depth jumping
	15	Weight training	Upper body, light weights 2 sets, 10 reps
	5	Warm-down	Jog 400, stretch
Saturday		Competition.	

Drills and plyometrics are the foundation of our training program. Tuesday is the only training day that we do all-out jumping. Of course, we jumped at 100% during competition. We found that all-out jumping more than twice a week was counterproductive. At this point in the season, our technique is pretty good, and the plyometric drills are included to manifest further development.

We usually take four days of complete rest between cycles. I discovered, quite by accident, that four days of restoration are necessary to potentiate the physical demands made on the body and recover from minor muscle trauma. Recently, I read an article written by Tom Platz and Leo Costa in the November 1996 issue of *Iron Man* magazine, about the physiological values of rest and restoration. The article stated that a brief cessation of vigorous exercise can result in an acceleration of physiological improvement. It seems that the body that receives regular exercise is conditioned to respond to these physical demands by adapting to the stress, and will continue to respond for a certain period of time in the absence of exercise. It is my empirical observation that this period of time is about four days. Taking a brief period of rest accelerates physiological improvement because the catabolic (tearing down), aspect of the athlete's body has been temporarily discontinued. Thus the anabolic (building up), aspect of the athlete's metabolism has prepotency. I call this physiological phenomenon *metabolic momentum*.

The peaking period is the final and probably the most crucial cycle in your jumpers' season. Each day has to be an entity within itself. By this time, your jumpers should be in top condition, and the focus is on competition. Workouts are planned based upon the outcome of previous competitions. It is a time to look for strengths and weaknesses in your jumper's condition and technique. All loose ends should be tied up from meet to meet.

The training emphasis is event-specific. Full run-throughs and jumps are the name of the game. Plyometrics are more difficult but workout time is much shorter. Weight training has switched to lighter weights but the lifts are more explosive. Be certain that the warm-ups are thorough before embarking on these explosive type exercises. Stretch before and after everything. This is the worst time to get any soft-tissue injury. You are too close to the end of the season. There is no tomorrow.

Our heaviest day of weight training is usually scheduled for Tuesday. Most of our meets are held on Saturday and we feel Monday is too soon to schedule an intense resistance workout. We also like to distance our heaviest workout from competitive jumping to optimize rest and recovery. We do just enough work on Monday to stimulate the jumpers' nervous system and musculature. For our purposes, Tuesday is the ideal day for heavy weight training.

Weekly training schedule for long jumpers during the peaking period

Day	Duration (min)	Training task	Training details
Monday	20	Warm-up	800 meter jog, stretch
	10	Sprint drills	High knees, chop downs, 1, 2, 3s
	20	Easy plyometrics	Box jumping, depth jumping, pop-ups
	5	Warm-down	Jog 400 meters, stretch

Day	Duration (min)	Training task	Training details
Tuesday	20	Warm-up	600 meter jog, stride 200 meters, stretch
	10	Sprint drills	High knees, quick steps, skipping
	30	Technique work	$7 \times$ pop-ups, $7 \times$ run-ups, 7 all-out jumps with a full run-up
	30	Weight training	Lower body, 6 sets, 3 reps, (60% of max) jumping squats, 2 sets, 10 reps
	5	Warm-down	Jog 400 meters, stretch
Wednesday	20	Warm-up	Jog 400 meters, 4×100 meter strides
	10	Sprint drills	High knees, butt kicks, form runs
	30	Plyometrics	Box jumping, depth jumping, pop-ups
	15	Weight training	Upper body, 3 sets, 4 reps
	5	Warm-down	Jog 400 meters, stretch
Thursday	20	Warm-up	Jog 800 meters, stretch
	10	Sprint drills	Same as Monday
	30	Technique work	Pop-ups off boxes for technique in air, landing drills
	20	Weight training	Lower body, light weights, 2 sets 8 reps (explosively)
	5	Warm-down	400 meter jog, stretch
Friday	20	Warm-up	Jog 400, walk 400, stretch
	10	Sprint drills	High knees, 1, 2, 3s, form runs
	20	Plyometrics	Run-ups $\times 4$, box jumping, depth jumping
	5	Warm-down	Jog 400, stretch
Saturday		Competition.	

LONG JUMPING UNDER DIFFICULT CONDITIONS

Successful long jumping is possible without all the modern conveniences. Let me repeat that Tom Tellez, Carl Lewis's long jump coach insists that the run-up to the takeoff board is the most important part of the event. I believe him.

Work on the runway can be done almost anywhere. Place a small mat or softball base, or make a mark the size of a takeoff board, on the corridor floor, gymnasium, playground, park, or pavement, and you can practice run-throughs whenever you feel like it. When you arrive at the meet site, be prepared to adjust the stride pattern because of the dissimilarity in facilities. Even if you have an ideal situation, you will have to make some adjustment. Most long jump runway surfaces are slightly different. However, if the run up is practiced diligently, your jumpers will experience little difficulty developing a consistent stride pattern.

The technique in air (hang or hitch kick) can be developed by doing a shortened run up (6–12 steps), and doing pop-ups into a high jump pit or mats. The most effective and safest way to practice this drill is to jump for height, *not* for distance. If you have a commercially made high jump pit, use an 18" box to jump into the pit. Occasionally, we practice our long jump technique into a swimming pool. Have your jumpers run off a low diving board and execute the hang or hitch kick technique. Most athletes love this change-of-pace workout. When you work with the jumpers in the pool, bring the rest of the team. Try to plan a water workout for the entire track team on these occasions — if they can swim.

To put all of the phases of the long jump together, plan to arrive at most of your indoor meets early and run your jumpers through the full technique. The only aspect of the event that has not been practiced is the landing. It is imperative that this part of the long jump be taught while you are working on the full technique. You will be surprised how quickly this skill will be learned. Your new jumpers will appear to be relatively unskilled in the earlier meets, but after a few indoor competitions, they will execute excellent technique.

During the outdoor season take your jumpers to a decent facility and practice the full technique at least once a week. Most suburban coaches will not object to your athletes' using their facility. There are also a few local facilities near our school, but their pits are not in good shape. You may have the same situation. Take a shovel and rake. We also try to use different sites so we won't wear out our welcome. We have gone as far as Evanston, Illinois, from Chicago to jump. This is a considerable distance to travel for practice, but our athletes felt this sacrifice was worth the effort.

CONCLUDING REMARKS

Every effort should be made to prevent injury while using alternative training equipment. The greatest possibility of injury will occur while working on the technique in the air. Pile mats as high as necessary for a safe landing. Gym mats are safe if there is no effort to do an all-out jump. Pop-ups are the best approach in any case. *Do not under any circumstances* practice landing techniques with alternative training facilities. If you don't have access to indoor facilities, use every opportunity available at dual meets to practice the full technique. If your jumpers are not participating in any running event, send them back to the long jump pit to practice phases of the event that may be hazardous to work on when you are at home.

You may have more opportunities to use various long jump facilities during the outdoor season. To potentiate your jumpers' development, you will need to visit a site that has reasonable long jumping facilities. If you schedule one meet a week, and visit a facility near you for practice once a week, your jumpers will have an opportunity to jump in a regulation pit twice a week. We have found in our situation, that all-out jumping more than twice a week is counterproductive.

We have developed outstanding jumpers with these makeshift facilities. The need to innovate, improvise, and invent is no deterrent to championship performance in the long jump. It may be inconvenient, and you and your athletes may have to make a few sacrifices, but how is that different from the way we seek to achieve success in any field of endeavor?

Section 16

THE TRIPLE JUMP
Sixty Feet?

Is nothing sacred in track and field? First it was the four-minute mile; then it was the seventy-foot shot put. After that came the twenty-foot pole vault. Before I could catch my breath, somebody cleared eight feet in the high jump. Then came the outrage of outrages — an Englishman jumped sixty feet in the triple jump! With scientific application of body mechanics, weight training, plyometrics, and periodization, no track and field record is sacred. A knowledgeable track coach, working in concert with a dedicated athlete, can be the consummate iconoclast.

When Jonathan Edwards triple-jumped 60 feet, I checked several newspapers for typographical errors. The lack of knowledge in regard to track and field in America is so abysmal you can never be certain if the facts are accurate. These were. I didn't expect this barrier to be broken so soon. Jonathan Edwards had been jumping in relative obscurity, so this remarkable effort was unexpected. I was still marveling at the 58-foot jumps registered by Mike Conley. World-class triple jumpers usually come from the United States, Eastern Europe, or Brazil. World-class triple jumpers from Great Britain are as scarce as a chicken with teeth. How did this happen?

As usual, when a barrier in track and field is broken, someone must have broken with tradition and done it a new way. So it is with Jonathan Edwards. I studied his films several times before I came to this conclusion. The differences in his technique are so subtle that they are difficult to detect, but they are there. First, Jonathan attacks the runway like a long jumper. Experts have been insisting that the triple jumper should employ a controlled run to the takeoff board. Judging from the films I saw, Jonathan's run-up looks like an all-out sprint. Second, most coaches teach a flattened or low hop, a higher step, and an even higher last jump into the pit. Not so with Edwards. He does a low hop and a low second phase or step, and a relatively high final jump. He broke with tradition and set a world record.

There is another factor that confuses me. Jonathan appears to be so frail physically. He may be on a weight program, but he sure doesn't look like it. Jonathan Edwards is a muscleless wonder. The triple jump is so hard on the lower extremities that most triple jumpers expect to be injured *at least once* in their athletic careers. Just think: All three jumps are made on a solid and unforgiving surface — and this skinny guy jumps 60 feet! Unbelievable.

TALENT IDENTIFICATION

The triple jump — also known as the hop, step, and jump — is probably the most physically demanding field event of all. A jumper has to take three obligatory jumps on a hard runway surface before landing into the long jump pit. If you count the prelims and finals, an athlete may have to take 18 bone-shattering jumps in every competition. During the NCAA finals many jumpers took 24 jumps in two days! Your triple jumpers may have to do this every week during the indoor and outdoor season. No other event in track and field exposes the lower extremities to this much trauma. Preparation for triple-jump competition had better be thorough. Injury can be a problem in this event.

It is difficult to define the necessary physical characteristics for championship triple jumping. Triple jumpers can emerge from various disciplines.

Many come from the ranks of outstanding long jumpers. Mike Conley is a world-class long jumper and sprinter. I have seen high jumpers excel in this event. Some, like Willie Banks, were not outstanding in any other event but the triple jump. You might expect these athletes to be extraordinary physical specimens, but this not the case. Mike Conley is an avid weight man; Willie Banks was not. All of these athletes, however, have a certain amount of speed and spring in their physical description. If a jumper has nearly equal jumping ability on both legs — this is a rare gift. Most jumpers have a disparity in leg strength. Here they take two jumps on their best leg and one on the weaker leg. If they are equal or nearly equal on both legs, the combined effort of the three jumps will be greater. So if a youngster can jump 21 feet on the stronger leg, he/she might hop 18 feet, step 16 feet, and jump 19 feet in a jump dominated effort. This would result in a 53 foot triple jump (with practice). That's a pretty good triple jump. His/her long jump is just average. The 53 triple jump is exceptional. Even if you use the formula of 21 feet multiplied by $3 \times .75 = 47' 3"$. That's a good jump also. A 47 foot jump will place in the NCAA Div. III nationals and if a woman jumped 47 feet, she would be world-class. Often, long jumpers will experience problems with the run-up and takeoff on the nondominant leg, and the distance achieved will not be much less than if they jumped off their dominant leg. Don't look a gift horse in the mouth. How many times have you seen a jumper clear 21 feet on the right leg and 20 feet with the left leg? This jumper may not set the world on fire in the long jump but with a little work, you may have a champion triple jumper in your midst.

HOW TO FIND TRIPLE JUMPERS

Triple jumpers may be on your team, hidden in another event. Try every jumper and sprinter in this event. An excellent test is the standing triple jump. Then try the triple jump from a 6-, 12-, and finally 18-step run up. Tell the athletes to forget about hitting the board every time; measure their effort from where they took off. If you don't have access to an indoor pit, pile up a few mats and go to work. After a few jumps, you will determine which candidates are triple jumpers.

I am assuming that you may not have a feeder system in your community. If this is the case, you may have to do a bit of detective work. I advised you in other sections to look at athletes on other teams, especially those sports that require explosiveness, sprinting speed, and quickness. The same advice is true for the triple jump. The triple jump is a strange event. The carryover from sprinting speed or jumping ability is not as certain as it is for other events — there is no one-to-one correlation here. If that were so, can you imagine how far Carl Lewis would triple-jump if he tried this event? Toni Nett of Germany calculated in the December 1961 issue of *Track Technique* that the ability to triple-jump is equal to 75% of one's best long jump × three. This means that Carl Lewis could have triple-jumped an incredible 65 feet! Other than Mike Conley, there have been very few world-class long jumpers who have excelled at the triple jump.

The odds are in your favor if the athlete you select has that difficult-to-define — but easy to observe — physical characteristic of quickness. This seems to be the trait that separates Jonathan Edwards from the rest of the triple jumpers. Mike Conley stated in the May 13, 1996, issue of *Sports Illustrated*, "There's no question I am faster than Jonathan, and I can jump higher. But nobody is quicker. "The same is true of Willie Banks, the former (1985) world record holder in the triple jump. Willie did not distinguish himself in any other track and field event, but none of that negatively impacted on his ability to triple-jump. Your triple jumper will need *some* speed, *some* natural jumping ability, *some* strength, and an *abundance* of quickness. Turtles with slow-twitch muscle fibers need not apply.

TECHNICAL ASPECTS

Success in all jumping events begins with a proper run-up. If there is no run up, there is no triple jump. For most jumpers there are minor differences between the run-up for the long jump and the run-up for the triple jump. Until Jonathan Edwards came along, most jumpers were taught to do a controlled run-up to the takeoff board. I think jumpers should run up to the takeoff board as fast as they can handle. Most beginners, because of their lack of strength and skill, should do a more controlled run-up or they will seldom make an optimum jump.

There are four ways you can tell if your triple jumper needs to control the run-up:

1. Have your jumper do a 6,- 12-, and 18-step run-up and measure each jump made from the various approaches to the board. If their is no significant difference between the distances jumped from the short run-ups (6 and 12), and the long run-up (18 steps), then a more controlled step pattern is in order.

2. If your jumpers seem to jump better when fatigue begins to set in, then you can assume that the subsequent slower run-ups are the causal factor. You can conclude that a more controlled run-up when the jumper is fresh will result in a longer jump.

3. Time the run-up; gradually decrease the velocity of the run-up and check the results. Determine the rate of speed of the run-up that resulted in the best jump.

4. The "gather" or preparation for the jump in the last 4 strides is more pronounced than it is for the long jump. This more deliberate approach may result in a longer triple jump. This is especially true for beginners.

As your jumpers become stronger and more accomplished, gradually increase the run-up. Your jumpers should be able to hit the takeoff board at full speed at some point in their career. The faster the run-up your jumpers can handle, the better the results. Remember, the speed of his run-up is one of the reasons that Jonathan Edwards holds the world record.

The Hop Phase, or the Takeoff

Before you begin teaching the triple jump, your jumpers have to establish which leg is dominant. After a few preliminary efforts, most jumpers will establish the leg they want to use for the hop or first phase of the triple jump. For our purposes, let's assume your jumpers choose the left leg for the hop. If this is the case, the jumpers in question will take off from the board with the left foot and land on the left foot. Every effort should be made in this phase of the jump to have a relatively flattened trajectory. Your jumper should work on this phase to determine the best distance that can be made with a flattened trajectory. If the heel strikes the board first, then the jumper is inadvertently executing a long jump takeoff, and excessive height will be the concomitant result. But if your jumper hits the board with the flat-footed landing, the trajectory of the parabolic curve through the body's center of gravity will be flattened. And if the jumper's speed at the board is adequate, the horizontal component of the run-up will also negate the tendency toward too much height on the hop.

The First Phase

Excessive height on the first phase will increase the "G" force when the jumper lands on the left foot at the culmination of the hop. This force will be several times greater than the jumper's body weight, and will obviously negate the effectiveness of the second phase, or the step. If the jumper settles into this phase too long, a decent step is almost impossible to execute. This is the reason that most neophyte triple jumpers have a ridiculously short second phase. Conversely, this is also why Jonathan Edwards is so adept in the triple jump; his transition from the hop to the step is so quick that he minimizes the effect of the "G" forces on the left leg and his step does not suffer the full effect of landing on the hard surface of most triple jump runways.

The drive from the takeoff mark in the triple jump, and the long jump as well, must exploit the physical law of "impulse." Simply put, the takeoff (left) foot must maintain contact with the ground as long as possible to develop greater force. This extra effort is not easily seen by the naked eye, but the jumper knows that it is there. If this technique is performed correctly, the right knee is driven high and out into the direction toward the pit before the takeoff (left) foot leaves the surface. Immediately following this effort, the takeoff leg is pulled through with a high knee action and lands on the runway beneath the jumper's center of gravity. The jumper lands on the flat of the foot in preparation for the step, or second, phase of the triple jump.

The Second Phase, or the Step

This is the most difficult phase of the triple jump to master. You can stand with your back to the competitors, hear the rhythm of the three phases of the triple jump, and determine who is aborting the second phase. You will hear **HOP!**, step, JUMP. A skillful jump will sound like this: HOP, STEP, JUMP! Getting a jumper to execute the proper rhythm, and hence a better jump, is one of the most frustrating coaching challenges in track and field — especially when at the outset, your triple jumper may initially jump farther with the wrong technique. In some respects, this is true of most track and field events. Most athletes will

Figure 16-1

TRIPLE JUMP TAKEOFF

HEAD IS TILTED SLIGHTLY AND THE EYES ARE LOOKING TOWARD THE HORIZON

THE TORSO IS ERECT

THE LEFT LEG WILL BE PULLED FORWARD IN PREPARATION FOR LANDING ON THE LEFT FOOT

RIGHT KNEE IS DRIVEN MORE FORWARD THAN UPWARD. THERE IS NO EFFORT TO GAIN HEIGHT ON THE FIRST PHASE OF THE TRIPLE JUMP

Figure 16-2

TRIPLE JUMP — FIRST PHASE

BOTH ARMS ARE BACK AND WILL DRIVE FORWARD TO INCREASE GROUND FORCE IMMEDIATELY FOLLOWING THE TOUCHDOWN OF THE LEFT (TAKE-OFF) LEG

THE TRAJECTORY OF THE HOP AND STEP IS FLAT. THE TRAJECTORY OF THE FINAL PHASE IS MUCH HIGHER

TORSO IS ERECT, THE LEFT KNEE IS HIGH

THE HOP AND STEP PHASES OF THE TRIPLE JUMP ARE SIMILAR. HOWEVER, THE POSITION OF THE LEGS ARE REVERSED

LEFT LEG (TAKEOFF LEG) WILL REACH FOR THE GROUND AND THE FOOT WILL LAND FLAT TO KEEP THE TRAJECTORY FLAT IN THE NEXT (STEP) PHASE

Figure 16-3

TRIPLE JUMP — SECOND PHASE

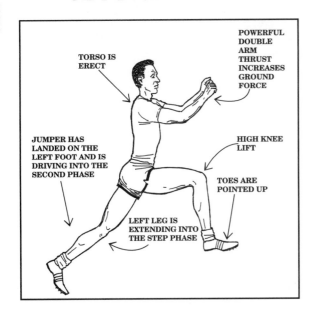

TORSO IS ERECT

POWERFUL DOUBLE ARM THRUST INCREASES GROUND FORCE

JUMPER HAS LANDED ON THE LEFT FOOT AND IS DRIVING INTO THE SECOND PHASE

HIGH KNEE LIFT

TOES ARE POINTED UP

LEFT LEG IS EXTENDING INTO THE STEP PHASE

Figure 16-4

TRIPLE JUMP — THIRD PHASE

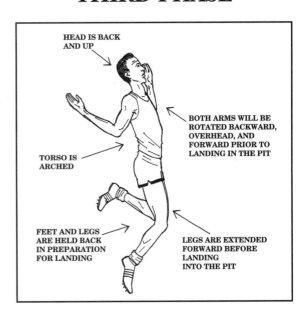

HEAD IS BACK AND UP

BOTH ARMS WILL BE ROTATED BACKWARD, OVERHEAD, AND FORWARD PRIOR TO LANDING IN THE PIT

TORSO IS ARCHED

FEET AND LEGS ARE HELD BACK IN PREPARATION FOR LANDING

LEGS ARE EXTENDED FORWARD BEFORE LANDING INTO THE PIT

Photo 16–1. The double-arm action in the second phase of the triple jump. This is the difficult-to-learn "step" phase of the triple jump.

feel uncomfortable with a corrected technique and may retrogress during the learning process. It is infinitely more difficult to unlearn bad technique than it is to do it right from the very beginning. Practice does not make perfect; *perfect* practice makes perfect.

A properly executed step should be about 30% of the total triple jump. When you look at the ratios of most world-record triple jumps, the hop is usually about 37%, the step is approximately 30%, and the jump is around 33%. These figures are not etched in stone; they are approximations. The ratios will vary somewhat from jumper to jumper. But if your jumper has an 18-foot hop, a 10-foot step, and a 17-foot jump, something is drastically wrong with the step phase.

There are several ways to improve the effectiveness of the step phase. Of the hundreds of drills I have tried over time, many were a waste of time. To save you from a lengthy ordeal of trial and error, I will list the best drills that helped most of our jumpers improve the effectiveness of the step phase:

1. Have each jumper do several standing long jumps. Notice that they naturally use a double-arm thrust to negotiate these jumps.

2. Ask each jumper to do a series of hops (about 7) on the dominant foot using the double-arm thrust. Repeat this drill with the other leg. Most jumpers will not experience too much difficulty with the drill. Incidentally, the athlete's torso should be vertical during all three phases of the triple jump.

3. Tell the jumpers to hop and lift their knees about waist high before each landing. Use the double-arm thrust with each hop.

4. Have the jumpers hop three times with the dominant leg and, without stopping, switch to the other leg and hop three times. Continue hopping and changing legs for 30–50 meters. Make sure that the knee is waist high on every hop when they change to the other foot. Without realizing it, your jumpers are doing the step movement every time they change legs. Place a series of cones on the ground about 6 feet apart. Repeat the above drill. Increase the distance between the cones as they improve.

5. Place seven hoops on the ground about 6 feet apart. Instruct the jumpers to do a series of "steps" from hoop to hoop. Increase the distance between the hoops as they improve. Use the double-arm thrust with each step.

6. Place three hoops on the ground 6 feet apart. Hop in the first, step to the second, jump in the last hoop. Increase the distance between hoops as the jumpers improve.

7. Place two hoops on the ground near the long jump pit (or mats). Hop into the first hoop, step to the next, jump into the pit.

Progress through these drills, making sure that the skills are executed correctly. It may take days, weeks, months, and even years before the correct triple jump technique is learned. If the triple jump were easy to learn, everybody would do it.

Many great jumpers in the early years of this event did not use the double-arm thrust and made some pretty decent marks, but every world-class jumper of the modern era uses the double-arm thrust. The reason? Physics. Because of the tremendous impact of the "G" forces on the lower extremities, the double-arm thrust improves the jumper's ability to launch the second phase. As the arms are driven upward (to shoulder height), the ground force and the subsequent raising of the center of gravity, is translated to lift the jumper from the ground and into the final "jump" phase of the triple jump. With all these forces at work, the step portion of the triple jump is potentiated.

The Third (Final) Phase, or Final Jump

The "jump" phase, also called the third or final phase, of the triple jump is the easiest to learn, but it should not be taken for granted. The triple jump is not over until it is over. Your jumpers should spend a considerable amount of time working on this aspect of the event. The triple jump is basically a continuum, and every effort should be toward making a smooth transition between phases. This is another reason that Jonathan Edwards does so well in this event.

Most triple jumpers use the hang style for the last phase. The foot plant for the hop and the step is on the flat of the foot — but to gain greater height on the jump phase, your triple jumper should plant the heel first. The planting of the heel should not be too pronounced, however, and definitely not ahead of the center of gravity. The jumper does this to avoid excessive forward rotation. Remember, the athlete's torso must remain vertical during all three phases of the jump.

The last phase of the triple jump is basically a long jump off the nondominant foot, which tends to have a negative effect on this portion of the triple jump. Most jumpers, however, chose to take the first two jumps with the dominant leg to optimize the triple jump effort. So it's six of one and half a dozen of the other. Bob Beamon, the former world record holder in the long, was alleged to jump 27 feet off the wrong foot. It boggles the mind to imagine that he could have jumped close to 27 feet on the final phase if he decided to specialize on the triple jump. Someday, an athlete of that caliber will appear on the scene and will not have to compromise on the last phase.

The Landing

The triple jump landing is exactly the same as the long jump landing. There is a deliberate attempt to land with the body's center of gravity as low as possible. Most jumpers accomplish this by dropping to the hips and landing on the side of the body. Jumpers can add nearly a foot to their jump by using this technique. This skill has to be practiced regularly in order to be safe and effective.

TRAINING PROGRAMS

The general preparation period for triple jumpers is similar to the general preparation period for all jumpers. The objective of this period and the specific preparation period is to build a foundation for the more demanding work that will occur during the precompetitive period. I delineate a specific preparation period training schedule, however, because of the uniquely difficult requirements of the triple jump. You will notice a great similarity to other jumping events; the big difference in this schedule will be the severity and intensity of the triple jump workouts.

Weekly training schedule for triple jumpers during the specific preparation period

Day	Duration (min)	Training task	Training details
Monday	20	Warm-up	800 meter jog, stretch
	10	Sprint drills	High knees, 1, 2, 3s, bounding
	20	Easy plyometrics	Rope jumping, dot drills, standing triple jump, box jumping, hop 50 meters×2 hop over 7 low hurdles×2 (right and left legs)
	30	Weight training	Lower body, 4×12 reps
	5	Warm-down	Jog 400, stretch
Tuesday	20	Warm-up	Jog 400, walk 200, stride 200, stretch
	10	Sprint drills	High knees, butt kicks, high knee skipping, overstrides
	10	Jump drills	Hop 3, change, hop 3, ×30 meters, repeat this drill×5
	30	Technique work	7×run-throughs
	20	Weight training	Upper body, 3 sets, 12 reps
	5	Warm-down	Jog 400 meters, stretch
Wednesday	20	Warm-up	Jog 600, walk 200, stride 200, stretch
	30	Games	Basketball or volleyball
	20	Weight training	Lower body, 3 sets, 10 reps
	5	Warm-down	Jog 400 meters, stretch
Thursday	20	Warm-up	Jog 800, stretch
	10	Sprint drills	Same as Monday
	30	Technique work	3 jumps, no run-up; 3 jumps, 3-step run-up; 3 jumps, 6- and 12-step run-up
	20	Weight training	Upper body, 3 sets, 10 reps
	5	Warm-down	Jog 400, stretch
Friday	20	Warm-up	Jog 800, stride 2×100, stretch
		Sprint drills	Same as Tuesday
	20	Plyometrics	Box jumping, 3 boxes, double and single leg, bounding 30 meters×3
	5	Warm-down	Jog 400, stretch
Saturday		Competition.	

The specific preparation occurs during the month of February — a time to begin putting all the triple jump pieces together. If you are working in a situation that is less than ideal, your only opportunity to execute the triple jump in its entirety is during competition — but don't feel underprivileged. More fortunate coaches in the suburbs may initially have an advantage, but after a few meets, your athletes will catch up. Take advantage of the facilities during these competitions. Most of our jumpers can be found working on their technique long after their events have culminated. Some of these athletes may be valued participants in a few running events, but we will often substitute someone else so we can take advantage of the available facilities. We may lose a few dual meets, but we must exploit every opportunity to practice our craft.

March is the most important part of the indoor season. It marks the important indoor invitationals culminating with an indoor conference championship. It is also the beginning of our precompetitive cycle. By this time, our jumping technique is becoming polished, and our jumpers have familiarized themselves with the total event. At this point, triple jump drills become increasingly relevant. As your jumpers obtain a feel for their events, drills may have a greater training effect on the jumpers' progress than competition. Marks made in competition become the way you measure effectiveness of your training program.

Weekly training schedule for triple jumpers during the precompetitive period

Day	Duration (min)	Training task	Training details
Monday	20	Warm-up	800 meter jog, stride 4×100, stretch
	10	Sprint drills	High knees, form runs, bounding
	20	Plyometrics	Box drills, depth jumping, hopping over low hurdles
	30	Weight training	Lower body, 4 sets, 8 reps, jumping squats, 2×10 reps
	5	Warm-down	400 jog, stretch
Tuesday	20	Warm-up	400 meter jog, 4×200 stride, stretch
	10	Sprint drills	High knees, 1, 2, 3s, chop downs
	30	Technique work	7×run throughs, 10×full jumps
	20	Weight training	Upper body, 4×8 reps
	5	Warm-down	Jog 400, stretch
Wednesday	20	Warm-up	Jog 800, 4×100 stride, stretch
	10	Sprint drills	High knees, quick steps, form runs

Day	Duration (min)	Training task	Training details
	30	Technique work	Hop runway $\times$ 3, hop 3 and change, runway $\times$ 7, pop-ups $\times$ 7
	30	Weight training	Lower body, 70%, 4 sets, 6 reps
	5	Warm-down	Jog 400 meters, stretch
Thursday	20	Warm-up	Jog 400, 800 wind sprints, stretch
	10	Sprint drills	Same as Monday
	20	Technique work	3-, 6-, 12-, 18-step run-up, 3 hops, 1 step, 1 jump $\times$ 3, 3 steps, 1 jump $\times$ 3
	15	Weight training	Lower body 2 $\times$ 10
	5	Warm-down	Jog 400, stretch
Friday	20	Warm-up	Jog 400, 4 $\times$ 70 strides
	10	Sprint drills	Same as Tuesday
	20	Plyometrics	Box drills (3 boxes $\times$ 7), depth jumping
	5	Warm-down	Jog 400, walk 400, stretch
Saturday		Competition.	

The next period initiates the outdoor campaign. In a large portion of the United States, inclement weather is a major consideration for jumpers and sprinters. The abrupt weather changes cannot be ignored, yet too many athletes from high school to the international level reach major competitions suffering from a plethora of major and minor injuries. We all know world-class athletes have to wait several years to recover from injuries that could have been easily avoided. When a wind comes from the north, send your jumpers and sprinters home! Finish the meet with your distance runners. Every drill and every work-out in the following schedule can be modified and completed indoors. Convince the school engineer, janitors, and others who may complain about indoor prac-tices, of the importance of track and field.

Weekly training schedule for triple jumpers during the competitive season

Day	Duration (min)	Training task	Training details
Monday	20	Warm-up	Jog 800 meters, stretch
	10	Sprint drills	High knees, 1, 2, 3s, form runs, bounding
	20	Plyometrics	Rope jumping, box jumping, depth jumping 3 hops and change drill, 50 meters $\times$ 3

Day	Duration (min)	Training task	Training details
	30	Weight training	Lower body 4 sets × 5 reps, jumping squats 2 sets × 10
	5	Warm-down	Jog 400 meters, stretch
Tuesday	20	Warm-up	Jog 400, walk 200, stride 200, stretch
	10	Sprint drills	High knees, chop downs, butt kicks, overstrides
	30	Technique work	Run throughs × 7, 7 jumps full runway
	20	Weight training	Upper body, 4 sets, 5 reps
	5	Warm-down	Jog 400, stretch
Wednesday	20	Warm-up	Jog 200, walk 100, stride 200, walk 200, 4 × 100, stretch
	10	Sprint drills	Same as Monday
	30	Jump drills	Hop 30 meters × 4, 3 hops and change — full runway × 7, hop, 3 steps and jump × 3
	5	Warm down	Jog 400, stretch
Thursday	20	Warm up	Jog 800, stretch
	10	Sprint drills	Same as Tuesday
	30	Technique work	3 × run-throughs, 6-step run-up and jump × 3 3 steps and jump × 7, pop-ups × 7
	30	Weight training	Lower body, 3 × 6, 60% of max
	5	Warm-down	Jog 400, stretch
Friday	20	Warm-up	Jog 800, stretch
	10	Sprint drills	High knees, 1, 2, 3s, form runs
	15	Plyometrics	Box drills, depth jumps (× 7)
	10	Weight training	Upper body, 2 × 10 reps
	5	Warm down	Jog 400, stretch

Saturday   Competition.

The next period is like the time during which an accomplished musician learns how to play by ear. Every day is an entity in and of itself. Most of the workouts up to this point have followed a predictable pattern. No such pattern exists during the peaking period. Each workout will depend upon how your athletes performed in previous competitions. Some of your jumpers may train harder, others will merely warm up and wait for the next meet, and a few might need to correct certain technical flaws. You will have to orchestrate all of this. At its best, the following training schedule is merely a guide.

Weekly training schedule for triple jumpers
during the peaking period

Day	Duration (min)	Training task	Training details
Monday	20	Warm-up	800 meter jog, stretch
	10	Sprint drills	High knees, chop downs, form runs
	20	Technique work — plyometrics	7×runway (18–20 steps), box jumping, bounding (use cones 10–15 feet apart)
	30	Weight training	Lower body, 6 sets×3 reps
	5	Warm-down	Jog 400, stretch
Tuesday	20	Warm-up	Jog 600 meters, stride 200 meters, stretch
	10	Sprint drills	High knees, 1, 2, 3s, form runs
	30	Technique work	7 runways, 10 full jumps (7 at 90%–95% effort, 3 at 100%)
	20	Weight training	Upper body, 3 sets×3, 1 set×8
	5	Warm-down	Jog 400, stretch
Wednesday	20	Warm-up	Jog 400, stride 200, jog 200
	10	Sprint drills	High knees, form runs
	30	Games	Basketball, volleyball
	5	Warm-down	Jog 400, stretch
Thursday	20	Warm-up	Jog 880, 4×100, stretch
	10	Sprint drills	Same as Monday
	30	Technique work	3 jumps from 3-, 6-, 12-, 18- steps run-ups
	30	Weight training	Lower body, 3 sets, 8 reps, jumping squats, 2×8 reps
	5	Warm-down	Jog 400, stretch
Friday	20	Warm-up	Jog 400, walk 200, jog 400
	10	Sprint drills	Same as Tuesday
	20	Plyometrics	Box jumping 7×3 boxes, depth jumping, 7×18" box
	10	Weight training	Upper body, 1 set, 10 reps
Saturday		Competition.	

Our jumpers will often spend more time on run-ups, especially if they get into foul trouble in competition. Our goal in practice is to be on the board 100% of the time. The only deviation we expect is how much of the board the jumper covers with each attempt. We found that most will hit the front edge of the board during their warm-up. We don't make any alteration of their steps; they will cover the board for their first official jump. The change in rhythm and the lengthening of the penultimate step in an actual jump will put a jumper on the board. By the third jump, our jumpers are completely warmed up and we move the athletes back a few inches to avoid fouling. As fatigue sets in, we may have to adjust a jumper's steps forward for the last two jumps in the finals. A jumper's stride pattern may be relatively consistent, but *slight* adjustments may have to be made during competition. Take note of your jumper's stride pattern in practice, and you will be able to predict certain inconsistencies in the runway and anticipate the need for minor adjustments, if any, in competition.

TRIPLE JUMP TRAINING UNDER DIFFICULT CONDITIONS

The run up is the most important part of any jumping event and the easiest to practice under difficult conditions. You can practice the triple jump runway in a corridor, gymnasium, playground, park, or just about anywhere. Make a chalk mark, use tape to fashion a takeoff board, or use a rubber softball base or linoleum strip as a substitute for a takeoff board. Measure the run-up distance and practice the runway until the jumper establishes a consistent stride pattern. If your area is not long enough, practice a short run-up of 6 and 12 steps and make this consistent. Add the remainder of the run-up at the meet.

Box jumping is a must in triple jump training. Ask the shop teacher to fashion three jump boxes. These boxes should be 18 inches high. If your school does not have wood shop, ask a nearby school to make a few boxes for you. If this is not feasible, make them yourself.

You can set up a few gym mats to facilitate triple jump practice. You can work on every phase of the triple jump except the landing with mats. Set up cones on a gymnasium floor to practice hopping and stepping drills. Move the cones farther apart as your jumpers improve. Your jumpers can also work on their hopping and stepping drills up stairs. Be careful.

If you have a commercially made high jump pit, your jumpers can safely practice landing skills. This is not the same as a regular long jump pit, but I was surprised how well this prepared our jumpers for competition.

Our indoor practices consist of various kinds of drills. We seldom do a full jump in practice. We subsequently put every thing together at meets. After a few competitions, our triple jump technique is first class. Most of the earlier training periods should emphasize drills anyway. As a result, our triple jumpers are not at any appreciable disadvantage at any time during the indoor track season.

During the outdoor season, we travel to several locations to work on the full triple jump technique. As our jumpers become more skillful, we continue to improve by practicing the full jump only once a week. We get all the triple jump exposure we need by practicing the triple jump on Tuesday and competing every Saturday.

We insist that our jumpers take every jump available in competition, whether they need to or not. This affords them the opportunity to practice their skills under meet conditions. As we enter the final weeks of the season, we change this tactic and take only as many jumps as we need to win the competition. Some of our jumpers are valuable competitors in other events, and they have to conserve their energy in several important late-season competitions.

Figure 16-5

BOX JUMPING DRILLS
(Plyometrics)

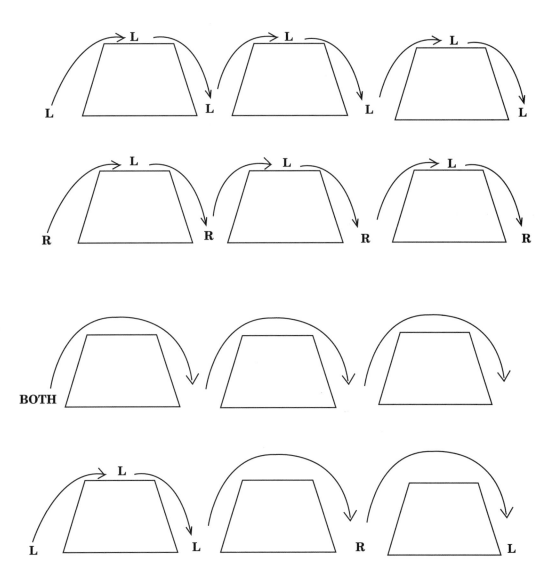

THESE DRILLLS CAN START WITH THE RIGHT OR LEFT FOOT. THESE DRILLS CAN BE PRACTICED BY LONG JUMPERS, TRIPLE JUMPERS, AND HIGH JUMPERS.

Your triple jumpers will be able to hold their own regardless of your lack of facilities and equipment. There will be little or no logistical problem in providing an adequate training environment for your jumpers. When you look at the performances of American jumpers in world-class competition, you realize that the best jumpers have come from every sort of situation — many that are far less than ideal. During the last decade, great jumpers have emerged from Brazil (Oliviera), Cuba (Quesada), Jamaica (Beckford), and Dominican Republic (Romain).

Section 17

THE POLE VAULT
The Daredevils

Pole vaulters are close cousins to skydivers and bungee jumpers. They love leaping off balconies, turning flop-flops on concrete sidewalks, and jumping off high diving boards. When you find this kind of athlete in your school, give that kid a fiber glass pole. Teach the daredevil every upside-down, wild, and death-defying drill you can think of. Take that athlete to a track meet, and let the competition beware!

When I was a high school athlete, the pole vault was a relatively inexpensive event. All you needed was a bamboo or steel pole and a sawdust pit or mats, and you could accommodate an entire cadre of vaulters. The vaulters of the early fifties were cut from the same cloth as the vaulters of the 1990s. Great pole vaulters have always been extraordinary athletes — probably the most versatile athletes on the track team. In addition, every pole vaulter must have the uncommon recklessness of a skydiver. They are the daredevils of track and field. There is at least one of these kids in every high school; however, the expense related to the event has increased to the extent that most of the poorer schools in America have abandoned the pole vault. The last time I ordered pole vault equipment (in 1980), it cost us over $7,000 to purchase the proper equipment. When I was a neophyte coach (in 1963), we were able with much enterprise and innovation to acquire some decent equipment without making a serious dent in the money we raised to keep our track and field program afloat. Our equipment was not the best possible, and we often competed in the affluent suburbs and held our own in the event. There were a few parochial schools in the city that developed state champions in the pole vault with our similar situation. Developing champion pole vaulters in a disadvantaged situation can be done, but every one has to participate in this effort or it won't happen. Nothing is impossible if you want it badly enough.

OBTAINING SAFE EQUIPMENT

The pole vault is an event that cannot be compromised. The event is loaded with hazards and risks, and you must have the best available equipment. When you have the best of equipment, your athletes will be able to vault without being overly concerned about possible disaster. This aspect of the pole vault is so important that I must cover this factor first. There is no need to talk about technique and modern training methods until we discuss how the forgotten coach can obtain decent equipment.

Early in my career, we bought net bags and filled them with foam rubber, but as our vaulters improved, we needed a safer landing area. After a few years, a generous college coach donated a used inflatable pit to our program. We repaired it and used this pit until it became illegal; a few athletes in our state were seriously injured using this pit, and many schools abandoned its use. The inflatable pit was declared dangerous because it would "bottom out" when the vaulter inadvertently landed feet first. With the demise of the inflatable pit, expensive commercial pits were mandated. Pole vaulting became too expensive for most athletic budgets.

Permit me to relate how a local coach and a dedicated parent solved the pole vault problem. This school (parochial), raised funds through a parents' club. Everyone became involved in the project. I am told that the school in question raised over $50,000 a year. They put on a boxing tournament (illegal in most public schools), and subsequently sold an ad book. Almost all of the local merchants contributed to this book. They did this project every year. This school also has a weight room that could rival Gold's Gym. Spending $7,000–$10,000 for pole vault equipment was a piece of cake. The coach dug a hole for the vaulting box and built an asphalt runway and they had state-of-the-art pole vaulting facilities!

This story had a happy ending. All of this effort ended with a third place in the state championships. What made this achievement so great was that no athlete from the city of Chicago had ever *placed* in this event since the advent of the fiber glass pole. If you want to develop a champion pole vaulter, you cannot compromise.

In 1961, Aubry Dooley of Oklahoma State was one of the first vaulters to use the fiber glass pole, and the event has never been the same since. Before the fiber glass pole became popular, world-class vaulters were happy to vault 15–16 feet. When the fiber glass pole became the only way to go, the event literally and figuratively took off. When the 20-foot barrier was broken by Sergei Bubka of Russia, I knew that American vaulters were in deep trouble. As this is written, only one American is ranked among the top ten vaulters in the world. The pole vault is no longer the private domain of American athletes.

A champion vaulter has to have the speed of a sprinter, the skill of an Olympic gymnast, and the reckless courage of a daredevil. A champion vaulter must also have an excellent work ethic. If a vaulter is not willing to work several years at this event, there is no chance for success. Talent is not enough in most track and field events, but an athlete cannot *begin* to pole vault without serious endeavor.

TALENT IDENTIFICATION

Look for the campus "stuntman"; every school has one. There is always some youngster around school trying dangerous stunts. The best vaulter I have ever coached was a skate board fanatic who would do flip flops at the slightest provocation. Another student would run up a wall and jump from a balcony backward (I never figured out how this stunt was done). Keep your eyes and ears open; these athletes' reputations are part of the campus gossip.

Vaulters are excellent sprinters. Sergei Bubka, the great Russian pole vaulter, allegedly runs the 100 meter dash in 10.1 seconds. Pole vaulters are excellent gymnasts. Most vaulters are at home on rings, horizontal bars, and tumbling mats. These athletes also possess excellent upper-body strength. If your pole vault candidates do not have these characteristics, it becomes your job to help them develop these skills. The potential vaulter will not be able to do anything of value on the pole whithout these physical requirements.

TECHNICAL ASPECTS

Most of our vaulters learned their technique by rope vaulting. We worked on this apparatus until they could rope vault at least a foot above their top hand hold. We taught them the proper hand hold, proper body position, and rock back on the rope before they touched a regular pole. We also use rope drills to develop upper-body strength. Our vaulters have to climb a rope without using their legs. As their strength improved, they would climb the rope in an inverted position.

Preliminary Pole Vault Instruction

When the potential vaulter's skills on the rope are satisfactory, drills with a fiber glass pole are introduced. Our most important drill is a 12-step run-up to a pole that is held by the coach at a 45 degree angle in the vaulting box. Have the vaulter run toward the pole. You stand to the left side of the pole (for a right-handed vaulter), grab the pole, and catapult the athlete into the pit. When the athlete can do this drill without taxing your strength, place a crossbar at a low height and continue this drill. Some of the more talented candidates will vault 10–11 feet using this method.

The Pole Plant

While you are working on bar clearance skills, you can devote part of your work-out to the pole plant. After 40–50 minutes working on clearing the bar, upper-body fatigue will set in. Spend the remainder of practice working the pole plant. If you do this, the vaulter will be ready to incorporate the pole plant and bar clearance much sooner.

One of the best methods to teach the pole plant is the towel drill. Place a towel on the gym floor; have the vaulter run toward the towel and plant the pole. Make sure the athlete learns to bring the pole directly above the head when the pole is planted. Spend about 20–30 minutes on this drill each day until it is per-fected. During the latter part of the season, the towel drill can be used as a part of the vaulter's warm-up.

Another planting drill can be done against the wall. Have the vaulter count three steps and plant on the fourth step. Teach the athlete to drive the right knee forward and upward as the pole is planted. Place your hands on the vaulter's back and lift the athlete slightly as the pole is planted. Continue this drill until the vaulter becomes easy to lift.

Combining the Pole Plant and Bar Clearance

Have your vaulters calculate a 6-step run-up by doing a series of run-ups with the pole. When the takeoff spot is established, stand to the left of this spot in order to assist the vaulters into the pit (from this point on, all instructions will be for right-handed vaulters). Instruct your vaulters to run at a controlled speed

Figure 17-1

POLE VAULT PLANT

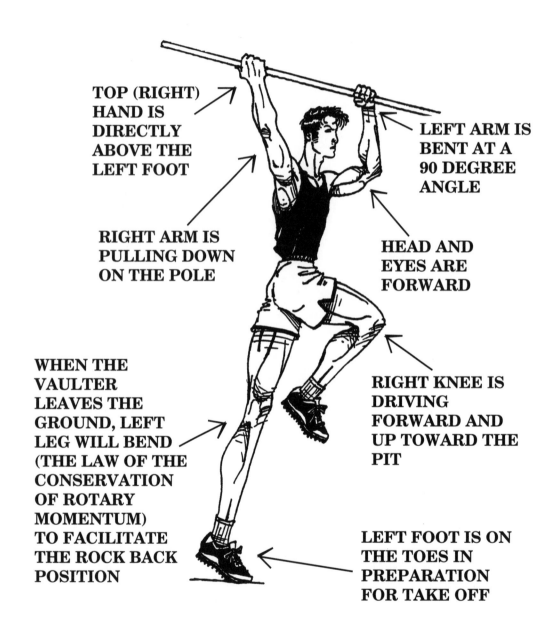

TOP (RIGHT) HAND IS DIRECTLY ABOVE THE LEFT FOOT

LEFT ARM IS BENT AT A 90 DEGREE ANGLE

RIGHT ARM IS PULLING DOWN ON THE POLE

HEAD AND EYES ARE FORWARD

WHEN THE VAULTER LEAVES THE GROUND, LEFT LEG WILL BEND (THE LAW OF THE CONSERVATION OF ROTARY MOMENTUM) TO FACILITATE THE ROCK BACK POSITION

RIGHT KNEE IS DRIVING FORWARD AND UP TOWARD THE PIT

LEFT FOOT IS ON THE TOES IN PREPARATION FOR TAKE OFF

and execute several assisted vaults into the pit without a crossbar. When the athletes' technique seems satisfactory, place a crossbar at 5 feet and continue to assist the vaulters by pulling the pole and catapulting them over the bar. When the candidate has successfully negotiated the assisted vaulting technique, you can move to the next step. Success means that the vaulters are clearing about 10–11 feet with very little assistance from you. You should not be exerting much effort as the vaulters clear the crossbar.

The Full Technique

It may take several days before an athlete can vault unassisted, but a vaulter should never vault alone. A reliable person should be present to spot the vaulter and catch the pole. That person may be the vault coach, a responsible adult, or an intelligent student athlete. If you are the only coach available, this becomes your job. But the best of all worlds is to find a knowledgeable vault coach. In most cases, you will have to be creative in finding someone to help you coach this event. If not, you will have to coach the pole vault in addition to the other 16 events. This is not an impossible task. I will discuss the logistics of coaching an entire track team without any assistant coaches in Section 22.

Teach your new vaulters to improve their technique by doing mostly low vaulting with a short run-up. The advantage of this approach is that your vaulters can spend most of their time working on the pole plant, rock back, and bar clearance in relative safety. The following steps must be automatic before moving back to a full run-up:

1. The pole should be held with hands slightly wider than shoulder width apart.

2. The right hand should be palms up and the left hand should be held palms down.

3. The pole should be carried with the tip held higher than the vaulter's head.

4. The pole plant should begin in the last 4 steps of the run-up.

5. When the pole is planted, the top hand, the center of gravity, and the left foot should be in a straight line.

6. As the vaulter leaves the ground, the right knee is driven forward and upward. The top arm is held straight; the bottom arm is bent at approximately 90 degrees.

7. During the rock back, the left leg joins the right leg in a bent position. This action will facilitate a greater rock back (conservation of rotary momentum). The athlete's back will be toward the ground. The right arm is still straight. The pole is bent to its maximum.

8. As the pole straightens, the body is held close to the pole in an inverted position. The vaulter simultaneously pulls and pushes the body upward and turns to the left to release the pole. The left hand is released first, followed immediately by the right, or top, hand. Every effort is made to keep the body in an inverted position.

Photo 17–1. The proper method of carrying the pole prior to planting the pole.

Photo 17–2. The "rock back" position in the pole vault.

Photo 17–3. The vaulter's body is beginning to extend to a vertical position. The athlete will subsequently turn counterclockwise after the body is completely vertical in preparation for bar clearance.

Photo 17–4. Pole vault finishing position. Both arms will be lifted to clear the bar.

9. Both hands are thrown to the rear and the vaulter lands on the back into the pit.

CHOOSING A POLE

Another expensive item that a vault coach must purchase is a fiber glass pole or poles. Most of the poles we had were for the average athlete. We seldom had a vaulter who was taller than 6 feet and weighed over 200 pounds. Since you select poles by hand hold and body weight, most of our poles were in a rather narrow range. We found that seven poles did the job for us. Our poles were based on a 10-, 11-, 12-, 13-, 14-foot hand hold for a 160 pound vaulter. Two additional stiff poles, for training new vaulters, were donated to us. These poles cost us around $750.00. We bought them over a period of several years. By manipulating hand holds with an athlete's body weight, we were able to accommodate every vaulter on our team. For example, a vaulter of a lighter body weight than 160 pounds, can hold a 13-foot pole at 14 feet and bend it without much difficulty. A heavier vaulter can use a 14-foot pole with a 13-foot hand hold. The largest pole was a recent purchase, when one of our better vaulters became too strong for the 13-foot pole. (The best way to determine if a vaulter has outgrown a pole is by observing the "snap" or recoil of the pole near the end of the vault.)

One of the most difficult transitions for a vaulter is to convert to a higher hand hold. Moving to a pole that is one foot higher makes it even more difficult. The transition to a higher pole should be gradual, but this was not financially feasible for us. Everybody had to move up one foot at a time. I discovered that a talented athlete could make this conversion in about two weeks. There will be several days of erratic vaulting and some serious trepidation but the conversion can be made. You will have to be exclusively at the pole vault area for several days to encourage your vaulters with positive affirmations and continual instruction until they are able to deal with the new hand hold. They will need your undivided attention. Every time a vaulter goes to a higher hand hold there is a minor difference in timing. A *substantial* change in the vaulter's hand hold will require an enormous adjustment in technique — the run-up, swing, rock back, and bar clearance.

Even suburban coaches are forced to improvise when it comes to pole vault equipment. I am told that they share and trade poles. If they need a pole that is not available in their supply, some of these innovative educators get on the phone and negotiate with their contemporaries for equipment. Apparently no one has an endless supply of funds.

Most coaches in affluent situations are eager to accommodate the less fortunate. I have never been refused use of facilities. One of our vaulters improved 2 feet in one week when we trained at a nearby suburban fieldhouse during our spring break.

THE POLE VAULT RUN-UP

Place a mark at the point of the vaulter's pole plant. Measure the run-up from point back to the start of the run-up and make another check mark. The pole vault stride pattern is basically the same as the long jump and triple jump runway. Most vaulters will use 18 steps, though this number will vary depending on the strength and skill of your vaulter.

This phase of the pole vault must be practiced assiduously. Without an effective run-up, there is no effective pole vault. The energy developed in the run-up determines the extent of energy that will be manifest in the bend of the fiber glass pole during the vault. The better and faster the run-up, the greater the amount of energy stored in the pole, the higher an athlete can vault. A faster vaulter can also hold the pole higher. The higher the hand hold, the higher an athlete can vault. Sprint speed is as important on the pole vault runway as it is in the other jumping events.

TRAINING PROGRAMS

The general preparation period for pole vaulters consists of extensive gymnastic work and sprint training. Gymnastic training should include horizontal bar, parallel bars, rings, tumbling, and rope climbing. Vaulters must feel at home in an inverted position on all of this equipment. The upper-body development gained from these activities will build an excellent physical foundation for the pole vaulting season.

Talented vaulters should also be able to compete favorably with your sprinters. During the specific preparation period, the vaulters will do most of the sprint drills carrying a pole. These drills will help them become accustomed to carrying a pole through the often long and exhausting competition awaiting them in most track meets.

The specific preparation period is the time when your vaulter's training program focuses on actual vaulting. Gymnastic exercises are continued, but as supplementary activities. Most of the training program will mirror actual pole vault mechanics:

Weekly training schedule for pole vaulters during the specific preparation period

Day	Duration (min)	Training task	Training details
Monday	20	Warm-up	4 × 100 (with pole), calisthenics, stretch, rope climbing

Day	Duration (min)	Training task	Training details
	10	Sprint drills (with pole)	High knees, form runs, butt kicks
	30	Technique work	Run-throughs, towel plants, rock back drills
	15	Gymnastic work	Hip circles, rope vaulting
	5	Warm-down	Jog 400 meters, stretch
Tuesday	20	Warm-up	Jog 800 meters, stretch
	10	Sprint drills (with pole)	High knees, chop downs, form runs
	40	Technique work	Vault for height from a 12-step run up
	5	Warm-down	Jog 400 meters, stretch
Wednesday	20	Warm-up	4×100 with pole, calisthenics, stretch
	10	Sprint drills (with pole)	High knees, high knee skip, form runs
	45	Technique work	Rope vaulting, pole bending drill with a surgical hose*
	5	Warm-down	Jog 400 meters, stretch
Thursday	20	Warm-up	Jog 400 meters, calisthenics and stretch
	10	Sprint drills (with a pole)	High knees, skipping, form runs
	45	Technique work	Run-ups, low vaulting from 12 steps
	5	Warm-down	Jog 400 meters, stretch
Friday	20	Warm-up	4×100 strides with a pole, stretch
	10	Sprint drills (with pole)	Same as Monday
	10	Technique work	Full run-throughs
	30	Gymnastics	Hip circles on horizontal bar, rope climbing, dips and chinning
	5	Warm-down	Jog 400, stretch

Saturday   Competition.

* Tie a surgical hose to a basketball goal support or a horizontal bar. Have your vaulters get into and *hold* the rock back position to accustom themselves to the sinking sensation of fiber glass pole vaulting. This is a fantastic drill for vaulters. Purchase a surgical hose that is similar in thickness to a fiber glass pole. I bought our rubber hose at a nearby factory.

The precompetitive period training program is very similar to our specific preparation period. The major difference between the two periods is the change from short runway vaulting to a full runway on Tuesday. Most of the drills are the same, and the vaulter continues to low vault for technique on Thursday. Earlier sections state that all-out jumping may be too demanding, and your athletes may leave their best jumps at home. More is not always better. In our situation, it was difficult to get the gym for all-out vaulting because of the basketball program. We often scheduled our full runway vaulting when the basketball team was at an away game. Most of our drills and short run-ups were done in a smaller auxiliary gym. Since we were working on polishing certain skills, we didn't need to do that many full run-up vaults. During our indoor season, drills and gymnastics were more important than all-out vaulting.

Weekly training schedule for pole vaulters during the precompetitive period

Day	Duration (min)	Training task	Training details
Monday	20	Warm-up	800 meter jog, 7×60 with pole
	10	Sprint drills	High knees, 1, 2, 3s with pole
	30	Technique work	7×runway, rock back drill, low vaults
	15	Gymnastics	Hip circles on the horizontal bar, handstand push ups, rope climbing
	5	Warm-down	Jog 400, stretch
Tuesday	20	Warm-up	Jog 400, 4×60, calisthenics
		Sprint drills	High knees, butt kicks, form run with pole
	45	Technique work	Vault with 6, 12, and full runway, maximum vaults
	5	Warm-down	Jog 400, stretch
Wednesday	20	Warm-up	Jog 800, stretch
	10	Sprint drills	High knees, form runs with pole
	40	Vaulting drills	Sinking drills with surgical hose, run-throughs, rock backs, low vaulting without a crossbar
	5	Warm-down	Jog 400, stretch
Thursday	20	Warm-up	Jog 400, stretch, 7×50 with pole
	10	Sprint drills	High knees, chop downs with pole

Day	Duration (min)	Training task	Training details
	30	Technique work	Short run-up, low vaulting
	20	Gymnastics	Hip circles to handstand on rings, cartwheel to round off, to back handspring on mats
	5	Warm-down	Jog 400, stretch
Friday	20	Warm-up	Jog 800, stretch
	10	Sprint drills	High knees, 1, 2, 3s, form runs
	30	Technique work	Low vaulting with a short run-up
	5	Warm-down	Jog 400, stretch
Saturday	Competition.		

The next four weeks is the early part of the outdoor season. There are several problems for vaulters at this time. The main problem is the weather; the conditions are not always the same. It is very difficult to conduct a decent practice if the weather is not cooperating with you. Athletes in some situations have a considerable advantage over everyone else; many schools with facilities never go outside to vault. In our case, when we had to vault outside, we would get the shot-putters to bring the vaulting pits across the street to a park, and after practice they'd take them back to the school. That effort was a good warm-up for their weight-training workout.

On other occasions, we would travel (about 16 miles) to the nearest Chicago Board of Education stadium to vault. We often shared this facility with several local schools. It was never too crowded; most public school coaches did not bother with the pole vault. Just the right amount of athletes (about 12) were usually working on the event. It was an occasion for our athletes to engage in friendly competition. This was a perfect situation for our vaulters.

We also used our spring break to travel to the nearest suburb. Most suburban coaches were eager to accommodate us. I have never been turned down by a suburban coaching staff when I called and made a formal request to train at their facility. I trained the majority of the team at the school in the morning and drove the vaulters to the suburbs in the afternoon for their workouts. This was one of the rare occasions that I could devote my undivided attention to the pole vaulters. Our vaulters usually improved 2 feet during this week. It caused me to wonder how much improvement they'd make if I could give them that kind of intensive coaching all the time.

Training schedule for pole vaulters during the competitive period

Day	Duration (min)	Training task	Training details
Monday	20	Warm-up	800 meter jog, 4 × 100 with a pole, calisthenics and stretch

Day	Duration (min)	Training task	Training details
	10	Sprint drills	Knee lifts, form runs with a pole
	40	Technique work	10×run-throughs, towel plant drill, rock back drill
	5	Warm-down	Jog 400 meters, stretch
Tuesday	20	Warm-up	Jog 400, 4×100 strides, stretch
	10	Sprint drills	High knees, 1, 2, 3s, form runs
	45	Technique work	Vault with a short run-up for 10–15 minutes, vault for height 30–35 minutes
	5	Warm-down	Jog 400, stretch
Wednesday	20	Warm-up	Jog 400. Stride 400
	10	Sprint drills	High knees, butt kicks, form runs
	40	Gymnastics	Rope climbing, sinking drill with a surgical hose, hip circles on the rings
	5	Warm-down	Jog 400, stretch
Thursday	20	Warm-up	Jog 400, wind sprint 400, stretch
	10	Sprint drills	High knees, chop downs with pole
	45	Technique work	10×runway, rope vaulting from a ladder or a balcony*
	5	Warm-down	Jog 400, stretch
Friday	20	Warm-up	Jog 800, calisthenics, stretch
	10	Sprint drills	High knees, 1,2,3s, form runs
	30	Technique work	Low vaulting, 12-step run up
	5	Warm-down	Jog 400, stretch

Saturday   Competition.

* This a valuable and fun drill — but it is also very dangerous. Handle with care.

During the peaking period, the vaulter's skill level is at its optimum for this season. All-out vaulting and competition are the name of the game in May. If your vaulter has matured to a higher hand hold, do it immediately. This is a bad time to encounter the problems associated with learning to use a new pole. If the change to a new hand hold is 12 inches, the vaulter will have a difficult time adjusting. This is one of the dilemmas; you may not have enough time to establish the timing for a new pole. You don't want a rush job; this situation should be resolved in previous cycles. Your athlete should be peaking for the important competitions with a familiar pole.

During the final weeks of the outdoor season, drills begin to assume a minor role in the training program. All-out vaulting is the name of the game in May.

Weekly training schedule for pole vaulters during the peaking period

Day	Duration (min)	Training task	Training details
Monday	20	Warm-up	800 meter jog, stretch
	10	Sprint drills	High knees, 1, 2, 3s, form runs
	30	Technique work	Full run-throughs with rock back, pull and push without a crossbar
	5	Warm-down	Jog 400, stretch
Tuesday	20	Warm-up	400 jog, stretch, 400 stride, stretch
	10	Sprint drills	High knees, chop downs, butt kicks
	45	Technique work	Full run-throughs, all-out vaulting
	5	Warm-down	Jog 400, stretch
Wednesday	20	Warm-up	Jog 400 meters, stretch
	10	Sprint drills	High knees, chop downs, form runs
	30	Technique work	Full run-throughs, rock backs
	15	Gymnastics	Hip circles, pull-ups and chinning on horizontal bar, handstand push-ups
	5	Warm-down	Jog 400, stretch
Thursday	20	Warm-up	Jog 400, stretch
	10	Sprint drills	Same as Monday
	30	Technique work	12-step run up and low vaulting
	5	Warm-down	Jog 400, stretch
Friday	20	Warm-up	Jog 400, 4 × 100 strides, stretch
	10	Sprint drills	Same as Tuesday
	30	Technique work	Full run-throughs with a rock back and a pull and push (no crossbar)
Saturday		Competition.	

You should be expecting your best vaulting at the end of this period. Emphasize competing, resting, and recovering. There is no "training through." Your vaulters' level of performance will be based primarily on the extent of their psychological readiness. Getting an athlete ready for intense competition is a never-ending project. If you wait until the week of major competition, it may be too late. There is no exact formula for getting vaulters mentally prepared. Each athlete is an individual. It may take several years to understand how your athletes respond to competition. If you learn how your vaulters function psychologically, you will be able to motivate them to perform under pressure. This, however, is the most difficult part of your coaching job. Psychological motivation is not an exact science.

POLE VAULTING UNDER DIFFICULT CIRCUMSTANCES

I offered several solutions to the pole vault problem throughout this section. Listed below is a summary of the methods we used to develop the vaulters in our program:

1. Gain access to the best of facilities and equipment. To do less than this is a disservice to your athletes. Purchase the best of everything for your vaulters. You may be able to pile up net bags and mats to train beginners, but as they improve, you will need better equipment.

2. If your financial situation does not permit the above, raise funds over a period of years until such a purchase is possible. *Do not vault with unsafe equipment.*

3. Until you can get the proper equipment, you can "borrow" facilities from your suburban friends, if they are agreeable.

4. Another solution is to work with your vaulters in the summer at a local college or university. This is an opportunity to develop your athletes' skills so that their skills will carry over into the next season.

5. We often vaulted underwater in the swimming pool. With a stiff pole anchored near the corner of the pool in deep water, your athletes can execute vaulting techniques and drills in slow motion. Be sure that all safety measures are in place before you attempt these underwater drills.

6. After pole vaulting technique is established, you may not need to vault everyday. Continue to work on pole vault drills during the track season, visit a suburban facility once a week, and vault primarily in competition. This method of training may not be the best of all worlds, but a talented vaulter can be produced from this system. You and your athletes may have to make a few sacrifices along the way, but the effort will be worth it.

Section 18

THE SHOT-PUT
Brian's Song

Several years ago, I had an opportunity to see track and field history being made. There was a shot-putter who refused to conform. He smoked cigarettes between throws and when he put the shot, and his technique was from Disneyland. He was using a then-revolutionary, rotational discus spin for the shot-put — and he was breaking world records. In the early 1950s, Parry O'Brien had faced backward in the ring prior to a throw, and now this Brian — Brian Oldfield — had the temerity to rotate and throw. Both men defied convention; both men broke world records. This section explains how to develop a shot-putter, using those techniques, within the boundaries of a limited budget.

Shot-put technique has undergone several major changes. Prior to 1952, athletes stood sideways and did everything they could to throw the 16-pound object beyond the 60-foot barrier. They increased speed across the 7-foot circle (Charles Fonville, 1948 and James Fuchs, 1950), and bent rearward almost to the ground in an effort to break the 60-foot barrier. Parry O' Brien broke with tradition — he turned his back to the throwing area and revolutionized the event. In 1952, Parry O'Brien put the shot 60' 11". Brian Oldfield broke with tradition again when he adopted a rotational (discus) style of putting the shot. Though he was never officially credited with a world record, Brian put the shot over 74 feet in 1975. Brian Oldfield marched to the beat of a different drummer. He could be seen stalking around the shot-put circle smoking a cigarette between throws. I guess this was his way of psyching up.

I have often wondered why American athletes seem to be so creative. Almost every innovation in track and field was started by an American. Fiber glass pole vaulting, the Fosbury Flop, the eastern, western, and straddle roll, the jet sprint relay pass, the crouch start in sprinting, 13 steps between the intermediate hurdles, and the two styles of shot-putting were developed by Americans. Could it be that a free country produces free thinkers?

THE IDEAL SHOT-PUTTER

Being able to identify a candidate for this event is crucial. Several well-meaning teachers and coaches brought me short, chubby, slow, and uncoordinated students as shot-put candidates. These are not the desirable physical characteristics. The ideal specimen for the shot-put is someone over 6 foot tall, muscular, coordinated, and quick. This person might be a tackle or defensive end on the football team, a power forward on the basketball squad, or a teenage super-heavyweight powerlifting champion.

Unless you are very fortunate, the ideal shot-put prototype does not appear often in your coaching career. You may have to take less gifted youngsters and develop them. This has also been the case on the world-class level. Al Fuerbach, former world record holder (1973) was not a very large man. He weighed only 240 pounds and was barely 6 feet in height. Most world record holders, including Brian Oldfield, were well over 6 feet and weighed around 270 pounds. One of our best shot-putters, a qualifier for the high school nationals, was dwarfed by the huge specimens at this competition. There were several much larger athletes in our school, but they didn't want to throw the shot. You take what you can get.

Championship shot-putting is all about basic physics. Newton's second law of motion states that Force = Mass × Acceleration — a big, fast shot-putter can manifest greater force. If your shot-putters are not big, then they should be *very* fast. This principle explains the success of the relatively small shot-putters like Al Fuerbach and Charles Fonville (world record holder, 1948) who weighed only 195 pounds.

Muscular power is also an important factor in the shot-put. Your shot-putter must be involved in a sensible weight-training program. However, the mission of the weight program should be toward building power (work divided by time) rather than just sheer strength. I have always thought of power as strength *plus* speed. Just lifting heavy weights is not enough; your shot-putter must lift explosively. White muscle fibers must be stimulated by your shot-putters' weight-training program. It also wouldn't hurt if your throwers were genetically gifted with an abundance of fast-twitch (white) muscle fibers.

Your weight program should focus on building power in the lower body. We were more concerned with our throwers' ability in the parallel squat and power clean than we were in their ability to bench press. The bench press and the standing press are an integral part of our weight program, but our major emphasis is on training the lower body. This approach is based on the physical law of *summation of forces*. All throwing events begin with the power delivered by the legs, lower back, and penultimately by the torso; the effectiveness of the arms in delivering the shot is the result of the forces delivered by the lower body. This explains why a relatively small man like Al Feurbach did so well in the shot-put: Al could power clean over 400 pounds. This lift is an excellent test of leg and lower-back power. Some of our better shot-putters could easily lift a car by the rear bumper. This is another extraordinary test of leg and lower-back power.

Shot-putters are fast. Most champion shot-putters could hold their own in a short sprint. Jim Fuchs, the former world record holder in the shot (1950) was the 1945 Illinois state champion in the 100 yard dash. Parry O'Brien and Brian Oldfield were also great sprinters. Most of the shot-putters on our team are excellent sprinters. A shot-putter's training program should also include a generous dose of speed work.

LEARNING TO PUT THE SHOT

Everything discussed from this point on will be for a right handed thrower. The first thing to learn about the shot-put is the proper grip. There are two ways to hold the shot.

1. *The O'Brien method*. Place the shot snugly against the neck — under the jawbone and just below the ear. The shot is placed in the first knuckle of the palm and rests on all four fingers of the right hand. The thumb points toward the ground.

2. *The Oldfield method*. Hold the shot on the shoulder snugly against the neck (like a waiter holding a tray of food). The thumb of the right hand is pointed toward the jawbone.

The next step is to learn the standing throw. The easiest way to teach the shot is to use an underweight implement. I have occasionally used a 16-inch softball to teach the technique, so that the weight of the ball will not interfere with good technique.

You can go through the throwing action in slow motion with a lighter implement. This will help establish correct motor pathways for proper technique:

1. Have the candidates face in the direction of throw, lean back slightly and push the shot. The feet should be a little more than shoulder width apart. The shot should leave the hand at approximately 43 degrees. Teach them to follow through or reach after the shot. Repeat this drill several times.

2. Instruct the putters to stand with the left shoulder facing the direction of throw. The feet are slightly wider than shoulder width apart. Have them put the shot, making sure the shot does not leave the neck or shoulder until the torso is facing the direction of the throwing area. The weight of the body should be over the right foot prior to the throw, and over the left foot as the shot is released.

3. Have the shot-putters stand facing away from the direction of throw in the "power" position. In the power position, the left hip is turned toward the direction of the throw, with the shoulders facing away from the throwing area. The feet are slightly more than shoulder width apart. Most of the weight of the body is over a partially bent right leg. The left leg is almost straight. Drive the hips toward the front of the circle, followed by the torso. When the torso is pulled to the front by the hips and legs, the arm puts the shot from the body at a 43 degree angle. Repeat this drill until it is mastered. This may take several days. Getting into the correct power position is the key to effective throwing. Every athlete in a throwing event must get into the power position prior to launching the shot.

Learning the "Glide" or "Shift"

Teaching a beginner to move across the shot-put ring effectively is often the most difficult aspect of this event. Most of our candidates for some reason seem to experience great difficulty in learning this phase of shot-putting. Brian Oldfield correctly stated that all throwing is the same, but somehow many youngsters have not learned the basic mechanics of throwing. This is why the movement across the shot-put circle should be taught from the beginning.

We usually teach the glide apart from the standing throw and combine the two skills when they are mastered. Occasionally, a few well-coordinated youngsters will learn the full technique almost immediately.

One of the best ways to introduce the glide is to have the shot-putters hop backwards for about 50 meters. This drill serves two purposes; it builds strength in the right or driving leg and it helps them to adjust to moving backward without losing balance. After they have become accustomed to this drill, teach the actual glide into the power position. Emphasize the importance of keeping the head and shoulders back and over the right leg as the left hip turns toward the direction of the throw. You may have to do these drills for several weeks before they are performed correctly.

One of the technical flaws common to most beginners is the premature transfer of body weight to the left leg. When the putter shifts to the power position, most of the weight is on the right leg. The left foot is lightly positioned against

Figure 18-1

SHOT-PUT — POSITION ONE

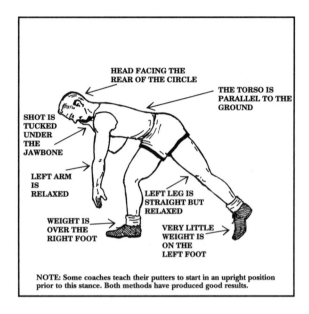

HEAD FACING THE REAR OF THE CIRCLE

THE TORSO IS PARALLEL TO THE GROUND

SHOT IS TUCKED UNDER THE JAWBONE

LEFT ARM IS RELAXED

LEFT LEG IS STRAIGHT BUT RELAXED

WEIGHT IS OVER THE RIGHT FOOT

VERY LITTLE WEIGHT IS ON THE LEFT FOOT

NOTE: Some coaches teach their putters to start in an upright position prior to this stance. Both methods have produced good results.

Figure 18-2

SHOT-PUT — POSITION TWO

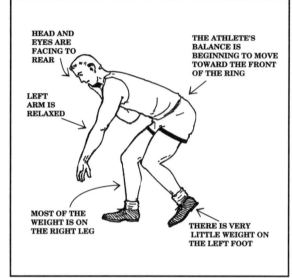

HEAD AND EYES ARE FACING TO REAR

THE ATHLETE'S BALANCE IS BEGINNING TO MOVE TOWARD THE FRONT OF THE RING

LEFT ARM IS RELAXED

MOST OF THE WEIGHT IS ON THE RIGHT LEG

THERE IS VERY LITTLE WEIGHT ON THE LEFT FOOT

Figure 18-3

SHOT-PUT — POSITION THREE

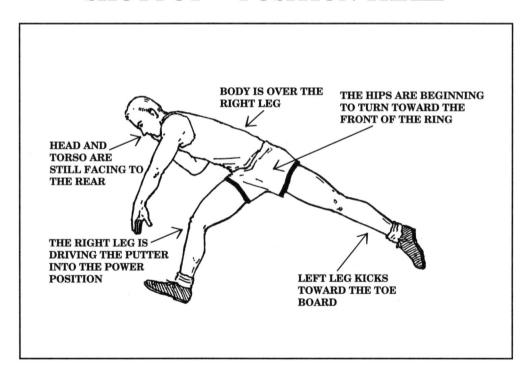

BODY IS OVER THE RIGHT LEG

THE HIPS ARE BEGINNING TO TURN TOWARD THE FRONT OF THE RING

HEAD AND TORSO ARE STILL FACING TO THE REAR

THE RIGHT LEG IS DRIVING THE PUTTER INTO THE POWER POSITION

LEFT LEG KICKS TOWARD THE TOE BOARD

Figure 18-4

POSITION FOUR — THE POWER POSITION

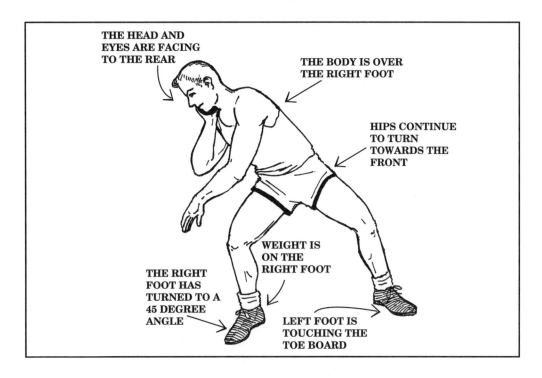

THE HEAD AND EYES ARE FACING TO THE REAR

THE BODY IS OVER THE RIGHT FOOT

HIPS CONTINUE TO TURN TOWARDS THE FRONT

WEIGHT IS ON THE RIGHT FOOT

THE RIGHT FOOT HAS TURNED TO A 45 DEGREE ANGLE

LEFT FOOT IS TOUCHING THE TOE BOARD

Figure 18-5

SHOT-PUT — POSITION FIVE

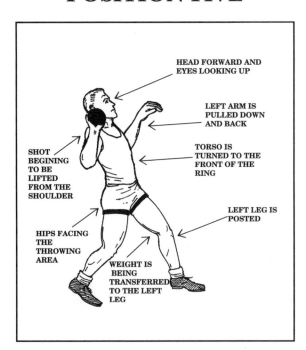

HEAD FORWARD AND EYES LOOKING UP

LEFT ARM IS PULLED DOWN AND BACK

TORSO IS TURNED TO THE FRONT OF THE RING

SHOT BEGINING TO BE LIFTED FROM THE SHOULDER

LEFT LEG IS POSTED

HIPS FACING THE THROWING AREA

WEIGHT IS BEING TRANSFERRED TO THE LEFT LEG

Figure 18-6

SHOT-PUT — POSITION SIX

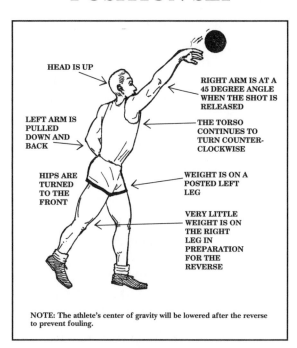

HEAD IS UP

RIGHT ARM IS AT A 45 DEGREE ANGLE WHEN THE SHOT IS RELEASED

LEFT ARM IS PULLED DOWN AND BACK

THE TORSO CONTINUES TO TURN COUNTER-CLOCKWISE

HIPS ARE TURNED TO THE FRONT

WEIGHT IS ON A POSTED LEFT LEG

VERY LITTLE WEIGHT IS ON THE RIGHT LEG IN PREPARATION FOR THE REVERSE

NOTE: The athlete's center of gravity will be lowered after the reverse to prevent fouling.

the bottom of the stop board to maintain balance. There is no transfer of weight until the torso turns toward the direction of the throw, accompanied by a subsequent delivery of the shot. When the torso is directly above the center of gravity there is a shift of weight to the left leg and the right arm immediately extends and puts the shot.

The Value of Videos

You may experience the frustration of trying to explain shot-put technique to your throwers and discover that you are not communicating anything of value. A picture is worth a thousand words. I am told that one of our state champions placed a track and field magazine at the rear of the shot-put ring and mimicked sequence pictures of shot-put technique. I often send the throwers to my office to look at loop films. One of our throwers improved 20 feet in the discus after studying these films. He told me that I did not tell him what he saw on the film. He was told this exact technique many times. What we had was a failure to communicate.

Incidentally, one of the best videos on the shot-put I have ever seen was by Brian Oldfield. The best video on discus technique is by John Powell.

Most school librarians will order videotapes and loop films for you. I submitted an order for films and videos of every event in track and field. When your athletes see Olympic champions performing world-class techniques, it reinforces and confirms everything you said. It also eliminates a lot of misunderstood rhetoric. I also purchased a number of videos for my personal library, so I could study the various techniques. All of these visual aids are worth their weight in gold — and they are tax deductible.

One of the most successful coaches in our area brings a video camera to every meet. Sometimes your athletes won't believe you when you point out a technical flaw. A video of their technical shortcomings will eliminate all doubt. I haven't needed to purchase a video camera yet. Several friends or parents bring video cameras to all our meets.

The O'Brien Shot-Put Form in a Nutshell

1. Stand to the rear of the circle with the back to the throwing area. Both feet are facing to the back of the circle with the left foot near the middle of the ring.

2. Bend forward until the torso is nearly parallel to the ground. Bend the right leg in a partial squat and bring the left foot near the right foot, while keeping most of the body weight on the right foot.

3. Kick the left leg toward the stop board and drive the right foot toward the middle of the circle.

4. Keep the torso low and over the right leg. Pull the right foot to the middle of the circle and quickly assume the power position. The right foot moves counterclockwise almost 90 degrees. The right leg is in a partial squat. The left foot is "in the bucket."

Figure 18-8

FOOT POSITION
IN THE SHOT-PUT
O'Brien Technique

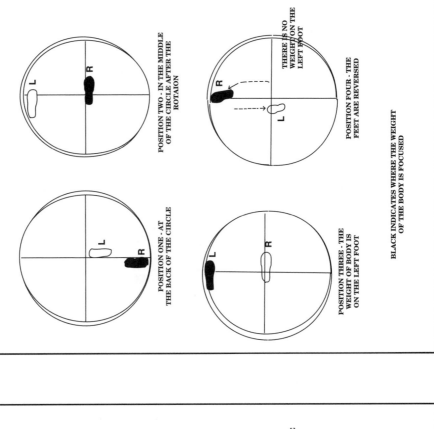

Figure 18-7

FOOT POSITION
IN THE SHOT-PUT
Rotational Technique

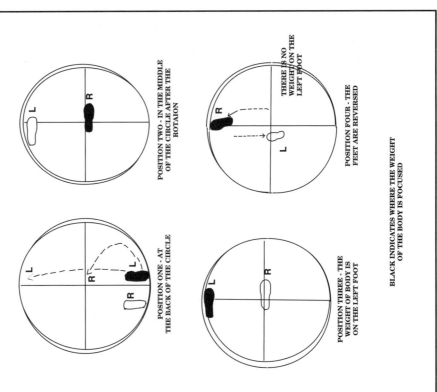

Photo 18–1. An excellent finishing position in the shot-put. The throwing arm is extended and the shot has left the hand. The rear (right) leg is beginning to move toward the inside of the stop board to prevent a foul and save the throw.

5. Without any hesitation in the middle of the circle, drive the right hip forward and upward, as the torso quickly rises to an upright position and simultaneously turns to the front of the circle. The weight of the body is still over the right leg.

6. As the torso rises to vertical, the body moves over the center of gravity and the weight is over the left leg. Both legs are slightly bent.

7. Drive the shot from the shoulder at a 43 degree angle. Follow through with the arms. Both legs are straightened. Reverse the position of the feet to avoid fouling.

The Discus or Rotational Style

1. Stand at the rear of the circle facing away from the direction of throw. The feet are parallel and shoulder width apart. The knees are bent in a partial squat position; the torso is erect.

2. Turn the body counterclockwise toward the direction of throw by pivoting on both feet while maintaining contact with the shot-put surface.

3. Transfer the weight of the body to the left leg. The right foot breaks contact with the shot-put surface and drives toward the center of the ring. The weight is on the ball of the left foot momentarily, and is quickly changed to the right foot.

4. Back into the middle of the circle with the weight of the body primarily on the right leg. Move into the "power" position. Do not hesitate in the power position, the transition to putting the shot should occur immediately after the legs, right hip, and torso move the body up and over the center of gravity.

5. Drive the shot from the shoulders in exactly the same manner as it is thrown in the O'Brien technique.

The rotational technique sounds rather complicated, but if you walk through the movement as it is written, it will not seem so difficult to learn.

The physical rationale for the O'Brien — and subsequently the discus technique is the concept of impulse. The length of time or distance that a force is applied determines how great the resultant power behind the shot will be. When Parry O'Brien and Brian Oldfield pioneered their respective techniques, they increased impulse, and therefore the possibility of throwing the shot greater distances.

TRAINING SCHEDULES

The general preparation period for shot-putters is a time for total conditioning. Games that involve jumping and running are emphasized. There are plenty of stretching and flexibility exercises. Strength training is potentiated when your throwers' range of motion is maximized.

Your throwers' weight program during this period consists of relatively moderate loads and higher repetitions. This is also a time to learn correct form in all the lifts. There is no attempt to lift maximum poundages. Build a foundation and your athletes will avoid injury later. Establishing a foundation will also enable your throwers to lift much heavier weights in April and May.

*Weekly training schedule for shot-putters during
the general preparation period*

Day	Duration (min)	Training task	Training details
Monday	20	Warm-up	400 meter jog, stretch
	10	Sprint drills	High knees, backward runs, grapevine, form runs
	30	Shot-put drills	Backwards hopping, medicine ball drills, standing throws, gliding drills
	40	Weight training	Lower body, squats, power cleans, etc. 3–4 sets × 12, crunches
	5	Warm-down	Jog 400 meters, stretch
Tuesday	20	Warm-up	400 meter jog, stretch
	10	Sprint drills	30 meter strides, 30 meter sprints
	40	Weight training	Upper body, bench press, standing press, etc. 3–4 sets × 12 reps
	30	Games	Basketball or volleyball
	5	Warm-down	Jog 400 meters, stretch
Wednesday	20	Warm-up	400 meter jog, stretch
	10	Sprint drills	High knees, backward run, grapevine, form runs, sliding sideways
	40	Shot-put drills	Overhead medicine ball throw, puts from a stand, shifts with and without the shot
	5	Warm-down	Jog 200 meters, stretch
Thursday	20	Warm-up	Jog 200, walk 200, jog 200, stretch
	10	Sprint drills	7 × 30 meters 80%–90% effort
	30	Shot-put drills	Standing throws with a surgical hose, vertical throws with an overweight shot*
	40	Weight training	Lower body, step-ups, leg press, rapid deadlift, sit-ups, 3 sets, 10 reps
	5	Warm-down	Jog 200, stretch

Day	Duration (min)	Training task	Training details
Friday	20	Warm-up	Jog 400 meters, stretch
	15	Games	Volleyball or basketball
	30	Shot-put drills	Standing throws, full technique without a reverse
	40	Weight training	Upper body, inclined press, push press, bent over rowing, curls, 3 sets, 10 reps
	5	Warm-down	Jog 200, stretch
Saturday		Competition.	

*We use surgical hoses for a number of shot-put drills. If the hoses are strong enough, they will force the putter to use proper form or the resistance of the hose will throw them off balance. We also have the throwers put an overweight shot straight upward toward the ceiling to train their legs to initiate the put. You will find that this drill helps them learn to "summate" their forces.

We also use underweight and overweight shots throughout the season. Using a variety of implements can stimulate the nervous system. I learned this concept from Angel Spassov, the Bulgarian strength coach. One of our throwers broke the 60-foot barrier after a week of practicing standing puts with a 20-pound shot. However, there is a tendency for heavier shots to negatively affect your throwers' timing if you use it for the full technique. It is best to occasionally use an overweight shot for standing throws.

Beginning putters learn correct technique more easily when you use underweight implements. When we used heavier shots, there was a tendency to use improper techniques in an effort to gain immediate distance. We often used a 16-inch softball in the beginning stages. It seemed that our newer candidates' egos were not at stake when they could demonstrate a certain amount of prowess with these lighter implements. When the correct motor pathways were established, they were switched to heavier equipment.

Weekly training schedule for shot-putters during the specific preparation period

Day	Duration (min)	Training task	Training details
Monday	20	Warm-up	400 meter jog, stretch
	10	Sprint drills	High knees, 30 meter sprints 90% effort
	40	Shot-put drills	Standing throws, gliding drills with and without the shot, vertical throws
	40	Weight training	Lower body, hyperextension, reverse hypers, leg extensions, squats, power cleans, 4 sets $\times$ 7 reps
	5	Warm-down	Jog 200, stretch

Day	Duration (min)	Training task	Training details
Tuesday	20	Warm-up	Jog 400, stretch
	40	Shot-put drills	Standing throws with a heavier shot, full technique with an underweight shot (for speed)
	40	Weight training	Upper body, bench press, standing
	10	Sprint drills	High knees, backward run, grapevine press, curls, sit-ups, 4 sets, 7 reps
	5	Warm-down	Jog 200, stretch
Wednesday	20	Warm-up	Jog 400 meters, stretch
	10	Sprint drills	High knees, form runs
	40	Shot-put drills	Standing and full form with a surgical hose, full technique throws
	20	Games	Basketball or volleyball
	5	Warm-down	Jog 200 meters, stretch
Thursday	20	Warm-up	Jog 400, stretch
	10	Sprint drills	High knees, butt kicks, chop downs
	40	Shot-put drills	Overhead throws (medicine ball), vertical throws, reversal drill*
	40	Weight training	Lower body, leg extensions and leg curls, step-ups and leg presses, power snatch, 3 sets, 8 reps
	5	Warm-down	Jog 200 meters, stretch
Friday	20	Warm-up	Half-court basketball, stretch
	10	Sprint drills	Form runs, grapevines. sliding
	30	Shot-put drills	7–10 full throws for form— 90% effort
	30	Weight training	Upper body, incline press, push press, 3 sets × 6 reps (60%) warm-down

Saturday   Competition.

* Reversal drill. Stand upright and turn the left side of the body facing the direction of throw. Drive the right hip toward the throwing area, followed by the torso. When the torso faces the front, the right arm drives the shot from the shoulder. The transition of body parts is rapid and smooth. When the arm is fully extended, reverse the feet to prevent fouling. The right foot hits the inside bottom of the stop board. Emphasize speed in this drill.

THE PRE-COMPETITIVE PERIOD

The pre-competitive period is a time that the shot-putters begin to work at perfecting the full technique. Some drills are discontinued, but the ones related to coordinating the movement across the circle with the throwing action are retained. If there are flaws in the putter's form, then we continue practicing the drills that are designed to correct these flaws. This may be different for each individual. There is also an increase in all-out efforts, but basically these throws are not done more than twice a week. We try to conserve our energy for competition. We may still train through, but there is a slight tapering off for the meet on Friday or Saturday.

Our heaviest weight training sessions are on Monday and Tuesday. This approach with certain modifications will continue through the final peaking period. The weights are beginning to be heavier and the repetitions are decreased to five or six, but there are no maximum attempts on the core lifts, e.g., the bench press, squat and the power clean.

We prepare the putters for competitions by simulating competitive procedures on Tuesdays or Wednesdays. All-out throws are held to a minimum. We are making every effort to retain energy and nerve force for Saturday's competition. It is for that reason that no workout lasts over 50 minutes. The best throws are recorded and counted: we want our putters to know when their best distances are made and we try to remember this number for competition. For example, if the athlete registers the best distance on the 10th attempt (after a warm-up) we try to arrange it so that effort will occur on the last preliminary throw or on the first throw in the finals. If everything goes according to how we planned it, we won't need to make a maximum effort on the last throw in the finals.

Weekly training for shot-putters during the pre-competitive period

Day	Duration (min)	Training task	Training details
Monday	20	Warm-up	Jog 400, stretch
	10	Sprint drills	High knees, backward hopping, 30 meter sprints (90% effort)
	40	Shot-put drills	Standing and full technique with a surgical hose, vertical throws
	40	Weight training	Lower body, leg extension and leg curls, squats, hyperextensions, power cleans, 4 sets, 5 reps
	5	Warm-down	Jog 200 meters, stretch
Tuesday	20	Warm-up	Jog 200, walk 200, stride 200, stretch
	10	Sprint drills	High knees, 1, 2, 3s, form runs
	40	Shot-put drills	Standing throws (overweight shot) full technique for distance

Day	Duration (min)	Training task	Training details
	40	Weight training	Upper body, bench press, standing press, curls, 4 sets 5 reps
	5	Warm-down	Jog 200, stretch
Wednesday	20	Warm-up	Jog 400, stretch
	10	Sprint drills	High knees, form runs, 30 meter sprints
	40	Games	Basketball or volleyball
	5	Warm-down	Jog 200, stretch
Thursday	20	Warm-up	Jog 400, stretch
	10	Sprint drills	1, 2, 3s, form runs, backward runs
	40	Shot-put drills	Medicine ball drills, step-and-throws* Reversal drill
	40	Weight training	Lower body, leg extension, leg curls lunges, leg press, power snatch, 3 sets, 6 reps, sit-ups
	5	Warm-down	Jog 200, stretch
Friday	20	Warm-up	Jog 400, stretch
	10	Sprint drills	High knees, backward runs, grapevine
	30	Shot-put drills	Standing throw $\times 7$, Full technique $\times 7$
	30	Weight training	Incline press, standing press 3×6
	5	Warm-down	Jog 200, stretch

Saturday   Competition.

* This is a transition from the standing throw to the full technique. Have your throwers stand in the circle facing the putting area. Then they step forward with the right foot and immediately back into the power position with the left foot. Without any hesitation, the shot is thrown from the power position. This is also an excellent drill to improve the rotational technique.

The next cycle opens the outdoor track season. We no longer train through. There will be a little tapering off for Saturday's competition. This approach also requires a slight adjustment in the weight-training schedule. Four workouts will be changed to three. There are also fewer days of maximum throwing and shot-put drills are not as intense. During the competitive cycle, marks made in meets are far more important than those made in training. The main physiological emphasis during this period is rest, restoration, and competition.

Weekly training schedule for shot-putters
during the competitive period

Day	Duration (min)	Training task	Training details
Monday	20	Warm-up	Jog two minutes, stretch
	10	Sprint drills	High knees, grapevine, slide sideways
	30	Shot-put drills	Overhead drill, reverse drill, step-and-throw, gliding with an overweight shot
	40	Weight training	Leg extensions and curls, squats and power cleans or pulls, 6 sets × 2 reps
	5	Warm-down	Jog 200, stretch
Tuesday	20	Warm-up	Jog 2 mins, stretch
	10	Sprint drills	7 × 30 meter sprints 80%–95%
	30	Shot-put drills	10 × standing (with overweight shot), 10 × full technique
	30	Weight training	Bench press, standing press, lat machine, 6 sets × 2 reps, sit-ups
	5	Warm-down	Jog 200 meters, stretch
Wednesday	20	Warm-up	Same as Monday
	10	Sprint drills	Same as Monday
	30	Restoration	Relaxed swimming
	5	Warm-down	Jog 200, stretch
Thursday	20	Warm-up	Jog 400, stretch
	10	Sprint drills	High knees, grapevine, backwards run
	30	Shot-put drills	Standing throw and full technique with a surgical hose
	30	Weight training	Power clean with a push press, power snatch 3 sets, 3 reps, crunches
	5	Warm-down	Jog 1 min, stretch
Friday	20	Warm-up	Jog 200, stretch
	10	Sprint drills	7 × 20 meters 80%–95%
	20	Shot-put drills	5 standing throws, 5 full throws with a lighter implement
	5	Warm-down	Jog 200, stretch
Saturday		Competition.	

The peaking cycle is the final and critical period of the year. If everything has gone according to your plans, there is probably no need to change the following schedule. The biggest alteration in your workouts might be a reduction in the volume of the work load. Two days should be devoted to heavy lifting, but the volume of the workout should be held to a minimum. Do not leave your strength in the gymnasium or workout area. Depend upon "metabolic momentum" to do the job — especially in the final weeks of training. Try to observe each athlete closely to be aware of individual differences.

Weekly training schedule for shot-putters during the peaking period

Day	Duration (min)	Training task	Training details
Monday	20	Warm-up	Jog 400 meters, stretch
	10	Sprint drills	High knees, butt kicks, 1, 2, 3s, form runs
	30	Shot-put drills	Full technique (underweight shot)
	30	Weight training	Leg curls and extensions, squat, power snatch, 5, 4, 3, 2, 1 repetitions
	5	Warm-down	Jog 200, stretch
Tuesday	20	Warm-up	Jog 400 meters, stretch
	10	Sprint drills	High knees, form runs, grapevine 7×20 meters,
	30	Shot-put drills	Step-and-throws, standing throws, full technique
	30	Weight training	Leg curls and extensions, 3×10 squats, power snatch, 7×1 rep
	5	Warm-down	Jog 200, stretch
Wednesday	20	Warm-up	Jog 2 minutes, stretch
	10	Sprint drills	High knees, backward run, hop 30 meters, grapevine
	30	Shot-put drills	Standing throws, overweight shot, full throws, underweight shot
	30	Weight training	Bench press, push press, 7×1
	5	Warm-down	Jog 200, stretch
Thursday	20	Warm-up	Jog 2 minutes, stretch
	10	Sprint drills	High knees, form runs
	30	Games	Basketball, volleyball, or swimming
	5	Warm-down	Jog 1 minute, stretch

Day	Duration (min)	Training task	Training details
Friday	20	Warm-up	Same as Monday
	10	Sprint drills	Same as Monday
	20	Shot-put drills	$7 \times$ standing throws, $7 \times$ regular throws
Saturday		Competition.	

If everything has gone according to your plan, your shot-putters will register personal bests at the conference championships and beyond. Most of these personal bests will be the result of your training program combined with your athletes' will to win. The mental and emotional drive in your throwers and their response is difficult to predict. I have often seen athletes perform superhuman efforts as a result of sound mental preparation. The best way to determine if they will come through under pressure is to schedule a few important competitions early in the season and observe the outcome. This may indicate who will come through when the chips are down. Also listen to their casual conversations; most athletes will reveal in one way or another who can be counted upon when you need them.

TRAINING FOR THE SHOT-PUT UNDER DIFFICULT CIRCUMSTANCES

Several pieces of equipment are necessary for shot-put workouts. Most are relatively inexpensive items that you should be able to purchase without much difficulty. Listed below are some of these items:

1. Indoor shots of various weights — 8, 12, 16 and 20 pounds.
2. Outdoor shots of various weights — 8, 12, 16 and 20 pounds.
3. Surgical hoses, 7 feet in length, 1/4 to 1/2 inch in thickness.
4. A wooden shot-put circle and stop board, which can be made in your school's wood shop or in a local lumber yard. I never needed to do this. We used an inverted beat board indoors and a sidewalk curbstone outdoors. We marked off a 7-foot shot-put circle with tape indoors and used chalk outdoors. Several exceptional shot-putters were developed using this "equipment."

After a few years, we accumulated enough shots to accommodate all of our throwers. Some of these implements were donated to us by our friends in the suburbs and we purchased the rest. Most of our weight equipment was fashioned from the junkyard. Most of our bars and plates were purchased or donated to us. The rest we made from various automobile parts. Rotors and flywheels make excellent barbell plates. Cement and pipes can be made into excellent barbells, our benches and racks were made in wood shop. I made an excellent squat rack out of pipes and tire rims. A community center had a few Olympic barbell plates and we made a crude Olympic bar from pipes and ball bearings. From time to time we purchased a few commercially made items. Our equipment was not fancy, but it got the job done. When our kids were throwing 55–60 feet in competition, we felt that our crude weight room was an advantage.

Occasionally, we would go to a local park for a training session. We spotted a few weight sets in the park district fieldhouse and asked the director if we could use their equipment. He refused. My car became a barbell. The putters did dead-lifts and bench presses with the rear bumper, and pushed the car to build their quads. We were having so much fun with this bizarre workout that the runners decided to join us. In two weeks, everybody was doing personal bests. The park district director happened to be at one of our meets and was so impressed with our prowess that he offered his weight room to us. We told him, "Thanks, but we don't need it now."

Resistance training with an automobile is a fantastic workout but proceed with caution. Make sure your team is thoroughly warmed up before attempting anything. Explain the possible hazards of these tremendous efforts. Straining with the bumper of a car can be dangerous.

We also used an empty bar and partner resistance. Sometimes I felt that this kind of exercise was more difficult than weights. We worked in groups of three. One athlete would lift while the other two resisted the lifter. They would change lifters after each set. In addition to this, we did a lot of freehand exercises. Some of these exercises are similar to those advocated by Hershel Walker in his book *Hershel Walker's Basic Training*. We also did exercises with one arm or one leg. Have you ever tried a one-legged squat?

Shot-putters can be developed anywhere, anyplace with a minimum of finances. Everything around you can be a facility. During the indoor season we would throw the shot up a flight of stairs if the gym wasn't available. On other occasions we covered a wall with mats and threw against the wall. There were times we threw the indoor shot in the swimming pool. We often sat on the floor in the corridor and threw the shot.

Most shot-put equipment is relatively inexpensive. The implements that you must purchase can fit any budget. If your school won't or can't buy what you need, raise the funds, appeal to the parents, or buy it yourself. A few 12-pound shots won't cost that much and they will last a lifetime.

Section 19

THE DISCUS THROW
It's Not a Frisbee

In the 1980s, a coach questioned me about discus technique. He was a phenomenal sprint coach, but he knew absolutely nothing about the discus throw. He thought the discus was thrown from the back of the hand. "It's not a Frisbee," I told him. When you read this section, you will learn that the discus is not a Frisbee, among other things. Newton's laws and the laws of aerodynamics as they relate to the discus throw are covered thoroughly. Several unique drills, born of necessity, are also discussed. Everyone knows necessity is the mother of invention.

Several years ago, I stood in a parking lot talking to a fellow coach about the discus throw. This man is a tremendous sprint and jump coach and has coached world-class athletes in those events. Some of his runners subsequently competed in the Olympics. He was a specialist and never knew much about the throwing events, and he knew even less about the discus throw. He thought that the discus was thrown from the back of the hand. I responded, "It's not a frisbee — it's a discus!"

In his defense, very few coaches are experts in all 18 track and field events and they often delegate the teaching of unfamiliar events to their assistants. But in many situations, there are no assistants and you may need to coach all events or forfeit 20–40 points to your more fortunate competitors. This coach never felt the need to bother with the throwing events because on the state level, it is possible to win a championship with a handful of sprinters. Many experts feel that it is a daunting and exhausting job for one person to coach an entire track team. In most of the Eastern European countries, one coach works with only four athletes! With a certain amount of innovation and enterprise it can be done, but many coaches are forced to compromise somewhere. On the other hand, the athletes are compromised, too. What are you going to do when a 6' 2", 230-pound freshman comes to you and asks to join the track team?

On one occasion, a coach brought his sprinters to the state meet in a Volkswagen and won second place. It is also possible to *win* a state championship with one thrower (discus and shot-put) and one jumper (triple jump and long jump). An additional advantage of the throwing events and the jumps is that an athlete has six attempts to win a championship. One mistake by a sprinter, and it's all over. Time spent developing athletes in the field events is time well spent.

TALENT IDENTIFICATION

It is difficult to talk about the discus throw without mentioning Al Oerter. No one in the history of track and field has dominated the discus throw like Al. This remarkable athlete won four gold medals in the Olympic games. What makes this achievement so memorable is that he had to train under difficult circumstances. Since this is one of the missions of this guide, it gives hope to those of us who train our charges under similar conditions. Lack of facilities is no excuse for poor discus throwing. It was stated in the Fall 1996 issue of *Track Coach* magazine, that Al Oerter had to wait until the local high school practice was over before he could use their facility.

World-class discus throwers, like most shot-putters, are big, tall, and fast. Al Oerter was 6' 4" and weighed 295 pounds when he won his fourth gold medal in

Figure 19-1

DISCUS THROW — PREPARATION FOR THE TURN

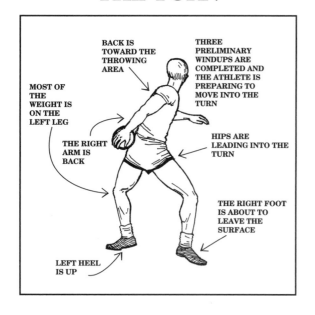

BACK IS TOWARD THE THROWING AREA

THREE PRELIMINARY WINDUPS ARE COMPLETED AND THE ATHLETE IS PREPARING TO MOVE INTO THE TURN

MOST OF THE WEIGHT IS ON THE LEFT LEG

THE RIGHT ARM IS BACK

HIPS ARE LEADING INTO THE TURN

THE RIGHT FOOT IS ABOUT TO LEAVE THE SURFACE

LEFT HEEL IS UP

Figure 19-2

DISCUS TURN OR SPIN

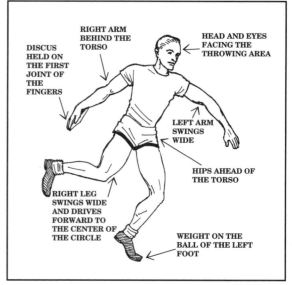

RIGHT ARM BEHIND THE TORSO

HEAD AND EYES FACING THE THROWING AREA

DISCUS HELD ON THE FIRST JOINT OF THE FINGERS

LEFT ARM SWINGS WIDE

HIPS AHEAD OF THE TORSO

RIGHT LEG SWINGS WIDE AND DRIVES FORWARD TO THE CENTER OF THE CIRCLE

WEIGHT ON THE BALL OF THE LEFT FOOT

Figure 19-3

DISCUS THROW — THE POWER POSITION

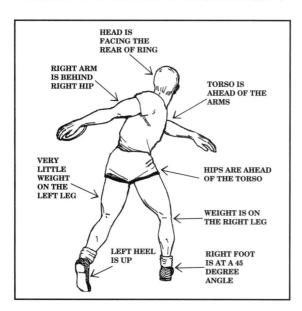

HEAD IS FACING THE REAR OF RING

RIGHT ARM IS BEHIND RIGHT HIP

TORSO IS AHEAD OF THE ARMS

VERY LITTLE WEIGHT ON THE LEFT LEG

HIPS ARE AHEAD OF THE TORSO

WEIGHT IS ON THE RIGHT LEG

LEFT HEEL IS UP

RIGHT FOOT IS AT A 45 DEGREE ANGLE

Figure 19-4

DISCUS RELEASE

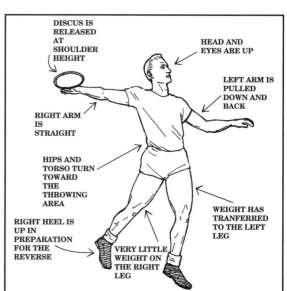

DISCUS IS RELEASED AT SHOULDER HEIGHT

HEAD AND EYES ARE UP

LEFT ARM IS PULLED DOWN AND BACK

RIGHT ARM IS STRAIGHT

HIPS AND TORSO TURN TOWARD THE THROWING AREA

RIGHT HEEL IS UP IN PREPARATION FOR THE REVERSE

VERY LITTLE WEIGHT ON THE RIGHT LEG

WEIGHT HAS TRANFERRED TO THE LEFT LEG

Figures 19-1 to 19-4 demonstrate the entire process for throwing the discus.

1968. There have been discus throwers of smaller stature, but they have to compensate for their lack of size with blinding speed and immaculate technique. Remember Force = Mass × Acceleration. If they don't have mass, then they must work to increase acceleration. Don't ignore the average sized, well-coordinated candidate.

On the high school and collegiate level, many discus throwers often double as shot-putters. Though most world-class discus throwers tend to specialize, many of these athletes have been known to make commendable efforts in the shot-put. A perfect example of this versatility is Mac Wilkins, the 1976 Olympic champion, who threw the discus 232' 10" and put the shot 69' 1". Brian Oldfield, of shot-put fame, could throw the discus 204' 3".

LEARNING TO THROW THE DISCUS

The first lesson in learning how to throw the discus is establishing the proper grip. The discus is held on the first joint of the fingers of the throwing hand. The fingers can be spread, or some throwers prefer to spread all fingers but the first two. The discus cannot be gripped in this position, it is the centrifugal force from the windup and subsequent throw that keeps the discus from falling to the ground. The discus is thrown from the outside joint of the index finger.

The best way to get the feeling of this action is to roll a discus on the ground, like a bowler. When this skill is perfected, pitch the discus in the air, like a softball pitcher. The next step is to work on a few standing throws. Your candidates should endeavor to spin the discus in a clockwise direction. All of these instructions are for a right-handed thrower.

If you are working indoors, you have several alternatives to practicing with a regular discus. Our throwers often work with a softball to learn the full technique. They can throw to their heart's content without damaging gymnasium walls. We also use a plastic discus and throw them against a wall reinforced with mats or you can borrow nets used by the baseball team for batting practice. Another alternative is to strap a discus to the athlete's hand and work the technique without actual throwing. There are times we throw an indoor shot or a medicine ball in a discus motion. A final method we use is to practice the various discus drills with surgical tubing. Most of these drills can be done in hallways, gymnasiums, swimming pools, or up a flight of stairs.

Technique

While athletes are learning the standing throw from the power position, they are also developing the discus turn or spin (or rotation). They begin this learning process with the South African drill, which has these six movements:

1. Stand at the back of the circle facing the direction of the throwing area.

2. Step forward with the right foot and place the ball of the right in the middle of the discus ring.

3. Pivot (counterclockwise) on the ball of the right foot into the power position. Drive the outside edge of the left foot toward the inside edge of the discus ring.

4. Drive the hips toward the front of the ring and pull the torso to the front, shift the bodyweight over the left leg.

5. Lift the body to vertical and "sling" the discus.

6. Reverse the feet to save the throw.

You can practice the South African drill with and without the discus. We have also tried this drill with underweight implements or a softball. If your throwers have difficulty learning the whole movement, walk them through parts of it. Some of your athletes can learn this technique during the first lesson; others will require several months.

When they have mastered the South African drill, have them stand in the regular starting position with the feet shoulder width apart. They must stand in a partial squat with their backs toward the throwing area. Have them pivot on the ball of the left foot, swing the right leg wide and subsequently drive toward the center of the ring. Add the South African drill to this maneuver and you have executed the full discus technique. The physical law "summation of forces," must be adhered to in the execution of the discus throw: The legs initiate the technique, then the hips, followed by the torso, and finally the arms. Each successive body part, starting with the largest and ending with the smallest, contributes to the acceleration of the implement.

The Release

The discus should be released at an angle of 25 to 35 degrees depending on the wind currents. The discus is an aerodynamic event and the angle of release depends upon the magnitude of the wind. The discus may stall if it is thrown at too high or too low an angle into a strong head wind. The direction and extent of wind currents have to be considered at every discus competition. The aerodynamic effects on the discus are so complicated that its flight is determined by the speed and angle of release, the ability of the athlete, and the direction and force of the wind. A comprehensive discussion of these factors can be found in Geoffrey Dyson's book *The Mechanics of Athletics*. According to his charts (page 194), an angle of release of 25 to 35 degrees (as suggested above) seems to produce optimum distances in most cases.

A BRIEF STATEMENT ABOUT PHYSICAL LAWS

All throwers must be aware of basic physical laws. An understanding of these laws can impact on the efficacy of their event. Several excellent books have been written on this subject. One of these books is *Track and Field: Technique Through Dynamics* by Tom Ecker, I focus here on the laws that made the most significant difference with our athletes:

1. *Summation of forces.* It is imperative that the athlete follow the correct sequence of body parts. An effective throw is initiated by the largest body part (legs), followed in rapid succession by smaller parts (hips, then arms). This is the same law that launches a space ship. The successful

launching of a shot or discus is the sum of the various parts moving in rapid sequence.

2. *Acceleration*. A positive rate of change of velocity. Once a thrower initiates movement, there must be a conscious effort to move increasingly faster. There is no settling or slowing down in the middle of the ring after the spin or glide. Moreover, a thrower should appear to explode at the end of a throw.

3. *The law of the conservation of rotary momentum*. The left arm (for a right-handed thrower) swings wide at the beginning of a discus throw or shot-put, and is brought closer to the body at the end of the throw. This is the same action that a skater uses in order to spin faster.

4. *Ground force*. Throwers should not leave the ground until the implement has left their hands. There is a force delivered from the ground that was initiated by the athlete during the throw. This law is extremely important to athletes who throw heavier implements.

5. *Center of gravity*. The higher the center of gravity, the more unstable the balance. Athletes must immediately lower their center of gravity after a throw to prevent falling out of the ring.

There are several other laws that may impact on successful throwing, but by emphasizing these five factors, everything else seems to fall into place.

TRAINING PROGRAMS

Discus throwers and shot-putters usually undergo identical general preparation periods. The only differences are in a few drills and weight-training exercises. For the rotational putter there are almost no differences. The differences in that case will be the inclusion on dumbbell flyes, a few simulated discus throws with surgical hoses, and a number of discus drills. It would be redundant to offer a detailed general preparation period for discus throwers. However, there are enough differences during the specific preparation period to require separate training schedules.

*Weekly training schedule for discuss throwers
during the specific preparation period*

Day	Duration (min)	Training task	Training details
Monday	20	Warm-up	Jog 400 meters, stretch
	10	Sprint drills	High knees, chop downs, grapevines
	40	Discus drills	Standing throws, South African drill, medicine ball drills (discus style)
	30	Weight training	Leg curls and extensions, squats and power cleans, 3 sets, 15 reps
	5	Warm-down	Jog 400 meters, stretch

Day	Duration (min)	Training task	Training details
Tuesday	20	Warm-up	Jog 200, stride 200, stretch
	10	Sprint drills	High knees, backward runs, form runs
	40	Discus drills	South African drill with and without discus, softball throw with full discus form.
	30	Weight training	Dumbbell flyes, bench press, regular press, 3 sets, 10 reps
	5	Warm-down	Jog 400, stretch
Wednesday	20	Warm-up	Jog 400 meters, stretch
	10	Sprint drills	High knees, form runs, grapevines
	40	Games	Volleyball or basketball
	5	Warm-down	Jog 400, stretch
Thursday	20	Warm-up	Jog 400, stretch
	10	Sprint drills	High knees, grapevine, backward run, form runs
	40	Discus drills	Standing throws with a 16-lb. shot and medicine balls, full form with a softball
	30	Weight training	Leg curls and extensions. step-ups and lunges, power snatch, 3 sets, 12 reps
	5	Warm-down	Jog 200, walk 200, stretch
Friday	20	Warm-up	Jog 200, stride 100, jog 200, stretch
	10	Sprint drills	High knees, 5 × 50 meter sprints, 90% effort
	40	Discus drills	Standing and full throws against mats using a plastic discus*
	30	Weight training	Bench flyes, bench press, standing press 3 sets, 10 reps
	5	Warm-down	Jog 200, walk 200, stretch
Saturday		Competition (shot-put).	

* We do this drill standing about 10–20 feet from a padded wall. Using a plastic discus eliminates the possibility of damaging the mat or the wall. Earlier in my career, we used a rubber discus, but they left marks that we subsequently had to remove. This is a great drill because the throwers do not have to chase after the disc between throws. You can get in 100 quality throws in a relatively short period of time.

There is no competition for the discus thrower until April. This means that the discus thrower has to continue practicing drills and competing in the shot-put during the precompetitive period. If the discus throw is the athletes' strongest event, we try to teach them the rotational shot-put technique in preparation for their outdoor competition. This period is usually scheduled for the month of March. Discus throwers must continue to rely on the shot as their primary outlet for competition. This will at least prepare them psychologically for the pressures of competition during the outdoor season.

Weekly training schedule for discuss throwers during the precompetitive period

Day	Duration (min)	Training task	Training details
Monday	20	Warm-up	Jog 400, stretch
	10	Sprint drills	High knees, grapevines, sliding sideways, form runs
	40	Discus drills	Surgical hose drills, discus technique with medicine ball, full throws with discus strap*
	30	Weight training	Leg curls and extensions, squats and power cleans, 4 sets × 8 reps
	5	Warm-down	Jog 200, stretch
Tuesday	20	Warm-up	Jog 200, stride 200, stretch
	10	Sprint drills	High knees, 7 × 30 meters, 95% effort
	40	Discus drills	Wall drills, standing throws and full technique
	5	Warm-down	Jog 200, stretch
Wednesday	20	Warm-up	Jog 400, stride 200, stretch
	10	Sprint drills	High knees, backwards run, chop downs, form runs
	40	Discus drills (in water)	Shot put rotational style, full discus form with a strap, surgical hose drills
	30	Recreation	Relaxed swimming
	5	Warm-down	Jog 400, stretch
Thursday	20	Warm-up	Jog 200, stride 200, stretch
	10	Sprint drills	High knees, grapevines, form runs
	40	Discus drills	South African drill, standing and full throws against mats
	30	Weight training	Leg curls and extensions, step-ups and leg press
	5	Warm-down	Jog 400, stride 200, stretch

Day	Duration (min)	Training task	Training details
Friday	20	Warm-up	Jog 300, stride 100, stretch
	10	Sprint drills	High knees, 7×30, 95% effort
	30	Discus drills	Shot put (rotational technique) wall drills, full discus technique
	30	Weight training	Incline bench flyes, incline bench press, curls, sit-ups
	5	Warm-down	Jog 400, stretch
Saturday		Competition in the shot-put.	

* Attach a leather strap to a discus. Make it tight enough to snugly secure your thrower's hand to the implement. This will permit your athletes to practice discus technique without actually releasing it. This is another way your throwers can execute a large number of "throws" without actually releasing the discus.

The competitive period is usually begun during the first week of April. This is your discus throwers' first opportunity to really know how far they can throw. Don't let their enthusiasm be the source of injuries. If the weather is extremely cold, your athletes must save their best efforts for warmer days. Throwers, unlike runners, can wear extra sweatsuits and function without fear of injury in practice and competition, but don't be disappointed if their efforts are not impressive during the first weeks of the outdoor season. Have them continue working on technique and when the weather breaks, the personal bests will come. They may have to work on a volume schedule on cold days. When the weather permits, gradually move toward quality training. The maxim "Make haste slowly" is apropos at this time.

Weekly training schedule for discus throwers during the competitive period

Day	Duration (min)	Training task	Training details
Monday	20	Warm-up	Jog 400, stretch
	10	Sprint drills	High knees, grapevines, backward run, form runs
	40	Discus drills	Continuous South African drill followed with a throw, standing throws
	30	Weight training	Leg curls and extensions, squats and power cleans, sit-ups
	5	Warm-down	Jog 400, stretch

Day	Duration (min)	Training task	Training details
Tuesday	20	Warm-up	Jog 400, stretch
	10	Sprint drills	High knees, stair running
	40	Discus drills	Standing throws, full technique throws
	30	Weight training	Bench flyes, bench presses, incline presses, 4 sets, 5 reps
	5	Warm-down	Jog 400, stretch
Wednesday	20	Warm-up	Jog 200, walk 200, stride 200, stretch
	10	Sprint drills	High knees, form runs, 5×30, 95% effort
	40	Discus drills	Standing and full technique with surgical hose, standing throws with an overweight implement
	5	Warm-down	Jog 400, stretch
Thursday	20	Warm-up	Jog 100, stride 100, jog 100, sprint 100, jog 100, stretch
	10	Sprint drills	High knees, grapevines, backward runs, form runs
	40	Discus drills	Standing throws (overweight discus), full technique (underweight discus)
	30	Weight training	Leg curls and extensions, leg press and lunges, 3 sets $\times$ 8 reps
	5	Warm-down	Jog 200, walk 200, stretch
Friday	20	Warm-up	Jog 400, stretch
	10	Sprint drills	High knees, 7×30 meters
	30	Discus drills	Standing and full technique throws $\times$ 20
	5	Warm-down	Jog 400, stretch
Saturday		Competition in the shot and discus.	

If you are coaching without assistants, it is best to set a specific time limit for each part of the training session. When we do this, practice can start and end at the same time for everyone on the team. It is also easy to tell where each athlete is supposed to be in the workout. You can check your watch, look around the field, and be certain that everything is going according to plan. There may be an occasional exception to this rule, but because of the planned schedule, the exceptions are easy to monitor. When you ascribe a specific number of throws for the throwers, some of the team will finish before the others, and the practice can become chaotic. This system also assures that the volume and intensity of work are adequate. Additionally, every athlete is aware that the practice session is not open-ended and they tend to work harder. If some of your highly motivated throwers request additional time to train — let them — but assess a time limit to this extra practice also.

The next period is the peaking cycle. This four-week period is a delicate phase. The intensity and volume of these final weeks are based on the outcome of Saturday's competition. Everything that is planned is based on your empirical assessment of the athletes' physical and psychological state during this period. Some athletes may need a heavier work load and others may require less work or none at all. The decision is yours.

The schedule below is based on the concept of competition, rest, and restoration. Weight training is limited to two days and much of this is explosive lifting with lighter poundages. The discus practice is usually specific, intense, and brief. The volume is low and the quality is high. The rest periods between throws and lifts are longer. We taper off earlier in the week. We no longer train through. We want peak performances on Saturday.

Weekly training schedule for discus throwers during the peaking period

Day	Duration (min)	Training task	Training details
Monday	20	Warm-up	Jog 400, stretch
	10	Sprint drills	High knees, grapevines, form runs
	40	Discus drills	Standing throws, South African drill, surgical hose drills
	30	Weight training	Leg curls and extensions, squats, power cleans, 6 sets ×2 reps
	5	Warm-down	Jog 400, stretch
Tuesday	20	Warm-up	Jog 2 mins, stretch
	10	Sprint drills	High knees, form runs, 5×30 meters
	40	Discus drills	Standing throws, full technique throws for distance
	30	Weight training	Incline flyes, bench press, standing press 6 sets ×2 reps
	5	Warm-down	Jog 2 mins, stretch
Wednesday	20	Warm-up	Jog 400, stretch
	10	Sprint drills	High knees, backward runs, form runs
	30	Discus drills	Easy full technique throws
	5	Warm-down	Jog 400, stretch

Day	Duration (min)	Training task	Training details
Thursday	20	Warm-up	Jog 2 mins, stretch
	10	Sprint drills	High knees, butt kicks, grapevines, form runs, backward runs
	30	Recreation	Relaxed swimming
	5	Warm-down	400 jog, stretch
Friday	20	Warm-up	Jog 2 mins, stretch
	10	Sprint drills	High knees, form runs, 5×30 meters, top speed
	30	Discus drills	Standing throws, $7 \times$ full technique
	5	Warm-down	Jog 2 mins., stretch
Saturday	Competition.		

DISCUS TRAINING UNDER DIFFICULT CONDITIONS

You can throw the discus just about anyplace. Permit me to cite an example of making the best of a bad situation. In 1969, our 800 meter runner qualified for the Golden West Invitational in Sacramento, California, and during our evening meal, I met two coaches who qualified discus throwers. The next morning, we went to a local park to train our respective athletes. I didn't see a discus circle anywhere in that park. These coaches found a narrow sidewalk located near a field house and used it for their practice. This area didn't look like a discus area but it served their purposes.

Get some chalk or tape and find a sidewalk, asphalt, or some solid surface; make two marks 8 feet apart and you're in business. You should use an area that has a surface similar to that of the discus circle. If you can't find a sidewalk surface smooth enough to do the job, try asphalt or dirt. Most parks and playgrounds will have some sort of surface that will suffice. We often found a deserted pavement near a park and threw the discus from the street into a grassy area.

During the indoor season, we throw the discus up a flight of stairs, in corridors, against walls, and in swimming pools. The best implement for these purposes is a plastic discus. The plastic won't leave marks on the walls or mats. To prevent damage, cover the intended areas with mats whenever possible. If it is not possible to secure a gymnasium, substitute a softball or medicine ball for the discus.

You can simulate the event with surgical hoses or indoor shots, or by strapping the discus to the thrower's hand. Practice rotational skills with hundreds of South African drills in a corridor or gymnasium. When your throwers weight train, incorporate exercises that affect the discus-throwing muscles. The best exercises for this purpose are flyes on a bench or the incline bench. A word of caution: Use a rubber or plastic discus during the learning process. You can save a great deal of money using these inexpensive implements. Most novice throwers will damage an expensive discus in a New York minute. After your throwers improve their skills, move them to a discus that has a wooden center and a metal rim. When they become accomplished in the event, try a disc that has a hollow center and most of the weight located on the outside rim. As they move to more aerodynamically constructed equipment, you may have to dig deep into your pockets or impact upon your "alleged" budget. To economize, and still prepare your throwers for competition, purchase several implements of similar specifications, but keep one of each to the side for inspection by meet officials. Never practice with one style of discus and expect to throw well with a discus of another design in competition. Your throwers need time to adjust to their discus of choice several weeks prior to an important track meet.

The discus throw is not an expensive event. A few dollars, a roll of tape, a box of chalk, and a pavement near a park, and you're ready to go. This is an event that can score a lot of points for your track team. When you find a talented athlete for this event, it can be the most consistent event on your schedule. Your discus thrower will have 12 attempts (in the shot-put and discus throw) to contribute 20 points to the team's total score. Don't look a gift horse in the mouth. With a few thoughtfully spent dollars, a talented discus thrower can be an invaluable addition to your track and field program.

Section 20

STRENGTH AND FLEXIBILITY TRAINING

Weight training is probably the most common exercise modality ever used. Old wives' tales regarding this valuable tool still abound in the 1990s. Ben Johnson did not take steroids to improve his leg speed; he took them to improve his strength. The attainment of strength is not a negative factor — it's always a plus. World records are falling at an unprecedented rate. The primary reason for this happy state of affairs is the acceptance of scientific weight training as a viable means of improving athletic prowess. Weight training is here to stay.

Incorrectly executed flexibility exercises can do irreparable harm to an athlete's musculature. An additional mission of this section is to determine the best way to do these often-misunderstood exercises.

When Ben Johnson blew Carl Lewis off the track in the 1986 Olympic games, the athletic world went into shock. No one expected a sprinter to beat the great Carl Lewis that easily in the 100 meter dash. When the officials subsequently discovered that Ben Johnson used steroids to accomplish this remarkable feat, the uninitiated thought that anabolic steroids were responsible for his dramatically augmented speed. People who know better realize that steroids didn't increase Ben Johnson's leg speed; they made him stronger. When records fall in a variety of sports — and they have — steroids are usually the culprit. In each case, the direct effect of steroid use is increased muscular strength. It is undeniable that steroids can increase muscular strength in a spectacular fashion — but that is all.

A well-designed weight-training program will accomplish the same thing. In the 1940s and 1950s, most athletes and coaches in all sports avoided weight training like a plague. My college physical education instructor was certain that if you touched a barbell, your body would turn into a mass of useless, musclebound, slow, and uncoordinated flesh. When I outran and outjumped everyone in our class, he refused to recognize the truth. Sadly, a few coaches still believe that enhanced muscular strength is a detriment.

In 1946, Otis Chandler a shot-putter at Stanford University, was the first track and field athlete of note to use weight training to improve performance. Though his coach initially objected to this "radical" approach to training, Dink Templeton finally bought the concept in Chandler's senior year. The rest is history.

Weight training is a miraculous training modality, but in the hands of the ignorant and misguided, this marvelous training aid can do irreparable damage to an athlete. If you don't know what you're doing, it is best to leave it alone. Weight training in the hands of an expert can produce results that will defy imagination. Clyde Hart, Michael Johnson's (current Olympic champion in the 200 and 400 meters) sprint coach is a staunch advocate of weight training for track and field. I think I have made my point.

Three major disciplines in weight training are Olympic weight lifting, power lifting, and bodybuilding. Weight training for athletics is none of the above and, paradoxically, it's all of the above. The best of all worlds is to borrow the most productive methods from all of these activities. For example, we can borrow the power clean and power snatch from the Olympic lifts; the squat, bench press, and deadlift from the power lifts, and several assistance exercises like curls, flyes, and calf raises from bodybuilding. From this amalgam of systems we can exploit the values of each and design a productive weight-training program specifically for track and field athletes.

WEIGHT-TRAINING GUIDELINES

The weight-training programs outlined in this section represent that mix of the various physiological approaches to training. Several programs based on these concepts will be listed on the following pages. But before they are submitted, these guidelines should be observed:

1. Slow lifting may make slow athletes, so lift with speed, but try to lift the weights in a smooth, controlled manner.
2. Train, don't strain.
3. Seldom attempt maximum singles. This is the quickest way to get injuries.
4. Always use correct form in the "core" lifts. The core lifts are the bench press, standing press, squat, deadlift, and the power clean.
5. Make haste slowly. Gradual gains are best. The body adapts more easily to smaller adjustments in poundages. An increase of 2 pounds per week in the bench press is over 100 pounds of improvement in one year. That's 1,000 pounds in 10 years!
6. Avoid monotony like a plague. The muscular and nervous systems are stimulated better by a constant change in repetitions, sets, exercises, and equipment. Variety is necessary for continued progress.
7. A workout should be less than an hour. The testosterone level begins to decrease after 50 minutes.
8. Periodize. Change workouts every 4-6 weeks.
9. Stretch before and after every workout.
10. Never work out alone.
11. Always warm up.
12. Never hold your breath during exertion.
13. The sequence of effort during the weeks should be medium, heavy, medium, light, medium, heavy, medium, light, etc.
14. Keep a written record of your workouts.
15. Exceptional strength development is possible without steroids; it just takes a little longer.

A Few Words About Steroids

Steroids appeared on the athletic scene in a big way during the 1960s. Rumors circulated among weight lifters and bodybuilders that a little blue pill was responsible for the remarkable improvement of certain competitors. Lifters were experimenting with these anabolic steroids oblivious of their deleterious side effects. Several years later, we discovered that steroid use could be hazardous to your health. These warnings fell on deaf ears, and athletes in other sports

Figure 20-1

A FEW EXAMPLES OF
BASIC WEIGHT-TRAINING EXERCISES

PARALLEL SQUAT

STARTING POSITION FOR THE
SNATCH, CLEAN, AND DEADLIFT

DUMBELL PRESS

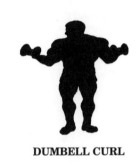

DUMBELL CURL

SIT-UP

LUNGE

BENCH PRESS

BENT-OVER ROWING

jumped on the bandwagon, with a concomitant outrage of continued drug use that caused exercise science to slow to a snail's pace. Nobody wanted to talk about scientific training anymore. Just take a few pills and a world record is yours.

World-class performances are possible without drugs. We have not exploited all the possibilities that scientific weight-training and proper nutrition have to offer. There is no need for athletes to risk permanent organic damage, and even death, in pursuit of a gold medal. It is possible to be world-class without the use of Dianabol, Ninevar, Wistrol, Deca-Derobolin, and HGH.

We must forget about steroids and do more research. The best research in regard to strength training can be found in Eastern European literature; this is probably one of the reasons why they dominate most of the strength sports. Athletes in various countries around the world are beginning to medal in events that were formerly monopolized by Americans. How often have we failed to medal in the 100 meter dash and lost the 400 meter relay in the same Olympics?

Weight-Training and Your Program

Weight-training suggestions were offered to give you a general idea of where weight-training should fit in each daily program, but there were very few details beyond that. You may have noticed, however, that weight-training was always done after the track workout, no weight program took more than 50 minutes to complete, and periodization and variety marked the entire season.

Of necessity, this is a brief version of the rather involved subject of weight training. If you feel a need to dig deeper, try *Soviet Training and Recovery Methods* by Bruner Tabachnik, or *Secrets of Soviet Sports Fitness and Training* by Michael Yessis, PhD. I will make every effort here to provide a philosophy and guidelines to lead you into a sensible and productive program for each category in track and field. These categories will be (1) sprinters and hurdlers, (2) jumpers, (3) distance runners and (4) throwers.

BASIC WORKOUTS

The workouts which follow should fit into your program. (See the exercise examples in Figure 20-1 on page 325.) Most are scheduled for Monday, Tuesday, Thursday, and Friday. Your athletes will train the lower body on Monday and Thursday and the upper body on Tuesday and Friday. There are other ways to schedule your workouts, but our athletes responded best to this system. We also tried to wait about 20 minutes between their track workout and weight-training.

According to Angel Spassov, the Bulgarian strength coach, this period of rest will permit the testosterone level to return to normal after a hard track and field regimen:

Weight program for sprinters and hurdlers

Lower body	Upper body
1. Leg extension	1. Bench press
2. Leg curl	2. Shoulder press
3. Squat or leg press	3. Upright rowing
4. Hyperextension	4. Bent-over rowing
5. Power clean	5. Lat machine pulls
6. Calf raise	6. Curls
7. Sit-ups	7. Crunches

Repetition scheme:
> General preparation period — 2 set, 15 reps
> Specific preparation period — 3 sets, 12 reps
> Precompetitive period — 4 sets, 8 reps
> Competitive period — 4 sets, 5 reps
> Peaking period — 6 sets, 3 reps

Weight program for jumpers

Lower body	Upper body
1. Leg extension	1. Forward raise with dumbbells
2. Leg curl	2. Bench press
3. Squat or jumping squats	3. Shoulder press
4. Hyperextension	4. Upright rowing
5. Power clean	5. Lat machine pulls
6. Calf raise	6. Curls
7. Sit-ups	7. Crunches

Periodization cycles, sets and reps are identical to the schedule suggested for sprinters and hurdlers.

Weight-training program for distance runners

Lower body	Upper body
1. Leg extensions	1. Standing press
2. Leg curls	2. Parallel bar dips
3. Step-ups	3. Pull-ups
4. Hyperextensions	4. Curls
5. Rapid deadlifts	5. Sit-ups
6. Sit-ups	

Repetition scheme:
> General preparation period — 1 set, 15 reps
> Specific preparation period — 2 sets, 12 reps
> Precompetitive period — 3 sets, 10 reps
> Competitive period — 3 sets, 8 reps
> Peaking period — 1 set, 10 reps

Weight-training program for throwers

Lower body	Upper body
1. Leg extension	1. Bench press
2. Leg curl	2. Incline press (flyes for discus)
3. Squat or leg press	3. Hyperextensions
4. Reverse hyperextensions	4. Hang snatches
5. Power cleans or rapid deadlifts	5. Curls
6. Sit-ups	6. Crunches

Repetition scheme:

General preparation period — 3 sets, 10 reps
Specific preparation period — 4 sets, 8 reps
Precompetitive period — 4 sets, 5 reps
Competitive period — 6 sets, 3 reps
Peaking period — 5, 4, 3, 2, reps

These programs are not the only productive exercise prescriptions; however, these will get the job done. Most of our athletes made phenomenal progress on these basic schedules. After a few months, you will need to adjust or change repetitions, equipment, exercises, and number of days you train. As your athletes improve and their intensity of training increases, you will have to be more creative in order to manifest continued progress.

For two years, variety will suffice. After that, you will have to look at what the experts are doing. There are two schools of thought for advanced training: (1) Train hard and heavy (about 90 minutes), but less often. For example, most advanced power lifters bench press and squat only *once per week*. (2) Train briefly at a percentage of max but more often, like the Bulgarian weight lifters who train several times a day *every day* with low reps (1-3 per set), for about 40 minutes. Since variety is a constant, you can use either system or both in your program. Don't try this with your beginners.

A Word of Caution

Weight-training is a supplement for track and field activity — not a substitute. When weight-training finally became accepted as a viable part of a track and field program there was a tendency in some quarters to drift into overemphasis on this valuable tool. Specificity should not be forgotten. The majority of your athletes' training time should be event-specific. You are not preparing them for a weight-lifting meet or bodybuilding contest.

ALTERNATIVES TO WEIGHT-TRAINING

When I received my first assignment as a track coach, there was no weight equipment in the building. The athletic director saw no need to order any, so I

Figure 20-2

VIABLE ALTERNATIVES TO WEIGHT-TRAINING

VIABLE ALTERNATIVES TO WEIGHT TRAINING

There are times when you may not have weights available, or at least no easy access to a weight-training facility. With a little innovation, a resistance-training program can be improvised with a mnimum of equipment. The nine photographs are a few examples demonstrating how a wooden or metal bar and a training partner can provide a viable alternative to weight equipment. If the athlete is very strong, station a teammate on each side of the bar for additional resistance. This unique approach to weight training can also be a refreshing substitute for the usual training program.

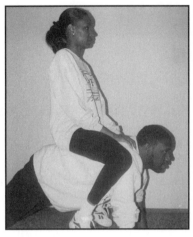

Photo 20–1. Push-ups with a partner providing resistance by sitting on the lifter's back. This exercise strengthens the triceps and pectoral muscles.

Photo 20–2. Partner-resisted shoulder press. This exercise develops the triceps and deltoids.

Photo 20–3. The one-legged squat. Twenty repetitions of this difficult exercise will build exceptional quadriceps strength.

Photo 20–4. A partner-resisted lunge. This is another quadriceps exercise.

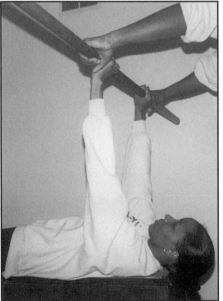

Photo 20–5. A bench press with partner resistance. This exercise builds the triceps and pectoral muscles.

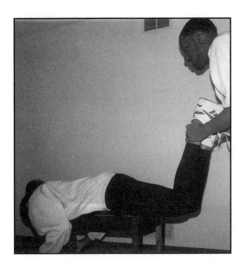

Photo 20–6. Hamstring curls with partner resistance.

Photo 20–7. The lifter is executing a squat for the quadriceps. The athlete behind her is providing resistance.

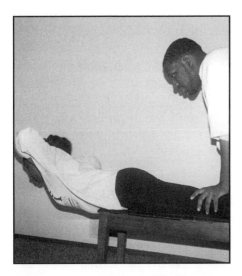

Photo 20–8. The prone hyperextension exercise for the lower back muscles, with legs held by a teammate.

Photo 20–9. The two-hand curl for the biceps. The lifter on the right is executing the lift. Resistance is given by the athlete on the left.

took the initiative and raised funds. In the meantime, we had to find a way to exercise until we had enough money to solve our problem. When the weights arrived, the athletes were amazed at how effective these temporary methods were. They could handle some serious poundages after they became adjusted to the new equipment. We still use some of these alternative methods when we practice in a local park or playground. Some of these exercises are listed below:

Upper body	*Lower body*
1. Parallel bar dips	1. One-leg squats
2. Push-ups with feet elevated	2. Piggyback walking up stairs
3. Isometrics with partner resistance	3. Lunges with partner resistance
4. Exercises with surgical hoses	4. Car pushing
5. Pull-ups on a horizontal bar	5. Exercises with surgical hoses
6. Automobile bench presses	6. Isometrics
7. Wheelbarrow walking up stairs	7. Partner-resisted running

MACHINES VERSUS FREE WEIGHTS

In the last decade, several resistance machines have appeared on the weight-training scene, making outrageous claims. Most strength coaches are quick to admit that no machine on the market can replace working with free weights. No machine can duplicate the results produced by multijoint exercises like the bench press, squat, and power clean, but machines can make a significant contribution toward the development of a complete athlete. Moreover, there are several exercises that can be done much better on a machine. Most machines can do a better job with single-joint exercises like the leg curl and leg extension.

Machines are safer. Athletes using free weights must have someone spotting them at all times. The possibility of injury can rear its ugly head when you least expect it. Conversely, an athlete can train alone (though I don't advise it) in complete safety with most machines. You have to try to get hurt on machines, but a few athletes will find a way to harm themselves. Spot them whether they need it or not.

The bottom line is to incorporate every piece of useful equipment into your weight program. Every modality can contribute to your athlete's progress; it depends upon how they are utilized.

FLEXIBILITY TRAINING

You can't stretch too often. Stretch before practice. Stretch during practice. Stretch after practice. Stretch between practices. Stretch. It is also possible, however, to stretch incorrectly. When you are not warmed up, you can stretch beyond the range of motion. You can use the wrong technique. You can use the wrong exercises. I have seen athletes hurt themselves while stretching. Listed below are a few guidelines for proper stretching:

1. Stretch after you have warmed up. Make sure your athletes have increased circulation by jogging a few laps. If jogging has not caused a little perspiration, they are not ready to stretch.

2. Stretch statically. Do not bounce into a stretch; gradually, and carefully, move into a stretch and hold that position for at least 20 seconds.

3. Use PNF (proprioceptive neuromuscular facilitation) techniques with care. Sounds impressive doesn't it? This is basically partner-assisted stretching. The athlete is pulled or pushed into a stretch and held as the stretchee pulls or pushes isometrically against the partner for 20 seconds or more. If your athletes don't fully understand this technique, skip it. This method can be dangerous if it is done incorrectly.

4. Your athletes may kick and swing their legs and arms after they have completed the above stretches, but be careful here also.

5. The only athletes on your squad who should do the hurdle stretch are hurdlers. This is not a natural position and the rest of the team should not do this exercise.

6. Stretch after each workout. The best time to stretch is often after a strenuous training session.

A FINAL WORD

A thoughtful weight-training schedule can work wonders in your conditioning program. Every athlete will benefit from this valuable supplement to your training schedule. Remember if you want to make rabbit stew, you have to start with a rabbit. A gifted athlete can go pretty far without doing anything special. But in these days of 19.4 200 meters, 9.8 100 meters, and 70-foot shot-puts, athletes will not reach their potential without scientific resistance training.

Your athletes are experiencing a tremendous growth spurt and weights can accelerate this growth process. Their talent may not be obvious to you when they are freshmen, but a few years of sensible weight-training will potentiate their ability. Weight-training is so effective that your competition may often accuse you of having more talented people than they. Just smile and continue with your weight program.

Section 21

CLERICAL WORK AND RECORD KEEPING

A necessary evil in coaching is the mountain of clerical work associated with our profession. Record keeping seems to increase every day. Included in this section are various forms and other information that confront most track coaches during a typical season. To be forewarned is to be forearmed.

I love coaching and everything associated with it — except record keeping — but I will be the first to admit that you cannot successfully coach, especially if you are the only coach, without a good system of record keeping. If you are working in a situation similar to mine, no one will assist you in keeping track of eligibility, medical records, inventory, team rosters, meet schedules, and such. But woe unto you if you don't have the proper records when your athletic director, principal, or the downtown office requests them. Included in this chapter are the necessary forms and information you need to survive as a track and field coach. Your situation may require more or less data, but every track coach will have to deal with this necessary evil from time to time. My advice is to take care of most of this early on and get it out of the way so you can coach.

KEEPING PARENTS AND TEACHERS INFORMED

One of the most important forms you must develop is a letter to the parents such as the one in Figure 21-1. This correspondence will eliminate a number of problems and may serve to get parents on your side. If you fail to communicate with parents or guardians in regard to your program, they will not be clear as to your training schedule, the amount of time you practice, or your meet schedule. A letter to the athlete's home can solve most problems before they become problems. This may be the first communication between you and the parents, and it will establish a positive connection from the beginning.

The letter that I suggest is not the only answer. Yours might be more detailed and lengthy. The nature and extent of the correspondence is up to you. I like to make a letter to the parents short and sweet. If it is too lengthy, it may be ignored.

To ensure that the athletes present the letter to the parent, have the parent sign the letter. If you do that, you don't have to worry about a failure to communicate.

Figure 21-1.   Sample Letter to Parents

ATHLETIC DEPARTMENT

Dear Parent:

Your son/daughter has been chosen as a member of the District 3030 High School's track team. He/she will be issued a uniform that will consist of a sweat suit, jersey, and shorts. We expect the student-athlete to keep this uniform clean and in order at all times. If this uniform is lost, stolen, or damaged, he/she is expected to reimburse our athletic department for the loss or damage of the uniform. The cost of each uniform is $205.75.

No academically ineligible student may compete for any high school in our district. Additionally, our students with failing grades cannot compete or practice with our team. One failing grade received in a major subject renders a student athletically ineligible for one week. A student-athlete receiving a failing grade in a major subject at the midterm is ineligible for the remainder of the track season.

Track practice begins at 3:00 P.M. and ends at 5:00 P.M. Most of our athletes live within District 3030; therefore you can expect your youngster to arrive home by 6:00 P.M. The only exceptions to this rule are the days we are involved in competition.

Please find enclosed with this letter a tentative meet schedule. Parents are encouraged to accompany the team to the track meets.

If you have any questions in regard to the above information, or if you have any suggestions that may help our program, call us at the athletic office. Our office hours are from 1:00 P.M. to 3:00 P.M. Monday through Friday. I can also be reached at home (phone number) after 8:00 P.M. Monday through Saturday.

Sincerely yours,

Track Coach

On the next several pages are a few forms related to meet competition. These are necessary for information and motivation. Athletes and parents must be informed about times, performances, and meet schedules (Figure 21-2). Teachers must also be informed (Figure 21-3). We usually schedule one meet a week. Most meets held during the week are over at 6:00 P.M. and Saturday competitions are finished around 1:00 P.M. These are submitted to give you a model of how we fit a track schedule into our training program:

Figure 21-2.   Sample Meet Schedule

UPCOMING MEETS

SATURDAY	MARCH 30	DENTON INVITATIONAL
FRI/SAT	APRIL 5, 6	CHICAGOLAND CHAMPIONSHIPS
SATURDAY	APRIL 13	@ WALTON DUAL
SATURDAY	APRIL 20	@ LEVANSTON-BROOKSIDE
FRIDAY	APRIL 26	CPS QUAD
FRI/SAT	APRIL 26/27	CITY RELAYS
FRI/SAT	MAY 3, 4	DISTRICT CHAMPIONSHIPS
FRIDAY	MAY 10	SECTIONALS
FRIDAY	MAY 17	SOUTH CENTRAL INVITATIONAL
WED - SAT	MAY 22–25	STATE CHAMPIONSHIPS

Figure 21-3.   Sample Track Meet Notice to Teachers

ATHLETIC DEPARTMENT

Dear Instructor,

Please excuse _____ from class

on _____. He/she is a member

of the District 3030 track and field team and will be competing on _____.

We will be departing from school at _____.

All work missed will be the responsibility of the student-athlete. If you have any

questions, please contact me. We appreciate your support and cooperation.

Sincerely,

Head Track Coach

KEEPING ATHLETES INFORMED

After each meet athletes are given a handout that informs them of the points (see Figure 21-4) scored and a coach's comment on their performance (See Figure 21-5) We always try to make positive, constructive statements. These comment sheets are the kinds of things that the late Ted Haydon did to motivate his athletes. We found this approach an invaluable asset to our program.

Figure 21-4.   Sample Sheet — Points Scored

EVENTS	POINTS	ATHLETE	POINTS
2 MILE (3200)	15	OSMAND	25
1 MILE (1600)	10	RYAN	20
400 HURDLES	16	REED	20
HIGH JUMP	15	WOODEN	19
100	15	MURCHISON	19
200	15	TAYLOR	16
800	15	WHITFIELD	15
TRIPLE JUMP	13	JONES	14
DISCUS	20	BROWN	13
SHOT	10	EVERETT	10
POLE VAULT	8	RICHARDS	10
110 HURDLES	8	STOVER	9
4 × 100	8	ANDERSON	7
4 × 400	8	SHEMANSKY	5
LONG JUMP	6	HUBBARD	5
4 × 800	8	WINT	4
400	7	RHODEN	4

Figure 21-5.   Sample Coach's Comment Sheet

CONFERENCE TRACK & FIELD CHAMPIONSHIPS
MAY 3 & 4

1. DISTRICT 3030 HIGH SCHOOL	275		5. NORTH H.S.	46
2. SOUTH DIVISION	253		6. ROOSEVELT	46
3. WESTSIDE	54		7. TAFT	35
4. EDGEWOOD	53		8. PARKWAY	14

100 METERS

Murchison	1st	10.6	Great start. Beautiful knee lift.
Jones	2nd	10.7	Personal best! Nice race.
Sipes	3rd	11.0	We needed the points. Good effort.

200 METERS

Stanfield	1st	21.4	Nice curve run. Good relaxation.
Carr	2nd	21.5	You need to work on your start.
Woodson	4th	22.0	Personal best!

400 METERS

Rhoden	2nd	47.8	School record. Nice going!
Wint	3rd	48.0	Beautiful stride pattern in the final 100.
Neighbors	4th	50.2	You made steady progress all year.

800 METERS

Courtney	1st	1:50	Your pace was perfect.
Thomas	2nd	1:50.2	Another 10 meters and you might have won.
Woodruff	4th	152.5	Avoid being boxed next time.

1600 METERS

Sheppard	1st	4:15	Just like we planned it!
Jackson	3rd	418.0	Your third quarter could have been faster.

110 METER HURDLES

Brown	1st	13.8	Your trail leg has improved. Great effort.
Smith	2nd	14.0	You have to work on the 7th hurdle.
Booker	5th	14.5	The first 3 hurdles gave you trouble.

400 METER HURDLES

Smith	3rd	55.4	You lost your steps on the curve.
Stevens	5th	56.2	Your lead leg hurt you on the last 3 hurdles.
Moore	6th	56.5	Personal best. Nice going!

Figure 21-5. Sample Coach's Comment Sheet

CONFERENCE TRACK & FIELD CHAMPIONSHIPS
(continued)

SHOT

Evans	1st	60-1	The weight training has made a difference.
Powell	4th	56-2	Try to accelerate from the power position.
Sawyer	5th	54-6	Your arm must wait for the legs and hips.

DISCUS

Robinson	3rd	170-2	The new disc gave you difficulties.
Thurman	4th	169-1	Personal best! The video helped.
Jackson	5th	165-3	Best hip drive I saw at the meet.

HIGH JUMP

Jones	1st	6-10	Your improved run-up helped.
Roberts	3rd	6-9	Plyometrics really gave you more spring.
Harris	5th	6-5	With a few technical adjustments, you'll do 6-8.

TRIPLE JUMP

Harris	1st	48-8	Personal best. Congratulations!
Brown	3rd	45-6	Improved second phase will add big distance.
Jones	5th	44-9	You need to work on your run-up.
Carson	6th	44-1	Good effort for an athlete new to this event.

The facts, names, and results given are fictional; the distances and times are offered to show you how we developed these handouts for our team. These handouts are more effective when the meet results are fresh in their minds. We present them to the team the following Monday when the results are current.

At least a day before each meet, we send a dismissal form to the team's instructors. If the athletes are diligent about their academics, they will not experience any difficulty getting this form signed. This form has another function: we can discover which athlete is not doing well in classes by the teacher's response to this request.

DEVELOPING A SYSTEM TO MEET YOUR NEEDS

You may not have to compose most of these forms. Most schools will have standardized forms for the athletic department. Check with your school's secretary or athletic director. If you are new to the school or to the district, consult with a veteran coach or athletic director in regard to the required forms and your clerical responsibilities. Get a sample of each and copy enough to last for the rest of the season.

The ensuing pages will be devoted to the kinds of forms and correspondence that you may need to negotiate successfully through a track season. Each school system is an entity within itself, and the number and kind will be different and unique. Some of these forms will seem unnecessary and redundant, but you will have to deal with them nevertheless.

Each year, clerical requirements seem to increase. Find or create a system to expedite this work. I have never been able to persuade our administrators to reduce the extent and amount of this requirement. The desktop computer has made much of my clerical work easier. If you don't have a personal secretary, become computer literate; it will cut your involvement in clerical work in half. The clerical work will be there when you are gone. What is, is.

You will need a roster of your team to keep an accurate record of your athletes and their events. There are several excellent ways to do this. Figure 21-6 is an example of our system. This roster served several purposes: (1) Everyone on this list was given a team uniform; (2) this list is used to check academic eligibility; (3) meet entries were easier; (4) practice organization was expedited; (5) their times can be on this list; (6) the faculty can be informed about team members; and (7) everyone seems to want a list of your team. Now you have one.

The Team Roster can be copied to assist in a multitude of responsibilities.

The names on the form on the following page are all fictitious, but this will give you an example of its value. Several events are also omitted; you can add them to your list.

The forms and letters in Figures 21-7 through 21-21 are familiar to most track coaches. They consist of eligibility sheets, entry forms, accident reports, meet information, supply requisitions, track score sheets, and so on. Most of these must be either responded to immediately or studied for future reference. These are not all of the forms you may encounter, but they are the most representative of the plethora of paper work that is common to most coaches.

"Clerical work and record keeping is my hobby. What's yours?"

Figure 21-6.

TEAM ROSTER

100 METERS

Aaron Williams

Matt Michaels

Ira Owens

200 METERS

Eric Crump

Joel Greer

Andy Fields

400 METERS

Jason Black

Jeff Donald

Herb Mack

800 METERS

Willie Lewis

Mal Wint

John Courtney

1600 METERS

Steve Johnson

Jim Sheppard

Dick Cunningham

3200 METERS

Harry Jackson

Frank Mills

Marty Shorter

HIGH HURDLES

Renaldo May

Mike Davenport

Jeff Norman

400 HURDLES

Edwin Jacobs

Martin Mack

Frank Pollard

HIGH JUMP

Valeri Hubbard

Nate Powell

Kevin Jones

SHOT PUT

Brian Young

Parry Fuchs

Gene Jordan

DISCUS

Mack Wills

Steve Powell

Sam Parker

LONG JUMP

Jesse Lewis

Nate White

Jim Mayer

TRIPLE JUMP

Pete Flowers

Jeff Stewart

Nate White

4×100

Eric Crump

Joel Greer

Matt Michaels

Ira Owens

4×400

Jason Black

Jeff Donald

Herb Mack

Willie Lewis

©1998 by Parker Publishing Company, Inc.

Figure 21-7. Sample Meet Verification Form

SIX-CONTEST VERIFICATION FORM

In accordance with High School Association bylaws, each member school entered in a High School Association Tournament Series must confirm that it has engaged in actual competition during this season in at least six (6) interscholastic contests for the sport it has entered, prior to the beginning of the state tournament series in order to be eligible to compete for team honors in the state tournament series. Competition by individuals will not be affected by this rule, except that individuals from schools that do not verify competition in at least six contests may not score team points.

This form MUST BE COMPLETED, SIGNED, AND DELIVERED to the manager of the beginning level of a state tournament series, prior to the beginning of competition in the tournament series. (Entry fees will not be refunded to those schools that are not eligible to compete for team honors in any tournament series.)

SEND TO SECTIONAL MEET MANAGER NOT TO ASSOCIATION OFFICE

THIS IS TO VERIFY THAT _____HIGH SCHOOL,
(name of school)

_____, HAS PARTICIPATED IN
(town, state)

ACTUAL COMPETITION IN AT LEAST SIX (6) INTERSCHOLASTIC CONTESTS IN

____**BOYS' TRACK AND FIELD**_____ DURING THE CURRENT SEASON.

Signed: _____, Principal

_____
Date

SEND TO SECTIONAL MEET MANAGER NOT TO ASSOCIATION OFFICE

349

Figure 21-8. Sample Permit for Use of Buildings or Grounds

APPLICATION FOR PERMIT TO USE SCHOOL BUILDINGS OR SCHOOL GROUNDS FOR OTHER THAN REGULAR SCHOOL PURPOSES

Applicants securing permits for use of school buildings shall not charge admission or permit subscription of any kind to be made. Any violation of this rule shall result in the immediate revocation of the permit and Engineer Custodian shall thereupon be notified not to open the doors of the school buildings.

APPLICATION FOR PERMIT TO USE SCHOOL BUILDINGS OR SCHOOL GROUNDS FOR OTHER THAN REGULAR SCHOOL PURPOSES

Date of application _____

Name or person and/or organization applying __BUREAU OF HEALTH, PHYSICAL EDUCATION, RECREATION AND SAFETY__

Name of school to be used ___HIGH SCHOOL_____ Mail Run No. _____

Address of School _____ Dist. _____ Zip Code _____

Room(s) or area of building desired ___OUTDOOR TRACK & WASHROOM FACILITY_____

Complete requested information as listed below:

PERMIT REQUESTED FOR: (Complete the following)

DATE	DAY OF WEEK	DOOR OPENING TIME	PROGRAM START	PROGRAM FINISH
4/19/88	Tuesday	3:00 p.m.	3:30 p.m.	7:30 p.m.
4/21/88	Thursday	3:00 p.m.	3:30 p.m.	7:30 p.m.
5/13/88	Friday	3:00 p.m.	3:30 p.m.	7:30 p.m.
5/21/88	Saturday	9:00 a.m.	9:00 a.m.	6:00 p.m.

Permit hours specify actual time of occupancy and program.

If those present are to be subjected to any expense by reason of their attendance, state particulars:_____

_____

_____

_____

_____

Purpose for use of building _____ PUBLIC HIGH SCHOOLS ATHLETIC ASSOCIATION _____

__ BOYS' OUTDOOR TRACK AND FIELD MEETS.__ _____

_____

The undersigned, applying for the use of the above named school property of the Board of Education of the City of Chicago, agrees to observe all the Regulations of the Board of Education for such cases made and provided: and to indemnify the said Board of Education for all expenses to which it may be subjected by reason of the use of said school property by the applicant, whether such expense shall be the extra cost of heating, lighting and caring for the said building, engaging extra service of custodial personnel, where required, according to the appended schedule, which sum the undersigned agrees to pay to the Department of Facilities ten days in advance of the day mentioned: or the expense of replacing property destroyed, repairing property injured, and otherwise putting the school building in the condition in which it was before the applicant made use of it.

Figure 21-9. Sample Contract for Interscholastic Athletic Contests

_____, Ill., _____ 19_____

This CONTRACT is made and subscribed to by the Principals and Coaches or Athletic Directors of _____

High School and of _____ High School, for _____ contests in _____ to be
played as follows: (Name of Sport)

	City	Date	Day	Hour	Hour
First Team Contest				Preliminary Game	
2nd Team Contest				Preliminary Game	

     The bylaws of the High School Association are a part of this contract. The suspension or termination of its membership in the Association by either of the contracting parties shall render this contract null and void.

Financial terms: _____

_____

(SIGNED) PRINCIPAL	COACH OR ATHLETIC DIRECTOR	SCHOOL
(SIGNED) PRINCIPAL	COACH OR ATHLETIC DIRECTOR	SCHOOL

Note 1. List suggested registered officials below. The visiting school Principal should scratch those not acceptable and number the others in order of preference under "Rating" column below.
Note 2. Cancellation of this contract must be mutually agreed to by the contracting parties or under other circumstances deemed acceptable by the Association Board of Directors.

LISTING OF SUGGESTED OFFICIALS

Name	Address	Rating

Figure 21-10. Athletic Awards Form

ATHLETIC DEPARTMENT

Southside High School

To Coaches:

  Please submit a list of the members of your team who have earned athletic awards for the 19____ season. Please submit this list to the athletic director before June____.

Thank you.

MAJOR AWARDS	MINOR AWARDS	NUMERALS
1._____	1._____	1._____
2._____	2._____	2._____
3._____	3._____	3._____
4._____	4._____	4._____
5._____	5._____	5._____
6._____	6._____	6._____
7._____	7._____	7._____
8._____	8._____	8._____
9._____	9._____	9._____
10._____	10._____	10._____
11._____	11._____	11._____
12._____	12._____	12._____
13._____	13._____	13._____
14._____	14._____	14._____
15._____	15._____	15._____
MVP._____	CAPTAIN _____	OTHER _____

Figure 21-11. Sample Players' Record Sheet

CENTRAL OFFICE RECORD SHEET

ATHLETIC ASSOCIATION

Sport _____   Year _____ High School _____

_____   Principal _____
(DATE SENT)   (SIGNATURE)

Original List _____   Board of Control Member _____
                                                                                   (SIGNATURE)

Supplemental List _____   Coach _____
              (PLEASE CHECK)   (SIGNATURE)

ALPHABETICAL LIST OF PROPOSED PLAYERS

NAMES OF CONTESTANTS				ADDRESS	BIRTH RECORD		SEMESTER IN SCHOOL
LAST NAME	FIRST	INITIAL	I.D. No.		MO.--DAY--YR.	PROOF*	
1.							
2.							
3.							
4.							
5.							
6.							
7.							
8.							
9.							
10.							
11.							
12.							
13.							
14.							
15.							
16.							

*Abbreviate as follows:
  Birth Certificate . . . . . . Bir. C.
  Baptismal Certificate . . . . Bapt. C.
  Elem. School Record . . . Sch. Rec.

Figure 21-11.   Sample Players' Record Sheet

CENTRAL OFFICE RECORD SHEET
(continued)

NAMES OF CONTESTANTS				ADDRESS	BIRTH RECORD		SEMESTER IN SCHOOL
LAST NAME	FIRST	INITIAL	I.D. No.		MO.--DAY--YR.	PROOF*	
17.							
18.							
19.							
20.							
21.							
22.							
23.							
24.							
25.							
26.							
27.							
28.							
29.							
30.							
31.							
32.							
33.							
34.							
35.							
36.							
37.							
38.							
39.							
40.							
41.							
42.							
43.							
44.							

Figure 21-12.   Sample Eligibility Certificate

OFFICIAL ELIGIBILITY CERTIFICATE

This is to certify that the following are eligible to represent the _____ High School,

in the Athletic Contest of _____

played with _____ at _____ P.M.
A.M.

on the _____ day of _____ Class _____

COACH _____ BOARD OF CONTROL MEMBER _____

FACULTY REPRESENTATIVE _____ PRINCIPAL _____

NAME OF CONTESTANTS			UNIFORM #		BIRTH DATE	STUDENT I. D. NUMBER	SEM. IN SCHOOL	SEASON NO.	DATE OF LATEST DOCTOR'S CERTIFICATE
LAST NAME	FIRST	INITIAL	HOME	AWAY	MO.--DAY--YR.				
1.									
2.									
3.									
4.									
5.									
6.									
7.									
8.									
9.									
10.									
11.									
12.									
13.									
14.									
15.									
16.									
17.									
18.									
19.									
20.									

PARK OR GYMNASIUM

VARSITY OR FROSH/SOPH

SIGNATURE

SIGNATURE

SIGNATURE

SIGNATURE

Figure 21-12.   Sample Eligibility Certificate

OFFICIAL ELIGIBILITY CERTIFICATE
(continued)

NAME OF CONTESTANTS			UNIFORM #		BIRTH DATE	STUDENT I. D. NUMBER	SEM. IN SCHOOL	SEASON NO.	DATE OF LATEST DOCTOR'S CERTIFICATE
LAST NAME	FIRST	INITIAL	HOME	AWAY	MO.--DAY--YR.				
21.									
22.									
23.									
24.									
25.									
26.									
27.									
28.									
29.									
30.									

PERSONAL REPORT OF BOARD OF CONTROL MEMBERS

Please send to Executive Secretary of the Board of Control of the Public High Schools Athletic Association immediately after a game. (See Note Below)

Date report sent in _____Contest in _____

Home Team _____ Score _____ Opponent _____ Score _____

NAMES OF OFFICIALS	ATTITUDE TOWARD PLAYERS	PERSONAL APPEARANCE	KNOWLEDGE OF RULES	CONTROL OF GAME
1.				
2.				
3.				
4.				
5.				

Remarks: _____
_____
_____

Board of Control Member _____ High School _____
                                      Signature

Principal _____
                         Signature

NOTICE — SECTION ____ BYLAWS

(a) The Board of Control members shall send to the Executive Secretary a complete report of the game or contest on regulation blanks, properly filled out. These lists must be sent to the Executive Secretary within one week after the date of the game or contest.

(b) In contests such as championship track and field meets, etc., where a number of schools are competing in the same contests, the chairman of that sport shall send in this report.

©1998 by Parker Publishing Company, Inc.

Figure 21-13.   Sample Accident or Injury Report

REPORT OF ACCIDENT OR INJURY — STUDENT OR VISITOR

EVERY UNDERLINED AREA / SECTION MUST BE COMPLETED AND TYPED OR PRINTED LEGIBLY

In the event of an accident, no matter how slight, to a student or visitor while under school supervision or on school property, the principal must immediately fill out this form and return as indicated. If the accident involves school buildings or grounds, please have the Engineer initial this report. If an accident involves a school bus, please prepare a separate accident report for each student and indicate the bus company name and route.

SECTION I

DATE OF ACCIDENT _____ SCHOOL _____ UNIT NO. _____ TIME OF ACCIDENT _____ (A.M.) (P.M.)

INJURED PERSON _____ STUDENT I.D. _____ AGE _____ SEX _____ GRADE _____

HOME ADDRESS _____ CITY & ZIP _____ DIVISION/CLASSROOM NO. _____

NAME OF GUARDIAN _____ HOME ADDRESS _____ PHONE NO. _____

TIME FAMILY NOTIFIED _____ HOW? _____ BY WHOM? _____ TITLE _____

FIRST AID GIVEN BY: _____

WHERE TAKEN AFTER ACCIDENT? _____ ABSENCE OF HALF DAY OR MORE ANTICIPATED? YES ☐ NO ☐

Was any person exposed to blood or other potentially infectious materials from another person? YES ☐ NO ☐   If yes, telephone Medical Health Services at (phone) and indicate person contacted _____

If applicable, was the incident reported to Safety & Security at (phone) and a Safety 103 — Incident Report (Misconduct) prepared? YES ☐ NO ☐   Was a Police Report prepared? YES ☐ NO ☐   If yes, give number _____

SECTION II

FULL NAME OF WITNESS	ADDRESS & PHONE, IF OTHER THAN SCHOOL	CHILD OR ADULT	AGE

1. _____

2. _____

3. _____

NAME OF PARTY FIRST TOLD OF ACCIDENT _____

SECTION III

Describe the accident completely beginning with "While", for example, "While walking across the playground during morning recess, Mary Smith was struck by a baseball which bruised her left jaw."

While...

Signature of Principal: _____ Date _____

Engineer's initials _____

Report prepared by: _____ Date _____

Original (WHITE) : School File   Copy (CANARY) : Risk Management

Figure 21-13.   Sample Accident or Injury Report

(continued)

Please check or circle any and all codes which describe the injury. Circle the letter "L" or "R" if applicable.

1. PART OF BODY

101	Abdomen	
102	Ankle	L R
104	Arm	L R
106	Back	
107	Chest	
108	Ear	L R
110	Elbow	L R
112	Eyes	L R
114	Face	
115	Fingers, thumb	
116	Foot	L R
118	Groin	
119	Hand	L R
121	Head	
122	Hips, buttocks	
123	Jaw	L R
125	Knee	L R
127	Leg	L R
129	Mouth-lips	
130	Nose	
131	Shoulder	L R
133	Teeth	
134	Toes	
135	Wrist	L R
137	Circulatory system	
138	Digestive system	
139	Nervous system	
140	Reproductive system	
141	Respiratory system	
199	Other	

2. NATURE OF INJURY

201 Abrasions, scratches
202 Allergic reaction
203 Amputation
204 Asphyxia [Oxygen deficiency]
205 Bite or sting
206 Brain injury
207 Bruise, contusion
208 Burn [including chemical]
209 Choking, strangulation
210 Concussion [brain, cerebral]
211 Cut, laceration, puncture
212 Death
213 Dental injury or disorder
214 Dermatitis [skin rash]
215 Diarrhea or vomiting
216 Disability-substantial
217 Disease
218 Disfigurement, scarring
219 Dislocation
220 Drowning
221 Ear injury-disorder
222 Electric shock
223 Eye injury-disorder
224 Fainting, dizziness
225 Foreign body in eye
226 Fracture
227 Freezing, frostbite
228 Hearing loss, impairment
229 Heat Stroke
230 Hemia, rupture
231 Infection
232 Inflammation-joints, muscles
233 Intoxication, overdose
234 Loss of limb
235 Nausea
236 Nerve injury
237 Paralysis, paraplegia, quadriplegia
238 Poisoned, poisoning
239 Radiation [X-ray, ultravioiet]
240 Reproductive organ-loss or impairment
241 Scratch, abrasion
242 Sensory organ - loss or impairment
243 Sexual misconduct-injury
244 Spinal cord, disc injury
245 Sprains, strains
246 Vision loss, impairment
298 PROPERTY DAMAGE
299 Other

3. CAUSE OF INJURY

ACTION OF PERSONS-INTENTIONAL
301 Assault
302 Assault with weapon
303 Horse play, fighting
304 Vandalism
305 Other

ACTION OF PERSONS-ACCIDENTAL
311 Act of Others
312 Act of Injured Person

CAUGHT IN, UNDER, BETWEEN
321 Equipment or machinery
322 Moving objects
323 Confined space

CONTACT WITH OR BY
331 Animal or insect
332 Hot or cold substances
333 Electricity
334 Chemicals, acids
335 Poisonous vegetation
336 Sharp object

INHALE, INGEST, ABSORB
341 Inhalation of substance
342 Ingestion of substance
343 Absorption of substance
344 Contamination or pollution

ACTIVITY, OVEREXERTION
351 Lifting, pulling, pushing
352 Twisting, turning, bending
353 Running, jumping, climbing

SLIP, TRIP, OR FALL
361 Same level
362 From other surface or level
363 On stairs
364 From ladder
365 Pits, shafts, holes
366 Recreation area
367 Parking lot
368 Entering or leaving vehicle

STRIKE AGAINST / RAN INTO
371 Another person
372 Moving object
373 Stationary object

STRIKE BY / HIT BY
381 Another person
382 Falling object
383 Flying object
384 Moving object
385 Moving vehicle

399 OTHER

4. AGENT OF INJURY

401 Alcoholic beverages, drugs
402 Animals, birds & insects
403 Boilers, pressure vessels
404 Boxes, containers, packages
405 Building-structure
406 Chemicals
407 Clothing
408 Conveyors, lifts & elevators
409 Doors and door hardware
410 Electricity, electrical wiring
411 Electrical equipment-not tools
412 Engines, motors, pumps
413 Fence
414 Flame, fire, smoke
415 Food & beverages
416 Food - knife, spoon, fork
417 Food - glassware, dishes, pots & pans
418 Furniture, furnishings & decorations
419 Hand tools - hammer, pliers
420 Hand tools - powered
421 Heating equip. - non-electric
422 Infectious, parasitic agents
423 Laboratory equip., supplies
424 Machines-stationary powered equipment
425 Mechanical belts, pulleys, hoists
426 Medicines
427 Metal Items [Nuts, bolts, pipe]
428 Noise
429 Paper materials
430 Pencils, pens
431 Person or persons
432 Plants, vegetation [not trees]
433 Plastic Items - sheets, rods.
434 Playground equipment
435 Poisonous gas, liquid, solid
436 Rocks/stones/gravel/dirt/ sand
437 Scissors
438 Scrap, debris, waste materials
439 Shop equipment
440 Sports - ball, football, puck
441 Sports - bat, racket, stick
442 Sports - equipment, other
443 Stair ramp, ladder
444 Tree
445 Unidentified particle
446 Vehicle - School Bus
447 Vehicle - Automobile
448 Vehicle - Truck
449 Vehicle - Wheelchair
450 Walking surface or floor
451 Wall
452 Water, steam
453 Weapon [With intent to harm]
454 Window, glass
455 Wood: stick, board, chips
499 Other

5. CONTRIBUTING FACTORS

500 None
599 Other

PERSONAL FACTORS
501 Alcohol or drug impairment
502 Disregarded Instructions
503 Equipment misused
504 Failed to use protective equipment
505 Fatigue
506 Fighting, horseplay, teasing
507 Gang activity
508 Inappropriate clothing
509 Inattention of injured person
510 Misjudged safe clearance
511 Overexertion
512 Unauthorized activity
513 Unsafe speed

EQUIPMENT / TOOL FACTORS
521 Equipment condition
522 Mechanical failure
523 Safety device inoperative
524 Unguarded equipment or tool

ENVIRONMENTAL FACTORS
531 Building condition
532 Grounds condition
533 Hazardous substance
534 Illumination
535 Inadequate work space
536 Unprotected energy source
537 Unsafe floor or work space
538 Ventilation
539 Weather - snow, ice, rain

6. ACTIVITY-TIME OF INJURY

601 Travel on school bus
602 Arriving at school
603 Waiting for school to open
604 Travel between classes
605 Attending classes
606 Lunch break
607 Recess-inside school
608 Recess-on school grounds
609 Restroom usage
610 Hall pass
611 Leaving school
612 Field trip
613 Extracurricular activity
614 Sports practice
615 Sports competition
616 Unauthorized activity
699 Other

7. LOCATION

INTERIOR
701 Art room
702 Auditorium, theater
703 Basement
704 Boiler, mechanical room
705 Class room
706 Coat room
707 Computer lab
708 Elevator
709 Gymnasium
710 Hallway
711 Home economics room
712 Kitchen
713 Laboratory - Biology
714 Laboratory - Chemistry
715 Laboratory - Other
716 Library, study hall
717 Locker, shower room
718 Lunch room
719 Office
720 Restroom, toilet
721 Science room
722 Shop - Auto
723 Shop - Metal
724 Shop - Wood
725 Shop - Other
726 Stage
727 Stairs [interior]
728 Storage area
729 Swimming pool
730 Vestibule, entrance
797 Other

EXTERIOR
741 Athletic track
742 Athletic field
743 Field house
744 Fence
745 Mobile class room
746 Parking lot
747 Playground equipment
748 Playground
749 Roof
750 School grounds
751 Sidewalk - City
752 Sidewalk - C. P. S.
753 Stadium
754 Steps, stairs [exterior]
798 Other

OFF PREMISES
761 Drivers education vehicle
762 Field trip
763 Park
764 School bus
799 Other

For "Other", either enter a short description following the code above or enter the number and description below:

Figure 21-14. Sample Parent/Guardian Information

(to be returned to School Coach)

A. Student / Athlete Name:	
B. Parent / Guardian Full Name and Address:	
C. Name, Address & Telephone of Father's Employer:	
D. Name, Address & Telephone of Mother's Employer:	
E. Name, Address, Policy No., Public Aid No., Social Security Recipient No. or Any Other Accident/Health Coverage:	

I hereby authorize any insurance company, prepayment organization, employer, hospital, physician, pharmacy, clinic or any other organization to release all information with respect to myself or any of my dependents which may have a bearing on the benefits payable under this or any other plan providing benefits or services. I certify that the above information in support of this claim is true and correct. A photostat of this authorization shall be as valid as the original.

DATE _____ SIGNATURE OF INJURED STUDENT _____

SIGNATURE OF PARENT/GUARDIAN _____

PHYSICIANS OR SUPPLIERS:
The Interscholastic Athletic Accident Benefit Plan is intended to be secondary to any Group Insurance parents may have.
The Public Schools will suggest the use of a First Aid Facility in the event of a student's athletic injury. If further care and treatment is necessary it should be provided by either the parent's Health Insurance through their approved Medical Facility or the parent's Health Maintenance Organization (HMO) by referral / approval through their designated Primary Care Physician. No Benefits are payable under this Plan for students covered by an HMO.
Please return completed form and bills to the School Coach. When submitting subsequent bills, please attach a copy of the Claim Form.
Questions regarding the Plan or claim payments should be directed to either the Board's Insurance Department, or_____.

14. DATE OF	ILLNESS (FIRST SYMPTOM) OR INJURY (ACCIDENT)	15. DATE FIRST CONSULTED YOU FOR THIS CONDITION	16. HAS PATIENT EVER HAD SAME OR SIMILAR SYMPTOMS? YES ☐ NO ☐
17. DATE ATHLETE ABLE TO RETURN TO COMPETITION	18. DATES OF TOTAL DISABILITY FROM	THROUGH	DATES OF PARTIAL DISABILITY FROM THROUGH
19. NAME OF REFERRING PHYSICIAN			20. FOR SERVICES RELATED TO HOSPITALIZATION GIVE HOSPITALIZATION DATES ADMITTED DISCHARGED
21. NAME & ADDRESS OF FACILITY WHERE SERVICES RENDERED (*if other than home or office*)			22. WAS LABORATORY WORK PERFORMED OUTSIDE YOUR OFFICE? YES ☐ NO ☐ CHARGES

23. DIAGNOSIS OR NATURE OF ILLNESS OR INJURY. <u>RELATED DIAGNOSIS TO PROCEDURE IN COLUMN D BY REFERENCE TO NUMBERS 1, 2, 3, OR DX CODE</u>

1.
2.
3.

24. A DATE OF SERVICE	B PLACE OF SERVICE	C FULLY DESCRIBE PROCEDURES, MEDICAL SERVICES OR SUPPLIES FURNISHED FOR EACH DATE GIVEN		D DIAGNOSIS CODE	E CHARGES	F
		PROCEDURE CODE (IDENTIFY)	(*EXPLAIN UNUSUAL SERVICES OR CIRCUMSTANCES*)			

25. SIGNATURE OF PHYSICIAN OR SUPPLIER	26. ACCEPT ASSIGNMENT (GOVERNMENT CLAIMS ONLY) YES NO	27. TOTAL CHARGE	28. AMOUNT PAID	29. BALANCE DUE
	30. YOUR SOCIAL SECURITY NO.	31. PHYSICIAN'S OR SUPPLIER'S NAME ADDRESS, ZIP CODE & TELEPHONE NO.		
SIGNED DATE				
32. YOUR PATIENT'S ACCOUNT NO.	33. YOUR EMPLOYER I.D. NO.			
		I.D. NO.		

PLACE OF SERVICE CODES
1 - (IH) - INPATIENT HOSPITAL   4 - (H) - PATIENT'S HOME   7 - (NH) - NURSING HOME   O - (OL)- OTHER LOCATIONS
2 - (OH)- OUTPATIENT HOSPITAL   5 -   DAY CARE FACILITY (PSY)   8 - (SNF) - SKILLED NURSING FACILITY   A - (IL) - INDEPENDENT LABORATORY
3 - (O) - DOCTOR'S OFFICE   6 -   NIGHT CARE FACILITY (PSY) 9 -   AMBULANCE   B-   OTHER MEDICAL SURGICAL FACILITY

Figure 21-15.   Sample Athletic Eligibility Certificate

Complete Eligibility Certificate for this school's team(s) in this sport may be typed on reverse side of this form, or a school may distribute in duplicated form information incorporating all data required on the Eligibility Certificate in addition, a school may include other roster information, particularly in the team sports, on its master eligibility list which is duplicated at the start of the sport season and distributed to all opponents in either case. ALL INFORMATION REQUIRED ON THE ELIGIBILITY PORTION OF THIS CERTIFICATE MUST BE PROVIDED. The high school PRINCIPAL MUST SIGN THE ELIGIBILITY CERTIFICATE IN ORDER FOR IT TO BE VALID.

The Contest information section is included as an additional vehicle to provide information for both Home and Away contests, but is not a Contract for Athletic Contest.

The supplemental List section (below) is designed to be used only when changes in the original Eligibility Certificate are necessary.

GENERAL INFORMATION

Class A _____ Class AA _____
(Check Which is Applicable)

Name of School: _____ High School, City _____ Zip _____
Sport of: Boys-Girls _____ School Phone (_____)_____ Coach _____
(Circle one)   (Name of Sport)

Level of Competition (for which this certificate is intended):   (Circle Where Applicable).
1) Varsity   2) Junior Varsity   3) Sophomore   4) Freshman   5) Other specify:_____

CONTEST INFORMATION

(Your)
HOME
Contest

Name of Opponent: _____ Date of Contest: _____, 19 _____

Site of Contest: _____ Site Address: _____
(Street Address)   (Name of Facility)

City: _____ State: _____ Starting Time: _____ a.m. / p.m.

(Your)
AWAY
Contest

Name of Opponent: _____ Date of Contest: _____, 19 _____

Site of Contest: _____ Site Address: _____
(Street Address)   (Name of Facility)

City: _____ State: _____ Starting Time: _____ a.m. / p.m.

OFFICIALS INFORMATION

(Must be completed by Host School: Not to be completed by Visiting School)

Officials listed below will be used in this contest as agreed between the two schools. They will be considered accepted unless protested by the visiting school immediately upon receipt of this notice.

Name of Official	Street Address	City	Level of Competition	Date of Contest
_____	_____	_____	_____	_____
_____	_____	_____	_____	_____
_____	_____	_____	_____	_____
_____	_____	_____	_____	_____

SUPPLEMENTAL LIST

(NOTE: To be used as necessary to update previously sent Eligibility List)

I hereby certify that each person whose name appears below has become eligible to participate or has become ineligible to participate. according to the provisions of all applicable School Association bylaws. on _____,19 _____
(Date)

Playing Nos.		Names of Students	Student Has Become Eligible or Ineligible	Student's Birth Record		Date Enrolled Present Term	(Based on) (grades 9-12) IS NOW IN Sem Season (No.) (No.)	Date Latest Physical Exam (3.071)	Check if Parents Do Not Live in District
Lt.	Dk.			Mo./Day/Yr.	County and State				

PRINCIPAL'S CERTIFICATION

I hereby certify that each person whose name appears on the Eligibility List for _____
(Name of School)
High School_____, is a bona fide student in regular attendance: has completed twenty (20) or more hours of recognized high school work in the last preceding semester while in any high school: has successfully carried twenty (20) or more hours during the present semester from the beginning up to the date of this certificate, has complied in all respects with the requirements of the Illinois High School Association, and is eligible to participate in interscholastic contests under said rules, and that the following data is correct
Signed _____ Principal   Date _____ 19 _____   Prepared on _____19 _____

Figure 21-16.   Sample Board of Education Tax Exempt Authorization

This form is to be used when authorizing purchase. Educational Fund Only.

SCHOOL NAME _____

LIST ALL ITEMS BELOW

			FOR RETAILER'S USE
QUANTITY	DESCRIPTION	ACTIVITY	PRICE
		TOTAL	

TO: Local Retailer

The Board of Education of the _____(city)_____ is an exempt purchaser under Section xx of the (state) Retail Occupation Tax Act.

As such, you are not required to collect sales tax for any purchases of instructional supplies for classroom use.

RETAILERS

FOR DEPARTMENT OF REVENUE AUDIT PURPOSES,
YOU MUST RETAIN THIS AUTHORIZATION FOR YOUR RECORDS

Certification

I certify that the purchase made under this authorization is on behalf of the Board of Education of the _____(city)_____ to be utilized only for student instruction.

Signature of Teacher	Soc. Sec. No.	Date

Signature of Principal	Date

Figure 21-17.   Heat Sheet — Track Events

MEET _____   DATE _____

EVENT _____   PRELIMS   SEMIS   FINALS (circle one)

NAME & TIME	PLACE	NAME & TIME	PLACE
HEAT		HEAT	
HEAT		HEAT	

Figure 21-18.   Team Score Chart

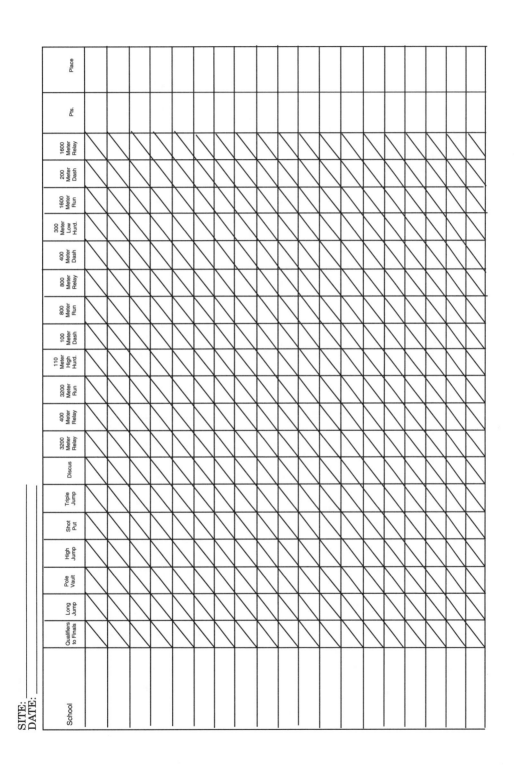

SITE: _____
DATE: _____

Figure 21-19.   Field Events for Distance

MEET_____ DATE_____

EVENT (circle one):   SHOT   DISCUS   LONG JUMP   TRIPLE JUMP

CONTESTANT		PRELIMINARIES				FINALS			BEST EFFORT
		1st	2nd	3rd		1st	2nd	3rd	

Figure 21-20.　Field Events for Height

MEET_____ DATE_____

EVENT (circle one):　　　HIGH JUMP　　　POLE VAULT

CONTESTANT		HEIGHT OF BAR																	BEST EFFORT

Figure 21-21.   Final Results

PLACE _____   DATE _____

School	Time		School	Time		School	Time	
		1			1			1
		2			2			2
		3			3			3
		4			4			4
		5			5			5
		6			6			6
		1			1			1
		2			2			2
		3			3			3
		4			4			4
		5			5			5
		6			6			6
		1			1			1
		2			2			2
		3			3			3
		4			4			4
		5			5			5
		6			6			6

OTHER RECORDS

Is there more record keeping? Yes. I have just scratched the surface. There will be demands placed on you by various administrations to submit forms, study mandates, and cope with endless red tape. Such a venture is unavoidable, but a systematic approach can expedite the situation.

Some coaches compile an annual yearbook for their team. Many successful coaches have been developing annual publications for their teams for decades. Athletes love to see their names in print, so we accommodate them. Our athletes eagerly look forward to our weekly handouts on meet results and comments. Its a great motivator for us.

If your school has an indoor or outdoor track, it is your bounden duty to schedule a few home meets. There is no greater means of publicizing your program and building team morale than a home meet. If all of your competitions are away meets, it is difficult to draw the uninitiated to your program. Home meets are an invaluable tool to showcase your team's prowess. If you schedule home meets, your record keeping and clerical responsibilities will take a quantum leap in volume. *Track and Field News* publishes a catalogue aptly named *Track and Field Market Place*, that has every thing you need to improve your track program, including forms for managing an efficient track meet. The address for *Track and Field News* is 2570 El Camino Real, Suite 606, Mountain View, CA 94040. Their phone number is (415) 948-8188. One of the best moves a track coach can make is to get involved with *Track and Field News* and their products.

Figure 21-22 gives you some typical guidelines for an indoor track meet, and Figure 21-23 is an example of an entry form for a district track meet. With a few minor adjustments, this model can be used for any type of meet you might want to organize.

Figure 21-22

Sample Guidelines for Indoor Track Meets

To: HIGH SCHOOL PRINCIPALS AND DISTRICT SUPERINTENDENTS

ATTENTION: BOARD OF ATHLETIC CONTROL REPRESENTATIVE,
TRACK COACHES, AND ATHLETIC COACHES

REF: INDOOR TRACK AND RUNNING IN HALLWAYS

The following guidelines are effective immediately for the conduct of indoor track meets and conditioning activities in hallways.

1. All track meets in school hallways are prohibited.

2. Track meets on school tracks specifically designed for running are permissible; these are located at Crane, Lake View, and Lindblom high schools. Track meets must be approved by the local principal and a report of the meet must be filed with the Executive Secretary on the Official Eligibility Form.

3. Track meets in schools with large gymnasia are permissible; these are located at Collins, Corliss, Julian, Westinhouse, and Young high schools. These meets must be approved as in item two above.

4. Indoor track practice and conditioning activities are permissible in school hallways and on stairwells providing the activity is properly supervised and the activity has been approved by the teacher-coach, board of control representative, principal, and district superintendent, and a record of these activities has been filed with the Executive Secretary of the Board of Athletic Control.

In implementing these guidelines it is imperative that no unsafe conditions exist throughout the course of the meet or practice session, and that the safety and well-being of the student-athlete are protected at all times.

Executive Secretary
Board of Athletic Control

Printed by permission of Chicago Public Schools, Dept. of Athletics, Physical Education & Recreation.

Figure 21-23

Sample Entry Form for a
District Track Meet

PUBLIC HIGH SCHOOLS ATHLETIC ASSOCIATION

Annual High School Interscholastic
Track and Field Championship

TO: High School Principals

ATTENTION: Track Coaches and Athletic Directors

SUBJECT: Boys State Qualifying Track Meet

I. QUALIFYING MEET

Friday, May 20   - 2:00 P.M.
Chicago State University (95th and King Drive)

PURPOSE: This is a qualifying meet for the Illinois High School Interscholastic Track
Field Championships. COACHES ARE REQUESTED TO ENTER ONLY
THOSE WHO WILL GO TO THE STATE FINALS IF THEY QUALIFY.
ONLY TOP ATHLETES SHOULD BE ENTERED.

II. STATE FINALS

Friday and Saturday, May 27 and 28
Eastern Illinois University, Charleston, Illinois

NOTE: All coaches are expected to remain in the stands and off the field. Only
people with field passes will be allowed on the field—this includes pho-
tographers. THIS IS A SINGLE-LEVEL MEET.

All schools must compete in at least 6 meets with IHSA member schools
in order to qualify for team points in this meet.

Figure 21-23

(Continued)

III. TIME SCHEDULE (Approximately)

<u>FIELD EVENTS</u>

2:00 P.M.	High Jump
	Pole Vault
	Long Jump
	Shot Put (Flight One)
	Discus (Flight One)
	Shot Put (Flight Two)
	Discus (Flight Two)
	Triple Jump

3:00 P.M.	100 Meter Dash Preliminaries
3:15 P.M.	High Hurdles Preliminaries
3:30 P.M.	100 Meter Dash Semifinals
3:45 P.M.	High Hurdles
4:00 P.M.	200 Meter Dash Preliminaries
4:20 P.M.	3200 Meter Run (slow heat) or 30-minute break
	(if needed because entries do not require
	2 heats in the Two Mile Run)
4:50 P.M.	200 Meter Dash Semifinals

<u>TRACK EVENTS</u>

5:00 P.M.	3200	Meter Relay	- Finals (R.A.T.)
	400	Meter Relay	- (R.A.T.)
	3200	Meter Run	- Finals (R.A.T.)
	110	Meter High Hurdles	- Finals
	100	Meter Dash	- Finals
	800	Meter Run	- Finals (R.A.T.)
	800	Meter Relay	- Finals (R.A.T.)
	400	Meter Run	- Finals (R.A.T.)
	300	Meter Intermediate Hurdles	- Finals (R.A.T.)
	1600	Meter Run	- Finals (R.A.T.)
	200	Meter Dash	- Finals
	1600	Meter Relay	- Finals (R.A.T.)

(R.A.T. = Run Against Time)

Coaches should advise their athletes of the time schedule and order of events. For the finals in the track events, the next event scheduled will start five minutes after completion of the preceding final. Please be aware that the exact time schedule cannot be determined without knowing the number of heats needed for each event.

Figure 21-23

(Continued)

IV. ORDER OF EVENTS

ORDER	EVENTS	QUALIFYING TIME	DISTANCE
1.	3200 Meter Relay	8:00.0	
2.	400 Meter Relay	0:43.0	
3.	3200 Meter Relay	9:30.0	
4.	110 Meter High Hurdles	0:14.7	
5.	100 Meter Dash	0:10.8	
6.	800 Meter Run	1:57.0	
7.	800 Meter Relay	1:30.3	
8.	400 Meter Run	0:50.0	
9.	300 Meter Intermediate Hurdles **	0:40.0	
10.	1600 Meter Run	4:24.0	
11.	200 Meter Dash **	0:22.2	
12.	1600 Meter Relay	3:24.0	

Discus		152' 0"
High Jump		6' 5"
Shot Put		52' 6"
Pole Vault		13' 6"
Long Jump		21' 10"
Triple Jump		44' 7"

** (Around one curve)

V. ENTRIES

1. Eligibility Certificates must accompany the attached Entry Sheet.

2. Not more than two (2) participants from the same school may be entered or strarted in any event.

3. Entries close on Monday, May16   at 4:30 P.M. with the Executive Secretary, Administration Central Service Center, 1819 W. Pershing Road, 6th Floor- Center, Chicago, Illinois, 60609. You may also use Mail Run #95, Bureau of Health, Physical Education, Recreation and Safety, 6th Floor- Center, Attn: Charles E. Frazier, Track Coordinator.

4. Enclosed please find sufficient event cards for individual running events and relay cards. Please include the full names (last, first), School, Event, and Times on each card. (Names on relay cards are optional.) *Please use State Qualifying Cards only.

5. Return the following to the Central Service Center:

   a. Entry Sheet - print all names
   b. Eligibility Certificate
   c. Entry cards (full name and year in school)
   d. Relay cards (names optional)

Figure 21-23

(Continued)

6. Seed Meeting, Tuesday, May 17   - 4:00 P.M., Central Service Center, 1819 West Pershing Road, Room TBA.

7. Seeding will be based on submitted times. These times must be verified by City results or written results from other approved Outdoor Track Meets.

VI.   ELIGIBILITY RULES: The Illinois High School Association, the Chicago Public High Schools Athletic Association Rules and Regulations, and the Interscholastic Section of the National Federation of State High School Associations and Field Meet Rules will govern this meet. Eligibility Certificates must accompany the entries. For those who qualify, State Eligibility Sheets must be sent to the State Office.

VII.   QUALIFIERS - STATE FINAL ENTRIES: The winner of the first, second, third, and fourth places in each event in the Chicago District Meet may be entered by their respective schools in the State Final Meet. In addition, contestants who equal a specified time, height, or distance in the Finals of each event are entitled to participate in the same events in the State Finals.

VIII.   SCORING: Five places will be counted in all events to determine the winning team. First, second, third, fourth, and fifth places will be awarded 10, 8, 6, 4, and 2 points respectively.

IX.   SPECIAL RULES:

A.   The high hurdles are 39 inches.
B.   Contestants must furnish their own vaulting poles.
C.   High Jump: The bar will start at 5' 10", and thereafter be raised one inch at a time.
D.   Pole Vault: The bar will start at 9' 6" and will be raised 6" at a time.

X.   AWARDS: The first five place winners will receive ribbons in each event. The first-and second-place teams will receive shields.

©1998 by Parker Publishing Company, Inc.

Figure 21-23 (Continued)

STATE QUALIFYING MEET

OFFICIAL ENTRY FORM

_____ SCHOOL   _____ COACH

ATHLETE'S NAME		YEAR IN SCHOOL	TIME
100 METERS			
_____ LAST	_____ FIRST	_____	_____
_____ LAST	_____ FIRST	_____	_____
200 METERS			
_____ LAST	_____ FIRST	_____	_____
_____ LAST	_____ FIRST	_____	_____
400 METERS			
_____ LAST	_____ FIRST	_____	_____
_____ LAST	_____ FIRST	_____	_____
800 METERS			
_____ LAST	_____ FIRST	_____	_____
_____ LAST	_____ FIRST	_____	_____
1600 METERS			
_____ LAST	_____ FIRST	_____	_____
_____ LAST	_____ FIRST	_____	_____
3200 METERS			
_____ LAST	_____ FIRST	_____	_____
_____ LAST	_____ FIRST	_____	_____
110 METER HIGH HURDLES			
_____ LAST	_____ FIRST	_____	_____
_____ LAST	_____ FIRST	_____	_____
300 METER INTERMEDIATE HURDLES			
_____ LAST	_____ FIRST	_____	_____
_____ LAST	_____ FIRST	_____	_____

Figure 21-23 *(Continued)*

SCHOOL		COACH	

ATHLETE'S NAME			
TRACK EVENTS	YES	NO	TIME
400 Meter Relay			
800 Meter Relay			
1600 Meter Relay			
3200 Meter Relay			

Figure 21-23 *(Continued)*

FIELD EVENTS		YEAR IN SCHOOL	DISTANCE HEIGHT
SHOT PUT			
LAST	FIRST		
LAST	FIRST		
LONG JUMP			
LAST	FIRST		
LAST	FIRST		
HIGH JUMP			
LAST	FIRST		
LAST	FIRST		
POLE VAULT			
LAST	FIRST		
LAST	FIRST		
DISCUS			
LAST	FIRST		
LAST	FIRST		
TRIPLE JUMP			
LAST	FIRST		
LAST	FIRST		

The form depicted in Figure 21–23 was developed by a committee of coaches and has been modified and improved over several years. This offering represents a considerable amount of debate, argument, and compromise by a number of experienced track coaches and administrators. You may need to be this detailed when you run a dual or triangular meet. If you choose to take on the considerable task of organizing a large invitational meet, then you might want to use some of this information as a guide.

Whenever you are faced with the responsibility of organizing any type of track meet, I suggest that you plan for it several weeks in advance. You will need the assistance of fellow coaches, faculty, students, and friends. You cannot have too many people involved in setting up an effective track meet. Most small meets will require 18–20 timers, 18–20 field event judges, 4 curve and relay officials, and at least 10–20 student helpers. This is a minimum; larger meets will need more.

You must meet with the officials and helpers several days prior to the competition to inform everyone of the specific logistics of your track meet. This necessary but tedious process will eliminate many of the problems that often occur at most competitions. The officials you choose should be certified, but often this is not the case. A brief discussion of the rules may be in order. If you have enough rule books, distribute them to those officials that are new to the job. Request that officials meet with you one hour before the meet begins. Try to have official tape measures, stopwatches, extra crossbars, and hurdles. There should also be rakes for long jump pits, yarn for the finish line, and weighing devices and measuring devices for the shot and discus. Is this all you need to know to run a successful meet? Absolutely not. You should purchase an official guide to help you in organizing a track meet. The one I use is "Planning and Administering a Home Track Meet," written by Bob Covey; it can be found in the 1981 issue of *The Track and Field Coaching Manual*, published by the Athletic Congress.

Section 22

PUTTING IT ALL TOGETHER

Several loose ends are tied together in these pages. In earlier sections, I explained how a coach can develop champions without facilities, equipment, supplies, or budget. Here, I discuss the most effective way to coach an entire team without assistant coaches. It makes me tired to think about it, but it can be done. It is possible to have outstanding performers in every track and field event if you are willing to work. It took me several years of trial and error to streamline this operation. The best of all worlds is to have knowledgeable assistants — or at least assistants who are willing to learn, but it is better to go it alone than to be surrounded by the inept; they will make you wish you had never met them. If you happen to be without competent assistant coaches, give this system a try. It works.

Your coaching endeavor will not be easy, but the gratification and personal satisfaction you will experience when you conquer its formidable odds cannot be matched!

The biggest problem you may have is how to manage a track team alone. It seems like the impossible dream, but it can be done. If you are given this difficult task, there are several ways this problem can be approached. It all depends upon which solution will fit your personality and inclinations. Coaching track and field with its 18 events and their obvious complexities is difficult, even if you have assistant coaches. I have known programs that have six or more coaches and they tell me how tough their job is. Can you imagine how crazy the situation can be if you are the only coach?

SOLUTIONS

Some of you out there have worked alone for years and the parents, administration — *no one* — has the slightest idea of what you are going through. You have the most exhausting job in the world. Listed here are six solutions that will help you do the impossible:

1. If you are a neophyte, coach what you know

One of my former runners graduated from college and was given a coaching assignment; he wisely aknowledged the formidable task he faced and came to me for advice. I told him to coach only those events that he knew.

Novice coaches need to make a good first impression. If you try to bite off more than you can chew, you may risk losing your team's confidence. By coaching only the events you have expertise in, you can gain the confidence of the team and move to unfamiliar events later on. Your athletes are more likely to accept a few mistakes in unfamiliar events after you have proven yourself. This coach took my suggestion, and his team won second place in the Illinois state meet that year.

After you have gained the team's confidence, try to learn at least two additional events *in depth* each year. This may be a slow process, but you will be knowledgeable in all of the events in a few years if you are willing to work at it.

2. Encourage your athletes to coach one another

Occasionally you will inherit a team with members who have certain skills. Most athletes are eager to participate in the teaching process. Since you cannot be everywhere at the same time, several of your veterans can be event leaders and assist you in your coaching duties. I am told that an Illinois state champion taught himself so well that he became a high school All-American.

If you are unfamiliar with an event, learn with the athlete. Try to stay ahead of the athlete by reading and studying as much as you can about the event. Purchase videotapes, hang around big competitions, and observe accomplished athletes. Don't be afraid to ask questions of top athletes. World-class athletes are happy to talk about their event. Most will be glad to answer your questions. In addition, attend every track clinic in your area or out of your area. I often flew out of state to learn something new.

3. Plan — Use a card system

You should not try to coach extemporaneously. A method that works wonders for me is a card system. I fill out 11 large (5″ × 8″), cards with every workout we do for a certain periodization cycle for every event. This means you will have to make 60 cards for the entire track season. It may take some time to develop these cards, but your job gets easier immediately when you have them for reference. You can also use 8″ × 11″ cards or take the workout sheets from this section, laminate them, and place them on a clipboard.

There are 25–30 workouts listed on each card for the runners. The workouts are numbered. If you cannot circulate to each group that day, instruct them to do a certain workout based on their needs for that particular stage in their development.

The field eventers are given cards with a list of drills that are relevant for their specific periodization cycle. If you are focusing on the runners that day, have them do the odd-numbered workouts or drills on odd-numbered days and the even-numbered workouts or drills on even-numbered days. You can also assign workouts based on a specific series of numbers.

The cards in this section are designed primarily for the competitive period. But with a little manipulation, these workouts could be applied to other cycles. If you change the intensity or volume of the suggested workouts, they could easily fit in four of the five cycles. You can also combine some of these drills into one workout. These cards are tools that you can use to fit your situation; however, you should make separate cards for the general preparation period. There are so many diverse recreational activities and drills during the general preparation period that you will need to create a separate set of cards for this cycle. If you are a veteran coach, you can get by with 24 cards. I suggest that inexperienced coaches make cards for all five periodization cycles.

Schedule a short team meeting prior to practice. Distribute the cards to your group leaders or captains, and assign the workouts. Initially, you will have to devote a considerable amount of time explaining the system, but this will eliminate a lot of grief and frustration later on. After they understand how to read the cards, the system will work smoothly.

The best way to handle team logistics is to start each workout with a few group activities such as jogging, calisthenics, and stretching. After this warm-up and a short team meeting, they take the cards to their respective event areas.

When the groups have embarked on their workouts, begin your coaching duties with the runners. The runners will need you to set the pace for their intervals or repeats. When they learn the routine and understand the purpose of your training schedules, your veterans will occasionally be able to anticipate what you have planned for them. When they learn the rationale behind your training program, some of your veteran runners can be encouraged to devise their group's workouts.

Schedule the distance runners for a long run on days when you need to time sprinters. On days when the sprinters are doing mostly drills and relay passes, you can focus your attention on the distance runners' interval or repetition workouts.

After the runners have started their program, and the rhythm of their workout is established, give a stopwatch and the workout card to a student manager and move to the field events. On Monday, your goal can be to supervise the throwing events for 25 minutes and move to the jumping events for the next 25 minutes. By this time, the runners should have finished their workout and the team can come together for a warm-down jog and a final stretch.

See the 11 examples of workout cards. The nature and sequence of the workouts can be designed based on the nature of your team, time of the year, climate, and the availability of your facilities. These cards will have to be upgraded from time to time as things change during the season. The easiest way to expedite this planning process is to become computer literate. I can't imagine how I ever managed to do this amount of work all these years without this marvelous device.

You can use these cards or make your own cards, based on your situation. You can also look at the workouts in the earlier sections and incorporate some of that information on your cards. When you are satisfied with your cards, have them laminated to protect them from the weather.

It will take considerable clerical work to develop an entire system of cards, but it will be worth the effort if you choose to use this system. This procedure is not the only way to conduct a practice, but it worked for us. Once the cards are made, you can file them away and use them for several years. If you save this information on a computer, the cards can be updated easily.

4. Use the Ted Haydon method

The late Ted Haydon, the venerable track coach of University of Chicago and the University of Chicago Track Club was revered and loved by the athletes he coached. He was the quintessential track coach. The methods and techniques he used to develop his athletes were years ahead of their time. His ability to successfully coach his college track team *and* the University of Chicago Track Club is a testimony to his genius and work ethic.

Like many coaches, Ted posted workouts on a bulletin board in the team's locker room. There was an additional comment sheet that critiqued every athlete's performance in competition. Each comment consisted of a brilliant one-liner that no one could forget. Every athlete knew where he stood with Ted Haydon.

Figure 22-1

SPRINTERS CARD
(COMPETITIVE PERIOD)

1. 12×100, walk back between 100s
2. 6×200, walk 200
3. 8×30, rest 5 mins 8×60, rest 5 mins, 1×400
4. 5×300
5. 10×150
6. Hill or stair running 30 minutes, walk back
7. Sprint drills, 4×100 relay drills
8. Sprint drills, 4×200 relay drills
9. Time trials
10. 600, 400, 300, 200, 100
11. 3×600
12. 4×500
13. Starts and finishes
14. Parlauf relays
15. 1 mile of windsprints
16. Swimming pool drills
17. 2×100, 80, 60, 40, 30
18. Resistance running
19. $8 \times$ acceleration 200s
20. 30–30 pickups
21. Mile relay baton passing, sprint the final 100
22. Towing
23. Piggyback up stairs
24. Car pushing
25. 15×50
26. 400 relay passes, sprint the final 50 meters
27. 800 meter passes, sprint the final 100
28. Plyometrics
29. 7×70, 100% effort
30. Uphill $\times 10$, downhill $\times 10$, level $\times 10$ (50 meters)

Figure 22-2

400 METERS CARD
(COMPETITIVE PERIOD)

1. 16×100, walk back between 100s
2. 8×200, walk back 200 between
3. 6×300
4. 12×150
5. Hill or stair running, 30 walk back
6. Sprint drills, 4×200 relay drills
7. Sprint drills, 4×400 relay drills
8. Time trials
9. 50 second run $\times 3$
10. 600, 400, 300, 200, 100
11. 4×500
12. 3×600
13. 4×800 relay drills
14. 400 meter simulators $\times 3$
15. Parlauf relays $\times 7$
16. Swimming pool drills
17. 4×100, 80, 60, 40, 30 meters
18. Resistance running
19. $8 \times$ acceleration 200s
20. 30–30 pickups $\times 12$
21. Stride patterns (stride 300, sprint 100) $\times 3$
22. Knee lifts over little hurdles $\times 16$
23. Towing
24. Piggyback up stairs
25. Weight training
26. Car pushing
27. Butt breakers 50 meters $\times 4$
28. Plyometrics
29. 2 mile wind sprints
30. Uphill $\times 16$, downhill $\times 16$, level $\times 16$ (50 meters)

Figure 22-3

HURDLES CARD
(COMPETITIVE PERIOD)

1. Trail leg drills
2. Lead leg drills
3. Scissors drill
4. 5-stepping drill
5. Starts to first hurdle
6. Three hurdles for time and rhythm
7. 100 hurdles workout
8. First 5 hurdles
9. Last 5 hurdles
10. Work on block starts with sprinters
11. 12 hurdles $\times$ 7
12. 200 meters $\times$ 8
13. 100 meters $\times$ 16
14. 300 $\times$ 6
15. 400 meter relay baton passes
16. 800 meter relay baton passes
17. 4 $\times$ 400 baton passes
18. Shuttle hurdle relay drills
19. Swimming pool drills
20. Resistance running
21. Hill or stair running, walk back recovery (30 mins)
22. Sprint drills
23. Plyometrics
24. Weight training
25. Time trials (5 hurdles)
26. Time trials (8 hurdles)
27. Time trials (10 hurdles)
28. Parlauf relays
29. Towing
30. Downhill $\times$ 10, uphill $\times$ 10, level $\times$ 10 (50 meters)

Figure 22-4

800 METERS CARD
(COMPETITIVE PERIOD)

1. 6×400, 2 mins rest between 100s
2. 16×200, walk 200 between
3. 8×300
4. 4×800 rest to recovery
5. Hill or stair running, 30 mins, walk back
6. Sprint drills, 4×400 relay drills
7. Sprint drills, 4×800 relay drills
8. Time trials
9. 2 minute run $\times 3$
10. 1600, 1200, 800, 400, 200
11. 4×600
12. 3×1200
13. 4×800 relay drills
14. 800 meter simulators $\times 3$
15. Parlauf relays $\times 7$
16. Swimming pool drills
17. 8×100, 80, 60, 40, 30 meters
18. Resistance running
19. $8 \times$ acceleration 400s
20. 30–30 pickups $\times 24$
21. Stride patterns (stride 600, sprint 200) $\times 3$
22. Knee lifts over little hurdles $\times 24$
23. Towing
24. 30 min fartlek
25. 24×100 at pace
26. Track soccer
27. 1 mile wind sprints $\times 3$
28. 7×70, 100% effort
29. 2 miles of 50 meter sprints
30. Uphill $\times 16$, downhill $\times 16$, level $\times 16$ (50 meters)

Figure 22-5

DISTANCE RUNNERS CARD
(COMPETITIVE PERIOD)

1. 8×400, 2 mins rest between
2. 16×200, walk 200
3. 4×800, rest 5 mins between
4. 10×300
5. 3×1600
6. Hill or stair running 30 minutes, walk back
7. Sprint drills, 4×800 relay drills
8. Sprint drills, 4×400 relay drills
9. Time trials
10. 1600, 1200, 800, 400, 200
11. 8×600
12. 10×500
13. 30 mins fartlek
14. 40 min run
15. 1 mile of windsprints×3
16. Swimming pool drills
17. 2×800, 400, 300, 200
18. Resistance running
19. 16×acceleration 200s
20. 3 miles of surges
21. 2 mile relay baton passing, sprint the final 400
22. Towing
23. 3×1600
24. 32×100 at pace
25. 2 min run×4
26. mile simulators×3
27. Long run (6 min/mile)
28. Track soccer (30 mins)
29. 7×70, 100% effort
30. Uphill×10, downhill×10, level×10 (50 meters)

©1998 by Parker Publishing Company, Inc.

Figure 22-6

SHOT-PUTTERS CARD
(COMPETITIVE PERIOD)

1. Medicine ball drills
2. Standing throws and full technique (surgical hose)
3. Overhead throws
4. Step and throw
5. Technique with underweight shot
6. Standing throw with overweight shot
7. Vertical throws
8. Backward hops with a shot
9. Throw for distance $\times 20$
10. Plyometrics
11. Work with the discus throwers
12. Shot put drills in the swimming pool
13. Standing throws up stairs
14. Standing throws with different weight shots
15. Shot-put explosions against mats
16. Sit-up and put
17. Hip drive and put the shot
18. Standing throw motion with a pulley
19. Bend and throw
20. Wrist flips with a shot
21. Isometrics
22. Car pushing
23. South African drill for discus technique throwers
24. Weight-training
25. Standing throws without a reverse
26. Drop to right leg and throw
27. Hip drive and throw
28. Step to a throw
29. Full technique with a softball
30. Standing throws with feet parallel

Figure 22-7

DISCUS CARD
(COMPETITIVE PERIOD)

1. Medicine ball drills
2. Standing throws and full technique (surgical hose)
3. Standing throws (overweight disc)
4. Step and throw
5. Full technique with underweight disc
6. Bench flyes with a 10-pound plate
7. South African drill
8. Throw for distance
9. Plyometrics
10. Work with shot-putters
11. Discus drills in the water
12. Standing throws against mats
13. Full technique against mats
14. Hip drive and throw
15. Standing throw with a pulley
16. Sit-up and throw
17. Bend and throw
18. Resistance running
19. Vertical throws
20. Isometrics
21. Car pushing
22. Series of South African drills and throw
23. Weight training
24. Standing throws without a reverse
25. Drop to right leg and throw
26. Grapevines and throw
27. Step to a throw
28. Full technique with a softball
29. Standing throws with feet parallel
30. Standing throws for distance

Figure 22-8

HIGH JUMPERS CARD
(COMPETITIVE PERIOD)

1. Box jumping, 5 boxes (both legs)
2. Hurdle jumping (both legs)
3. Rope jumping (100 jumps)
4. Dot drill (both legs)
5. Dot drill (single leg)
6. Volleyball dunk — 7-step approach
7. Depth jumping (20 jumps)
8. Backward jumps over a crossbar
9. Single-leg hops (50 meters)
10. Low jumps for technique
11. Box drills (single leg)
12. Triple jump drills
13. Walking lunge
14. Walking lunge with dumbbells
15. Run-throughs without a crossbar
16. Depth jump and dunk
17. Jump for height
18. Jump at 90% effort × 7
19. High jump (1 step)
20. High jump (3 steps)
21. High jump (5 steps)
22. Backward jump from 18" box
23. Jumping squats — light weight, 2 sets × 10 reps
24. Figure 8 runs
25. Weight training
26. Vertical jumps in shallow water
27. Backward jumps with a crossbar in water
28. Depth jumps (single leg)
29. Jumping squats with surgical tubing
30. Depth jump into high jump pit

Figure 22-9

LONG JUMPERS CARD
(COMPETITIVE PERIOD)

1. Box jumping, 5 boxes (both legs)
2. Hurdle jumping (both legs)
3. Rope jumping (100 jumps)
4. Dot drill (both legs)
5. Dot drill (single leg)
6. Runway work — 18-step approach
7. Depth jumping (20 jumps)
8. Pop-ups, 6-step run-up
9. Single-leg hops (50 meters)
10. Landing drills
11. Box drills (single leg)
12. Long jump, leg drills off box
13. Walking lunge
14. Walking lunge with dumbbells
15. Run throughs × 7
16. Depth jumps (one leg)
17. Long jump into high jump pit
18. Single-leg hops up stairs
19. Long jump for distance
20. Long jump (12 steps)
21. Pop-up off incline board
22. Hop over little hurdles × 10
23. Jumping squats — light weight, 2 sets × 10 reps
24. Split jumps
25. Weight training
26. Vertical jumps in shallow water
27. Butt breakers 50 meters × 4
28. Depth jumps from 3 feet
29. Jumping squats with surgical tubing
30. Side-to-side jumping over 2′ crossbar

©1998 by Parker Publishing Company, Inc.

Figure 22-10

TRIPLE JUMPERS CARD (COMPETITIVE PERIOD)

1. Box jumping, 5 boxes (both legs)
2. Hurdle jumping (both legs)
3. Rope jumping (100 jumps)
4. Dot drill (both legs)
5. Dot drill (single leg)
6. Runway work — 18-step approach
7. Depth jumping (20 jumps)
8. Triple jump, 6-step run-up
9. Single-leg hops (50 meters)
10. Landing drills
11. Box drills (single leg)
12. Two hops, one step, two hops, etc. $\times 7$
13. Walking lunge
14. Walking lunge with dumbbells
15. Run-throughs $\times 7$
16. Depth jumps (one leg)
17. Bounding 50 meters $\times 4$
18. Single-leg hops up stairs
19. Triple jump for distance
20. Triple jump (12 steps)
21. Hop, 3 steps, jump $\times 7$
22. Hop over little hurdles $\times 10$
23. Jumping squats — light weight, 2 sets $\times 10$ reps
24. Split jumps
25. Weight training
26. Vertical hops in shallow water
27. Butt breakers 50 meters $\times 4$
28. Depth jumps from 3 feet
29. Jumping squats with surgical tubing
30. Side-to-side jumping over 2' crossbar

Figure 22-11

POLE VAULT CARD
(COMPETITIVE PERIOD)

1. Towel plant drill
2. Run-throughs
3. Rock-back drill without crossbar
4. Rock-back drill with surgical tubing
5. Low vaulting (short run-up)
6. Rope vaulting
7. Pole plant without vaulting
8. Rope vault from a balcony
9. Full technique without crossbar
10. Vault for height
11. Sprint drills carrying pole
12. Gymnastics
13. Weight training
14. Pull-and-turn drill against the wall
15. Vaulting technique in deep water
16. Short run-up, rock back to a back flip
17. Short run-up, rock back, land on back
18. Full vault to 90% of best vault $\times 7$
19. Rope climbing, regular and inverted
20. Tumbling drills over low crossbar
21. Gymnastic drills over crossbar
22. Simulated drills on gymnastic equipment
23. Pole vault drills on ropes
24. Hip circles on gymnastic equipment
25. Pole plant against wall

The way he conducted practice was amazing. I saw him time and train the entire track team in a manner that defied imagination. He would line up the team, from sprinters to distance runners, and time them simultaneously. Most of his workouts were finished in less than an hour.

Coach Haydon had the sprinters line up on the track (according to ability), using all eight lanes. He told the quarter-milers to line up 10 meters behind the sprinters. The half-milers stood 10 meters behind the quarter-milers. The milers were 10 meters behind the half-milers. When the runners were organized and ready, Ted shot the starting pistol. The sprinters would run 100 meters and immediately leave the track. The quarter-milers ran 200 meters and cleared the track. The half-milers moved to the infield after running 400 meters. And finally, the distance runners ran 800 meters and walked 400 meters to recover. During the rest period, Ted would walk over to one of the field events and coach somebody. After a brief rest, this process would be repeated.

Coach Haydon was a staunch believer in recording accurate times and measurements. All athletes knew exactly how fast they ran or how far they threw or jumped after every meet. Every split and every series of throws was recorded. A positive comment was made about every athlete's effort, regardless of ability. Ted never had an assistant coach. I don't know how he did all of this record keeping without a computer. He was a remarkable man.

5. Recruit student managers

There are always students who want to be involved with a good track program. The best people for this job are intelligent students who love to time and keep records, and are dependable. Most of the time, female students fit this job description, but make a special effort to get a reliable male or two to help with the equipment. You can also teach your managers a few basic fundamentals of track and field. They can be a tremendous asset to your program, if you show them how to look for a few technical flaws. Student help can often be better than some assistant coaches because they will do exactly what you tell them.

6. Look for adult volunteers

If your school does not have a budget for assistant coaches, keep your eyes open for interested adults. Be wary of the "sidewalk experts"; they can sabotage your program. I made the mistake of accepting the services of an individual who thought he knew everything, totally ignored my directions, and caused us to lose a few close meets. When volunteers offer their services and proceed to tell you how great they are — RUN. Alexander Pope, aptly stated, in his *Essay on Criticism*, "A little learning is a dangerous thing."

The best assistant I ever had was a volunteer from the FCA (Fellowship of Christian Athletes). He told me that he knew nothing about track and field. After a few weeks of instruction, I gave him full responsibility for sprints and relays. Initially, I would casually check on his coaching. If there was a problem he couldn't solve, he would always ask. I could tell that he was going to be good. He turned out to be the best sprint coach I ever had.

Another outstanding volunteer was the school's head custodian. His best quality was his love of kids. He would show up at our meets and encourage the athletes. He came so regularly, I asked him to help with the coaching. He said the magic words, "I don't know anything about track." His biggest asset was his positive attitude. He would circulate among the team and tell everybody how good they were. He literally encouraged our team into a championship. He also had a ton of common sense. He would stand around and point out technical flaws based on nothing but plain common sense. He would often tell me that "something" didn't look right about an athlete's technique and he would be right. It is too easy to overlook technical flaws when you are the only coach.

My youngest brother, who is an inveterate track nut, would come to every meet and critique our track team. Sometimes you can overlook the obvious because you see it every day. Because he knows and loves track and field, and because he did not see these kids all year long, he could immediately spot something that I'd missed. After one meet, he ran across the infield screaming at the top of his voice that I had a boy in the wrong event. I took his advice and in a few months, the athlete won the state championship in the 400 meters. You need another set of eyes.

LAMENTATIONS

Can an experienced coach outcoach a coaching staff of five or more dedicated coaches? Absolutely not. You may be able to win big championships and develop state champions by yourself, but all your kids are not getting what they need with one coach. You need help. Our kids are being shortchanged — pure and simple. The bottom line indicates that this uninspired approach to track and field is beginning to affect us on the international scene. In the 1996 Olympics, our athletes didn't earn a medal in events we used to dominate. We were shut out of every event longer than the 800 meters. We didn't score a point in the pole vault. As a consequence, the media coverage on track and field left much to be desired. The average citizen never realized how poorly we did because the media covered only those American athletes who earned medals or broke world records. Beyond Michael Johnson, Carl Lewis, Dan O'Brien, and a few women like Jackie Joyner Kersee and Gail Devers — what else did the media show?

Most of our gold medal winners are on the verge of retirement. Who will take their place? We *must* upgrade the track and field program in the United States. It is patently unfair to require a coach to do it all alone; however, the mission of this survival guide is to help the forgotten coach do the impossible. This book is an effort to equip a coach who is faced with a difficult situation with the tools to survive — and possibly thrive — under circumstances that are less than ideal. It also provides information on how to make your budget (if you have one) go a lot further, as well as helping a coach upgrade a program that has all of the amenities. This is the way it is supposed to be. It is unfair to threaten the fortunate few with a decreased budget because some unusually innovative, creative, and overworked coach managed to win a few track meets with no visible means of support.

Even with the most exhaustive work schedule you can imagine, many kids are hurt because they happen to live in communities that cannot financially support a decent track and field program. I do not for a moment believe that a better sports program will solve all of our problems, but it will definitely remediate many of them.

Finally, don't let this be the only track and field publication you read. Offerings in this book can turn your program around, but new research, both scientific and empirical, will be developed. Some of what we do today in the name of physical conditioning will be obsolete in the year 2000. Continue to read, study, and think. Keep a record of your workouts, and you may discover something of value. No one, regardless of expertise or experience, has all of the answers. Continue to learn. If you had the patience to read this far, I commend you. You are the kind of coach our kids need.

ABOUT ATTITUDE

Coaching these days is more difficult than it has ever been. Most qualified coaches have abandoned the profession for greener and less stressful pastures. Everything I have suggested or written about coaching is worthless if the potential athlete doesn't want to pay the price for success. Motivation is important, but you can't do it all yourself. You and the athlete have to be on the same page. Don't assume that every kid really wants to excel. Some may have a different agenda from yours. Ask them to write their goals. Assure them of their confidentiality. Most athletes will not lie to themselves. Once you read their goals, you and the athletes will be on the same page. I never dismiss athletes because they have strange goals, but I do schedule a private conference in an effort to comprehend the student's unusual philosophy.

It is difficult to understand why a youngster will come to practice every day and put up with a grueling training program, but have no desire to excel. Such athletes may be running track for a variety of reasons, including psychological ones. If their attitudes don't impact on the rest of the team or sabotage our goals, I will keep them on the squad and try to provide for their needs — whatever they are. I have coached hundreds of kids who never won a race — but they became good citizens, and I like to believe it was because of my influence on their behavior.

I don't have a lot of complicated rules for the team to follow. My philosophy is based on a statement that Bobby Knight, the head basketball coach at the University of Indiana, made on his television program regarding athletes on his team:

1. You have to do what you have to do.

2. You have to do it when you have to do it.

3. You have to do the best you can when you do it.

4. You have to do it all the time.

All the outstanding athletes I have ever coached told me up front what they wanted to do. Most of them walked up to me and boldly stated that they wanted to be champions. Some of these athletes showed no physical evidence of being as good as they said, but I never told them that it wasn't possible. They believed, and so I kept my mouth shut and believed. In these days of New Age meditation, hypnosis, EST, biofeedback, and chanting, these kids just *believed*. All you need is a positive attitude.

When an athlete changes his or her attitude in a positive direction, the results are miraculous. One of our half-milers improved from a 1:59 to a 1:52 in one week because he wanted to. Another went from a 2:04 to 1:53 in three weeks because something I said finally began to make sense to him. Another rather ordinary athlete ran a 47.9 400, 37.5 intermediate hurdles, and 14.1 hurdles because our school head custodian told him every day how good he was. An oft-injured triple jumper came to me and said, "I want to be an All-American." He exceeded his personal best by 4 feet and was second in the NCAA Division III finals. It is written, "Death and life is in the power of the tongue and for as he thinketh in his heart so is he." (Proverbs. 18:21 and Proverbs 23:7).

When athletes believe, you don't have to be concerned about their work ethic or their commitment to your program. They will be there every day, on time and you will have to make them go home. They will find a way to excel. It is hard to define this wonderful attitude, but you will know when it is there. When it is there, it transcends genetics, workouts, and training. It takes a coach and athlete working together to create a miracle. You can't measure, weigh, or touch attitude. It is just there.

There *are* occasions when you must dismiss an athlete from your team. Some youngsters have no intention of following your rules. They are usually talented and they may have some sort of hidden agenda. They can affect the morale of the rest of the team if you let them get away with this nonsense. Be proactive about these people; they will let you know early on that they have a poor attitude. Read their behavior quickly and send them on their way. There is always someone to take their place.

A FINAL WORD

Successful coaching is hard work. I don't care if you have the best of equipment and facilities; it is still hard work. Young coaches often come to me looking for a quick and easy answer to their coaching problems, and occasionally a few meaningful words will solve the dilemma. At times, however, there are no easy solutions. It may take blood, sweat, and tears to iron out a technical flaw or a difficult coaching situation. I can remember when a sophomore hurdler could not negotiate the 3 steps between the barriers; it was 9:00 PM before we finally solved the problem. This athlete eventually ran 13.8 in the high hurdles and 19.1 in the 180-yard low hurdles. He subsequently became an NCAA All-American. You have to hang in there with many of your athletes' difficulties. They won't go away unless you work at it, so roll up your sleeves and make it happen!

Everything you do and every sacrifice you make in this noble profession is worth the time you take working with a youngster. They may not all become champions in track and field, but they may become champions in life. There are — or will be — hundreds of doctors, lawyers, teachers, and other gainfully employed good citizens who benefited by being involved in your program. Track coaches, and coaches in general, are making a tremendous positive impact in the lives of multitudes of young people. The media and your administration may never realize how you and your sport have influenced young people's lives. The athletes know — and that's all that matters. You are in the right profession.

BIBLIOGRAPHY

Among the following books are some older ones that may be out of print but many libraries and organizations still have them. I've included them on the list because they are, in my opinion, the most definitive for track and field coaches. Many were also published in other countries. If you can get your hands on them, I highly recommend them.

Arnot, Robert, M.D. *Sports Talent.* New York: Viking, Penguin Inc., 1966.

Banister, Roger. *The Four Minute Mile.* New York: Dodd, Mead & Co., 1955.

Bowerman, William J. *Coaching Track and Field.* Boston: Houghton Mifflin Co., 1974.

Brauman, Ken. *The Art of Coaching Track and Field.* West Nyack, NY: Parker Publishing Co., Inc., 1986.

Bresnahan & Tuttle. *Track and Field Athletics.* St.Louis: The C.V. Mosby Co., 1969.

Brock, Greg. *How High School Runners Train.* Los Altos, CA: Tafnews Press, 1976.

Bruner & Tabachnik. *Soviet Training and Recovery Methods.* Pleasant Hills, CA: Sports Focus Publishing, 1990.

Bush, Jim. *Inside Track.* Chicago: Henry Regnery Co., 1974.

Cerutty, Percy Wells. *Middle Distance Running.* London: Pelham Books Ltd., 1964.

Clarke, Ron. *The Unforgiving Minute.* London: Pelham Books, 1966.

Collins, Dick. *Coaching a Championship High School Track and Field Team.* West Nyack, NY: Parker Publishing Co., Inc., 1984.

Cooper, John. *Track and Field for Coach and Athlete.* Englewood Cliffs, NJ: Prentice Hall, 1970.

Costa, Leo. *Serious Growth.* Visalia, CA: Optimum Training Systems, 1989.

Cretzmeyer, Alley & Tipton. *Track and Field Athletics.* St. Louis: The C.V. Mosby Co., 1969.

Dellinger, Bill. *The Competitive Runner's Training Book.* New York: Macmillan Publishing Co., 1984.

Doherty, Ken, Ph.D. *Track and Field Omnibook.* Swarthmore, PA: Tafmop, 1971.

Dominquez and Gajda. *Total Body Training.* New York: Charles Scribner & Sons, 1982.

Dunn, George Jr. & McGill, Kevin. *The Throws Manual.* Mountain View, CA: Track and Field News, 1994.

Ecker, Tom. *Track and Field Technique Through Dynamics.* Los Altos, CA: Tafnews Press, 1976.

Editore, Rizzoli. *Encyclopedia of Track and Field.* Englewood Cliffs, NJ: Prentice Hall, 1986.

Editors of Runner's World. *Running with Style.* Mountain View, CA: World Publications, 1974.

Francis, Charlie. *The Charlie Francis Training System.* Ottawa, Ontario, Canada: TBLI Publications Inc., 1992.

Gambetta, Vern. *Hurdling and Steeplechasing.* Mountain View, CA: World Publications, 1974.

Gambetta, Vern. *Track and Field Coaching Manual.* West Point, NY: Leisure Press, 1981.

Ganslen, Richard. *Mechanics of the Pole Vault.* Denton, Texas: Dick Ganslen, 1970.

Gilbert, Doug. *The Miracle Machine.* New York: Cowaed, McCann, Inc., 1980.

Gironda, Vince. *Unleashing the Wild Physique.* New York: Blandford Press, 1984.

Gretton, George. *Out in Front.* London: Pelham Books, Ltd., 1968.

Hannus, Matti. *Finnish Running Secrets.* Mountain View, CA: World Publications, 1983.

Hatfield, Frederick C., Ph.D. *Powerlifting: A Scientific Approach.* Chicago: Contemporary Books, Inc., 1989.

Hay, James G. *The Biomechanics of Sports Techniques.* Englewood Cliffs, NJ: Prentice Hall, Inc., 1989.

Henderson, Joe. *Long, Slow Distance.* Los Altos, CA: Tafnews Press, 1969.

Henderson, Joe. *Run Further, Faster.* Mountain View, CA: Anderson World Books, Inc. 1984.

Henning, Joel. *Holistic Running.* Canada: McClelland and Stewart Ltd., 1978.

Hettinger, Theodore. *Physiology of Strength.* Springfield, IL: Charles C. Thomas, 1961.

Hoffman, Bob. *Weight Training for Athletes.* New York: The Ronald Press, 1961.

Hyman, Martin. *Long Distance Running.* London: King and Jarrett Ltd. 1966.

Jarver, Jess. *The Hurdlers.* Los Altos, CA: Tafnews Press, 1981.

Jerome, John. *The Sweet Spot in Time.* New York: Summit Books, 1980.

Jesse, John. *Strength, Power and Endurance for Runners.* Pasadena, CA: The Athletic Press, 1971.

Johnson, Brooks. *The Winning Edge.* New York: Macmillan Publishing, 1988.

Johnson, Michael. *Slaying the Dragon.* New York: Harper Collins Publishers, 1996.

Jones, Arthur. *Nautilus Training Principles, Bulletin No. Two.* Deland, FL: 1971: Arthur Jones.

Jones, Charles. *What Makes a Winner Win.* Secaucus, NJ: Carol Publishing Group, 1997.

Koehler, Mike and Bruce Hanson. *Building the Total Athlete.* Englewood Cliffs, NJ: Prentice Hall, 1995.

LeMasurier, John. *Discus Throwing.* London: Amateur Athletic Association, 1967.

LeMasurier, John. *Hurdling.* London: Amateur Athletic Association, 1966.

Leonard, George. *The Ultimate Athlete.* New York: The Viking Press. 1974.

Levy, Allen M., M.D. *Sports Injury Handbook.* New York: John Wiley and Sons, Inc., 1993.

Lewis, Carl and Marx, Jeffrey. *One More Victory Lap.* Flushing, NY: The Manifestation Glow Press, 1996.

Little, John and Sisco, Peter. *Power Factor Training*. Sylmar, CA: Power Factor Training System, 1993.

Lovesay, Peter. *Five Kings of Distance*. New York: St. Martin's Press, 1981.

Lydiard, Arthur. *Run to the Top*. London: Herbert Jenkins Ltd., 1962.

Lydiard, Arthur. *Running Training Schedules*. Los Altos, CA: Track and Field News, 1970

Maxwell Maltz Foundation & Bobbe Sommer. *Psycho Cybernetics 2000*. Paramus, NJ: Prentice Hall 1997.

Marlow, Bill. *Sprinting and Relay Racing*. London: Amateur Athletic Association, 1966.

Masurier, John. *Track Speed*. London: Stanley Paul Ltd., 1972.

Matthews, Vincent. *My Race Be Won*. New York: Charterhouse, 1974.

Matveyev, L. *Fundamentals of Sports Training*. Moscow: Progress Publishers, 1977.

McNab, Tom. *The Complete Book of Track and Field*. New York: Wm. Exeter Books, 1980.

McNeff, J.D. *High School Runners and Their Training Programs*. Los Altos, CA: Tafnews Press, 1968.

Miller, Carl. *Olympic Lifting Manual*. Alliance, NE: Iron Man Magazine, 1975.

Miller, David. *Sebastian Coe Coming Back*. London: Sidwick and Jackson, 1984.

Moore, Bobbie. *Sports Illustrated: Field Events*. New York: Lippencott Co., 1977.

Myles, John. *Hepburn's Law*. Vancouver B.C. Canada: Kodiak Enterprises, 1980.

Newton, Joe. *The Long Green Line*. Oak Brook, Il: All American Publishing Co., 1969.

Noronha, Francis. *Kipshoge of Kenya*. Kenya: Elimu Publishers, 1970.

Olson, Tom. *Vaulting Handbook*. Salina, KS: Thermo-Flex, Inc., 1966.

Ostrander, Sheila. *Super Learning*. Great Britain: Sphere Books Ltd., 1981.

Pearl, Bill. *Keys to the Inner Universe*. Padadena, CA: Physical Fitness Architects, 1979.

Pickering, Ron. *Shot Putting*. London: Amateur Athletic Association, 1968.

Prokop, Dave. *The African Running Revolution*. Mountain View, CA: World Publications, 1975.

Raiport, Grigori, M.D., Ph.D. *Red Gold*. Los Angeles: Jeremy P. Tarcher, 1988.

Reilly, Secher, Snell & Williams. *Physiology of Sports*. Great Britain: St. Edmunsbury Press, 1990.

Roman, R.A. *The Training of the Weightlifter*. Livonia, MI: Sportivny Press, 1988.

Rosandich, Thomas. *Olympia Cross Country Notes*. Upson, WI: Olympia Sport Publications, 1967.

Ross, Wilber L. *The Hurdler's Bible*. Arlington, VA: Yates Printing Co., 1969.

Santos, Jim. *Sports Illustrated Track and Field*. Philadelphia and New York: Sports Illustrated Books, 1991.

Schwartz, Leonard, M.D. *Heavy Hands*. Boston: Little, Brown and Co., 1982.

Sellitz, Claire. *Research Methods in Social Relations*. New York: Holt, Rinehart and Winston, 1965.

Shepard, Greg. *Bigger, Faster, Stronger*. Salt Lake City: Hawkes Publishing, Inc., 1985.

Shmolinski, Gerhardt. *Track and Field*. Berlin, Germany: Leipzig College, 1977.

Smith, Connie. *Smith Encyclopedia of Computerized Workouts*. West Frankfort, IL: Track Books Sales, 1974.

Snell, Peter. *No Bugles, No Drums*. Aukland N.Z: Minerva Ltd., 1965.

Spener, Bud. *High Above the Olympians.* Los Altos, CA: Tafnews Press. 1966.

Stampfl, Franz. *Franz Stampfl on Running.* London: Herbert Jenkins, Ltd., 1960.

Winter, Lloyd C. *The Jet Sprint Relay Pass.* San Jose, CA: Winter Enterprises, 1964.

Yates, Dorian. *Blood and Guts.* Woodland Hills, CA: Wolff Creative Group, 1993.

Yessis, Michael, Ph.D. *Plyometric Training.* Canoga Park, CA: Fitness Systems, 1986.

Yessis, Michael, Ph.D. *Secrets of Soviet Sports Fitness and Training.* New York: Arbor House, 1987.

Zekov, Ilya Pavlovich. *Weightlifting Technique and Training.* Livonia, MI: Sportviny Press, 1992.